# Pedagogical and Andragogical Teaching and Learning with Information Communication Technologies

Victor C.X. Wang
*California State University Long Beach, USA*

Lesley Farmer
*California State University Long Beach, USA*

Judith Parker
*Columbia University, USA*

Pamela M. Golubski
*Carnegie Mellon University, USA*

Information Science
REFERENCE

Senior Editorial Director: Kristin Klinger
Director of Book Publications: Julia Mosemann
Editorial Director: Lindsay Johnston
Acquisitions Editor: Erika Carter
Development Editor: Joel Gamon
Production Editor: Sean Woznicki
Typesetters: Keith Glazewski, Natalie Pronio, Jennifer Romanchak, Milan Vracarich, Jr.
Print Coordinator: Jamie Snavely
Cover Design: Nick Newcomer

Published in the United States of America by
Information Science Publishing (an imprint of IGI Global)
701 E. Chocolate Avenue
Hershey PA 17033
Tel: 717-533-8845
Fax: 717-533-8661
E-mail: cust@igi-global.com
Web site: http://www.igi-global.com



Library of Congress Cataloging-in-Publication Data
Pedagogical and andragogical teaching and learning with information communication technologies / by Victor C.X. Wang ... [et al.].
p. cm.
Includes bibliographical references and index.
Summary: "This book shows how teachers can further their art by considering both pedagogy and andragogy in light of the each other, specifically in the modern classroom, highlighting the future possibilities opened by technology when teachers are not bound by the constraints of traditional attitudes toward time, space, age and experience"--Provided by publisher.
ISBN 978-1-60960-791-3 (hardcover) -- ISBN 978-1-60960-792-0 (ebook) -- ISBN 978-1-60960-793-7 (print & perpetual access) 1. Adult education--Computer-assisted instruction. 2. Educational technology. 3. Information technology.
I. Wang, Victor C. X.
LC5225.D38P43 2011
371.33--dc22
2011010739

British Cataloguing in Publication Data
A Cataloguing in Publication record for this book is available from the British Library.

# Table of Contents

# Preface

Traditionally, due to the distinction between pedagogy (art and science of teaching children) and andragogy (art and science of helping adults learn), scholars have written books for K-12 learners while other scholars have written books for adult learners. Clearly, the two fields are separated. Nowhere can we find a book that addresses both pedagogical and andragogical issues. By studying pedagogy, we learn more about andragogy, and by studying andragogy, we learn more about pedagogy. Since we live in this learning society, lifelong learning has become the goal in education. Why separate the two fields from each other? After all, from pedagogy to andragogy, it should be seen as a continuum of one's education as an integral part of lifelong learning process. As two distinctively different scientific disciplines, pedagogy and andragogy should be knitted together into one book so that teachers and school administrators can study both approaches to teaching and learning and select the ones that fit their particular teaching and learning situations. Teaching and learning with information communication technologies also require different approaches. Pedagogy and andragogy should be translated into online teaching and learning in the new century. It is our utmost pleasure to give birth to such a book titled *Pedagogical and Andragogical Teaching and Learning with Information Communication Technologies* after months of research in the two separate, yet closely related disciplines, pedagogy and andragogy. Indeed, this book has advanced a framework, a process, and meaningful approaches for teaching and learning with information communication technologies.

Everyone who teaches knows that pedagogy and andragogy emerged as soon as famous educators such as Socrates, Plato, and Confucius began teaching. These two concepts are used every day by ordinary teachers and educators from any educational establishments on any campus from any countries. While pedagogy is defined as instructional methods in the educational field, it is defined in particular as the art and science of teaching children (please note in the general field of education, it is defined as the overarching concept of teaching, though) as opposed to andragogy, which is defined as the art and science of helping adults in adult education. In any educational leadership/counseling programs, the most commonly asked question is what kinds of knowledge/skills should school teachers and administrators (principals/counselors) possess in order to be effective instructors and administrators? The primary answer to this question will be school instructors and administrators need to be equipped with the knowledge of pedagogy as well as andragogy. In other words, they need to know how children and adults learn in order to teach those children and help those adults learn effectively. Without knowledge of pedagogy and andragogy, any instructional/administrative activities would lead to mindless activism, let alone effective teaching or administrative leadership. As two closely related fields of study, pedagogy and andragogy have been studied by teachers, scholars, and practitioners for centuries. Some scholars argue that pedagogy preceded andragogy, and others argue that andragogy preceded pedagogy by saying that the students of Socrates, Plato, or Confucius were of adults, not of children.

Some even say although these prominent educators educated and trained adults first, andragogy was not coined until 1833 in Germany. As a field of study, it was advanced only around the 1920s. Later in the 1970s, as a strikingly different concept from pedagogy, it was popularized by Malcolm Knowles in North America. Pedagogy as field of study had matured long before andragogy was introduced to North America. The father of pedagogy, John Amos Comenius (1592-1670), advocated that children should learn from things to words and then from words to things. Principles of pedagogy were well documented for teachers and school leaders long before the term andragogy was coined. Then, Jean Piaget's (1896-1980) advancedtheory of cognitive development and epistemological view, together called "genetic epistemology," laid great importance to the education of children. He declared in 1934 that "only education is capable of saving our societies from possible collapse, whether violent, or gradual."

Naturally, education should encompass the education of children and the education of adults. Otherwise, "democracy based on well-informed citizenry" would become an empty slogan. Back to the question what kinds of knowledge/skills should school teachers and administrators (principals/counselors) possess in order to be effective instructors and administrators? The secondary answer to this question should be school teachers and administrators need to be equipped with their own preparation from their own fields, whether they be math, biology, history or nursing. In other words, teachers and school administrators need to be subject matter experts. Knowledge of pedagogy and andragogy will only equip them with the right kinds of instructional strategies. Subject matter knowledge should come from their former school preparation or real world experience.

Even well equipped with the aforementioned two kinds of knowledge, a plethora of other kinds of knowledge are needed in order for teachers and administrators to be effective instructional and administrative leaders. For example, as e-learning has become a major force in education on any campus in any country in the new century, acquiring knowledge through technology, especially Web 2.0's interactivity, can occur anywhere, at any time. Most schools and universities have seized this historic opportunity to engage teaching and learning via technology. Information communication technology as an enhancing instructional tool has become the buzz term. Indeed, both school teachers and administrators can help learners, young and old, acquire knowledge with information communication technologies. In other words, teaching and learning either pedagogically or andragogically online can happen. Likewise, pedagogical and andragogical assessment online can happen.

# Acknowledgment

Reading, critiquing, and making edits of unpublished chapters to help the authors is truly an act of friendship and colleagueship. Our colleagues spent hours proofreading certain chapters in the book. Therefore, in alphabetical order, we wish to thank Beth Kania-Gosche, Lindenwood University; Karen Weller Swanson, Mercer University; and Mary C. Ware, State University of NY – Cortland. These three colleagues read certain chapters based on their research expertise and their suggestions, critiques, and encouragement were essential to the book's completion.

The publisher, IGI Global's goal is to publish high quality books for readers from around the globe and their editorial team provides first rate editorial work. There is no doubt that this publisher has become one of the best publishers whose essential duty is also to disseminate knowledge. We thank all the members from IGI Global and may our cooperation last many years to come. Finally, thanks to Anthony, Anni, and Katie for their continued support and tolerance.

*Victor C.X. Wang*
*California State University Long Beach, USA*
*June 25, 2010*

# Chapter 1
# Pedagogical Teaching and Learning

**Victor C.X. Wang**
*California State University Long Beach, USA*

## ABSTRACT

*From infancy to adolescence, the degree of dependency on the part of learners requires pedagogical teaching and learning. To teach pedagogically, teachers are required to employ the so termed Stimulus-Response theory and some other related theories. To learn pedagogically, learners are accustomed to the so called top down education. With the advent of information communication technologies, there has emerged teaching and learning styles online. This chapter discusses pedagogical teaching and learning in comparison with andragogical teaching and learning. It should be a highly relevant chapter for teachers from K-12, as well as for teachers from adult education settings.*

## INTRODUCTION

Teaching and learning have paralleled humanity from the Stone Age to modern civilization. When human beings were hunters and gatherers, teaching and learning had their very beginning. To survive, older, more experienced human beings passed their knowledge and skills to the younger generations. Inexperienced human beings learned from those more experienced people by observation or by what we (teachers) call "job shadowing" in its modern terms. After centuries of teaching and learning or informal teaching and learning, societies made progress. As early as the seventh and twelfth centuries, organized teaching and learning began to occur in Europe where young boys were trained to be clergymen or a nation's leaders. It was around the twelfth century that more people began to establish their own countries.

After countries were established, formal schools of all types were established to teach a nation's young people. The world's earliest universities were set up in Europe (e.g., Italy or France). The ideas of great philosophers or educators such as Socrates, Plato, and Confucius have shaped teaching and learning. Their influence is still be-

DOI: 10.4018/978-1-60960-791-3.ch001

ing felt today. The teaching method by Socrates implies that teachers are to question learners, trying to formulate a definition of something and then attempting to test its accuracy by a careful analysis of its meaning. Via this type of questioning, the learners are expected to arrive at a better personal understanding, a closer examination to the truth. To Socrates, no one knows the truth before using his or her own kind of questioning (Brownhill, 2002).

Plato introduced the authoritarian approach to teaching. To Plato, there exist two worlds: a world of material things and a world of absolutes. While the world of material things is the source of belief and opinion, the world of absolutes is the source of knowledge. Definitions were accepted through the skills of the more persuasive debaters, whose main concern were to further their own or faction's interests. Plato considered teachers as charlatans who offered the rhetorical skills to control versions of the truth for the payment of fees (Brownhill, 2002, p. 71).

Confucius' main teaching method lies in his quest for self-realization or self-criticism, the rectification of the mind. He wants his learners to be authentic persons that are to be truthful to both their selfhood and their sociality (Wang & King, 2007). Confucius considers learning as emphasizing meditation to control oneself as well as an internal integration between self and nature. Through dialogue with others, the learning process facilitates the development of this meditative and integrated self. The dialogue approach is a mutual search among peers for answers and should not be considered an authoritarian approach to teaching and learning.

However, in Confucius-Heritage countries, teachers are invested with a great deal of authority as they are the ones who define the rules and requirements of courses offered. Teachers are considered judges and assessors of the learners participating in the dialogue. Learners consider teachers authority figures who set the agenda and the way of procedure, and decide the aim of the exercise and how it might be achieved. The Socrates method enabled the process of discussion to become a joint exploration of a given topic, as Socrates never claimed to be an authority figure. He respected the contribution of others, not only as human beings, but for their ideas. Therefore, his teaching method should be considered anti-authoritarianism. While we have inherited different approaches to teaching and learning, the question remains which teaching method has influenced modern teaching more, Plato's authoritarian teaching, Confucius' self-criticism, or Socrates' anti-authoritarianism? Although K-12 schools do not offer the rhetorical skills to control versions of the truth for the payment of fees as Plato describes, what is their predominant teaching approach? As more modern scholars are trying to advance other teaching and learning approaches rather than Plato's authoritarian approach, has the educational enterprise bought into these modern scholars' notion concerning teaching and learning?

The reality is that the whole educational enterprise has been frozen into the very pedagogical teaching and learning (Knowles, Holton, & Swanson, 2005). Pedagogy can be defined as the art and science of teaching children. As the art and science, how has pedagogy prevailed in the educational enterprise? We have to say that the ideologies revolving around pedagogy do make sense to many teachers and learners. Another primary reason is that pedagogy as an educational model was the only model available to teachers even prior to World War II (Knowles, Holton, & Swanson, 2005). Basically, as more experienced human beings, teachers enjoy the full responsibility for making all decisions about what to learn, how to learn, when to learn and how learning can be assessed. This teacher-directed education has prevailed simply because the pedagogical model considers learners as submissive followers of instructors' instruction.

## BACKGROUND

From infancy to adolescence, learners possess a high degree of dependency.. Thus, learners are seldom self-directed in their education. Teachers need to supervise and direct learners. Between their adolescence and adulthood, however, learners should become self-directed and rely far less on teachers. At this point, teacher-directed education does not seem to be relevant. The teacher-directed education is akin to Platonic authoritarian approach. The teacher was the expert and his function was to lead and assess the ability of his students to achieve a knowledge of those absolutes (Brownhill, 2002, p. 74). For centuries, educators have been conforming to Platonic authoritarian approach. Now educators refer to Platonic authoritarian approach as the pedagogical model. Pedagogy means the art and science of teaching children simply because the term is derived from the Greek words paid, meaning "child" and agogus, meaning "leader of." To teach pedagogically, educators have to rely on a particular model or rationale or know exactly how to develop curriculums. Then, Tylerian rationale became popular after 1949 (Tyler, 1949). The rationale includes four questions to answer when developing a curriculum in order to teach pedagogically:

- What educational purposes should the school seek to attain? At the heart of the purpose are learners' performance objectives. The teachers must be able to write these objectives and they must be stated in relationship to a norm or standard so that these objectives are quantifiable in behavioral terms. When instructors select their teaching methods, they have to choose the pedagogical model because of the way the objectives are formulated.
- What educational experience can be provided that are likely to attain these purposes? Tyler's second question concerns deciding what experiences will lead to achievement of the learners' performance objectives. Criteria for choosing these experiences must provide opportunities to practice the behavior implied by the learners' performance objectives (Ziegler, 2008, p. 149). In terms of selecting the teaching methods, educators must select the pedagogical model because educators always keep the norm and standard in mind.
- How can these educational experiences be effectively organized? The third question addresses the criteria for organizing learning experiences. Because learners are considered dependent learners, educators are required to use the pedagogical model to teach learners.
- How can we determine whether these purposes are being attained? The fourth question concerns evaluation of learning. Educators are required to assess the learners' performance objectives in behavioral terms. Tyler's four questions form the foundation of the pedagogical model.

Most K-12 educators do not deviate from this model simply because this is the model they have been familiar with and it is the way they were taught. It is convenient for these educators to conform to this model. In addition, administrators and accreditation bodies are always looking for accountability of teaching and learning. To measure learners' performance objectives in quantifiable terms seems to be the norm and practice in the education system. After World War II, especially when the andragogical model began to attract the attention of educators, the pedagogical model was discussed in relationship to the six principles of andragogy:

1. The need to know. Learners only need to know that they must learn what the teacher teaches if they want to pass and get promoted. They do not have a deep psychological need

to know what to learn or if anything has been learned.

2. The learner's self-concept. The teacher believes that the learner is a dependent learner. Therefore, the teacher must direct his or her learning.
3. The role of experience. The learner's experience is of little value as a resource for learning as he or she has not accumulated nearly enough experience as a young learner. What counts is the experience of the instructor. Therefore, the teacher must rely on the textbook, lectures or assigned readings to teach the learners.
4. Readiness to learn. Again, learners are ready to learn when their teachers tell them what to learn if they wish to pass and get promoted.
5. Orientation to learning. These young learners have a subject-centered orientation to learning. They focus on certain subjects. Learning experiences are organized according to the content of the subjects.
6. Motivation. Young learners are motivated to learn by external motivators such as grades, the teachers' approval or parental pressures.

The bottom line of this pedagogical model is that the teacher is seen to have the knowledge whereas the students are manipulated so that they will look at the world through the teacher's epistemological spectacles. In the modern society, teachers try to lead their students to some "aha moments." What they want to do is really to have students see the world the way they see it. That is why educators nowadays talk about "competency-based" education. If learners are to achieve those specified competent skills, criteria set by teachers must be met in quantifiable terms. Between infancy and adolescence, learners are not considered the fount of all wisdom. They have to acquire knowledge through all their senses and their teachers represent the fount of all wisdom given the number of years and education they put behind them. Naturally, teachers traditionally are expected to possess the following characteristics:

- Have a monopoly on transmitting knowledge.
- Determine or legislate on matters of knowledge but they may be interpreters of different systems of knowledge.
- Deal with truth but they certainly teach truths.
- Teach with unchanging knowledge but now they deal with scientific knowledge that is transient.
- Are confined to the classroom, but like the ancient teachers they may have to function where their learners are.
- Teach only theoretical knowledge but now they also help learners acquire practical knowledge.
- Can assume that their learners know nothing about the subject that they teach but must learn to build on knowledge acquired by their learners from a wide variety of sources. (Jarvis, 2002, p. 20)

The pedagogical model or Platonic authoritarian education is marked throughout by regimentation demanding obedient conformity to patterns of conduct handed down from authority. Behavior is expected to be predictable, standardized. Perhaps, the model is predetermined by Habermas' (1971) instrumental knowledge, which allows teachers to manipulate and control the environment, predict observable and social events, and take appropriate actions. Based on this school of thought, learners acquire instrumental knowledge through teacher-centered strategies such as lecture and demonstration (Cranton, 2010, p. 5). Also, worthy of note is that the pedagogical model has been translated into S-R theory (S stands for stimuli; R stands for responses) by scholars. The principles emphasized in S-R theory by Hilgard and Bower (1966, pp. 562-564) are listed in Table 1 for reference.

## WHY PEDAGOGICAL TEACHING AND LEARNING WITH INFORMATION COMMUNICATION TECHNOLOGIES?

Web 2.0 technologies provide a teaching and learning environment for pedagogical instructors. Pedagogical instructors need a teaching and learning environment, whether in the traditional classroom setting or the virtual environment. For centuries, teachers have been expected to provide a safe, conducive environment for learners. Once an environment is available, it does not mean teachers can just go ahead to dump their courses onto the computer screens. To impart knowledge to learners in the virtual environment, teachers are required to demonstrate their teaching methods. In addition, course design requires teachers to teach in a certain way. The pedagogical model is not a bad model used to teach traditional age learners in the virtual environment.

First, all instructors need to post their online syllabi via which learners' performance objectives are communicated to the learners. Due to accountability and accreditation, instructors are required to write learners' performance objectives in quantifiable terms and align them to existing mandated standards. In other words, instructors are responsible for observing and measuring learners' performance objectives. In most cases, schools require teachers to possess certain teaching philosophies. It is not surprising that parents see many children bring home candy or other tangible rewards from schools. We (authors) can tell that their teachers prefer using the so termed behaviorist philosophy, which mirrors the American teaching philosophy at the turn of the twentieth century (Knowles, Holton, & Swanson, 2005). After Watson (1967) and Skinner (1968) popularized behaviorism in North America, most teachers began to adhere to this philosophy.

When applied to teaching online, instructors began to use "programmed instruction" in the 1960s (Based on programmed instruction in the 1960s, current instructors have developed online teaching). Again, teachers prescribe learners' performance objectives in behaviorist terms, organize learning activities online according to those objectives and determine the means to evaluate those learners' performance objectives. Teachers who believe in behaviorism are bona fide pedagogical instructors who may prefer the art and science of teaching children (pedagogy). Talking to most K-12 instructors in North America, they will say, "it is teachers' responsibility to provide stimuli in either traditional classroom setting or the virtual classroom setting; then teachers expect responses from learners; once a correct response is received, teachers award the learner who has provided the correct response." The principles (Hilgard &

*Table 1. Principles emphasized in S-R Theory*

| |
|---|
| 1. The learner should be an active, rather than a passive listener or viewer. |
| 2. Frequency of repetition is still important in acquiring skill and for retention through overlearning. |
| 3. Reinforcement is important; that is, repetition's desirable and correct responses should be rewarded. |
| 4. Generalization and discrimination suggest the importance of practice in varied contexts, so that learning will become (or remain) appropriate to a wider (or more restricted) range of stimuli. |
| 5. Novelty in behavior can be enhanced through imitation of models, through cueing, through shaping, and is not inconsistent with a liberalized S-R approach. |
| 6. Drive is important in learning, but all personal-social motives do not conform to the drive-reduction principles based on food-deprivation experiments. |
| 7. Conflicts and frustrations arise inevitably in the process of learning difficult discriminations and in social situations in which irrelevant motives may be aroused. Hence we must recognize and provide for their resolution or accommodation. |

Bower, 1966, pp. 562-564) emphasized in S-R theory were derived from this behaviorist philosophy. Tylerian rational was also derived from behaviorism. The pedagogical model, behaviorism or Tylerian rationale all speak to Platonic authoritarian approach or teacher-directed education. In other words, teachers are considered the fount of all wisdom or authority figures and their job is to impart knowledge to the younger learners.

In the present day to day teaching, the pedagogical model has been translated into "four step instruction" (Wang, 2010). The first step is called motivation. Teachers are supposed to say or do something to get the learners interested in their subject matter. Naturally, anything they say or do must be closely related to the subject matter they want to teach. Once teachers determine that learners are motivated to focus on the subject matter, teachers begin their second step, which is called presentation. During this phase, teachers begin to teach even those quantifiable learners' performance objectives as well as any key points they want to share with learners. It is during this phase that teachers can adhere to their pedagogical instructional method such as lecture or providing heavy stimuli or cues. The second step takes the bulk of an instructor's time during a class. Then comes the third step, which is called homework. Pedagogical teachers are supposed to give out homework to learners. The homework must be closely related to those learners' performance objectives and content of a certain subject matter. Homework is done by learners for the sake of reinforcing competency on the part of learners. Often times, homework is related to exams. The last step of the four step instruction is follow-up. Another way to explain follow-up is Tylerian evaluation. Learners' performance objectives or mastery of content must be assessed by teachers. Here evaluation of learning by teachers is of primary importance. Learner self-evaluation has no place in this pedagogical model.

In the online environment, most exams are timed and learners can be given one or two times to complete an exam. Computation of exam scores is easy because computerized exams can be considered part of programmed instruction. Today, computer programs are readily available to be used to help assess learning.

As an enhancing teaching and learning tool, web 2.0 technologies can do many things for teachers in addition to providing one access point to knowledge. First, text, audio, and video based pedagogical lectures can be created and posted for learners. Pedagogical instructors can require their learners to listen to their lectures. Second, instructors can prescribe course assignments according to their behaviorist teaching philosophies. In other words, assignments can be graded by using grading rubrics or in quantifiable terms only. Third, any learning resources or activities online can be organized effectively in a sequential manner. These resources or activities must be closely related to those learners' performance objectives. Finally, pedagogical online instructors may believe in standardized exams used to assess learning on the part of learners.

Then the question remains why we (teachers) have to stick to pedagogical teaching and learning online? The answer is we (teachers) do not have to. However, the focus of this chapter is all about pedagogical teaching and learning. The theme of the book is about pedagogical and andragogical teaching and learning with information communication technologies. We (teachers) have to address those factors that predetermine pedagogical teaching and learning. That was why we (teachers) addressed those leaders such as Plato who advanced Platonic authoritarian approach, which is akin to the pedagogical model. The primary reason the whole educational enterprise has been frozen into the pedagogical model is that between infancy and adolescence, no other model is better than the pedagogical teaching and learning model. Further, scientists have done more experiments with children and on animals. Naturally, we (teachers) do know more about this pedagogical teaching and learning model.

As soon as we (teachers) began to teach online in the new century, teachers quickly moved their pedagogical model onto the computer screens. Has this model worked? Yes, in certain cultures, the pedagogical model is the only available model used to teach both children and adults. Teachers have never heard of the distinction between the education of children and the education of adults. We (teachers) all tend to have such belief that if we know the aims and objectives of the lesson and the content to be taught, then the teachers are in better control. Note here, teachers want to be in better control. No teachers want to be known as "disorganized." To be in better control of a certain lesson, teachers have to prescribe a certain teaching method or methods. If those aims, objectives and content are meant to be taught, then, the pedagogical model is adopted by most teachers. Like discussed earlier in this chapter, this pedagogical model is simply easy and convenient for most teachers. It is the way they were taught previously. It is also true that many curriculum studies nowadays include teaching methods and teaching philosophies as part of the discussion of the curriculum.

Think of Tyler's four questions. One of them is How can these educational experiences be effectively organized? Evidently, this question requires teachers to prescribe certain teaching methods that strive to address learners' performance objectives. These teaching methods should also address evaluation and assessment of learning. Because Tyler emphasized the pedagogical model used in the education of children, teachers have no choice but to stick to behaviorist teaching philosophy. Based on Jarvis's writing in 2002, if teaching involved the transmission of knowledge/theory or the teaching of a skill (e.g., in vocational education) – it was an instrumentally rational activity, the outcomes could be measured and the techniques employed could be assessed (p. 24). If teachers are to follow this school of thought, they will use the most efficient methods to achieve their specified objectives. If teaching is designed to achieve specified ends, teaching methods must be prescribed. For centuries, the pedagogical model has worked well for learners between infancy and adolescence. Over the years, scholars keep raising questions about the validity and legitimacy of the model. However, this model seems to have its place in the whole educational enterprise. At least up to this point, this pedagogical model has not been replaced with another model.

Scholars keep experimenting with other methods, but those novel methods including the andragogical model (addressed in other chapters of the book) have been use on a trial and error basis and by a very small number of educators, mostly in the field of adult education. Although research one universities emphasize student-centered methods, in actualuality, they have not been practiced very well by many teachers. Indeed, the student-centered methods have been over-rated. On the other hand, school administrators always want teachers to achieve specified ends due to accountability and accreditation or national/international standards. There is no question that the pedagogical model is too formal and that it provides little opportunities for self expression and for recognition of individual differences. It focuses on the skills of the learners rather than aesthetic and creative side of work. It promotes competency-based education. As noted by Jarvis (2002, p. 26), the pedagogical model fails to take into consideration the difference of classes, cultures and teachers themselves:

- Omits consideration of value rationality, as opposed to instrumental rationality.
- Is instrumental and assumes that the achievement of the specified objectives is always a sign of good teaching.
- Emphasizes outcomes and omits consideration of the unintended learning outcomes.
- Is universalistic and downplays social, cultural and individual differences.
- Assumes that learning is always measurable, and so on.

While Jarvis's criticisms of the pedagogical model are valid, the Platonic authoritarian leaders create a sense of group dependence on the leader, that their presence held the group together and that in their absence no work was done. Many factors contribute to this authoritarian teaching style. The primary reason is that between infancy and adolescence, learners are mostly dependent learners, unable to initiate self-directed learning. Then societal/cultural and political factors also contribute to this pedagogical model. Often times, teachers have no choice but to conform to this pedagogical model. In addition, during the course of authoritarian teaching, teachers can be didactic, friendly or Socratic, and so on.

Back to the pedagogical teaching and learning with information communication technology issue, does technology allow for other teaching methods such as andragogical teaching methods? As an enhancing tool, technology provides environments for all kinds of teaching methods. However, environments must be created by teachers at the direction of school administrators. Should the nature of learners, school's mandate and preferences of teachers predetermine the pedagogical model to be used in the virtual environment, technology serves as the best vehicle for the pedagogical teaching and learning. Programmed instruction dictated by behaviorism works best for learners between infancy and adolescence to achieve certain learning aims and objectives. Programmed instruction also facilitates the evaluation and assessment of learning for teachers. Programmed instruction supports the directing relationship between teachers and learners. Teachers want to observe and measure those learners' performance objectives in behaviorist terms to determine that learners have changed in three domains of educational objectives: Cognitive Domain, Psychomotor Domain, and Affective Domain. Habermas's theory on instrumental knowledge indeed supports this pedagogical teaching and learning in the virtual environment—after all, which teacher does not want to manipulate and control the environment, predict observable and social events, and take appropriate actions via technology? Competition for grades and accreditation leaves schools no room for other teaching methods such as facilitation methods. Finally, it is safe to say although other methods are pursued by scholars, there have been many realistic situations for the pedagogical model in many school settings including university settings. Despite its criticisms, the model will continue to survive and thrive as a solid teaching method in the field of education.

## FUTURE TRENDS

To most teachers, the behaviorist approach to teaching and learning represents the best approach simply because it stems from the work of Watson (1967) and Skinner (1968). Of course, there are other influential behaviorists in education. The behaviorist approach is seen as the most common theoretical perspective used in education. The primary reason is that it is functional and scientific. Because behaviorist instructors focus on the measurable behavioral outcomes of learning, rather than on knowledge, attitudes, values, beliefs and so on, this objective in teaching and learning seems to be well liked by school administrators and accreditation bodies who place emphasis on accountability and the reliability of standardized assessments. Since its sole concern is behavior, it is a limited approach to teaching and learning. It concerns any form of response to a stimulus that can be measured. Nowadays, teachers do know that learners, whether traditional age or non traditional age, learn via other learning methods such as critical reflection, even silence. One trend in education could be that scholars and researchers will continue to study other approaches problem-solving, experiential learning, reflectivity, and silence in relationship to behaviorism.

The pedagogical model has become so well known in education simply because humans have the propensity to measure intelligence and learning by tests and examination. These tests will give teachers and administrators a clearer understanding of what learners have learned so that intervention will be prescribed. Think of the imperial examination system that has existed for centuries in China and some other Confucius-Heritage countries. That is the only way governmental officials were selected for hundreds of years and only the small group of well educated elite were allowed to run the country like China. Even in the Western societies, governmental officials were selected from those well educated scholars who majored in either political science or mathematics. Consider what the early Greeks had said, "working people didn't think and thinking people didn't work" (as cited in Kacirek, Beck, & Grover, 2010, p. 32). When different societies placed greater emphasis on well educated people, they did rely on the well known behaviorism to educate and train their learners. Another trend in education is to compare other well known teaching and learning approaches with the pedagogical model to determine why no other approaches could replace behaviorism in teaching and learning.

One concern about the pedagogical model is that it does not give learners freedom to learn what they want to learn, how they want to learn and how learners can evaluate their own learning. Everything including aims and objectives has been prescribed. Learners have the submissive role of following their course instructors. When course are moved to the computer screens, everything is designed revolving around course aims and objectives. Evaluation is conducted by course instructors. Learner freedom, and learner self-evaluation are not common terms used by behaviorist instructors online. Programmed instruction remains the buzz term in the virtual environment. Do behaviorist online instructors allow for learner self-expression? Do behaviorist online instructors allow for aesthetic and creative side of work? Well, they may wish so. In actuality, because of the aims and learning objectives specified, because of their fixed behaviorist approaches to teaching, they take away the freedom from learners. On the other hand, we do talk about scholars and researchers offering whatever freedom to learners. In the adult education field, teachers conform to what we (teachers) call "facilitation methods." As noted by Rogers (1951, 1961, 1969), "we cannot teach another individual; we can only facilitate his/her learning." It could be a trend that scholars and researchers may look into Rogers' other hypotheses to find out if the facilitation methods could possibly replace the pedagogical model where learner freedom is taken away by instructors. Regarding granting freedom to learners, Jarvis, Holford and Griffin (1998, pp. 25-26) vehemently said the following:

*Teachers and learners can allow students considerable freedom to undertake projects and experiments and discover for themselves the outcomes of their work. Much problem-based learning focuses on trial-and-error-type approaches to learning situations. When trial and error is a project without a great deal of teacher intervention, then the only conditioning that occurs is that which occurs as a result of learning in the process. Students are conditioned by the positive outcomes—pleasurable or satisfaction—of their experience.*

The key aspect of behaviorism is that teachers are required to provide intervention to change any learning situation by providing reinforcement when learners can provide correct responses. However, more mature and intelligent learners may already know the correct responses. One more trend in education could be what behaviorist instructors would do if they know some learners may already have correct responses. Should these instructors still stick to the pedagogical model given the fact that their learners are still moving from infancy to adolescence?

Instrumental teaching has become the most common form of learning in today's schools and colleges because learning outcomes are specified in behavioral terms. Teachers and new instructors are expected to write their lesson plans in terms of: By the end of the lesson, the student will be able to do what under what conditions by what standards. The verb "do" should be replaced by action verbs found from Bloom's (1956) taxonomy reflecting higher order thinking skills (verbs must be taken from the levels reflecting analysis, synthesis and evaluation). Any vague or squish terms such as know, understand, demonstrate the knowledge of, or demonstrate the understanding of must be avoided. Gagne, Wager, Golas and Keller (2005) have specified more components in writing learners' performance objectives. They suggest that teachers and new teachers write objectives that communicate:

1. Situation (context in which the learned outcome will be performed).
2. The type of learning being performed (a "learned capability" verb classifying the type of learning).
3. The content or object of the performance.
4. The observable part of the behavior (action verb).
5. The tools, constraints or special conditions applied to the performance (acceptable performance). (p. 134)

No one is to argue that the pedagogical model displays a high degree of precision, prescribing teachers' role in terms of what to teach and how to teach. And there is nothing wrong with this popular approach to teaching and learning. The question remains how much freedom, or learners' autonomy is left? One last trend in education could be that scholars and researchers may challenge the pedagogical model with well established approaches in educational psychology.

## CONCLUSION

In our classes, we (teachers) often see learners reach some "aha moments" by saying, "that is the approach I have been using, teaching ESL learners; that is the approach I have been using, teaching mathematics in this community college and so forth." If we don't address educational approaches such as pedagogical teaching and learning or facilitation methods, our learners may never reach those "aha moments," let alone discuss these approaches with course instructors. There has been such as shortage of teachers of all kinds. Some learners aspire to be teachers after graduation. It is important and necessary to address different teaching and learning approaches so that teachers and new teachers may follow a general direction regarding what approaches may best fit their teaching and learning situation. As education is delivered electronically in the new century, it is all the more important for teachers and new teachers to possess the right teaching methods in the virtual environment. Otherwise, we may fail to convince school administrators and accreditation bodies that learning can not occur in the online environment.

In this chapter, we have demonstrated that programmed instruction is the preferred mode of instruction by most instructors. We (authors) have illustrated that programmed instruction is part of behaviorism that makes up the pedagogical instructional model. The model did not emerge overnight. Rather, it has been used in the education and training of learners from infancy to adolescence probably prior to the beginning of formal education in our school systems in different societies. We (authors) also addressed the contributions regarding teaching and learning approaches by those historic figures such as Socrates, Confucius and Plato. More recent contributions by Rogers, Knowles, and those behaviorists were also discussed in this chapter. If we agree that we live in an instrumentally rational age as discussed by Habermas (1971) where end-product have always been more important than the means, then, teachers should be expected to get immediate and measurable results and schools and colleges should do the same. If this is the considered the case, we should conform to the pedagogical model characterized by behaviorism. Therefore, what has been practiced for centuries should be continued in our school system.

As competency education has become the norm in education, as the national vocational qualifications of instructors are required by accreditation bodies, there is no reason to discard the pedagogical model which has served well traditional age learners for centuries. After all, the ends justify the means (Jarvis, Holford, & Griffin, 1998, p. 27). However popular the pedagogical teaching and learning as discussed in this chapter, we remind our teachers and readers to think about this question: Are short-term ends always the best ones? Are our learners' better scores indicative of their true abilities to learn and to cope with our modern society? We (authors) are not suggesting that the pedagogical teaching and learning approaches be replaced by other educational approaches. Rather, we (authors) are suggesting what teachers and researchers do to make the model better serve our learners from infancy to adolescence. Are there other approaches rather than just the programmed instruction for online instructors? With these remarks, we (authors) invite you to read other chapters in this book and share with us your feedback about our discussions of pedagogical and andragogical teaching with information communication technologies.

## REFERENCES

Bloom, B. S. (Ed.). (1956). *Taxonomy of educational objectives*. London, UK: Longman.

Brownhill, B. (2002). The Socratic method. In Jarvis, P. (Ed.), *The theory & practice of teaching* (pp. 70–78). London, UK: Kogan Page.

Cranton, P. (2010). Working towards self-evaluation. In Wang, V. C. X. (Ed.), *Assessing and evaluating adult learning in career and technical education* (pp. 1–11). Hangzhou, China & Hershey, PA: ZUP & Information Science Reference. doi:10.4018/978-1-61520-745-9.ch001

Gagne, R. M., Wager, W. W., Golas, K. C., & Keller, J. M. (2005). *Principles of instructional design* (5th ed.). Belmont, CA: Wadsworth/Thomson Learning.

Habermas, J. (1971). *Knowledge and human interests*. Boston, MA: Beacon Press.

Hilgard, E. R., & Bower, G. H. (1966). *Theories of learning*. New York, NY: Appleton-Century-Crofts.

Jarvis, P. (Ed.). (2002). *The theory & practice of teaching*. London, UK: Kogan Page.

Jarvis, P., Holford, J., & Griffin, C. (1998). *The theory and practice of learning*. London, UK: Kogan Page.

Kacirek, K., Beck, J. K., & Grover, K. S. (2010). Career and technical education: Myths, metrics, and metamorphosis. In Wang, V. C. X. (Ed.), *Definitive readings in the history, philosophy, practice and theories of career and technical education* (pp. 31–49). Hangzhou, China & Hershey, PA: ZUP & Information Science Reference.

Knowles, M. S., Holton, E., & Swanson, A. (2005). *The adult learner* (6th ed.). Boston, MA: Elsevier Butterworth Heinemann.

Rogers, C. R. (1951). *Client-centered therapy*. Boston, MA: Houghton-Mifflin.

Rogers, C. R. (1961). *On become a person*. Boston, MA: Houghton-Mifflin.

Rogers, C. R. (1969). *Freedom to learn*. Columbus, OH: Merrill.

Skinner, B. F. (1968). *The technology of teaching*. New York, NY: Appleton-Century-Crofts.

Tyler, R. W. (1949). *Basic principles of curriculum and instruction*. Chicago, IL: The University of Chicago Press.

Wang, V. C. X. (2010). Critical components of curriculum development for career and technical education instructors in the United States. *International Journal of Adult Vocational Education and Technology*, *1*(1), 72–89. doi:10.4018/javet.2010100905

Wang, V. C. X., & King, K. P. (2007). Confucius and Mezirow—understanding Mezirow's theory of reflectivity from Confucian perspectives: A model and perspective. In King, K. P., & Wang, V. C. X. (Eds.), *Comparative adult education around the globe: International portraits and readings of the history, practice, philosophy, and theories of adult learning* (pp. 253–275). Hangzhou, China: Zhejiang University Press.

Watson, G. (Ed.). (1967). *Concepts for social change*. Washington, DC: National Training Laboratories Institute for Applied Behavioral Science, N. E. A.

Ziegler, M. (2008). Expanding curriculum development models. In V. C. X. Wang (Ed.), *Curriculum development for adult learners in the global community, volume I: Strategic approaches* (pp. 146-170). Malabar, FL: Krieger Publishing Company.

# Chapter 2
# Utilizing Interactive Technologies to Engage, Integrate, Involve, and Increase Community amongst College Students

**Pamela M. Golubski**
*Carnegie Mellon University, USA*

## ABSTRACT

*Retention in higher education is a forefront goal for most administration, staff, and faculty members. For this goal to be achieved, college professionals must go above and beyond to ensure students are engaged socially, successfully integrated into the campus community, and actively involved during college. When these interactions occur, students are more likely to experience a sense of belonging, as, evident from developmental research theories, an institution could experience an increase in overall retention rates. However, to achieve engagement, integration, involvement, and feelings of belonging, it requires staff and faculty members to offer and encourage continuous interactions with students, both inside and outside the classroom. While these interactions in the past usually happened through face-to-face methods, today, the Web 2.0 and virtual technological tools have extended opportunities for college professionals to interact more often with students. Two such virtual technologies are Google Wave and Wimba Collaboration Suite (Voice, Pronto, and Classroom).*

DOI: 10.4018/978-1-60960-791-3.ch002

## RETENTION OVERVIEW

Retention of students is a pinnacle goal for any higher education institution. This is most likely due to the fact that only approximately 58 percent of students who enter a four-year institution will persist to earn bachelor degrees within six years (U.S. Department of Education, National Center for Education Statistics, 2009). If college administrators, staff and faculty members do not strive to make retention a priority, rates could continue to drop (Tinto, 1993). This means that staff and faculty members have to actively engage, integrate, involve, and increase social presence (socialization) of students during college. Research has found when these actions occur inside and outside the classroom a reduction in attritions rates is most often experienced by an institution. However, achieving student active engagement, integration, involvement, socialization, and sense of affinity/belonging to an institution requires staff and faculty members to offer and encourage continuous interactions with students. So the question becomes how can these interactions occur in an already over-scheduled, time deprived world? The answer might lie in utilizing and interacting with students through virtual technologies and tools. In order to better understand how to effectively interact effectively with students it is essential to first understand retention from a theoretical perspective.

### Tinto's Model of Student Departure

Tinto's (1975, 1987, 1993) Model of Student Departure has been the theoretical foundation for retention research in higher education. Tinto's model views student departure as a complex relationship between student involvement, academic achievement, and social integration while at college. The conceptual framework of Tinto's theory was developed through Pantages and Creedon's 25 years of attrition research, Durkheim's model of suicide, Spady's research on social system departures, and Van Gennep's research on an individual's rites of passage from childhood to adulthood (Tinto, 1993).

Tinto discovered that a student's departure from an institution was due to five critical factors that include (1) a lack of personal commitment, (2) time and resource adjustment issues, (3) the lack of a social network or social integration, (4) academic difficulty, and (5) the lack of clear academic and career goals (Tinto, 1975, 1993). In past research, when students left college, the term used to define these students was "dropout" or "failure" which assumed students did not have the capabilities or characteristics to succeed in college (Tinto, 1993). Today, students who leave an institution are viewed from an attrition standpoint, and rarely termed "failures" (Tinto, 1975, 1987, 1993).

In an effort to better understand student departure, Tinto's (1993) model further divides the causes of departure into three critical areas: (1) individual characteristics prior to entering college, (2) the experiences of the individual upon entry into the college community, and (3) external forces that hinder the college experience.

Individual characteristics (1) include intention and commitment towards earning the degree and learning. Intention is the individual's personal goal(s) that guides his/her related educational activity. According to Tinto, the higher a student sets his/her goal(s) the more likely the student will persist. Commitment is the level of motivation that influences a student's drive to complete a degree program in that commitment "not only help set the boundaries of individual attainment but also serve to color the character of individual experiences within the institution following entry" (Tinto, 1993, p. 37).

For the college experiences (2) critical area, Tinto separated the area into four clusters of occurrences or circumstances that effect the student's decision to either depart or remain enrolled at a college. These clusters were entitled (a) adjustment, (b) difficulty, (c) incongruence, and (d) isolation.

Each describes how the individual interacts within the institutional environment. Adjustment (a) is the process of transitioning from one environment to another, such as being a stay at home mother to being a full-time college student or a high school student having her own bedroom to attending a college out of state and living with a roommate in a campus resident hall. The transition to college is difficult for most students regardless of age. Therefore, offering additional assistance, interaction, and support during this transitional time to students is important to combat attrition.

During the difficulty (b) period/cluster, a student might withdrawal if he/she can't meet minimal academic standards/requirements. A student experiencing difficulty must be tended to immediately to avoid feelings of frustration and despair (Tinto, 1993). For example, an adult learner experiencing the difficulty cluster would be further frustrated if tutoring was only available during the traditional weekday (9 am to 5 pm), when many adults are working full-time jobs. Colleges would need to offer support services during non-traditional hours such as evening and weekends, which can effectively happen now with the proliferation of virtual and Web 2.0 technologies. Tinto (1993) discovered that the difficulty cluster affects all students at some point during their college tenure. Therefore, faculty and staff members must have support services and communication efforts in place to combat the difficulty cluster.

The third cluster, Tinto termed incongruence (c) which refers to the lack of fit between the needs, interests, and/or preferences of an individual and the higher education institution. Students, who have undeclared majors are extremely susceptible to feelings of incongruence. These students often need individual guidance on major and career choice. When a student experiences incongruence, he/she doesn't feel a sense of belonging or affinity to the college community. This incongruence is usually reflected in peer relationships where the student doesn't feel his/her values and interests match those of classmates. This can be extremely challenging when adult learners are in courses where the enrollment is primarily traditional-aged students.

The final cluster is isolation (d). Isolation occurs when a student cannot establish himself/herself into a social network and lacks the "personal bonds that are the basis for membership in the communities of the institution" (Tinto, 1993, p. 56). This network can include classmates, staff and faculty members. The absence of meaningful relationship with peers and other institutional members contributes to this sense of isolation, thus potentially leading to departure.

The third cause of student departure according to Tinto's research is due to the influence of external forces (3) that interfere with the student's college experience. Tinto identified these as competing obligations and multiple roles that can contribute to early withdrawal decisions. This can range from a student that is caring for small children and managing a home to a student who has to work full-time to finance his/her education. External forces causes, according to Tinto, are most often experienced by students who do not reside on campus, such as adult students or commuter students. This is due to their lives being more complicated by external forces such as family, work, and the community in which they reside (Tinto, 1993).

Lastly, Tinto never asserts that if colleges successfully integrate and involve students academically and socially that they won't leave. He does confirm that organized college integration and interaction does lead to lower student departure rates. This being stated, it is crucial that colleges use as many interactive technologies inside and outside the classroom to encourage students to acclimate, engage, and be involved during college. One way to ensure students become acclimated, engaged, and integrated in college is through socialization and involvement with their peers, staff, and faculty members.

## SOCIALIZATION IN COLLEGE

Braxton and Lee (2005) have described college social integration as the harmonious relationship between a student and the social system within an institution of higher education. If a student doesn't successfully become integrated into a college's social system, there is an increased risk of attrition (Bean, 2005). Therefore, it is not surprising that a large body of research exists that supports the need for social integration and the development of positive relationships during college (Astin, 1984; Light, 2001; Pascarella & Terenzini, 2005; Schlossberg, 1989; Spady, 1971; Tinto, 1975, 1987, 1993). College students' peer interactions in some cases have a greater influence on a student's college experience than their classroom experience (Astin 1993; Terenzini, Springer, Yaeger, Pascarelle, & Nora (1996). For example, Strage (2000) discovered that the development of positive relationships with peers accounted for higher levels of confidence in students, regarding their ability to succeed in college. In addition, Upcraft and Gardner (1989) identified the relationships students had with peers during college was a predictor of both student success and retention. College friendships can help students gain independence, support personal goals, aid in the development of interpersonal skills, influence career, and support appropriate behaviors (Upcraft & Gardner, 1989). Social interaction involves sharing interests, experiences, activities, and conversations both inside and outside the classroom. Today, peer interaction is viewed as a campus-wide entity in which interactions occur within a variety of interpersonal environments. These interactions do not necessarily need to occur in person, as there are virtual tools such as Google Wave and Wimba Collaboration Suite that encourage and enable virtual interaction to resemble those of face-to-face communication (Astin, 1993; Kuh, 1995; Pascarella & Terenzini, 2005). Regardless if socialization occurs online or in-person, it is one of the necessary actions to retain students. In addition to socialization, a student needs to become actively involved during college. The need for this involvement can further be explained by reviewing Astin's extensive research in the topic.

## INVOLVEMENT IN COLLEGE

### Astin's Theory of Involvement

Astin's (1984, 1993, 1996, 1999) Theory of Involvement states that students learn more when actively involved in both the academic and social aspects of the collegiate experience. "An involved student who devotes considerable energy to academics, spends more time on campus, participates actively in student organizations and activities, and interacts often with faculty" (Astin, 1984, p. 292). "The quality and quantity of the student's involvement will influence the amount of student learning and development (Astin, 1984, p. 297). The Theory of Involvement assumes that the student plays an integral role in determining his/her own degree of involvement in educational classes, meta-curricular and social activities, but faculty and staff can influence those decisions by offering and suggesting a variety of ways to become actively involved (Astin, 1993).

Astin (1993) found that students who had positive interactions and relationships with peers, faculty, and staff members on campus were more likely to experience higher cognitive development and academic success. More importantly, involvement or lack of involvement with individuals on campus can influence if a student persists or departs. Astin's (1984) theory incorporated five basic foundations necessary to ensure quality involvement. (1) Involvement must be an investment of physical and psychological energy towards an object. The object can be anything from an in-class group project, a fraternity/sorority to a religious activity. (2) Student involvement during college occurs along a continuum. At any given time, students will invest more energy than others due to class rigor and other personal challenges/ commitments. (3) Involvement should be viewed as both quantitative (amount of hours time devoted) and qualitative (the quality or seriousness towards the activity). (4) Student learning and personal development that is associated with any educational program is directly proportional to the quality and quantity of student involvement in that program. This means the more a student puts into an activity or interaction the more he/ she gets out of it. Finally, the (5) effectiveness of any college practice or initiative is directly related to the capacity that the initiative has to increase student involvement while decreasing the potential of attrition (Astin, 1984).

Other than Astin, many researchers have found a strong positive correlation between student involvement on campus and student retention in higher education (Light, 2001; Pascarella & Terenzini, 2005; Schlosseberg, 1989; Spady, 1971; Tinto, 1975, 1987, 1993). This research provides evidence of the need for students to be provided with ample opportunities to become actively involved on campus. It is imperative that involvement with peers, staff, and faculty members extend beyond the classroom (Astin, 1984). Therefore, faculty and staff member interactions play a pertinent role in student involvement and growth. It was discovered through Schlossberg's (1984) research that when students become actively involved on campus, this engagement often leads to an increased sense of mattering or belonging on campus. When a student experiences a sense of belonging, this can lead to less students wanting to leave or attrite from an institution (Tinto, 1993). In an effort to better understand the importance of belonging in college Schlossberg Sense of Mattering will be reviewed.

## SENSE OF BELONGING IN COLLEGE

### Schlossberg Sense of Mattering

Schlossberg (1989) suggested that a student's sense of belonging, mattering, marginality, or affinity to the institution was crucial in his/her successful transition and persistence. When a student enters college, he/she does not feel a sense of belonging and if these feelings are prolonged, it may lead to an increase in the likelihood of attrition of that student (Tinto, 1993). Schlossberg (1989) defined the five constructs of mattering for college students to include feelings of (1) attention, (2) importance, (3) ego-extension, (4) dependence, and (5) belonging. Attention (1) is when an individual needs to feel that someone is paying attention to his/her presence or absence, whether it is in class or at an organization meeting. Students need to feel they are important (2) to another and that someone cares about their well-being. Ego-extension (3) is the feeling that others share in one's successes and saddened by one's failures. The component of dependence (4) is the feeling that one is needed by others and one makes a difference in someone else's life. Lastly, belonging (5) happens when others appreciate the contribution that a person brings to an environment. Institutions that focus on ensuring that students feel a sense of belonging will most likely experience greater student involvement, learning, and increased retention because students believe that they have a purpose at the institution (Schlossberg, 1989). In addition, Habley and McClanahan (2004) surveyed 2,995 colleges and found that institution fit was the second highest intuitional factor that contributed to student retention. Students have to believe that they "fit in" in order to want to continue at that institution and the need to feel a sense of belonging is evident in human basic needs as highlighted by Maslow's (1943) Hierarchy of Needs. The third basic need on Maslow's scale hierarchy is the need for affection and belongingness, which includes giving and receiving love, and affection.

The research conducted by Astin, Tinto, Schlossberg, and Maslow, highlighted in this chapter demonstrates the importance of socialization, involvement, and the feeling of belonging has on student retention and overall satisfaction. For faculty and staff members to increase the occurrence of socialization, involvement, and the feelings of belonging, this requires increasing, encouraging, and offering essential student interactions. This could pose a problem as there are only so many hours available in a traditional college work week, usually Monday through Friday from 9 am to 5 pm. However, these interactions can be extended outside the four walls of the classroom or professional office by utilizing virtual methods.

## VIRTUAL TOOLS

There are many new virtual tools that resemble that of face-to-face interactions and communication that possess the ability to encourage student involvement, socialization, and sense of belong, thus leading to higher retention rates of students. Educators need to be made aware of such virtual offerings, as well as provided with ample application-based and hands on training to ensure effective use. The first virtual tool that will be addressed is a free tool that was developed and is powered by Google.

### Google Wave

Google Wave (https://wave.google.com/wave/) is the newest free online communication platform that is both a synchronous communication and collaboration document sharing virtual tool. Stated simply, Google Wave is like combining the features of e-mail, threaded discussions, wikis, and instant message (IM) with multiple users all in one location. The virtual tool allows users to create "waves" which act as message documents and portals that include all replies, changes, and/or threads in one central location. This virtual tool reduces the need for individuals to send e-mails and attachments back and forth in an effort to try to collaborate on a document or project. Any of us that have tried the back and forth approach knows that it typically becomes problematic and confusing.

Through a shared "wave" individuals can access a document and have mutual conversations using richly formatted text, photos, videos, and more. Within a wave a participant can reply, edit, and add content at any given time within any part of the document. Since the wave is live, as participants reply or access the document the other members of the wave will see those edits in real time. Literately, in the wave you can watch as a user in type (letter by letter). Additionally, Google Wave will notify users who are members of a wave when replies or edits occur and displays those in chronological order. The best thing is that in a wave each reply or edit is recorded as an individual blip and users within that wave can utilize the playback feature to determine the order to which blips (replies and edits) were added, as well as what member was responsible for each blip. Waves can also be searched by users to determine what blips were specific to that participant. Lastly, waves can also be linked to other waves for additional collaboration and sharing to occur. Thus waves increase students' involvement in the course material and communication with peers.

So how can Google Wave improve and encourage socialization, involvement, and sense of belonging in higher education? Simple, through Google Wave instructors can assign groups projects in which collaboration can occur effortlessly outside the classroom through a virtual method. Through working in various waves, students can brainstorm ideas, create documents, discuss concepts, assign tasks to group members, attend virtual meetings, and solicit feedback in one central location. The professor can observe, reply, and make edits as the group is working on the project.

On Google Wave, ideas can come to life through virtual interactions. This interactive tool will allow students who are commuters, adult learners, and traditional learners who would otherwise be separated by distance outside the classroom to work together on teams without having to meet in person. After each group has completed their project, various waves (student groups) can be linked and classmates can comment on other group projects in an effort to build community and learn from each other.

Education is about learning, not only from the professor but also from other students. Gaining feedback, which leads to increased student socialization and involvement which according to Astin (1984, 1993, 1996), Schlossberg (1989), and Tinto (1993) are components of that lead to a sense of belonging thus making a student less likely to leave an institution. Google Wave is virtual tool that can help educators accomplish the above goals.

In education it is not difficult to locate critics when it comes to encouraging students to utilize virtual communication. Though the virtual tools in this chapter are use as supplemental resources to extend the learning that occurs in the classroom to increase student, faculty and staff member interactions outside the classroom. However, with use of any technology, risks can be associated with virtual communication and those will be briefly addressed.

### Virtual Communication Risks

When students utilize technology as their primary means of communication, their face-to-face verbal, non-verbal, and written communication skills are potentially reduced (Wilkinson & Buboltz, 1998). Communication often has less to do with the actual words, and more to do with the nonverbal cues that are incorporated into the exchange (McQuillen, 2003). Internet usage has been shown to be less effective in developing and maintaining social relationships than face-to-face communication. However, new virtual tools have made it possible for students, staff, and faculty members to communicate, interact, and collaborate in rich environments. One such tool is Wimba Collaboration Suite which was created to resemble and offer similar benefits associated with in-person communication utilizing a virtual environment.

## WIMBA COLLABORATION SUITE

Wimba Collaboration Suite (www.www.wimba.com) is a synchronous and asynchronous collaboration tool that enables and supports audio/voice (VOIP), text, instant messaging, application sharing, polling, and content display in one location. Through the use of this suite interactions between faculty members and students, as well as between classmates, can be extended beyond the four walls of a classroom. The options offered through Wimba have the ability to appeal to students who learn best through different learning styles such as auditory, visual, kinesthetic, and linguistic learners. Wimba Collaboration Suite (former named HorizonLive) offers Wimba Voice, Wimba Pronto, and Wimba Classroom. Wimba, unfortunately is not a free technology and does have a fee associated with each of the various components. The Wimba products are integrated and synchronized to an institution's Learning or Course Management Systems (LMS or CMS) such as Blackboard, ANGEL, and Moodle.

### Wimba Voice

Wimba Voice allows for voice or audio to be incorporated into most features or functions of the LMS/CMS, from the discussion board to the Gradebook. It combines speaking, writing, and listening in one location. Wimba Voice will particularly appeal and benefit those who learn best through audio information (aural/auditory or verbal/linguistic learners). The package has several features including, Voice Podcaster, Voice

Presentation, Voice Discussion Board, and Voice E-mail.

The first feature of review is Voice Podcaster which enables a user to create, edit, upload, and distribute podcasts. Professors could record podcasts for students to use as supplemental learning and instruction. For example if a student is taking a Principles of Accounting course, and the professor knew from previous classes that students often struggle with the concept of depreciation, he could produce a podcast that reviews the concept by discussing the causes, methods (straight-line, reducing balance, sum-of-the-years digits, or units of production), and proper disposal of property/equipment. While the topic was covered in class, a student has the added option of reviewing the concept prior to the midterm exam or another student might have been out sick with the flu and can listen to the content that she missed. Some critics may be leery of podcasting, but Jenkins, Goel, and Morrell (2008) concluded technology-based instruction such as podcasting was as effective as traditional classroom-based instruction. Of course this does not mean lecture-style teaching should be completely replaced, but podcasting does offer a great supplemental review or explanation of course materials for students. The added benefit of podcasting is students can listen to the information virtually anywhere, as they walk to class or drive home for the weekend. Lastly, Bennett and Cooper (2006) found that using podcasting in a college course improved both students' interest and understanding of course content. On U.S. campuses, most students come to college equipped with i-pods or MP3 players so the technology is readily available.

Voice Presentation allows a professor to upload content that is accompanied by vocals to function similar to an in-person presentation as opposed to static PowerPoint slides. These vocals can reiterate important class notes, provide helpful tips on completing homework, or aid a student in preparing for an upcoming exam. Imagine a modern language professor having the ability to show a word on a student's computer screen and then properly pronouncing the word to ensure students learn correct dialect and articulation. The student could further be required to send the instructor a message where he or she demonstrates the pronunciation of the word or the use of the word in a sentence.

Another use of the Voice Presentation would allow an instructor to provide supplementary explanation to a challenging concept of a recent lecture. For example a Physics professor could upload audio to accompany her PowerPoint that would further explain the Theory of Relativity for students to access if they need a review of the topic. It is not surprising that during an average 50 to 75 minute college lecture period, there is not enough time for a professor to offer individual clarification of a topic, but through this vocal feature the professor can upload this content after class for students to review.

Through the Voice Discussion Board, a user can record and listen to audio messages on a class virtual discussion board. This feature adds more depth and interactions to the typical text based postings and threads found on LMS discussion boards. Higher education professionals have been worried that technology usage has the potential to reduce students' speaking skills, but Wimba Voice has the added benefit of combining text with voice to ensure students can not only write what they mean but can orally communicate and articulate the message effectively to others. As most professors require students to adhere to the use of professional language and appropriate grammar on course discussion boards, a speaking component could be added to better strengthen a students' verbal communication as well. International students or non-native English speakers often need extra practice in oral communication skills, in that many universities are have established programs where an international student is matched with an English speaking as a conversational partner. The ended purpose of the conversational partner is to help a student practice speaking English in a casual environment, while giving the native speaker the opportunity to meet students from different parts of the world. In the past the pair met in person, but with Wimba Voice this conversation can occur virtually. The program can be expanded to include community members or alumni who may like to volunteer but were unable to get to campus due to work schedules or family commitments. Now conversations can be actively added, played, and returned through Voice Discussion Board.

Voice E-mail allows professors and students to record, send, and listen to audio email messages. Through this medium, messages can entail complex details and explanations that would be rather difficult and time consuming to write. Additionally, with the Integrated Gradebook feature of Wimba Voice, a LMS/CMS grade function is enhanced by permitting faculty to record voice messages and feedback in regard to assignments, quizzes, or tests. This audio feature will essentially eliminate the need for a professor to type detailed explanations of issues, comments, or suggestions. It can also simplify the grading process by allowing a professor to record comments as he/she reads through the paper. These verbal messages could better assist students in understanding details that might be difficult to get across with written words alone. Lastly, now that everyone is typing with the help of a computer, student's often struggle to read the professor's handwritten notes on tests and assignments, so verbal feedback can eliminate that challenge. Grading becomes as easy as pressing a record button. The next component in the Collaboration Suite is called Wimba Pronto.

## Wimba Pronto

Wimba Pronto offers instant (synchronous) communication to encourage collaborative learning. The features include instant messaging, combined audio and video conferencing, application sharing (real-time sharing of documents or computer applications on a user's screen), and a virtual interactive whiteboard. While you may think IM is not a unique feature, the difference is that Pronto automatically connects all users enrolled in a course, such as students, the professor, and/or a teaching assistant to each other for easy class collaboration and interactions. This differs in comparison to other IM programs that require users to become a member of the person's buddy list (AIM, MSN) or social network (Facebook) prior to exchanging messages. Pronto automatically connects the class, therefore allowing the instructor to encourage or require students to share ideas and concepts off line through the IM feature. The Wimba feature also provided an excellent portal for an instructor to hold virtual office hours via the system to answer any last minute questions the evening before an exam.

Now imagine trying to explain a complicated calculus solution to a student via e-mail using only text. It doesn't sound easy, but through Pronto a professor can work with the student by using the interactive whiteboard feature where he/she can enter text, draw freehand, import content, and make notes directly on the board as the student watches virtually on his/her computer. This type of instruction will particularly appeal to visual learners. Pronto even offers interactive tools such as a laser pointer, a semi-transparent highlighter, various shapes, colors, graphics, backgrounds, and font styles.

After a whiteboard session, the information can be saved as a pdf, png, jpg, or bmp. Upon saving the information, it can be uploaded and the student can access the information when needed or other classmates who might be experiencing a similar issue can open and review the notes from the session. The whiteboard session can be conducted one-on-one, in small groups, or to the entire class. There is a built in whiteboard navigation control that helps the professor save, organize, and locate various slides and sessions. This navigation feature is a great benefit because most full-time professors are teaching four classes a semester, having multiple daily interactions with students, and may struggle to keep content organized.

Lastly, the combined audio and video conferencing option can increase faculty to student interactions by extending office hours outside the traditional face-to-face times when a professor is on campus. The professor from the comforts of his/her own home could offer a variety of times when he/she is available virtually, such as in the evenings or on the weekends. Virtual conferencing is beneficial to adult learners who do not spend a lot of time on campus outside of attending classes or may not be able to make a professor's office hours if those are scheduled at a time that the student is at his/her full-time job. The conferencing option might be preferred by more than adult learners, because Jones (2002) discovered that 46 percent of traditional-aged students felt more comfortable expressing ideas to professors through virtual methods as opposed to face-to-face interactions. So it seems interacting virtually with a faculty member might be a welcomed opportunity by both adults and traditional-aged students. Whatever methods of interaction appeals to students, a faculty member should make an effort to appeal to a vast majority of the student population in an effort to further engage, integrate, and involve the student during college, in an effort to increase a student's sense of belonging. The final program in the Wimba Suite is called Wimba Classroom.

## Wimba Classroom

Wimba Classroom incorporates verbal and non-verbal communication to resemble that of face-to-face interactions; therefore these interactions can effortlessly occur outside the four walls of the classroom. Some interactive features of Wimba Classroom include instant polling, computer to computer application and document sharing, electronic whiteboard, presenter on-the-fly, MP3 and MP4 downloads to YouTube, iTunes University, or Facebook. Professors, who once could only share Word and PowerPoint documents with students can now share additional files like HTML, web pages, images, movie clips, PDF, whiteboard sessions, and Flash options.

Imagine the possibilities of adding interaction and involvement with classmates and professors through using one-on-one and multi-way video and audio features. This feature encourages and extends interactions outside the classroom. For example a professor could meet with various student groups in the evening to discuss the progress of class projects. A professor might also wish to have office hours or one-on-one advising sessions from the comforts of his/her own home, which would be done during non-traditional hours. The virtual interactions that occur through Wimba Classroom could be beneficial for meeting students that are separated by distance, for example an advisor could continue to communicate with her advisor as she spends a semester studying abroad in China. A PhD student might use the virtual Classroom as a suitable location to arrange weekly meetings with his dissertation committee, where it once seemed impossible to coordinate a time when the entire team was available on campus to meet in person. Finally, it gives student the extra confidence in knowing that he/she has the potential of being able to touch base with a professor on the weekend if he/she was experiencing a struggle in understanding an assignment.

While email (text) is feasible for answering student questions, Wimba Classroom combines text and voice by providing students with a full range of options of expressing themselves and developing verbal communication skills. As mentioned previously in this chapter, communication skills are essential for student to develop during college. It is no secret that employers are looking to recruit and hire students who have effective written and verbal skills, so faculty members can make sure students strengthen these skills through virtual interactions outside the classroom. For example many professors require students to write an original post and reply on a weekly discussion board or thread, now an oral component can be added to the weekly assignments.

The "live classroom" feature resembles that of a real classroom but in a virtual environment. In this classroom, students can virtually raise their hands, ask questions, and view information as it is posted on an interactive whiteboard. The live classroom has made bringing in guest speakers from around the world effortless. Guest speakers can add practical knowledge and provide application to what is being taught in the classroom. In the past it was often difficult to arrange a convenient time when a speaker could arrive on campus to address a class. Through technology, the speaker can remain locally and be broadcasted live where students can log on to see, hear, and ask questions. Wimba has a classroom archiving option that would allow for the speaker's session to be recorded (voice, chat, content, question and answer session, etc.) and saved to be used in a future course or available for students to access who might have been unable to attend. Lastly, Wimba Classroom has features that assist students who have disabilities to experience academic success by viewing information in a closed-caption format or through a screen reader that aids a student who is visually impaired.

The live classroom feature could also benefit institutions that host speaker series on campus. Most institutions are experiencing a challenge of locating interesting and engaging speakers that adhere to a college's strict budget. Through the use of a live virtual interactive option, it eliminates the need to pay for the speaker's travel expenses, campus facility and media technology support fees, as well as other expenses associated with the visit such as catering (refreshment) costs. This approach provides students with the opportunity to attend a speaker series from their dorm rooms and perhaps this would appeal to students and increase participation rates. It is no surprise that institutions are finding it increasing difficult to fill an audience when a speaker is on campus. This method would avoid the embarrassment an institution feels when a speaker is on campus, and only a handful of students show up, and the speaker is forced to talk to an almost empty audience.

Finally, with the popularity of first-year reading or summer common reading programs, this virtual method could also work well in allowing and encouraging students to interact with the author of the book in which they are reading. The newest trend is for colleges to bring the author to campus to discuss the book. However, with technology such as Wimba this could be completed in the summer as students are engaged in reading the book as opposed to after the students have arrived on campus and their focus and interest is now on meeting classmates, attending classes, and adjusting to college life.

Additionally, Wimba Classroom has incorporated the popular student response systems (SRS) or "clicker" feature into the system. The interactive polling option can be used as a strategy to increase active engagement of course content and materials. Draper and Brown (2004) identified the most important benefit of in-class polling was in its ability to provide instructors with immediate feedback about whether students were able to understand and conceptualize course content. Several researchers have determined that polling increases a student's focus, engagement, processing, and application of course concepts and ideas (Hidi, 2000; Schiefele, 1999). The polling on Wimba can be as simple as yes or no questions to advanced options such as multiple choice and open ended assessments.

Another great option of Wimba classroom is a professor can arrange virtual breakout rooms to enable and encourage outside the classroom peer interactions and discussions. T break out rooms would be perfect for group projects where each group would have their own break out room and the professor would be able to monitor participation and progress. Another use for break out rooms would be to create theme based rooms. For example if a professor discovered students in his class were having trouble referencing citations using APA style, a breakout room might be created to cover that concept for students who needed additional help. The student would enter the room during open hours and receive support, perhaps from a professional staff member from the campus writing center. These virtual breakout sessions have the potential to increase student collaborations, socialization, and involvement, which as we learned earlier in the chapter can lead to increased student retention rates. This is due to the fact students are supporting and cooperating with each other, while demonstrating a shared commitment to accomplishing a team goal (Dede, 2000). Through these breakout groups, a professor can encourage and facilitate peer interactions outside the classroom to ensure all learners feel included and valued as part of the class, potentially leading to an increases sense of social presence and belonging. It is important that instructors begin to understand the difference of being physically present (passive) is not the same as being mentally (active) engaged. Therefore, students must be monitored by the professor from time to time during virtual group sessions to ensure equal student collaboration and team work. When students interact and work collaboratively to achieve a common goal the process fosters feelings of community or belonging by enriching interactions between students, while contributing to group cohesion. One way for a professor to manage students who are working virtually on a project is require the group to turn in a project management weekly summary. This summary (workflow) highlights how project tasks were divided amongst teammates, as well collaborate efforts that occurred between members. This provides a general view to the instructor if group cohesion and team commitment is taking place, and a way to better ensure students are actively engaged in the learning process. As more colleges incorporate practical application of knowledge and learning through assigning projects as opposed to giving rote memorization exams, there will be an increased need for students to interact outside the classroom. Therefore, the student breakout sessions in effect extend classroom interactions but allow the professor to continue to oversee and provide feedback to each group without consuming valuable class time. The breakout rooms can be further enhanced with the document sharing that eliminates the need for sending attachments back and forth between students and instructors for comments, edits, and brainstorming. Goodbye Microsoft track changes, hello live editing capabilities.

The last feature of Wimba Classroom that is beneficial in increasing student interactions is the live chat and eBoard. The chat feature can be used to have individual meetings with students regarding assignments, class performance, semester academic advising meetings, or project progress. The added perk is the chat function creates a transcript of the chat and this can be saved or printed to be placed in a student's file as in the case of academic advising. It would serve as a record of the various items covered during the session, especially if there was an issue that needed documented.

Lastly, the eBoard would allow a professor to take control of the student's computer anything on your computer, thus turning the computer into an electronic whiteboard. Students and professors can now type, draw, import, and share desktop applications through eBoard (which acts as a whiteboard). Instructors might find this function useful in troubleshooting because as the student performs the function the professor can watch online to ensure that he/she is following protocol. For example, students often struggle on how to create a table of contents for a report, few realize there is a function in Microsoft Word in which if the user defines all headers throughout the document the software will create the table of contents. The process can be demonstrated via an eBoard as it is difficult to explain using text or audio alone. This chapter briefly demonstrated that with Web 2.0 and virtual technologies the sky is the limit.

## FUTURE RESEARCH DIRECTIONS

In an effort to increase retention rates, college administrators, professional staff and faculty members implement and utilize many of the recommendations, suggestions, and findings from past retention research studies. It might be rare to locate higher education professionals who have not heard or reviewed the research of Vincent Tinto, the guru of college student retention and dropout literature. However, most of the longitudinal research that exists on attrition and retention has been conducted utilizing the traditional environment, whereas interactions are assumed to take place through face-to-face methods. Since we are living in a technological world more robust research studies need to be conducted on how virtual and Web 2.0 technologies can be used to retain, orient, socialize, engage, involve, and create a sense of belonging for college student, both students living on and off campus.

Lastly, it must be statistically (quantitative and qualitative) determined if virtual interactions are presumed as valuable (significant) or perhaps in some cases more beneficial in the mind of today's college students. With more students enrolling in blended learning or distance education degree programs, it becomes increasing difficult to retain students who are rarely or never available for in-person interactions. The question to answer becomes how can staff and faculty members effectively supplement and/or replace face-to-face interactions by using virtual and Web 2.0 alternatives?

## CONCLUSION

Learning is an interactional process whereas communications should occur between and amongst students and instructors. Osguthorpe and Graham (2003) discovered that when students actively share questions, insights, ideas, suggestions, and engage in content, they experience higher levels of comprehension and sense of being a member of a group. Therefore, professors must encourage and enable collaborative interactions to occur inside and outside the classroom. While in the past in-person interactions might have been enough, today, with the proliferation of the Web 2.0 and virtual technologies these can be used to supplement face-to-face meetings, ensure continuous interactions, and active collaborations. By increasing interactions between peers, faculty and staff members, the process may lead to a student experiencing an increase sense of socialization, involvement, engagement, and belonging in an overall attempt to increase retention rates. The days of only offering students face-to-face interactions in the classroom are a thing of the past. Many universities have realized the potential of utilizing and incorporating virtual technologies to extend classroom interactions outside the brick and mortar walls of the college building. Currently, many virtual tools exist to encourage interactions between classmates, professional staff, and/or faculty members, and as technology develops the options will continue to expand. It is up to educators to continuously take advantage and make use of available options.

## REFERENCES

Astin, A. W. (1984). Student involvement: A developmental theory for higher education. *Journal of College Student Personnel*, *25*, 297–308.

Astin, A. W. (1993). *What matters most in college: Four critical years revisited*. San Francisco, CA: Jossey-Bass.

Astin, A. W. (1996). Involvement in learning revisited: Lessons we have learned. *Journal of College Student Development*, *37*, 123–134.

Astin, A. W. (1999). Student involvement: A developmental theory for higher education. *Journal of College Student Development*, *40*, 518–529.

Bean, J. P. (2005). Nine themes of college student retention. In Seidman, A. (Ed.), *College student retention: Formula for student success* (pp. 215–243). Westport, CT: Praeger Publishers.

Bennett, J. F., & Cooper, P. A. (2006). EdPod: Adding classroom richness to the on-line experience. *The Proceedings of ISECON 2006* (vol. 23). Dallas, TX.

Braxton, J. M., & Lee, S. D. (2005). Toward reliable knowledge about college student departure. In Seidman, A. (Ed.), *College student retention: Formula for student success* (pp. 107–128). Westport, CT: Praeger Publishers.

Dede, C. (2000, March). Emerging influences of information technology on school curriculum. *Journal of Curriculum Studies, 32*(2), 281–303. doi:10.1080/002202700182763

Draper, S. W., & Brown, M. I. (2004). Increasing interactivity in lectures using an electronic voting system. *Journal of Computer Assisted Learning, 20*, 81–94. doi:10.1111/j.1365-2729.2004.00074.x

Habley, W. R., & McClanahan, R. (2004). *What works in student retention? All survey colleges.* American College Testing.

Hidi, S. (2000). An interest researcher's perspective on the effects of extrinsic and intrinsic factors on motivation. In Sansone, C., & Harackiewicz, J. M. (Eds.), *Instrinsic and extrinsic motivation. The secret for optimal motivation and performance* (pp. 311–339). New York, NY: Academic Press. doi:10.1016/B978-012619070-0/50033-7

Jenkins, S., Goel, R., & Morrell, D. S. (2008). Computer-assisted instruction versus traditional lecture for medical student teaching of dermatology morphology: A randomized control trial. *Journal of the American Academy of Dermatology, 59*(2), 255–259. doi:10.1016/j.jaad.2008.04.026

Jones, S. (2002). *The internet goes to college: How students are living in the future with today's technology.* Retrieved from http://www.pewinternet.org/pdfs/PIP_College_Report.pdf

Kuh, G. D. (1995). The other curriculum: Out-of-class experiences associated with student learning and professional development. *The Journal of Higher Education, 66*, 123–135. doi:10.2307/2943909

Light, R. J. (2001). *Making the most of college: Students speak their minds.* Boston, MA: Harvard University Press.

Maslow, A. H. (1943). *Motivation and personality.* New York, NY: Harper.

McQuillen, J. S. (2003). The influence of technology on the initiation of interpersonal relationships. *Education, 123*, 616.

Osguthorpe, R. T., & Graham, C. R. (2003). Blended learning environments: Definitions and directions. *The Quarterly Review of Distance Education, 4*(3), 227–233.

Pascarella, E. T., & Terenzini, P. T. (2005). *How college affects students: A third generation of research* (*Vol. 2*). San Francisco, CA: Jossey-Bass.

Schiefele, U. (1999). Interest and learning from text. *Scientific Studies of Reading, 3*, 25–279. doi:10.1207/s1532799xssr0303_4

Schlossberg, N. K. (1984). *Counseling adults in transition: Linking practice with theory.* New York, NY: Springer.

Schlossberg, N. K. (1989). Marginality and mattering: Key issues in building community. In Roberts, D. C. (Ed.), *Designing campus activities to foster a sense of community. New directions in student services* (pp. 5–15). San Francisco, CA: Jossey Bass.

Spady, W. (1971). Dropouts from higher education: Interdisciplinary review and synthesis. *Interchange*, *1*, 64–85. doi:10.1007/BF02214313

Strage, A. (2000). Predictors of college adjustment and success: Similarities and differences among Southeast-Asian American, Hispanic, and White students. *Education*, *120*, 731–741.

Terenzini, P., Springer, L., Yaeger, P., Pascarelle, E., & Nora, A. (1996). First-generation college students: Characteristics, experience, and cognitive development. *Research in Higher Education*, *37*, 1–22. doi:10.1007/BF01680039

Tinto, V. (1975). Dropouts from higher education: A theoretical synthesis of recent research. *Review of Educational Research*, *45*, 89–125.

Tinto, V. (1987). *Leaving college: Rethinking the causes and cures of student attrition*. Chicago, IL: The University of Chicago Press.

Tinto, V. (1993). *Leaving college: Rethinking the causes and cures of student retention*. Chicago, IL: The University of Chicago Press.

United Sates Department of Education, National Center for Education Statistics. (2009). *The condition of education 2009* (NCES 2009-081). *Indicator (Minnesota Mining and Manfuacturing Company)*, 22.

Upcraft, M. L., & Gardner, J. N. (1989). A comprehensive approach to enhancing freshmen success. In Gardner, L. M. (Ed.), *The freshman year experience, helping students survive and succeed in college* (pp. 1–12). San Francisco, CA: Jossey-Bass.

Wilkinson, L., & Buboltz, W. C., Jr. (1998, March). E-mail: Communication of the future? *Proceedings (IR 018 794) at SITE 98: Society for Information Technology & Teacher Education International Conference*, Washington, D.C.

# Chapter 3
# E-Learning for K-12 Learners and Adult Learners

**Lesley Farmer**
*California State University Long Beach, USA*

## ABSTRACT

*E-learning uses online networks to enable learners to interact meaningfully with their educational environment. E-learning is explained in terms of the communication cycle and its application in a learning cycle. Social and developmental aspects of e-learning are addressed. Strategies to scaffold e-learning are also provided.*

## INTRODUCTION

The number one goal of education is to help people learn. How does learning occur, and how do conditions of technology-based education impact learning? Does e-learning, in fact, differ from conventional learning? These issues are addressed in this chapter.

## THE COMMUNICATION CYCLE AND LEARNING

E-learning is not an isolated process, but occurs within the context of society. At the most elemental stage, e-learning reflects the interaction between an individual and his or her environment, between the internal and external world. When this interaction occurs between two people, it is called a communication cycle. One person externalizes information, and another person receives that information. For the communication to complete the cycle, the receiving party needs to process the information and respond to the sender. If the receiver changes his or her behavior in the process, it can be said that the person *learned*. Costa (1985) asserted that learning as any stimulus of change for which the response is not readily apparent. If the process is digitally based, usually involving a network (such as a LAN, WAN, or broadcast network), then the term e-learning can be applied.

DOI: 10.4018/978-1-60960-791-3.ch003

The communications cycle adds another layer of complexity when technology is incorporated. For instance, the information may be expressed digitally: as a text file, a podcast, a video, or a jpg image. To create that expression, the originator has to have access to, and be able to use, some kind of hardware and software. To send that information, equipment is also required as a communication channel. The potential or target party needs physical access to compatible communication channel equipment and software to translate that information into a recognizable format. Only then can the receiver sense the information, and process it. The receiver, like the sender, would also need to be able to use technology in order to respond to the information digitally.

The communication cycle can be applied to the teaching process. The teacher has information that s/he wants to communicate to the student with the conscious intent of teaching the student so that the student can learn. For the teacher to know if her/his intent was successful, the student needs to respond in a way that demonstrates learning: a change in behavior. Teachers can incorporate technology into the communication cycle when communicating information as well as communicating about technology explicitly. Each aspect can impact how the student receives the information and responds – or not.

It should be noted that learning can occur without the presence of a teacher. Indeed, a communication cycle itself is not necessary. Theoretically, a *learning* cycle could begin with a person sensing some stimulus, such as a raindrop. However, the raindrop is not sentient and is not communicating anything. On the other hand, a raindrop is an indicator of rain; it has a meaning, potentially. If the person knows what a raindrop represents, he or she is likely to react to it, perhaps by running inside, opening an umbrella, or waiting for a puddle to form. If that person has no knowledge of a raindrop, the experience of sensing it and seeing how one's body and clothes become wet, the person will probably learn the meaning of the raindrop, and hopefully will have enough sense to get out of the rain, literally.

Communication implies intelligence on both ends, with a conscious intent to convey information, be it an idea or an emotion, with the expectation that the receiving party will respond. Additionally, when technology is involved, some human is behind it at some point. Mass media, for instance, involves a communications channel and some kind of message that has the intent of influencing the audience, even if a specific individual is not targeted. Thus, for the purposes of discussion in this chapter, elearning can be connected with the communications cycle. The elements of that process are detailed in terms of ways that show how technology impacts learning.

## INTERACTING WITH INFORMATION

At this point, it is useful to focus on the more generic issues of individual engagement with information: attention, processing, evaluating information, manipulating information, and acting on information, Each step impacts learning. Furthermore, technology impacts each step as well.

### Attention

Each person has life experiences prior to contact with a specific piece of information within a specific situation of space and time. Concurrently, information has been created by billions of people over time. That information has been expressed and disseminated in myriad ways: from cave drawings and singing to movies and holographic images.

Humans are constantly bombarded by stimuli, even before they are born. They become aware of stimuli through their senses, and make decisions as to whether to ignore the stimuli or deal with them. What causes them to pay attention? Novelty (such as an unknown sound) or impact on themselves (such as a protruding nail). It should be noted that the individual has to be conscious and receptive to the stimulus as well (a counter example being the person who closes his eyes and ears to avoid hearing bad news). Even if the person is receptive, other competing stimuli might distract or counteract the specific stimulus. Furthermore, a person might not be able sense the stimulus; hence the phrase "Falling on deaf eyes."

In face-to-face education, the teacher is likely to activate curriculum-based stimulus, and call attention to it, In e-learning situations, the teacher sets up the structures that provide stimula for the information-interaction process, but the student might have to pro-actively seek the stimulus.

## Processing

Persons take that external stimuli and internally process it. They to make sense of that stimuli; they have to decode it (that is, determine the communication protocols of linguistics, visual principles, etc.) and understand the content being communicated (that is, the vocabulary, semiotics, concepts, etc.). Biologically, the brain's sensory cortex receives the information, and the integrate cortex makes meaning of the information. The frontal integrative cortex creates ideas form the meaning, and the motor cortex acts on the ideas (Zull, 2004). The brain has to store the incoming information first in immediate memory, and then long enough in the working memory to make sense of the information (Sousa, 2000). Adding to the picture are brain processing propensities; some people have more developed, specialized brain areas that favor linguistic or musical processing, for instance. Some people process information in light of its context (such as who said it or in what room the information was expressed) while others process information independently of any context (known as field-independence). Some people can process abstract information more easily than concrete information, and vice versa. In each other these cases, when information is novel, being able to build on well-developed processing methods can help individuals to pay more attention to the content. On the other hand, when the content is familiar, the person can focus attention on processing in novel ways.

Motivation is a key factor at this point. Without it, persons may ignore the stimulus. Motivation draws from prior experience, and is contextually situated: what is happening to the person at the time that the stimulus is sensed. Pintrich and Linnenbrink (2002) posited four components of motivation: self-efficacy, attribute theory, locus of motivation, and achievement goal theory. Self-efficacy is the feeling of competency, that the person can deal with the stimulus. Attribute theory addresses the basis for success or failure; females are more likely than males to attribute success to others (for example, "computers are so smart") and attribute failure to themselves ("I'm so stupid about technology"). Motivation may be external (such as getting good grades or looking good in front of others) or internal. Achievement goal theory addresses the reason for achievement: performance-oriented or master-oriented, for example. Motivation involves feelings. Biologically, the chemicals associated with feelings – adrenalin, dopamine, serotonin – interact with and reinforce neuron connections, which influence the processing of the stimuli. A pleasant surprise can stimulate the person to process the information and derive pleasure from figuring out the surprise. On the other hand, too much emotion, such as overwhelming fear, can paralyze a person's processing.

Thus, for persons to successfully process the information, they have to be able to intellectually access that information (make sense of it), which entails both biological processes as well as mental and psychological processes. Learning disabilities, such as dyslexia or ADHD, jeopardize internal processing in that sensory connections may be impaired or memory may be affected. Several internal intellectual barriers exist to comprehension: language, illiteracy, lack of prior content knowledge. If persons disengage with the information, out of frustration or lack of motivation, they might short circuit processing.

Sometimes processing requires external scaffolding. Students may ask for help from other people: "What does this word mean?" "Can you open this file?" Students might consult other sources to help them understand the information, such as dictionaries or encyclopedias. Students might use tools to highlight passages or draw diagrams to better comprehend the information.

Technology tools may be used in such situations: Internet-connected computers, mind-mapping software applications, telephones. The choice of tool depends on the person's prior knowledge and experience since without that knowledge, the technology would be useless.

In any case, with this external processing, a micro-communication cycle occurs within the larger communication cycle, pro-actively seeking additional information or communication channels to complement or supplement existing internal resources. When students self-regulate their learning, they are able to see the learning cycle as a whole and step-by-step, identify the miss-steps and try to identify how to address them. Likewise, educators are trained to analyze the learning cycle. If they know what processing problems students have, educators can provide the relevant scaffolding based on their academic and professional experience.

Even if the stimulus makes sense, the question remains: "Does it have meaning?" Is it relevant? This question is a personal judgment call. If it does not affect the person, that information might not be very meaningful. For instance, knowing the formula for salt might not be very meaningful unless one is involved in chemistry. In all likelihood, unmeaningful information is usually forgotten and not learned. Biologically, only if the brain stores the information in long-term memory is learning possible. Therefore, if educators want students to learn, the information needs to be made meaningful. Educators have to show how the information has potential value, that it can make a positive difference in their students' own lives.

## Evaluating Information

Next, the person relates the "new" information with his/her existing knowledge. If the information is the same, it can be forgotten or it can reinforce existing long-term memory, which strengthens neuron connections. The person also has to determine the value of the interaction; it is worth the effort to continue the relationship?

Learning only happens when the stimulus is understandable as well as new/novel or contradicting existing knowledge; a disequilibrium exists. In response, the person tries to regain equilibrium by either rejecting or adding the new information, or reconciling it with current information (which might result in rejecting or modifying the existing information). Both cognitive and affective factors come into play. For instance, if the person dislikes the information's messenger, then the message itself may be rejected. On the other hand, if a new discovery delights a person, old ideas might be easily shed.

The more important the information (both mentally and psychologically), the greater impact the learning (or decision to *not* learn) has. For example, information about evolution might contradict a person's belief in a literal interpretation of the Bible; if religious faith is more important than scientific evidence – or the fear of religious doubt is too troubling, that person might well reject evolutionary theory. Contradictory new information considered to be trivial to an individual (such as the ingredients in suntan lotion) might be easier to accept because it does not negatively impact one's personal identity or way of life; of course, that new information might also be easily ignored or rejected *because* it makes no difference. To add complexity to the issue, one person's trivial information might be critical to another person (such as severe allergic reaction to some types of suntan lotion, to continue the example).

As with processing step, educators try to help student grapple with new information and incorporate it into their long-term memory for later action. Educator efforts need to address both the cognitive and affective aspects of evaluating. They can provide criteria for evaluation information, tools for comparing such as T-charts, and additional resources to reinforce the validity of the new information. They can also offer external incentives for accepting the new information, such as grades and career opportunities.

Technology can help students evaluate information in several ways. Obviously, technology facilitates physical or virtual access to resources globally. Students and educators can find additional information to corroborate existing or new information, depending on the person's desired intention. Networked information has the potential for being practically instantaneous, so if timeliness or currency is highly-valued by the student, then that information may be more highly regarded. Depending on the person's attitude about technology, presenting information electronically can influence a person's acceptance of that information; some people give more credence to information on the Internet while others may scoff at such online resources, assuming that little critical review is involved.

## Manipulating Information

Individuals also need to determine what to DO with that information, if anything. Typically, doing implies an externalization process: the next part of the communications cycle as it applies to learning. If the person just parrots back that information, no change occurs. On the other hand, for learning to occur, that information needs to be transformed in some way: through interpretation, organization, synthesis, reformatting, relating. In any case, information manipulation consists of four processing skills: 1) extracting the information, 2) deciding how to represent it, 3) determining the method of manipulating it, 4) knowing how to do the manipulation. Throughout this surprisingly complex interaction with information, individuals need to make decisions that are based on prior knowledge -- or lack thereof. They cannot continue to interact and act unless they have the prerequisite knowledge and skills to build upon.

In formal educational situations, educators tend to stipulate the parameters for the student to manipulate the information. For any of the four processing skills, educators need to make sure that students have the intellectual and physical tools necessary to complete each task. Finely targeted diagnostic abilities are called for, as well as interventions that help students gain those skills. In some cases, the focus of learning is actually in such processing skills. For instance, students may know about biomes, but have to extract pertinent information about biomes from a given article about birds. Their teacher may need to explain now to take notes or locate key phrases in a text. Likewise, that teacher might focus on showing students how to create a concept map as a way to represent their knowledge.

Technology provides many tools for manipulating information. In fact, computers were created originally to compute: to "crunch" or process numbers. Ideally, technology can do the "grunt" or mechanical work so that the student can focus on the cognitive work. It should be noted that technology can also help store and retrieve information for use. Here are just a few technological tools and ways that they help people manipulate information.

- Spreadsheets enable one to organize and sort information data by category, create and use formulas, generate charts. Spreadsheets can be used to test hypotheses and make predictions. For instance, students can determine if household income might be correlated to infant mortality or other health issues.
- Databases enable one to organize and sort information data by category, and link related databases of information such as demographics and politics. Databases help one test hypotheses and analyze groups

of data. For instance, a database of plants and chemicals might lead to medicinal discoveries.

- Presentation tools (e.g., PowerPoint, KeyNote, HyperStudio) enable one to organize and sequence information, and combine media to more effective represent knowledge. Presentation tools can be used to outline information and relate ideas. For instance, a PowerPoint presentation can tell about an author's life.
- Graphic programs (e.g., PhotoShop, Illustrator, iPhoto) enable one to produce and modify images. Graphic programs foster visual literacy. For instance, students can see how different color schemes can affect perceptions about interior design.
- Audio tools (e.g., Audacity, GarageBand) enable one to record, capture, and manipulate sounds. Audio applications foster aural literacy so that one can be used to perceive poetic rhythm or distinguish linguistic features. For instance, students can use different music to convey different interpretations of an advertisement.
- Video tools (e.g., Movie Maker, Photo Story, iMovie, Premiere) enable one to record, capture, and manipulate a combination of sound, image and movement (image in space and time). Video tools help one process realistic information and procedures such as chemical reactions. For instance, students can make a video to explain how to repair a car.

Identifying which technology is the most appropriate to manipulate information requires learning about the technology itself. For instance, as students make sense of a video and its visual language, they are better poised to use video to manipulate information. If the focus of learning is on creating a video, students experience what processes are involved, and how they impact the video product. They become fluent in the "language" and "grammar" of video (and sound and image) to that they can comprehend its meaning and ways to manipulate that meaning more subtly.

While students can explore different technologies on their own, testing which media work best, educators can mandate appropriate technologies as they understand how each technology operates. In such situations, students can focus on the information manipulation rather than on the technology manipulation. However, educators would be remiss if they did not point out the features of the technology on hand so that students can learn how to identify appropriate technologies independently.

## Acting on Information

Still another decision needs to be made after the manipulation: how to act upon that information if at all. While information may be meaningful and interesting in itself, such as the elegance of a mathematical proof, it derives power when contextualized and related to other information. Learners may apply the information to a familiar or novel situation, they might solve a problem or answer a question, they might change their environment or themselves. In terms of the communication cycle, the individual becomes the creator or initiator. Taking the information that has been the focus of attention, the individual links it to other information or source of information, including other people. The act can also be the generation of new information. The cycle spirals. Not only does the information have meaning, but the learning itself gains meaning as it impacts the individual who can then impact others.

Educators can prime the action pump by identifying the information task in the first place, which also motivates the student to engage with the information and resolve the underlying problem. Educators can also critique–and help learners self-critique–their efforts with the intent of reaching an optimal conclusion. For instance, a student might know how chemicals react, and might know how

*Table 1.*

| ELEMENT | E-LEARNER | INFORMATION | TECHNOLOGY | EDUCATOR SCAFFOLD OR INTERVENTION |
|---|---|---|---|---|
| *Pre-engagement.* | Background, knowledge, capabilities, situation | What are its characteristics? What are the characteristics of the environment in general and at that moment? | What hardware and software is available? What are its characteristics and status? | Knowledge, role, situation |
| *Origin of need:* | Personal, academic | Producer wants to influence or gain power | Producer wants to gain profit | Standards, values |
| *Task determinator:* | Brainstorming, concept map, strategy choice | Format parameters | Availability, operational status, connectivity | Giving directions |
| *First contact:* | Attention (may choose to ignore it) | Physical access issues (equipment, availability) | Availability, operational status, connectivity | Introduction, motivation |
| *Comprehension/ intellectual access:* | Decoding (e.g., visuals, sound, linguistic language); Understanding content (e.g., vocabulary, semiotics, concepts) | Layout, cues to understanding, glossary, dual coding | Software/ application features | Phonics instruction; oral reading; simplification; deconstruction; contextualization |
| *Evaluation:* | Agreement/ rejection/ incorporation of ideas (based on cognitive, affective, behavioral); Determination of use; Task or need change | Comparative information; peer review | Comparative hardware and software | Criteria lists, rubrics; critical thinking skills instruction |
| *Manipulation of information:* | Interpretation; Organization; Synthesis; Re-Formatting; Changing; Relating or Combining with other information | Characteristics of information and its representation; malleability | Characteristics of hardware/ equipment and software/ applications; connectivity issues | Analytical and manipulation skills diagnosis and instruction; Stipulating end product format or desired result; Provision of tools |
| *Application/ use:* | Problem-solving; Learning; Self-change; Adding to knowledge base | Generation of new information; Change in environment; Change in power | Hardware, software, connectivity changes | Critique; Providing venue for implementation |

to use the appropriate equipment, but still might have a chemical spill that the teacher might need to address – and help students to learn how to deal with. Alternatively, a student might know how to create a web page with relevant content, but might still need to submit the material for the teacher or administrator to upload unto the server, or learn how to upload the information independently.

As with information manipulation, technology can facilitate applying the information by serving as the communications channel and storage mechanism. Probably the greatest impact that technology has in this respect is the enormous potential for reaching people around the world. Today's students have many more opportunities to communicate with a wide and authentic audience. Especially as student can pass on their learning to others so that they in turn can learn is an amazing and empowering experience for all parties.

Table 1 summarizes the interaction between the e-learner and the information, and the role that technology and educators can play.

Educators set the preconditions along each step, with the conscious intent to facilitate learning. As they establish the learning environment for information interaction, educations need to address the following questions.

- Where will the interaction occur: in the classroom, in the library, in the lab, in the community, at home?
- What is the time frame?
- Who will instruct: the classroom teacher, other school staff, students, community experts?
- What networked information sources will be used? What should be their characteristics and quantity? What hardware and software is needed to transmit the information?
- What learning aids or scaffolding is needed to facilitate physical and intellectual access and manipulation of information?

Additionally, along the way, educators can optimize the possibilities for learning by providing scaffolds that bridge the students' lack of knowledge or skill with the desired learning outcome, which is detailed below.

## LEARNING WITH TECHNOLOGY, LEARNING ABOUT TECHNOLOGY

Learning *with* technology differs from learning *about* technology. The former focuses on process while the latter emphasizes content matter. When technology is integrated into the learning environment, its manipulation needs to be taken into account as well as the academic concepts to be mastered. A separate, and sometimes related, set of knowledge and skills must be addressed. If students do not know how to create a PowerPoint, then they will need to opportunity -- and the time -- to learn and practice that skill. Teachers need to figure out how that learning will occur. Do students have access to the hardware and software at home or at school? Do they have the time outside of class to access and learn the application? Does class time have to be dedicated to that learning? Could students work in groups so that one student would input the information but other students would do the research and writing?

In e-learning situations, educators should frontload the conditions for e-learning.

- **Physical access**. Instructional resources should be accessed by low-performance equipment and dial-up connectivity. Text needs to be saved in formats that can be read by open source software;.rtf files are usually an acceptable format. Unfortunately, while image-rich and multimedia documents take advantage of multiple learning styles, they also require broader bandwidth and may need plug-ins in order to play correctly. Furthermore, instructional materials should be accessible for individuals with disabilities.
- **Intellectual access**. Educators may need to provide directions on the use of technology tools such as spreadsheets or authoring programs. In some cases, even simple operations such as attaching files need to be explained. Educators can help students be self-sufficient learners by showing them how to get technical assistance through help screens, manuals, web FAQs, and online tutorials. While some students are motivated to use technology, and will make the extra effort to process information, others have a negative attitude toward technology that will impede information processing.
- **Building community**. One of the main drawbacks of e-learning can be the feeling of isolation. With the advent of Web 2.0, students can interact with their online peers to build a community of learners. Educators need to set up the conditions for interactive learning by designing opportunities for group discussion and collaborative learning activities. Threaded discussion forums, wikis, blogs, and online conferencing are just a few of the tools available. These community-based struc-

tures have to be supported through the online training of these tools.

Even with these general provisions, e-learning might not succeed because students have differing pre-existing attitudes and experiences with technology, particularly if they are adult learners. By its nature, e-learning can be a very personalized experience, and technology can support such differentiation. At the very least, educators need to provide students with a variety of instructional materials and learning activities to choose from. Relating to technology is affected by emotional states, so educators need to make sure that students can feel safe in taking intellectual risks in trying technology, and are rewarded for their efforts as well as their final products (Rogers, 1962).

In addition, though, educators may have to deal a spectrum of student comfort levels vis-à-vis technology. The Center for Research and Development in Teaching at the University of Texas at Austin (Hall & Loucks, 1979) developed a seven-step model that identifies issues that concern lenders as they process form unawareness to full integration of technology. The developers assert that educators need to modify instruction to align with each person's stage of concern. Ideally, educators should conduct a needs assessment to ascertain the stage of their students in order to design activities accordingly. Stages and suggested approaches follow.

1. **Awareness**. Learners start from ignorance. Educators have to get their attention. Online features need to draw attention to the relevant technology.
2. **Information**. Learners receive technology via one-way communication. Educators give objective information about the relevant technology, perhaps giving a video demonstration. http://www.commoncraft.com is a good source of user-friendly technology information.
3. **Personal**. Learners react to technology from a personal perspective. Educators need to know the immediate benefit of using technology, such as peer sharing. Having students share a photo of themselves and a brief introduction can serve as a good ice-breaker.
4. **Management**. Learners try to fit technology into their overall learning experience and practice. Educators need to show how the technology concretely contributes to their educational goal.
5. **Consequence**. Learners determine whether the effort to learn the technology is worth the effort. At this point, choosing the most appropriate technology for the learning task is a key competence.
6. **Collaboration**. Leaders work with others to leverage the impact of technology. Educators should introduce Web 2.0 tools at this point.
7. **Refocus**. Learners become pro-active experts. Educators should give them opportunities to teach others about technology.

## COOPERATIVE E-LEARNING

The social aspect of learning needs to be acknowledged and leveraged. As noted above, e-learning can facilitate peer interaction and coaching. Vygotsky (1978) asserted that learning exists first between people and then is internalized. The most common way to learn socially is through collaboration: typically, small groups working together towards a common goal or solution. Other features of collaborative learning include group and individual accountability, distributed leadership, and group autonomy. Collaboration provides opportunities for individuals to think aloud and engage both intellectually and emotionally, and incorporates both academic and social objectives. Another basic tenet of collaborative learning is that students have significant control over learning through automany and key decision-making.

Today's technology can facilitate collaborative e-learning because it transcends time and space. People can work with each other both in real time and asynchronously. Web 2.0 tools have greatly expanded the ways that collaboration can occur to support e-learning.

- **Threaded discussions** archive individual contributions and responses chronologically by subject.
- **Blogs** (web logs) enable individuals to write about their experiences chronologically, and others can comment on the entries.
- **Wikis** (quick-edit web pages) facilitate joint production of web pages that reflect collaborative knowledge.
- **Multimedia** programs such as Voicethread enable users to develop and share online group albums.
- **Image sharing** programs such as Flickr enable users to upload and share photos and other images; these items can be combined into albums that reflect conent matter leadned.
- **Online chats** enable individuals to discuss issues in real time. Some chat programs include features that allow documents and web pages to be viewed in common.
- **Web-based conferencing** incorporate text, image and sound to more closely approximate physical interaction.
- **Virtual environments** (object-oriented online environments) enable individuals to interact virtually using avatars. Virtual environments usually have ways for applications to be embedded and documents to be stored.

It should be noted that collaboration is a set of learned skills in itself. For individuals to work together as a group effectively, all members need to share information, listen, follow directions, keep on track, clarify and check for information, share leadership and decision-making, and show respect (Dishon & O'Leary, 1994). While collaboration can be learned informally, educators should provide explicit instruction and feedback for each skill, and teach self-governing techniques. At the beginning, educators provide a structure in which groups work, dividing the task into small, manageable steps. Monitoring is close and extensive, and groups spend significant time discussion group dynamics and brainstorming ways to improve group management.

In e-learning environments, such structure for learning depends on effective instructional design. Directions can be provided in several formats, such as guide documents, web tutorials, and videos. Learning activities need to generate ongoing evidence that can be monitored for timely, specific feedback so that individual roles can be practiced correctly and the group as a whole can function effectively. For instance, wikis archive all changes so educators can assess each person's contributions. Groups can also monitor their own governance, giving each other feedback, which reinforces collaborative learning.

## DEVELOPMENTAL ISSUES IN E-LEARNING

Beyond the obvious issue of prior experience, educators sometimes overlook the developmental issues that compound the difficulties students encounter in e-learning situations. Youngsters deal with concrete reality and so may make false generalizations about abstract concepts such as volume conservation. Sometimes they cannot distinguish between main concepts and distracting details, and have difficulty categorizing information. Moreover, young children have a difficult time when faced with conflicting information such as maps with different keys or terms with different meanings (Moore, 1995; Leong & Jerred, 2001).

As children mature cognitively, how they interact with information to learn changes. Norris and Foxcroft (1996) examined the questioning behavior of 44 matched normal and learning disabled persons ages 10 to 14. The researchers noted that with cognitive growth, youth:

- asked more abstract questions
- developed more questions based on abstract categories
- built on prior questions more systematically
- used more inferential reasoning in their questions
- self-regulate their questions more.

They suggested that educators should target adolescents in learning sophisticated questioning strategies because teenagers are most likely to have developed their formal logic and have more experiences to draw upon. Nevertheless, Glaubman and Glaubman (1997) found that even kindergartners could understand and use metacognitive methods to generate high-level questions; explicit training in questioning also improved reading comprehension and retention. These questioning behaviors reflect engagement with information, which occur in e-learning environments as well. Educators just need to make sure that online tools such as e-mail, instant messaging, threaded discussion, online chats, and web conferencing provide opportunities for ongoing questioning throughout the e-learning process.

## Adolescents

Other factors emerge in adolescence, particularly since development is significantly gender-linked. While biology continues to play a role in differentiated e-learning, psychological and social factors assume greater importance. The American Association of University Women (1992, 2000) note several differences. Girls tend to lose their "voice, confidence, and self-esteem as they try to fit in and relate to their peers. As a result, girls tend to approach problem-solving more cautiously and reflectively than boys. Girls tend to contextualize meaning, which favors collaborative learning, while boys are more able to separate emotion from reason, and favor abstract reasoning. Girls tend to appreciate process, while boys tend to focus on product.

Youth also vary in the amount of information they need to learn. Some individuals are high risk-takers, critically evaluating the source as soon as they encounter information. Others need to know enough facts or background information before they can determine whether to accept or reject that information. Especially among this latter group, the amount of prior experience impacts their learning behavior significantly.

Sadly, the socialization process of education can negatively impacts students' e-learning. Low-achieving kindergarten males interact more than their female counterparts or high-achieving kindergarteners. However, over the years, lower-achieving students tend to engage less with information than higher-achieving students, becoming more passive learners; they do not want to look stupid. In observing the questioning patterns of students in twenty-two classroom, Good, et al. (1997) noted that adolescent girls tended to ask fewer questions than boys because they do not want to appear aggressive In both studies mentioned above, students changed their behaviors based on peer response.

Technology exacerbates these gendered adolescent e-learning behaviors. While today's youth have always lived in the digital world, their attitudes towards technology reflect gendered expectation with puberty (Hackbarth, 2001). Girls report less positive attitudes, and both sexes consider technology to be the male's domain. Girls are less critical of Internet content, and are more likely to attribute e-learning success to the equipment (Cooper & Weaver, 2003). On the other hand, girls constitute the majority of social networking users, particularly as a way to keep in touch with friends (Lenhart & Madden, 2007). As such, e-learning that incorporates collaborative learning and allows for reflective responses can play to teenage girls' strengths.

To compensate for this social "norming," educators should also set a positive e-learning atmosphere that encourages intellectual risk taking. Nevertheless, the degree and quality of online participation may betray the student's inner feelings of frustration, defensiveness, or condescension towards e-learning. Therefore, educators should also facilitate confidential ways for students to seek help through writing or private online conversations, especially since girls are more likely to ask for help.

## Millennial E-Learners

Traditional college age students in their early twenties are digital natives, shaped by globalization and technology. For them, the Web is an interpersonal experience more than surfing the Net, and they are likely to multi-task with technology tools. Technology also reinforces their desire for choice, customization, and immediate results (Carlson, 2005).

Although strong in digital communication skills, these millennials are not necessarily strong e-learners. They often do not understand research processes, and are more likely to use the first entries in a Google search or Wikipedia than to perform a Boolean search on subscription databases. In examining the information processes of undergraduates, Holliday and Li (2004) noted how the ease of federated searching and cut-and-paste word processing results in sidestepping critical thinking and other reflective e-learning practices; students tend to settle for "good enough" information.

Some gender differences also exist for this generation of e-learners, according to Morley (2007). He reported that females exerted more effort and made more commitments relative to technology, although males spent more time on computers and had more positive attitudes about digital libraries.

## Adult E-Learners

As a review, adult learning or andragogy builds on the experiences and needs of adult. Knowles (1990) identified factors that need to be considered when designing instruction for this population. The following list explains adult factors that apply to e-learning situations.

- **Self-direction.** Adults want to be treated as responsible, self-directed learners. They want to be in control of their use of information. Therefore, educators should develop am e-learning environment that provides adults choices in how they identify, access, and use information according to their needs.
- **Experience.** Adults have extensive and diverse experiences, which influence how they construct meaning from their engagement with information. Educators should help adult learners identify what they already know and then build on that knowledge. Educators should also realize that adult learners might have little digital information experience so explicit instruction on technological use is necessary.
- **Motivation.** Adults are motivated internally: by job needs, personal desire, and self-esteem. Whenever possible, e-learning activities should be developed in response to adult interests and needs. For instance, adults may want information in order to improve their economic statues or to solve personal health problems. In these scenarios, adults are willing, committed learners, thus offering a positive online atmosphere.
- **Need to know.** Adults need to know what they are going to learn and why they are learning it before they commit to the learning. An information need determined by adult learners offers an ideal opportunity for instructors should leverage the oppor-

tunity to design and introduce learning activities.

- **Readiness.** Adults learn when they see a need to learn in order to cope with their lives or improve them. As with motivation, readiness should dictate the creation of e-learning opportunities. It should also be noted that instructors need to incorporate methods of dealing with change since that aspect of e-learning may be unexpected and uncomfortable. Particularly when new information contradicts adults' existing knowledge base, the most likely outcome is rejection of the new information, especially if it impacts adults' livelihood or established values.
- **Timing.** Adults have many demands for their time, so they need to fit learning within the framework of the rest of their lives. E-learning activities have the benefit of typically being able to adjust to existing schedule demands, offering options for self-pacing.
- **Practicality.** Adults appreciate immediate and close transfer of learning and practical instruction. Hands-on, concrete e-learning activities that address needed information work well with adults, especially if adults can apply that information to their lives immediately. Service learning offers a concrete way to contextualize online instruction via community applications.
- **Socialization.** Adults want their social needs to be met as well as their informational needs. Moreover, adults learn through shared knowledge construction. Educators should provide online opportunities for adult learners to share information, and build in networking time. By offering these outlets, instructors find that e-learners are more satisfied with their coursework and learn more.

Technology has made incredible advances in the last decades, and many adults have not experienced technology-infused learning. Sometimes an adult learner may consider taking an online course, only to discover that this medium was not a good instructional "match." While online instruction varies wildly because of its design, its content, and its deliverer, the overall process does exhibit some stable characteristics. Adults who prefer to learn online, for instance, tend to exhibit certain characteristics (Harley & Bendixen, 2001; Wilson, 2000):

- self-directed and self-regulated
- persistent
- autonomous
- prefer anonymity
- independent
- egalitarian
- believe in flexible ability
- value convenience
- self-paced
- work outside 9 to 5 timeframe
- technologically comfortable
- comfortable with complex and ill-defined knowledge domains
- may have "traditional" language or physical barriers
- tend to be a different population than face-to-face learners.

Other studies have examined the characteristics of successful distance education student, who differ somewhat from generic online learners (Simonson, 2002):

- have advanced education
- tend to be younger
- have support from family or friends
- emotionally stable
- trusting
- passive and conforming
- introverted.

## SCAFFOLDING E-LEARNING

Educators have to factor in developmental variables when designing instruction for e-learning, but differentiation extends beyond these age-specific trends. Educators need to provide timely and individualized feedback, scaffolding, and interventions so that e-learning can be optimized. Scaffolding (that is, specialized instructional support) needs to take into account what knowledge and skills are needed at a specific point in the learning process for a specific person. The extent to which the educator knows the e-learning environment, with its resources and processes in light of the intended outcome and the student will help identify the appropriate scaffold. For instance, to deal with the English learner, the educator might provide relevant information that is written in the student's home language or is communicated visually rather than in text. If that class has several students with the same home language, the educator might well locate alternative texts in that language for the entire year. If educators have taught the same content matter before, or had students produce a specific type of product previously, they can leverage that prior experience to identify probable problem areas. In some cases, educator s can choose more understandable resources or demonstrate desired skills more clearly so that all students will be more likely to engage meaningfully in the task. Once educator s know those sticking points, lack of knowledge or stills, they can identify ways to measure those pre-requisite competencies and administer pre-tests or diagnostic tests so that an appropriate scaffold can be provided in a timely manner. For instance, if students are supposed to write a haiku about weather, but do not know what a haiku is, then the educator can provide that information via an information sheet, book reference, online tutorial, or website. Depending on what access students have to information, educator s can determine what format is more useful and accessible to the student.

Clearly, determining what scaffold to use and how to provide it are complex decisions. Even when teachers thoughtfully design instruction and the learning environment to include scaffolds to differentiate learning with an intent to provide universal instructional design, those scaffolds might not work with a specific student in a specific situation. For instance, a student might get distracted by blinking images. Perhaps the topic is a sensitive one for the student, such as cancer if that child's mother died from it. What if the student breaks her wrist and is supposed to type? In these unforeseen cases, scaffolding is usually called an intervention, and is done on a case-by-case situation. Teachers need to have a deep understanding of subject matter and associated processes in order to bridge the gap between students and the intended goal, to help students demonstrate competence.

Fortunately, the designated instructor is not alone in this process of scaffolding. For one thing, students themselves may be able to identify their own gaps. This process of being able to think about and articulate learning processes is called metacognition, and is another skill that students should learn. The more that they can identify learning gaps and self-regulate their learning processes, the more able students are to take responsibility and control their learning. Along with identifying the learning gap, if students can identify a way to bridge that gap themselves, they can become self-sufficient learners. Even if they can only identify what does NOT work can help the educator determine possible interventions (or work-arounds) that will help students proceed productively. For instance, a student may say that he does not know what a Venn diagram is or how to use it. The educator can either give the student that information or suggest another way to compare two concepts. Sometimes another student may suggest the intervention; potentially, everyone in the course can assume the role of teacher or expert learner. Perhaps the instructor is trying to explain a concept that is foreign to some students, such as parabolas. Another student in the course might be able to translate that concept into terms that are more familiar and concrete, such as trajectories in sports. In that respect, interaction is not just between the student and the information but also between students as intermediaries or gap bridgers.

## CONCLUSION

E-learning enables students to engage with information, transcending time and space. Furthermore, the social aspects of learning increases as students have more ways to interact with their peers as well as their instructors. Such expanded learning environments demands that educators expand their own design of instruction to incorporate technology resources. Instructors have to diagnose students' physical and intellectual access to technology, and make accommodations accordingly, such as choosing applications that all learners can use or adding learning aids so that students can gain technological skills to use the designated technology.

Additionally, because e-learning can broaden the student base, instructional designers also have to find out the experiences and perspectives of students in order to scaffold their learning as well as provide them opportunities to contribute their knowledge to enrich the e-learning environment. Fortunately, collaboration can be leveraged in e-learning environments to support peer teaching and learning.

In the final analysis, e-learning facilitates student engagement with information not only that which educators provide, but also information that their peers share in that environment. Instructors need to make sure that the informational cycle includes both sources – and provides a means for learners to generate new cycles of information that they share with their colleagues outside of the learning experience.

## REFERENCES

American Association of University Women. (1992). *Shortchanging girls, shortchanging America*. Washington, DC: American Association of University Women.

American Association of University Women. (2000). *Tech-savvy: Educating girls in the new computer age*. Washington, DC: American Association of University Women.

Cooper, J., & Weaver, K. (2003). *Gender and computers: Understanding the digital divide*. Mahway, NJ: Erlbaum.

Costa, A. (Ed.). (1985). *Developing minds: A resource book for teaching thinking*. Alexandria, VA: Association for Supervision and Curriculum Development.

Dishon, D., & O'Leary, P. (1994). *Guidebook of cooperative learning*. Holmes Beach, FL: Learning Publications.

Glaubman, R., & Glaubman, H. (1997). Effects of self-directed learning, story comprehension, and self-questioning in kindergarten. *The Journal of Educational Research*, *90*(6), 361–374.

Good, T. (1997). Student passivity: A study of question asking in K-12 classrooms. *Sociology of Education*, *60*, 181–199. doi:10.2307/2112275

Hackbarth, S. (2001). Changes in primary students' computer literacy as a function of classroom use and gender. *TechTrends*, *45*(4), 19–27. doi:10.1007/BF02784821

Hall, G., & Loucks, S. (1979). *Implementing innovations in schools: A concerns-based approach*. Austin, TX: Research and Development Center for Teacher Education, University of Texas.

Harley, K., & Bendixen, L. (2001). Educational research in the Internet age: Examining the role of individual characteristics. *Educational Researcher*, *30*(9), 22–25. doi:10.3102/0013189X030009022

Holliday, W., & Li, Q. (2004). Understanding the millennials: Updating our knowledge about students. *RSR. Reference Services Review*, *32*(4), 356–366. doi:10.1108/00907320410569707

Knowles, M. (1990). *The adult learner: A neglected species*. Houston, TX: Gulf Publishing.

Lenhart, A., & Madden, M. (2007). *Social networking websites and teens*. Washington, DC: Pew Internet & American Life Project.

Leong, C., & Jerred, W. (2001). Effects of consistency and adequacy of language on understanding elementary mathematics word problems. *Annals of Dyslexia*, *51*, 277–298. doi:10.1007/s11881-001-0014-1

Moore, P. (1995). Information problem-solving: A wider view of library skills. *Journal of Contemporary Educational Psychology*, *20*, 1–31. doi:10.1006/ceps.1995.1001

Morley, J. (2000). Gender differences and distance education. *Journal of Education for Library and Information Science*, *48*(1), 13–20.

Norris, C., & Foxcroft, C. (1996). Cognitive maturity and the questioning strategies used by learning disabled and normal subjects: A comparative study. *South African Journal of Psychology. Suid-Afrikaanse Tydskrif vir Sielkunde*, *26*(4), 243–247.

Rogers, E. (1962). *Diffusion of innovation*. New York, NY: Free Press.

Simonson, M. (2002). *Teaching and learning at a distance* (2nd ed.). Upper Saddle River, NJ: Merrill.

Sousa, D. (2000). *How the brain learns* (2nd ed.). Thousand Oaks, CA: Corwin Press.

Vygotsky, L. (1978). *Mind in society*. Cambridge, MA: Harvard University Press.

Wilson, M. (2000). Evolution or entropy: Changing reference/user culture and the future of reference librarians. *Reference and User Services Quarterly*, *39*(4), 387–390.

Zull, J. (2004). The art of changing the brain. *Educational Leadership*, *29*(5), 4–13.

# Chapter 4
# Assessing Online Learning Pedagogically and Andragogically

**Victor C.X. Wang**
*California State University Long Beach, USA*

## ABSTRACT

*Online learning occurs among traditional age students as well as among non-traditional age students. Because traditional age students learn differently from non-traditional age students, especially in the virtual environment, educators are required to employ either pedagogical or andragogical assessment methods accordingly. Using pedagogical assessment methods may not work for non-traditional age learners. Likewise, trying to apply andragogical methods to traditional age students may not work for younger learners. Available assessment methods such as objectively-scored tests, subjectively-rated tests and criterion referenced tests will be discussed as well as a new form of assessment-learner self-evaluation. To use the proper tests to assess online learning, educators are required to possess both pedagogical and andragogical knowledge.*

## INTRODUCTION

The primaryreason we say that we know more about how children learn than about how adults learn is that pedagogy (the art and science of teaching children) preceded andragogy (i.e., the art and science of helping adults learn, as defined by the father of adult education, Malcolm Knowles). Why do teachers need to know how learners, whether children or adults, learn? It is commonly argued that if teachers don't know how learners learn, how can we expect teachers to access learning.

Once learning is successfully assessed, teachers can identify the gap between learners' present

DOI: 10.4018/978-1-60960-791-3.ch004

level of knowledge and the desired level. In other words, a gap is successfully identified so that teachers know exactly how to teach learners and what to help learners learn in order to close that gap. Without identifying that gap, instruction on the part of teachers will be aimless.

Learning can be categorized as organized learning and unorganized learning. Organized learning can occur in the traditional classroom or a traditional lab or even on the Internet. Likewise, unorganized learning can occur in the same aforementioned places. Because of the wide utilization of the Internet, learning can occur anywhere, anytime in today's so called information age. It is no exaggeration to claim that nearly every course imaginable is available via the Blackboard program or WebCT program in North America. Although some instructors may not use cutting edge technology to deliver their courses, most universities choose to make their courses available online in order to provide the needed convenience and flexibility desired by learners. While education is being delivered electronically, instructors have common concerns, for instance, how do we teachers assess learning?

Can we use the same assessment and evaluation methods to assess learning of children and adults? Are there different assessment and evaluation methods that teachers can follow when teaching primarily adult learners? Because of the web 2.0 technologies and economic downturn in the United States of America, 47% of students are returning students (adult learners who have worked for some time and now have decided to retool their knowledge by attending universities) on campuses. We are experiencing what we call the graying of American campuses. Since these returning students may know how to assess their own learning, what would be the role of faculty members who help them learn especially in an online environment?, More than likely instructors would assess learning using the traditional assessment and evaluation methods in their repertoire. We have to understand there are other innovative, andragogical assessment and evaluation methods that we can use when assessing adult learning. It is true that we have to assess learning pedagogically when assessing learning on the part of children. However, if we use the same assessment and evaluation methods to assess learning on the part of adult learners, we will more than likely frustrate adult learners who may already know how to assess their own learning.

According to Rogers (1951, 1961, 1969), adult learners know exactly how to assess their own learning andwhether learning has illuminated any areas of confusion. Based on this school of thought, Knowles (1970) began to encourage "self evaluation" in the field of adult education. Other prominent scholars such as Patricia Cranton also encouraged "self-evaluation" in the field of adult education. Can this method be applied to assessing learning on the part of children? It will all depend on the maturity level of children. If we turn towritten references for the answer, most books address the assessment of learning pedagogically. When it comes to assessing learning online, most instructors would utilize the same pedagogical assessment and evaluation methods, leaving adult learners wondering why they have been treated as traditional age learners.

Some reasons why instructors are so dependent on pedagogical assessment and evaluation methods can be as follows:

1. Instructors have never heard of andragogical assessment and evaluation methods.
2. Instructors are accustomed to using pedagogical assessment and evaluation methods.
3. Instructors may not believe in the distinction between pedagogy and andragogy.
4. Instructors may assume that all learners, whether young or old, acquire knowledge the same way.
5. Instructors may believe that learners learn the same way whether in an online learning environment or in the traditional classroom setting.

6. Instructors may not believe that learners can "honestly" assess their own learning.
7. Administrators may not be familiar with andragogical assessment and evaluation methods; how can we expect them to support instructors who wish to use andragogical assessment and evaluation methods?
8. There is a lack of research supporting innovative/andragogical assessment and evaluation methods.
9. Some senior faculty resist teaching or helping learners learn online, let alone assessing learning via technology.
10. Andragogical assessment and evaluation methods involve more work on the part of instructors.
11. Because of reason number 10, faculty workload may become an issue.

From the above listed reasons, we can assume that innovative and andragogical assessment and evaluation methods are under researched. On the one hand, prominent leaders such as Knowles, Rogers, Cranton encourage instructors to apply andragogical assessment and evaluation methods when assessing adult learning. On the other hand, the number of instructors who actually use these methods remains unknown. Some instructors with degrees in adult education refuse to use andragogical assessment and evaluation methods when it comes to assessing learning online. Who is to blame? This chapter is to illustrate to our readers that learning can be assessed either pedagogically or andragogically, depending on the characteristics of our learners. Some history and philosophy of teaching children and helping adults learn will be addressed in order to gain insights into how learning should be assessed. The goal in assessing learning is to ensure that learners will be able to make progress. A secondary goal in assessing learning is to ensure that instructors will be able to diagnose learning and then provide needed instruction to close the gap between the present level of knowledge and the future desired level of learners. Since online learning has become one of the chief modes of learning in the new century, it is critical that both instructors and learners become well versed in assessing online learning pedagogically and andragogically. Only by assessing learning accordingly can our learners say, "our course instructors really care about student success."

## BACKGROUND

Assessment is needed to determine whether learners have achieved change in three domains: Cognitive domain, psychomotor domain and affective domain. To break down the three domains into more specific areas, Gagne, Wager, Golas and Keller (2005) call these domains: intellectual skills, cognitive strategies, information, motor skills, and attitudes. As soon as human societies had schools, it was the schools' responsibility to provide opportunities to organize and provide curriculum, instruction and assessment methods to bring about the learning of those kinds of capabilities as described by Gagne, Wager, Golas and Keller. Evaluation is a crucial part of instructional design. Without it, no instructors know for sure whether instruction has helped learners achieve change in those learning capabilities. When Tyler (1949) published his classic book on curriculum development, he advised all educators to ask four basic questions.

These four questions form a comprehensive view with the four questions as integral parts. Each part is important. Without it, instruction has taken place in vain. The other three questions are as follows:

1. What educational purposes should the school seek to attain?
2. What educational experiences can be provided that are likely to attain these purposes?
3. How can these educational experiences can be effectively organized?

The fourth question is: How can we determine whether these purposes are being attained? The fourth part is in the author's view, the most important because it is used to attain educational purposes. Further analysis of these questions and this topic of the chapter will continue in the subsequent sections of this chapter.

If we take a look at other instructional design models, the last part of these models is about assessment and evaluation. Instructional design and evaluation texts go in depth to describe the different kinds of tests available to educators in order to answer the last question of Tyler's model: how can we determine whether these purposes are being attained, that is, whether instruction has brought about the learning which was desired.

The most commonly talked about assessment methods can be multiple choice, true-false, essay, short answer, objectively-scored assessments, subjectively-rated assessment, assessment rubrics, learner self-evaluation and the like. Objectively-scored tests can be multiple-choice, true-false, and some short answer tests (such as fill-in-the blank tests where there is only one possible word or phrase considered to be right, or problem-solving questions where only the answer and not the work leading to the answer is evaluated (Cranton, 2010, p. 2). Objectively-scored tests are most popular among K-12 settings as our youth are encouraged to accept the belief that "objective is good," that rational is better than irrational and that they should be striving to nail down the right answer in their endeavors. This school of thinking has prompted educators to value objectively-scored tests. Further, educators in K-12 settings set the standard for student performance before assessment. This century old practice can be called criterion-referenced evaluation. In addition, most educators in K-12 settings are trained to be behaviorists. Behaviorists value programmed instruction and objectively-scored tests can be used to meet their previously set standards. On the contrary, subjectively-rated assessments are those that call on the educator or evaluator to judge the quality of the student performance or product. For those subjectively-rated assessments such as essays or short answer tests, there is no one right answer. Oral examinations, theses, dissertations, artistic performances and products, and the performance of skills in technical and professional fields, including the trades, nursing, medicine, dentistry, education, social work, and so on are examples of these (Cranton, 2010, p. 3). Although subjectively-rated tests allow for a depth and richness, to be fair, these tests depend heavily on the expertise, fairness, and openness of the evaluator. If the evaluators are prejudiced, the learners will suffer as they won't receive fair judgment on the learners' performance. The primary reason assessment rubrics have become popular in recent years is that two features stand out: 1, a list of criteria specified by the evaluator; 2, gradations of quality, with descriptions of strong, satisfactory, and problematic student work.

Andrade (2003) describes the following reasons why rubrics have become popular in education:

- They are easy to use and to explain. Rubrics make sense to people at a glance; they are concise and digestible.
- Rubrics make teachers' expectations very clear. When students are given written expectations—such as the form of a rubric—they will have a better understanding of the basis for their grades.
- Rubrics provide students with more information-- feedback about their strengths and areas in need of improvement than do traditional forms of assessment.
- Rubrics increase inter-rater reliability for grading. When multiple graders are assessing student work, it is important that they are all using the same standards.
- Rubrics support learning, the development of skills, and understanding.

Learner-self-evaluation may be frowned upon in K-12 settings as these educators have never heard of such a concept. As Rogers (1951, 1961, 1969) and Knowles (1970) described such an assessment method, they based this concept on their own instructional design model (setting objectives, finding resources, choosing methods, and evaluating the results). One might ask, is this model drastically different from that which Tyler advanced in 1949? How is learner-self-evaluation possible? Learner self-evaluation takes place when the learner makes some or all of the decisions regarding the evaluation and grading of his or her learning. Adult learners are capable of teaching themselves because often, they are able to be self-directed in learning. If they make decisions about their own learning, they are the ones that should know whether learning has illuminated the dark areas of their brain (Rogers, 1969). According to Cranton (2010, p. 3), learner self-evaluation can be done in a structured way, where the learner sets goals, criteria for meeting these goals, and finds evidence of doing so. The learner then assigns a grade to the learning.

As soon as information communication technologies were available to assist teaching and learning online, educators simply began transfer those available assessment methods onto their computer screens without realizing that certain assessment methods may work well for children and that certain assessment methods may not work well for adult learners. They also might not have realized that some assessment methods would work better (or worse) in an online setting. Assessment methods that work well for children should be called pedagogical evaluation and likewise, methods that work well for adults should be called andragogical evaluation. In the virtual environment, as soon as instructors tell us about their assessment approaches, we know for sure whether they cling to pedagogical evaluation or andragogical evaluation. For instance, if they depend heavily on true-false, multiple choice and short answers tests and if their tests are all timed and graded using computers, then we label these instructors as pedagogues and their assessment method as pedagogical evaluation. If instructors give out learning contracts and independent learning projects and if instructors encourage learner self-evaluation, then we label them as andragoguges and their assessment methods as andragogical evaluation. As a basic rule of thumb, instructors of adults tend to stick to andragogical evaluation and instructors of children tend to stick to pedagogical evaluation. There are always exceptions given one's particular teaching/learning situations, plus the preferences of particular schools or school districts. It is the intent of this chapter to reveal to our readers that there are some particular patterns we can follow in terms of how to assess online learning pedagogically and andragogically. Although instructors may have their own pedagogical or andragogical preferences, the nature of learners do determine which approach they can use to effectively assess online learning. It is crucial for instructors to employ the right method to assess online learning because learners and instructors are physically separated from one another. The wrong assessment method will frustrate learners and eventually learners may not want to take more classes with the same instructors. The bottom line of using the correct assessment is to find out whether online instruction has helped learners achieve change in those three domains of capabilities. If no change has taken place on the part of the learners, instructors need to consider switching to alternative assessment methods.

## ASSESSING ONLINE LEARNING VIA BLOOM'S TAXONOMY

Based on Tyler's (1949) model, all instructors are required to engage in assessment and evaluation of learning in order to determine whether educational purposes have been attained. Evaluation of learning is required both in the traditional classroom setting and the virtual environment, that is, the online teaching and learning environment. Assessment has become an integral part of the instructional and design process. Some instructors prefer objectively-scored tests because they wish to seek the one right answer. Some instructors prefer subjectively-rated tests because there may not be right or wrong answers students can seek. Yet other instructors may prefer learner self-evaluation not because they are lazy, but because these instructors know that learners know exactly whether learning has illuminated the dark areas on the part of the learners.

For centuries, the Chinese depended on the imperial examination system to select their governmental officials. Koreans and Japanese have followed the Chinese in their footsteps. Westerners have gone great length to examine whether tests have "validity, reliability, and practicality". While the Chinese educators are known for "teaching to the tests, encouraging rote learning and memorization," researchers from United Kingdom recently concluded that rote learning or memorization precedes critical thinking or creativity. Without rote learning or memorization, deeper thinking or learning cannot take place (Biggs, 1996). Some say that learning is shaped by one's culture.. Some say that the "ruthless" imperial examination system in the Eastern Hemisphere contributes to a higher suicide rate in those Confucius Heritage Societies. Despite the different views on learning and tests, we seem to agree that educators in the Eastern Hemisphere tend to teach to tests in order for learners to "master" lower order thinking skills characterized by the first three levels of Bloom's (1956) Taxonomy (Knowledge, Comprehension, Application,) Educators in the Western Hemisphere emphasize that tests should be used to evaluate learners' higher order thinking skills characterized by Analysis, Synthesis and Evaluation in Bloom's Taxonomy. Scholars recently added one more level, Knowledge Creation, to Bloom's Taxonomy (Fisher, 2007). Bloom's original taxonomy looks like Figure 1.

With the seventh level added to the taxonomy, the current Bloom's taxonomy looks like Table 1.

Over the years, people's epistemological positions have been changed. While evaluation was the highest level in the instructional design process in the past, in the information age, knowledge creation has become the highest level based on Bloom's revised taxonomy. Indeed evaluation

*Figure 1. Adapted from Wang and Farmer (2008, p. 2)*

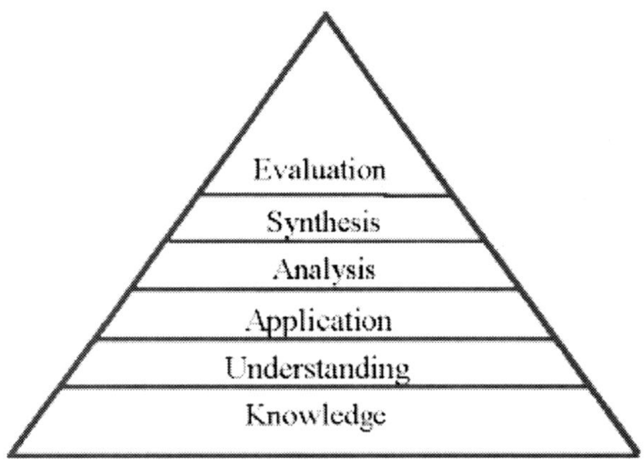


*Table 1. Instructional design: The taxonomy table (Fisher, 2007)*

| KNOWLEDGE DOMAIN | *Remember* | *Understand* | *Apply* | *Analyze* | *Evaluate* | *Create* |
|---|---|---|---|---|---|---|
| Factual Knowledge | List | Summarize | Classify | Order | Rank | Combine |
| Conceptual Knowledge | Describe | Interpret | Experiment | Explain | Assess | Plan |
| Procedural Knowledge | Tabulate | Predict | Calculate | Differentiate | Conclude | Compose |
| Metacognitive Knowledge | Appropriate Use | Execute | Construct | Achieve | Action | Actualize |

Adapted from Wang and Farmer (2008, p. 3).

must come before knowledge creation. Neither educators nor learners can create knowledge without evaluating previous learning first. Perhaps because of Bloom's original and current taxonomy, online learning and assessment have become so popular among returning students. We have been experiencing what we call the "graying of American campuses" in the 21st century. With 47% of the student body as adult learners, adult learners have been taking advantage of information communication technologies to enhance their learning and evaluation of learning online. Not only can these adult learners teach themselves, but also they are teachers of others in their fields. Can they evaluate their own learning online by using learner self-evaluation in order to create knowledge? Of course, they can. How about those learners between 16 and 25 years of age? Can they create knowledge by using learner self-evaluation? If directed correctly and positively, yes, they can. Learners regardless of their age, who can assess their own learning and create knowledge, are often labeled as "super learners". In the Western Hemisphere, they may be called "gifted learners."

Confucius twenty-five centuries ago emphasized "learning and evaluation" by advancing the following thought provoking philosophy:

*"Study without thought is labor lost; thought without study is perilous."*

*"By nature men are nearly alike, but through experience they grow wide apart."*

*"Those who are born wise are the highest type of men;*

*those who become wise through learning come next;*

*those who are dull-witted and yet strive to learn come after that.*

*Those who are dull-witted and yet make no effort to learn are the lowest type of men"*

*(as cited in Chai & Chai, 1965, pp. 44-45). Confucius or Kong Fuzi (551-479 BC)*

While Confucius' major concern lies in his quest for self-realization, Western educators' major concerns lies in knowledge creation, supported by critical thinking skills and critical reflection (Wang & King, 2006). Returning to our main concern regarding assessing online learning pedagogically and andragogically, Bloom's original taxonomy is revealing. When educators emphasize the lower thinking order skills, they tend to use tests to assess knowledge, comprehension and application. Then, they use pedagogical assessment methods characterized by objectively-scored or criterion-referenced tests. When children are not so experienced with certain subject matters and when they are not so self-directed in learning, pedagogical assessment methods may be the best methods that can be used to assess their learning. When educators emphasize the higher order thinking skills such as analysis, synthesis and evaluation, they tend to use subjectively-rated tests or learner self-evaluation to assess learning. When adult learners are capable of teaching themselves, giving meaning to their prior experience and internally motivated to learn, andragogical assessment methods may be the best methods to assess their learning.

Teaching online does not mean that instructors can just transfer their traditional assessment methods to the computer screens. There is a choice that they can make: either select pedagogical assessment methods or andragogical assessment methods based on the characteristics of their learners. There is not such a thing as one size fits all assessment method. If instructors confuse pedagogical assessment methods with andragogical assessment methods, they don't recognize the distinction between the education of children and the education of adults as described by Knowles

(1970). It is important for instructors to select the right assessment methods to fit their respective learners.

If you are in k-12 settings, this does not mean that you don't have returning students to take your classes. GED students are bone fide adult learners. Even some older adult learners may enjoy taking classes in the K-12 setting to find out what they have missed when they were young. In a typical college class, it is hard to tell which learners are traditional age students and which learners are non-traditional age students. The dividing line is getting more and more blurred. Therefore, recognizing the difference between pedagogical and andragogical assessment is not enough. Instructors who are engaged in online teaching should be able to develop pedagogical assessment methods such as grading rubrics based on Bloom's taxonomy. Below is an example of how to develop the pedagogical assessment method that emphasizes the lower order thinking skills reflected in Bloom's taxonomy:

## GRADING RUBRIC

Grading based on 100 Total Points per Course is determined using the percentages listed in the following rubric. This percentage is determined by dividing the total number of points possible for an activity by the actual points earned, with the resulting percentage determining the letter grade for the activity or course according to the DSC Grading Rubric. 70% of each grade represents Learner's content understanding, and 30% of each grade represents Learner's ability to convey such understanding in academic format (See Table 2).

On the contrary, an andragogical assessment method can be developed in the form of a learning contract, which emphasizes learner self-evaluation. See Table 3 for an example.

Clearly, the author of this learning contract did not feel the need to specify well defined rubrics. Possibly the author was guiding graduate students -- adult learners learning via WebCT, an integral part of information communication technologies. This contract did not even mention Bloom's taxonomy. However,these advanced students knew that the course instructor would assess their high order thinking skills characterized by the higher levels of Bloom's taxonomy.

Nowadays, educators bombard learners with educational terms such as critical thinking skills, problem solving skills and postmodernism. Educators believe that these terms are closely associated with the higher levels of Bloom's taxonomy. If knowledge creation is the highest level, then andragogical assessment methods may prove to be more powerful than pedagogical assessment methods that focus on the lower levels of Bloom's taxonomy. Online learning is complicated by the physical separation between instructors and learners. If we know the nature of our learners and their specific learning styles, we should select the right assessment method to assess their learning. Without recognizing the distinction between pedagogical and andragogical assessment methods, we may probably frustrate our learners by using the wrong assessment method. If the correctly selected assessment method can really help learners learn in the online environment, perhaps the physical separation will not matter too much. Although face to face interaction may inspire learning, the goal in learning is to result in change in those five domains as specified by Gagne (2005). The goal in evaluation of learning is to ensure that educational purposes can be attained. To attain our educational purposes, we need to choose between pedagogical assessment methods and andragogical assessment methods. If we confuse one with the other, we are not helping our learners learn. Out of the many assessment methods, we have shown our readers that basically they fall under two big umbrellas, either pedagogical or andragogical approaches.

## FUTURE TRENDS

Assessing online learning pedagogically and andragogically is no easy task. It requires instructors to have thorough knowledge of both pedagogy and andragogy. While pedagogy is defined as the art and science of teaching children, andragogy is defined by Knowles (1984) as the art and science of helping adult learners learn As the dividing line between pedagogy and andragogy is getting blurred, instructors should be equipping themselves with pedagogical and andragogical

*Table 2.*

| | 70% of grade - Content | | 30% of grade - Presentation |
|---|---|---|---|
| | **Discussion Activities** | **Coursework Activities** | **Style and Conventions** |
| | Includes evaluation of Focus, Development, and Organization | Includes evaluation of Focus, Development, and Organization | Includes evaluation of Style and Conventions |
| ***Excellent*** **100%-94%** | Learner demonstrates a well-developed focus, thorough points of development, and a logical pattern of organization of ideas and concepts. The original posting covers the topic thoroughly, demonstrates substantial reflection and/or self assessment, exhibits a broad integration of readings, and reveals conceptual knowledge and skills. | Learner demonstrates a well-developed focus, thorough points of development, and a logical pattern or organization of discussion ideas and concepts required in assigned activity.<br><br>• Substantially achieved stated learning outcome(s)<br>• Substantially integrated key concepts and terms from course materials<br>• Substantially evaluated, concluded, and applied concepts learned-demonstrated learning through use of examples and/or illustrations<br>• Supported insights and assertions through research and use of additional outside academic resources | Learner demonstrates exemplary accomplishment of task.<br><br>• Consistently appropriate and precise language for the assignment<br>• Consistently clear divisions between the writer's voice and the sources used to support claims<br>• Consistent and clear use of standard American English in grammar and punctuation<br>• Consistent use of APA formatting |
| ***Above Average*** **93%-87%** | Learner demonstrates a clear focus, substantive points of development, and a logical pattern of organization of discussion ideas and concepts. The original posting covers the topic in some detail, demonstrates reflection and/or self assessment, exhibits integration of readings, and reveals adequate conceptual knowledge. | Learner demonstrates a clear focus, substantive points of development, and a logical pattern of organization of ideas and concepts required in assigned activity.<br><br>• Above-average achievement of stated learning outcome(s)<br>• Above-average integration of key concepts and terms from course materials<br>• Above-average evaluation, conclusion, and application of concepts learned-demonstrated learning through use of examples and/or illustrations<br>• Above-average support of insights and assertions through research and use of outside academic resources | Learner demonstrates above average accomplishment of the task.<br><br>• Appropriate and precise language with occasional lapses<br>• Mostly clear divisions between the writer's voice and the sources used to support claims<br>• Somewhat consistent use of standard American English in grammar and punctuation<br>• Somewhat consistent use of APA formatting |

*continued on following page*

*Table 2. continued*

| | 70% of grade - Content | | 30% of grade - Presentation |
|---|---|---|---|
| ***Adequate* *86%-80%*** | Learner demonstrates noticeable focus, adequate points of development, and a noticeable pattern of organization of discussion ideas and concepts. The original posting partially covers the topic, demonstrates some reflection and/or self-assessment, exhibits a sporadic integration of readings, and reveals incomplete conceptual knowledge and skills. | Learner demonstrates a noticeable focus, adequate points of development, and a noticeable pattern of organization of ideas and concepts required in assigned activity.<br><br>• Adequately achieved learning outcomes<br>• Partially integrated key concepts and terms from course materials<br>• Analyzed and applied concepts learned-limited use of examples and illustrations<br>• Limited use of outside references or use of non-academic resources | Learner demonstrates adequate accomplishment of task.<br><br>• Somewhat precise language<br>• Irregular divisions between the writer's voice and the sources used to support claims<br>• Lapses in use of standard American English in grammar and punctuation<br>• Lapses in use of APA formatting |
| ***Needs Improvement* 79%-70%** | Learner demonstrates some focus, irregular points of development, and lapses in the pattern of organization of discussion ideas and concepts. The original posting is unrelated to the assigned topic, demonstrates little to no reflection or self-assessment, exhibits little to no integration of readings, and reveals deficient conceptual knowledge and skills. | Learner demonstrates some focus, irregular points of development, and lapses in the pattern of organization of ideas and concepts required in assigned activity.<br><br>• Minimal to no learning outcomes achieved<br>• Key concepts and terms from course materials lacking or omitted<br>• Does not describe and/or summarize course materials<br>• No references or inclusion of additional outside academic sources | Learner demonstrates incomplete attempt to address the task.<br><br>• Frequent lapses in concrete language,<br>• Consistent irregularity in divisions between the writer's voice and the sources used to support claims<br>• Consistent lapses in use of standard American English in grammar and punctuation<br>• Consistent lapses in use of APA formatting |
| ***Not acceptable* 69% or below** | Learner demonstrates no clear focus, no clear development, and no clear organizational pattern of discussion ideas and concepts. Learner fails to post or original posting demonstrates no reflection or self-assessment, did not exhibit integration of reading, is deficient in conceptual knowledge and/or skills. | Learner demonstrates no clear focus, no clear development, and no clear organizational pattern of ideas and concepts required in assigned activity. Learner fails to submit or submission fails to demonstrate learning outcome(s). | Learner demonstrates incomplete attempt to address the task.<br><br>• Consistent lapses in concrete language; regular use of slang, etc.<br>• Little to no division between the writer's voice and the sources used to support claims<br>• Failure to use standard American English in grammar and punctuation<br>• Failure to use APA formatting |

assessment knowledge in order to assess online learning. Online learning won't be effective if it is not assessed in a timely manner either pedagogically or andragogically. Knowledge of pedagogical and andragogical assessment drives instructors' teaching in the virtual environment. For example, those who wish to assess learning pedagogically must provide sequenced step-by-step instruction. Those who wish to assess learning andragogically must "negotiate" their course syllabi with their learners at the beginning of a semester via technologies. Although there exists in the literature the distinction between pedagogical and andragogical evaluation of learning, not many instructors have bought into the dichotomy. In addition, may schools or school districts may

*Table 3. Sample Contract: EDU 671 – Issues in Foundations of Education*

| |
|---|
| **Summary of requirements for A contract** |
| Quality participation (in class when we meet and on WebCT) |
| Philosophy draft and *revisions* |
| Quality participation in Design a School Activity |
| History timelines and reflection |
| Participation in Issues Presentation with group |
| *In-Depth Paper on issue chosen above (relating the issue to philosophical, historical or social foundations perspectives) (7-10 pp)* |
| *Poster and short paper (3-5 pp)* on chosen book (relating book's content to the foundations studied in class) |
| Reflection paper based on journaling throughout semester |
| **Summary of requirements for B contract** |
| Quality participation (in class when we meet and on WebCT) |
| Philosophy draft |
| Participation in Design a School Activity |
| History timelines and reflection |
| Participation in Issues presentation with group |
| *Annotated Bibliography* on the issue presented |
| *Issues Applied paper* (A **brief** paper (2-3 pp) on a current issue with your commentary) |
| *Brief summary* of chosen book |
| Reflection paper |
| Items in italics are unique to the grading contract in which they appear. |
| I reserve the right to assign + or – grades (e.g., if you contract for an A, you might receive an A+ or A-) |

Adapted from Ware (2010, p. 116).

not believe in this dichotomy. As Knowles noted, "the whole educational enterprise has been frozen into the pedagogical model" (Knowles, Holton, & Swanson, 2005). In terms of assessment of learning, it seems that pedagogical evaluation has been encouraged for learning at all levels. Many high schoolshave begun to implement "exit exams." Many schools use more standardized tests with their students in order to keep up with students from other industrialized nations. In the past, Westerners frowned upon the Chinese imperial examination system. Now scores of Confucius Institutes have been imported into the United States. Many educators look up to these testing system, especially their standardized tests to assess learning on the part of students. It seems that relying on standardized tests will remain a strong trend in the near future. One obvious advantage of using standardized tests is that it is easy for educators to determine which students excel and which students do not perform as well. In those cases, educators can use remedial instruction to help students to catch up with those who excel. Also, it is easy to seta national standard by using standardized tests. No Child Left Behind, a controversial educational reform, depends highly on "high stakes testing"–most of which are objective tests.Every learner needs to work hard to meet the national standard. In the past, decentralization was characterized by the testing system in the United States. As most universities deliver their courses via Blackboard or WebCT programs, it is easier to apply pedagogical assessment methods. Instructors with the help of technicians can easily upload their tests by performing a few strokes on the keyboard and students' tests will be graded easily by computers. Encouraging educators to conform to pedagogical assessment methods will continue to be a trend in the field of education. Objectively-scored tests seem to school administrators a step towardaccountability.

On the other hand, it may be difficult to offer subjectively-graded tests. As there are no right or wrong answers, these tests can be controversial. Also learners may challenge those test givers based on their own critical thinking skills. Even in the adult education arena, not many educators currently believe in learner self-evaluation. Sometimes, educators simply do not trust their learners. Learner self-evaluation will continue to spark subsequent research.

## CONCLUSION

Assessment or evaluation of online learning takes many forms. To date, educators have employed objectively-scored tests, subjectively-rated tests, criterion-referenced tests and learner self-evaluation. Learner self-evaluation has been relatively new in the field of education as it was advanced in the field of adult education. Educators such as Rogers (1969) and Knowles (1970) advocated learner self-evaluation because they realized that learners are capable of evaluating their own learning. Learner self-evaluation also appears in the form of a learning contract that instructors assign to learners at the beginning of a course. Since most universities in the 21st century began to deliver their courses via Web 2.0 technologies, learner self-evaluation has been used considerably to assess online learning. This is not to say that pedagogical assessment characterized by objectively-scored tests or criterion-referenced tests is not being used. r Some administrators may not believe in learner self-evaluation because of accountability or accreditation issues. The intent of writing such as a chapter as this one was to show to our readers that in addition to pedagogical assessment methods, there are andragogical assessment methods characterized by subjectively-rated tests or learner self-evaluation. When scholars address Habermas's (1971) emancipatory knowledge, Mezirow's (1990, 1991, 1997, 2000) critical reflection or constructivism, they are talking about learners' making sense out of their prior experience or existing knowledge. If learners can indeed learn from their prior experience or existing knowledge via critical reflection, they should be able to assess their learning via learner self-evaluation. To Rogers, and Knowles, evaluation by the educators is of secondary importance to learners who are capable of teaching themselves. Learner self-evaluation is of primary importance. It will benefit even traditional age learners if they are encouraged to assess their own learning and taught, with scaffolding, how to accomplish it.. If learners can tell their instructors where instruction is needed, instructors' diagnosis is omitted. Then, instructors can be fully engaged in designing that needed instruction to help learners close that gap between what it is and what it should be. It has been demonstrated in this chapter that in order for instructors to employ either pedagogical or andragogical assessment methods, they need to familiarize themselves with both. Pedagogy and andragogy have distinctively different definitions and each represents a different core body of knowledge. Recognizing the dichotomy is the first step in studying the two distinctively different bodies of knowledge. Thorough knowledge of pedagogy and andragogy will prompt educators to move freely from pedagogical assessment to andragogical assessment and vice versa. It is understandable that educators have been relying on Bloom's taxonomy when it comes to assessment and evaluation of learning simply because the six levels clearly are related to pedagogy and andragogy. When educators emphasize the lower order thinking skills, they are using pedagogical assessment approaches. Likewise when educators emphasize the higher order thinking skills, they are using andragogical assessment approaches. The goal in assessing learning is to achieve change in those learning capabilities or three domains of educational objectives. In the virtual environment, the goal in assessing learning is the same.

## REFERENCES


Biggs, J. (1996). Western misconceptions of the Confucian-heritage learning culture. In Watkins, D., & Biggs, J. (Eds.), *The Chinese learner* (pp. 46–47). Hong Kong: University of Hong Kong Comparative Education Research Center.

Bloom, B. S. (Ed.). (1956). *Taxonomy of educational objectives*. London, UK: Longman.

Chai, C., & Chai, W. (1965). *The sacred books of Confucius and other Confucian classics*. New York, NY: University Books.

Cranton, P. (2010). Working towards self-evaluation. In Wang, V. C. X. (Ed.), *Assessing and evaluating adult learning in career and technical education* (pp. 1–11). Hangzhou, China & Hershey, PA: ZUP & Information Science Reference. doi:10.4018/978-1-61520-745-9.ch001

Fisher, D. (2007). *Instructional design: The taxonomy table*. Corvallis: OR: Oregon State University. Retrieved from http://oregonstate.edu/instruct/coursedev/models/id/taxonomy/#table

Gagne, R. M., Wager, W. W., Golas, K. C., & Keller, J. M. (2005). *Principles of instructional design* (5th ed.). USA: Thomson Learning Inc.

Habermas, J. (1971). *Knowledge and human interests*. Boston, MA: Beacon Press.

Knowles, M. S. (1970). *The modern practice of adult education: Andragogy versus pedagogy*. New York, NY: Association Press.

Knowles, M. S. (1984). *Andragogy in action*. San Francisco, CA: Jossey-Bass.

Knowles, M. S., Holton, E., & Swanson, A. (2005). *The adult learner* (6th ed.). Boston, MA: Elsevier Butterworth Heinemann.

Mezirow, J. (1990). *Fostering critical reflection in adulthood: A guide to transformative and emancipatory learning*. San Francisco, CA: Jossey-Bass.

Mezirow, J. (1991). *Transformative dimensions of adult learning*. San Francisco, CA: Jossey-Bass.

Mezirow, J. (1997). Transformative learning: Theory to practice. In Cranton, P. (Ed.), *Transformative learning in action. New directions in adult and continuing education, no. 74* (pp. 5–12). San Francisco, CA: Jossey-Bass.

Mezirow, J. (Ed.). (2000). *Learning as transformation: Critical perspectives on a theory in progress*. San Francisco, CA: Jossey-Bass.

Rogers, C. R. (1951). *Client-centered therapy*. Boston, MA: Houghton-Mifflin.

Rogers, C. R. (1961). *On becoming a person*. Boston, MA: Houghton-Mifflin.

Rogers, C. R. (1969). *Freedom to learn*. Columbus, OH: Merrill.

Tyler, R. (1949). *Basic principles of curriculum and instruction*. Chicago, IL: University of Chicago Press.

Wang, V., & Farmer, L. (2008). Adult learning methods in China and Bloom's taxonomy. *International Journal for the Scholarship of Teaching and Learning*, *2*(2), 1–15.

Wang, V., & King, K. P. (2006). Understanding Mezirow's theory of reflectivity from Confucian perspectives: A model and perspective. *Radical Pedagogy*, *8*(1), 1–17.

Ware, M. (2010). Learning contracts as part of instructional design and evaluation. In Wang, V. C. X. (Ed.), *Assessing and evaluation adult learning in career and technical education* (pp. 107–128). Hangzhou, China & Hershey, PA: ZUP & Information Science Reference.

# Chapter 5
# Utilizing a Virtual Environment for Academic Advising

**Pamela M. Golubski**
*Carnegie Mellon University, USA*

## ABSTRACT

*Students, regardless of age, need access to an assigned academic advisor with which they can develop a long term, mutual relationship during their college tenure. An academic advisor assists students with the difficult transition into college, and ensures that each advisee has the opportunity to gain the professional, personal, interpersonal, career, and/or academic skills necessary for college success. In the past, academic advising was viewed as a prescriptive, non developmental service; today academic advisors are making every effort to support students' holistic growth. The development approach of advising will require an advisor to have a greater presence in the student's life, thus meaning an increased time commitment, availability, and interaction with advisees. While traditional, face-to-face methods have been effectively used since the 1900's to advise students, in a virtual world, more advisors are utilizing virtual and Web 2.0 technologies in an effort to educate, empower, interact, and inform students. These technologies include: Facebook, Instant Message (IM), Skype, chat sessions, electronic mailing lists, blogs, Twitter, online testing, and training.*

## TRANSITION TO COLLEGE OVERVIEW

The transition to college is difficult for most students. For a traditional-aged student this transition means leaving behind his/her high school network of friends, and for an adult learner it might mean making arrangements to secure daycare for children that she has been caring for over an extended period of time. Schlossberg (1984) researched how transition affects a person's ability to adapt to a changing environment. According to Schlossberg's Transition Theory (1984), transition is "any event or nonevent that results in change in

DOI: 10.4018/978-1-60960-791-3.ch005

relationships, routines, assumptions, and/or roles within the settings of self, work, family, health, and/or economics" (p. 43).

Thus, when a student enters college, he/she begins to embark on a new experience that will most likely require a change in his/her past identity (Chickering & Schlossberg, 2002). Tinto (1993) describes the college transition as a time when a student moves "between membership in past communities and membership in the new communities of the college" (p. 125). During this transition it is essential that students have access to support services, mentors, and academic advisors who can assist in alleviating some of the challenges and stress associated with the transition. Together this network can offer assistance in the areas of social, emotional, academic, and career decisions in an effort to increase a student's chance of experiencing a successful college transition while decreasing the potential of departure (Tinto, 1993). Departure is a serious concern, as only about 58 percent of students who enter a four-year institution will persist to earn bachelor degrees within six years (U.S. Department of Education, National Center for Education Statistics, 2009). Therefore, more than ever an academic advisor plays a pertinent role in acclimating and ensuring student success in college.

## ASSISTING STUDENTS WITH THE COLLEGE TRANSITION

It is necessary for academic advisors to intervene and assist in the college transition, because many students arrive on campus lacking the academic skills necessary for success (Light, 2001). A traditional-aged student may struggle with deciding on a possible major of study, while an adult learner may need additional support in locating classes that fit into her schedule to enable her to balance a part-time work schedule, college, and a family. In the past, students were often required to learn how to be successful in college largely on their own. Tinto (1993) determined that successes and/or failures that a student experiences may positively or negatively influence the student's entire higher education experience. Furthermore, it is not surprising that Tinto (1993) also discerned that when a student fails to become integrated into the institutional environment, he/she is at a higher risk for departure. Lack of integration mostly affects students who do not reside on campus such as commuter students and adult learners.

Today, the need for students to acclimate and integrate successfully into college is a distant memory. Academic advisors are making every effort to support students traditionally through face-to-face methods as well as utilizing virtual and Web 2.0 technologies to advise, educate, register, and inform students. Gone are the days when a student had to present a proposed paper schedule to his/her advisor in person to receive approval to take semester courses, then upon approval wait in line at another office to have the Registrar enter those courses. Technology has given students the option to perform tasks such as interacting with an advisor, registering for class, and accessing grades without ever having to leave the comforts of their dorm room, homes, or offices. Though, technology has the potential to improve the effectiveness, efficiency, and overall student satisfaction of academic advising. It is essential to first understand the history and foundational need of academic advising to be able to make use of virtual and Web 2.0 technologies.

## ACADEMIC ADVISING OVERVIEW

Academic advising began in the 19th century as a way for faculty members to assist students in making appropriate academic choices (Frost, 2000). Early advising involved a faculty member supervising a student's academic studies, living environment, and religious worship as opposed to student development (Frost, 2000). Advising was viewed as a form of parenting and referred to as *in loco parenti,* which is Latin for "in place of a parent" (Frost, 1991).

In the 1960s, college experienced the highest growth in enrollments in three decades, with a more diverse, robust population arriving on campus (Frost, 2000). At this time, "academic advising became an important vehicle for individualizing academic adjustment and planning" (Gordon, Habley, & Associates, 2000, p. 4). In an attempt to meet students' diverse needs, colleges began to hire additional academic advisors to ensure academic success of students.

With the passing of the Civil Rights Act of 1964, the Vocational Education Act, the Higher Education Facilities Act, the Higher Education Act, Title IX, and the Family Educational Rights and Privacy Act, the shift in the advisor/advisee relationship changed from an informational to a developmental focus (Becker, 2000; Thelin, 2003; Winston, Miller, Erder, & Grites, 1994). Students additionally wanted to be treated as adults, (Melear, 2003) and the Supreme Court responded to this demand by rendering "for the most part, persons above the age of eighteen are legally adults and that students at public colleges do not relinquish their fundamental constitutional rights by accepting student status" (Nuss, 2003, p. 74).

Shortly after, in 1979, the first comprehensive national study of academic advising was completed by the American College Testing Program (ACT) with support from the National Academic Advising Association (NACADA) (Carstensen & Silberhorn, 1979). Through the survey results, it became apparent that colleges had an increased interest in supporting and offering academic advising to students (Habley, 1988). According to research conducted by Light (2001), academic advising was discovered to be the single most underestimated characteristic of a successful college experience. Therefore, more colleges were shifting to the belief that "retention is a key objective of the advising effort" (Tuttle, 2000, p. 16).

Today academic advising offers a unique opportunity for faculty and staff members to develop long-term, positive relationships with advisees in an effort to promote student development (King, 1993; King & Kerr, 2005; Upcraft, Gardner, & Barefoot, 2005). In addition, academic advising is a process that assists students in developing professional, personal, interpersonal, career, and/or academic success through a paired relationship with an advisor on campus (Habley, 2004). The advising relationship allows for an advisor to empower students to make suitable decisions that best accomplish their individual personal and professional growth (Creamer, 2000).

## National Academic Advising Association

In an effort to enhance the student's holistic college learning experience academic advising standards were set forth by the Council for the Advancement of Standards in higher education (CAS) and the National Academic Advising Association (NACADA). The eight goals for academic advising that were developed by NACADA (2008) include assisting students in the following areas: (1) self-understanding and self-acceptance, (2) considering life goals by relating interests, skills, abilities, and values to careers, the world of work, and the nature and purpose of higher education, (3) developing an educational plan consistent with life goals and objectives, (4) developing decision-making skills, (5) obtaining accurate information about institutional policies, procedures, resources, and programs, (6) making referrals to other institutional or community support services, (7) evaluating or reevaluating progress toward established goals and educational plans, and (8) obtaining information about students to the institution, college, and/or academic departments (Habley, 2004). Today, these standards still act as the foundation of academic advising in higher education. Though, most colleges have moved from the outdated prescriptive method of advising to the more interactive and developmental style of advising.

## Prescriptive vs. Developmental Advising

The prescriptive model views the advisor as the deliverer of basic information associated with registration, policies, and procedures (Laff, 1994). Academic advising is viewed as the process of signing forms and communicating policies to students (Winston, et al., 1984). The approach is a top-down, hierarchical relationship. In prescriptive advising there is a one-directional flow of information and ideas from the advisor to the advisee. The student is viewed as a passive recipient. Prescriptive advising assumes that students are irresponsible, need close supervision, and the advisor should serve as the person of authority and knowledge (Crookston, 1972).

On the other hand, advising should not be reduced to the tasks of processing a clearance for a student to register for classes. Grites (1979) first began to define academic advising as "assisting students to realize the maximum educational benefits available to them by helping them to better understand themselves and to learn to use the resources of an educational institution to meet their special needs and aspirations" (p. 1). Developmental or collaborative advising was presented by Crookston (1972) and O'Banion (1972) as an alternative to prescriptive advising. O'Banion defined advising as "a process in which advisor and advisee enter a dynamic relationship respectful of the student's concerns. Ideally, the advisor serves as teacher and guide in an interactive partnership aimed at enhancing the student's self-awareness and fulfillment" (p. 63). Developmental advising included the exploration of life, educational and career goals, along with the basic functions of scheduling and choosing courses. Additionally, advising was an interactive teaching process that incorporated professional development, behavior awareness, problem solving, and decision making (Crookston, 1972). In developmental advising "the advisor and the student differentially engage in a series of developmental tasks, the successful completion of which results in varying degrees of learning by both parties" (Crookston, 1972, p. 13). This style of advising assumes students are active learners who are self-directed, and the relationship between advisor and advisee is one of collaboration. Lastly, the focus of advising is on identifying the advisee's academic, personal, and career goals, designing a plan to accomplish those goals, and assisting the advisee in acquiring the skills that will enhance intellectual and personal growth (Ender, Winston, & Miller, 1984).

With the growth of prescriptive advising students need, want, and expect more from an advisor than basic registration tasks and information. An advisor needs to provide the students with (1) active involvement where together the pair engages in intellectual and life discussions of learning and development both inside and outside the classroom. Secondly, an advisee expects an advisor to help him/her achieve (2) social integration, which is the need to become connected, integrated, and significant within the college community. Students need to be able to find (3) personal meaning, purpose, and value in college, to enable them to make relevant connections between current college experience and future life plans. The student wants an advisor to help them understand how to apply what is being taught in the classroom to the real world (not solely within the four walls of a classroom). Lastly, advisors need to assist a student with (4) personal validation and ensuring he/she feels empowered and capable of succeeding in college. This personal validation is accomplished by the student knowing that the advisor cares about him/her as an individual, is available, and committed to the student's success. Therefore, to better satisfy the student's four core needs, the developmental method of advising needs to be invoked. This method will require an advisor to have a great presence in the student's life, thus meaning an increased time commitment, availability, and interaction with advisors. This will require advisors to get creative in being able to serve students. One way to better serve students is through the utilization of virtual and Web 2.0 technologies.

## VIRTUAL ALTERNATIVE TO TRADITIONAL ADVISING

In an over scheduled, time deprived world, students are demanding that support services and advising be offered in accordance with their availability. This may require a shift in traditional face-to-face, in office meeting to a virtual venue. All students must experience equal access to campus support services and advising, regardless of the learning delivery system (classroom versus online), age (traditional-aged versus adult learner), and living situation (on campus in a resident hall or commuter). More often than not, student support services and advising have been designed with the focus of successfully serving the traditional student, who uses a service in-person on a brick and mortar campus (Gaide, 2005). As a result, student services are often ineffective and underdeveloped for the online or adult student population (Yalama & Aydin, 2004).

However, in an effort to better serve traditional and distant learners alike, colleges need to utilize an array of virtual and Web 2.0 technologies. Since the introduction of developmental advising, higher education professionals will find it necessary to learn and implement new technologies by reexamining and redesigning past methods in an effort to better serve, support, and advise students (Meyer, 2002). Technologies that advisors can make use of include Facebook, Instant Messaging (IM), Skype (video conferencing), chat sessions, electronic mailing lists, blogs, Twitter, online testing and training.

## INTRODUCTION OF VIRTUAL COUNSELING

The use of technology was first used by the field of counseling in the 1960's. Since academic advising tends to take its cues from psychology and the mental health field, it is not surprising that academic advisors also began to utilize virtual methods to serve college students. The growth of the virtual information highway has made a profound difference on the way people communicate with one another in order to obtain information as part of the learning process. Most households own a computer with reliable Internet access, therefore; technology has changed the field of counseling. Though, little research exists regarding the lasting impact on clients who were treated virtually as opposed to using a traditional, face-to-face format (Carlson, 2002).

Gore, Leuwerke, and Krumboltz (2002) stated that the computer might represent one of the biggest paradigm shifts the field of counseling and psychology has experienced in treating mental health. Today, many therapists are conducting e-therapy or e-counseling over the Internet. Counselors offer therapy via synchronized chats, audio and video conferencing. Virtual counseling allows clients to engage in therapy at a distance, using a format that is easily accessible, cost effective, and time efficient. Clients can access professional counseling from the comforts of their own home. This type of counseling is beneficial and convenient for those who do not live near specialized counseling services or are unable to leave their home due to a disability or medical challenge. In addition, virtual counseling services are also becoming more prevalent and useful on college campuses to better serve students.

### Virtual Counseling on College Campuses

A number of campus counseling centers are utilizing an online venue to administer services to students. Through these virtual centers students can receive help through e-mail, web video, chat sessions, or on-line information libraries and assessments. College counseling and physiological services discovered that students often don't seek help due to embarrassment or time constraints, and perhaps the best venue to reach students is through technology (Carlson, 2002). College counseling centers can successfully offer online screening for depression, alcohol abuse, and eating disorders. The on-line screening provides students with immediate results to determine if they should seek professional counseling.

As the virtual explosion continues to enhance and change the way counseling is conducted, one might predict that technology will impact how other college support services such as academic advising will be offered to students (Howe & Strauss, 2000, 2003, 2007). Even in person meetings can be greatly enhanced by the use of technology (Granello, 2000). For example, a follow up e-mail can be sent after a meeting reminding the student to visit the career center to sign up for Myer Briggs testing, or additional information regarding a major four-year curriculum plan can be distributed effortlessly through e-mail. The process of offering guidance, counseling, or advising to students is being called virtual, web-based, cyber, or online advising or counseling (National Board for Certified Counselors, 2007). It can be described simply as the delivery of information, instruction, and/or advice that occurs when a student (advisee) and advisor are in remote locations. This virtual communication can be asynchronous, occurring at different times, or synchronous, occurring simultaneously.

While viewing student support services in higher education, it is clear that both counseling and academic advising support the need to utilize technology to better serve college students; especially adult, distance learners and millennial students. Virtual and Web 2.0 technologies that have been found beneficial in advising students including, Facebook, Instant Message (IM), Skype, chat sessions, electronic mailing lists, blogs, Twitter, online testing and training.

## Facebook

There are several beneficial ways advisors can utilize Facebook. The group feature allows an advisor to create an advising network. For example, a Facebook group could be created by an advisor for all students who currently have an undeclared major or a group for the advisor's assigned advisees. Through this group the advisor can interact with students by making announcements on the "Wall" or initial an active dialogue on a specific topic through the site's threaded discussion option. As mentioned in the example above, a Facebook group could be created especially for students with undeclared majors. The advisor could disseminate information about different support services offered in the career center that help students declare a major, such as available career testing, an exploration career course, or various workshops. The wall could also be used to post changes to curriculum or reminders about an upcoming deadlines, such as semester add or drop course deadlines. Students should also be encouraged to post questions and concerns to the wall for the advisor to answer. Since the wall is viewable to all group members, students will be able to read and access answers to an array of questions.

The "My Message" option lets an advisor send a message through a private venue between the advisor and the student. This might be congratulating the student on his/her excellent mid-term grades, which would be an easy way to encourage and demonstrate to student you care. When an advisor creates a Facebook profile, it allows his/her advisees to get to know him/her as a person, and through this profile perhaps it is realized that you both share the same favorite reality show. Relationship building is about letting people get to know you as you are also getting to know them. This means the greatest reward of Facebook from an advising standpoint is being socially networked with students in an effort to build and maintain a relationship. Mottarella, Fritzsche, and Cerabino (2004) determined that students were more concerned with an advisors willingness to develop a relationship with them, than with the specific method of advising the advisor utilized (in person versus online).

The "My Events" feature is a location where an advisor could publicize and invite student to an event. For example, if the college was hosting a career fair which would allow students to pre-screen and interview for part-time, full-time, and internship opportunities, an advisor could invite all his/her advisees by creating an event page in Facebook. Through the RSVP feature of the page, students could register to attend the career fair. On the event page students could also access a list of employers that would be attending the career fair, as well as other relevant information (resume writing, interviewing, and/or professional dress tips). Finally, the new "Online Friends" feature allows an advisor to connect with a student who has logged into his/her account. Through the Facebook chat function, an advisor and advisee can asynchronously exchange messages. The chat makes identifying students effortless, and if the advisor needs a quick reminder of who the student is, there is a direct link to the student's Facebook profile.

## Instant Messaging

Instant Messaging (IM) allows users to share digitally-based information such as text, audio, and video over a network of computers (Internet) with another user (Baron, 2005). While Facebook has a chat feature, there are other available programs that host free chat software such as AOL/AIM Instant Messenger (dashboard.aim.com/aim), Yahoo Messenger (messenger.yahoo.com), Google chat (www.google.com/talk/), Skype (www.skype.com), and Microsoft (MSN) Messenger (im.live.com/messenger/im/home). It might be noted that International students prefer MSN, while U.S. students prefer AOL/AIM, so an advisor should determine what IM program he/she will be using to communicate with students. There are programs like Meebo (www.meebo.com) or Trillan (www.ceruleanstudios.com) that support multiple IM services in one place.

IM is an excellent communication and interaction tool for advisors. It provides genuine social negotiation because users decide when and whether an interaction will and should take place (Nardi, Whittaker, & Bradner, 2000). An advantage to IM is communication happens synchronously which allows a student to retrieve answers to questions concurrently. Students and advisors alike have to accept and partake in an IM session, it is not a forced medium, similar to in person interactions. Baron (2005) analyzed 2185 undergraduate students' IM conversations and discovered that IM language resembled natural patterns of speech better than writing, in that one thought builds off another to digitally mirror natural conversation. The communication during IM functions differently than face-to-face conversations, in that the user typically is doing various other activities while holding IM conversations, such as listening to music or talking to a roommate.

Carnevale (2006) found that millenials preferred IM interactions over in person and e-mail. Therefore, it becomes essential that advisors begin to understand this important communication modality in order to better connect with students using their preferred method of interaction (Lipschultz & Musser, 2007). Through IM, advisors can set up specific times when he/she is available to receive IMs from students. Since this type of communication/interaction is virtual, an advisor can hold hours in the evening from the comforts of his/her home. IM hours allow students to get answers quickly to non-complex questions, thus providing a more service-oriented approach to advising. At some colleges upper-class students host IM sessions to answer questions that perspective or new students might have regarding the institution.

A disadvantage with this technology is when an advisor has a large caseload of advisees it becomes cumbersome for IM to accommodate more than one student at a given time. At peek times, such as advising week, this technology could create a backlog of advisees wanting to IM, with the advisor only being able to engage in one online conversation at a time. Also with the exception of Facebook, recognizing or negotiating students' identification is challenging because IM user names are usually nicknames, such as a student's initials, "jhk2012". Therefore, confidentiality issues can arise. This medium is most efficient if there are predetermined times during the week that an advisor will be available to IM students. If an advisor and advisee prefer to add the visual component to a conversation then Skype may be a feasible option.

## Skype

When students utilize technology as their primary means of communication, their face-to-face verbal and non-verbal communication skills are potentially reduced (Wilkinson & Buboltz, 1998). Communication often has less to do with the actual words, but more to do with the non-verbal cues that are incorporated into the exchange (McQuillen, 2003) and Internet usage has been documented to be less effective in developing and maintaining social relationships than face-to-face communication. However, Skype (http://www.skype.com) has the potential to add those non-verbal cues into the conversation. An advisor and advisee can make arrangements to engage electronically by utilizing the video option in Skype. The student and advisor would need to possess a computer, Internet connection, web camera, and microphone. After connected through Skype, the student and advisor will be able to virtually see and talk to each other over the Internet. The advantage of Skype is that the majority of voice and video calls are free even to international locations. If an advisor wants to serve more students in a specific time frame, then a chat session might be an alternative option to IM and Skype.

## Chat Sessions

Chat sessions function similar to IMs. However, instead of one user communicating to another user, multiple users can communicate with any user that enters the chat session. Usually chat sessions are designated areas where people with similar interests can come together to interact. Like IM, the conversation happens in real time. In most cases a predetermined time is arranged for all interested users to log in and enter the chat session. Most of the IM providers previously mentioned in this chapter, Yahoo, MSN, and AOL/AIM host a chat function. Unlike IM, where only two people are exchanging messages, chat sessions messages are not posted in an orderly manner. Messages appear in the temporal order that the chat server receives them. This leads to a question being asked but the answer might not appear until several lines later. There are no mechanisms available to ensure the orderly exchange of messages and at times discussion threads may be difficult to follow (Werry, 1996). Setting a limit on the number of people allowed in a chat session can greatly alleviate the confusion that may occur in conversational threading. A group of 15 users or less has been researched to be the most successful (Smith, Cadiz, & Burkhalter, 2002).

In chat session it is often difficult to determine the identity of a user, whereas IM interactions usually occur through approved buddy lists or a linked social network as in Facebook, where one can identify the user prior to accepting or receiving a message. Herring (1999) determined that the multiple conversations that occur in a chat session mimic a face-to-face interaction as opposed to writing.

Advisors or upper-class students (peer advisors) can hold chat sessions for incoming students regarding different topics like core curriculum, student support services offered on campus, what to bring to college (traditional-aged students), or the local community. Chat sessions can also act as support groups. A group could be set up where single mothers can talk about the challenges associated with balancing college, a career, and a family with the advisor offering helpful services available on campus or in the local community. Those representing the services could also be invited to attend and participate in the chat session to further explain the benefits and services offered. During the chat session the advisor should act as the moderator by answering questions, monitoring content, and encouraging group conversation. The schedule of chat sessions are predetermined and arranged by topic. It is important to establish a time limit for how long each chat session will last. One hour to two hours in length is often best. Another option to effortlessly reach a large volume of students is through developing topic specific electronic mailing lists (ListServs).

## Electronic Mailing Lists

Electronic mailing lists are an effective tool for advisors to use, in an effort to send messages, announcements, and information through one e-mail to a large group of students. Electronic mailing lists, often called ListServs are Internet forums that allow a student to subscribe (join) a distribution list that is of interest to him/her. Typically electronic lists are set up according to topics. For example, an advisor can have ListServs set up for a student to subscribe to and receive messages regarding registration information, scholarships, internships, full-time jobs, and changes in curriculum. It provides students the option to subscribe to topics that they feel are most relevant and beneficial to their educational needs. Students determine what messages he/she receives from an advisor, as opposed to an advisor sending e-mails to his/her entire assigned advisee d-list, with the majority of those messages being deleted without ever being read. The electronic mailing list provides students with some sense of ownership as to what information they will receive and therefore increases reading rates. Students at any time can also unsubscribe (be removed) from a ListServ. For example when a student was looking for an internship he was a member of the internship ListServ, but after securing an internship he could remove himself from getting those e-mails regarding that topic.

## Advisor Blog

Blogs are online, archived logs that serve as a form of journaling and were introduced on the Internet in approximately 1997 (Blood, 2000). Blogs are usually written regarding a specific topic or subject, but have the added benefit of readers adding and posting comments, opinions, ideas, and/or experiences. Thus as readers comment, they become interactive and engaged in the virtual asynchronous conversation and a topic begins to deepen, broaden, and take additional meaning as to where is started (Blood, 2002).

An advisor's blog is a free, simple, and easy way for advisors to establish a connection with their advisees. This web-based communication tool can be written in a less-formal, light-hearted manner or in a formal, structured manner. There are a variety of free sites where an advisor can host a blog such as WordPress (http://wordpress.com), Blogger (https://www.blogger.com), and myblogsite (http://www.myblogsite.com). Information can incorporate text, images, and links. Blogs are displayed in reverse chronological order and work especially well for incoming students who are probably overwhelmed with questions, concerns, and worry. The advisor can blog about the process of getting acclimated to college from every aspect of completing financial aid forms to buying text books. The online venue acts as a non threatening way a student can interact and engage with his/her advisor and classmates. Advising blogs should be written to invoke empowerment and encourage students' personal, academic, and career success.

When writing and managing a blog, an advisor should remember to (1) make sure the topic/subject is interesting and engaging to the student population. For instance, if the advisees are undeclared students it might be focused around helpful tips and practices on declaring a major. Secondly, (2) the blog should be meaningful and relevant to the audience in which the advisor hopes to attract. Adult learners have different needs, interests, and concerns than those of a traditional-aged students residing on campus. If an advisor advises two different populations of students, such as undergraduates and graduate students, then he/she should create and manage two blogs, each relevant and valuable to the specific population. Thirdly, (3) the topics/subjects of a blog should appeal to and engage a variety of students (Blood, 2002). If blog comments are only coming from a handful of students, then the blog will not be deepened by reflections and personal experience. A best practice would be for an advisor to ask upper-class students to participate in an advisor's blog to offer advice from an experience standpoint. For example, have an upper-class student, who was at one time an undeclared major, comment on how he/she was able to finally declare a major. This personal experience is vital in increasing student knowledge, learning, and engagement. An effective blog will encourage a high level of participation where the conversation between students extends beyond the electronic medium and perhaps into the classroom, resident halls, and/or cafeteria (Blood, 2002).

## Twitter

Twitter is a social networking and micro-blogging technology that enables users to send and read posts from others. Posts cannot be greater than 140 characters. These computer generated text like messages are called "Tweets". The users who join your network and read your messages are called "Followers". The specific function of this technology allow for sharing of quick informative messages, posts, or links. Tweets can be either public or private and a user chooses the level of security.

Twitter can be used to disseminate short tidbits of information quickly. Thus Twitter is an excellent resource in getting a quick message blast out to advisees. For example, a Tweet can let students know that the deadline is approaching to drop a course for the semester or remind them about a workshop on time management. Twitter accounts for college students should be arranged by topics of interest. So if a student is interested in learning more about available majors then he/she will become a follower of that Twitter account, which might be called "majorsatstateU".

Since most students, traditional and adult learners, have over-extended lives, Twitter can be used to keep students on task to meet important deadlines. For example, an advisor can send out Tweets about items that should be completed in preparation for fall registration, placement testing, or the FASFA form deadline for financial aid. Tweets can help students think of things they might have otherwise forgotten or not considered. This approach is completed by posting a question to followers. An example might be, "Do you need some additional help in your College Writing Course?" This might get students interested and thinking about attending walk-in tutoring or supplement instruction (SI) sessions.

Twitter can also effectively be used to promote and publicize an event, like an upcoming group advising sessions. This Web 2.0 technology can better ensure that those living on and off campus are informed on college happenings, thus potentially leading to an increased sense of community. When students feel connected and integrated into a college community, retention rates are usually increased due to this affinity to the institution (Tinto, 1993).

## Online Placement Testing

For incoming students that need to complete placement testing, online testing can become an effective and efficient tool for academic course assignment. A student can say goodbye to the old paper and pencil format, and often the anxiety of taking a test in a classroom. During the summer, students can be directed to complete a required Mathematics, English, Modern language, and/or Writing placement test, via an online format. The test is then administered through a Learning Management System (LMS) such as Blackboard or eCollege or through a packaged software system such as the ACT COMPASS (http://www.act.org/compass). A student logs into the system, at their convenience, with either a student id or an assigned code. The student can take the test via an online venue. The results are then compiled and either sent or accessed directly by advisors or the system displays the results. For an advisor, viewing all the scores at one time makes compiling statistics, course assignments, or comparisons easy.

Additionally, online placement testing saves time, as it eliminates the need for a student to spend countless hours completing tests during orientation or make a trip to campus in the summer to have placement tests proctored to them. Virtual testing, eliminates the need for a staff member to administer the test time and time again in the summer as students sign up for various testing sessions. Finally, students can be located all over the country and/or world and still complete the testing effortlessly in the comfort of their own home.

Advisors should keep in mind the potential to cheat, plagiarize, or use assistance from a calculator or dictionary is increased with online placement testing. Students should be required to read a statement regarding ethical behavior in test taking, academic integrity, and acknowledge that they will abide by the policies set forth. To deter potential devious acts, students can be required to mail their scratch paper or outline to the institution in a postage- paid envelope that can be attached with the initial mailing about the online placement tests.

After a student completes placement testing, the advisor can post student results in a gradebook like those found on Blackboard and eCollege, or register the student for the appropriate course. A best practice regarding online placement testing would be to have troubleshooting information available for students, which provided answers to questions such as what to do if the system times out or if an Internet connection becomes disconnected during testing, which can happen often to international students. Students who are not familiar with using a LMS or an online testing system will need training on everything from how to log in, to how to review and understand placement test results. That is where virtual training becomes a valuable advising tool.

## Virtual Training

Lastly, online computer-based training can assist students in learning how to use various online student information systems, such as Learning Management Systems (LMS), or institution specific online registration and grade systems. Web shots, virtual instruction, and video or audio demonstrations can walk students through a series of steps, such as how to log onto their accounts, view class schedule, retrieve grades, change mailing information, register for classes, and print an academic audit. Students can move at their own speed through the material and can use it as a quick reference in the future, instead of burdening an advisor with basic questions. This online technology can encompass, visual, audio, and hands-on learning elements, which is sure to appeal to every type of learning style. For example there are many free web shot software, such as ScreenHunter, that an advisor can use to create a training guide using screen shot images to add visuals to text. Podcasting is also an effective way for an advisor to walk students through directions using an audio method. Lastly, for advisors who want to try an advanced online training method they may consider virtual hands-on training, that is delivered using a web based application, like Adobe Acrobat Connect or Webex. While virtual and Web 2.0 technologies have been able to offer students increased access to advising and support services, there are still privacy laws that govern student information.

## LEGAL ISSUES RELATED TO VIRTUAL ADVISING

### The Family Educational Rights and Privacy Act

Whether an advisor is communicating with a student virtually or face-to-face, all academic advisors must adhere to and abide by the laws that govern activities and communication occurring in the higher education settings. The Family Educational Rights and Privacy Act of 1974, also known as FERPA, mandates procedures for managing and maintaining students' educational records (www.ed.gov/policy/gen/guid/fpco/ferpa/index.html). Any institution, public or private, who receives funding through a program associated with the Department of Education falls under the constraints of FERPA.

An "educational record" is any record maintained by an institution about a student (U.S. Department of Education). An educational record encompasses all records related to the student, paper and virtual, including e-mails, photographs, microfilm/microfiche, videos, podcasts, and audio tapes (Van Dusen, 2004). All educational records are to be kept in the sole possession of the advisor (institution) and not to be revealed or accessed by any other person (Office of Family Policy Compliance, Family Education Rights and Privacy Act).

While the Internet and Web 2.0 provide advisors with a venue to easily communicate and disseminate information to students, the practice can lead to violations in privacy from a FERPA standpoint. Most academic advisors maintain academic records or files regarding their assigned advisee. The advising file usually hosts meeting notes, an academic record, semester schedules, SAT/AP scores, recommendation letters, transcripts, probation and medical issues, as well as a wealth of personal information such as social security or student identification numbers. Electronic records are required to be maintained following the federal privacy guidelines, which require all programs and information to be password protected (Office of Family Policy Compliance, Family Education Rights and Privacy Act). Electronic advising, while useful and efficient, has higher education institutions implementing new policies and regulations specifically addressing virtual records management. The only information academic advisors can disclose online or in-person is termed "directory information". This includes name, e-mail addresses, telephone numbers, major(s), degree(s), honors, awards received, as well as participation in recognized activities and sports (McDonald, 2008). So for example an advisor could not post student placement scores on a Facebook group account even if the group was deemed private or tells students the results through IM.

### Technological Violations

While technology breaches of student information can occur though so called illegal hacking, more often violations in data privacy occur through human error. This can happen when an advisor uses a personal e-mail instead of a campus e-mail (.edu) and a third party, such as a parent or roommate intercepts the message. Staff and faculty members should only be corresponding with students using a secured institution issued e-mail addresses (Steele, 2005). However, other violations happen by accident, such as when a staff member loses a flash drive, has a laptop stolen, or inadvertently sends an e-mail message with private student information using an unencrypted site or to another student with a similar e-mail address (Cate, McDonald, & Mitrano, 2008). As in any venue an advisor has to be cautious in utilizing and communicating through a virtual or Web 2.0 technology.

## FUTURE RESEARCH DIRECTIONS

Higher education institutions can use the information of this chapter as a framework to create the necessary dialogue for college administrations to begin thinking about the possibilities of utilizing virtual and Web 2.0 technologies for academic advising. While the technologies that were addressed in this chapter were cost effective, there are many additional options that could be considered if an institution had a more robust operating budget. These technologies include: streaming video, podcasting, and Blackboard or eCollege (Learning Management Systems).

However, the question still remains if the virtual academic advising has the same benefits associated with traditional, face-to-face methods that have been successfully used and researched since 1909. A comparison study would have to be performed to determine any statistical significance differences that may exist between both methods or if one method was preferred by students over the other. As more virtual technologies and tools are developed there will come a time when colleges will want to consider using those as a component of their advising offerings to students. The traditional way of advising using a face-to-face method during scheduled office hours may be a thing of the past.

## CONCLUSION

Virtual advising may always be viewed by some as an unconventional form of supporting students during college. Online methods may never entirely replace traditional, face-to- face methods, though if used effectively advising can be further enhance through the use of virtual and Web 2.0 technologies. It may not be unforeseen that academic advising and other student support services can experience greater student satisfaction and reduced attritions rates with the use of virtual technologies and tools. Technologies such as Facebook, Instant Message (IM), Skype, chat sessions, electronic mailing lists, blogs, Twitter, online testing and training have the potential to offer students increased access to advising, and convenient methods of interacting and communication with advisors. In the future, as more technologies become available, user friendly, and cost effective, advisors should plan on utilizing those as a way to interact more easily with students. In the end, the more options advisees (students) have available to engage with advisors the better colleges can ensure that students are provided with advice, empowerment, and support. Lastly, when students have solid relationships with advisors and are actively conversing with them regarding challenges and academic concerns this may lead to higher retention rates.

## REFERENCES

Baron, N. S. (2005). Instant Messaging by American college students: A case study in computer-mediated communication. *Conference Proceeding from the American Association for the Advancement of Science*, Washington, DC.

Becker, B. A. (2000). Legal issues in academic advising. In Gordon, V. N., & Habley, W. R. (Eds.), *Academic advising: A comprehensive handbook* (pp. 58–70). San Francisco, CA: Jossey-Bass.

Blood, R. (2002). *The weblog handbook: Practical advice on creating and maintaining your blog*. Jackson, TN: Perseus Books Group.

Carlson, C. (2002, November). 15). Virtual counseling: As campus psychologists go online, they reach more students, but may also risk lawsuits. *The Chronicle of Higher Education*, *49*(12), A35–A36.

Carnevale, D. (2006, October 6). E-mail is for old people. *The Chronicle of Higher Education*, *53*(7), A27.

Carstensen, D. J., & Silberhorn, C. (1979). *A national survey of academic advising*. Iowa City, IA: American College Testing Program.

Cate, B., McDonald, S. J., & Mitrano, T. (2008, April 4). The law, digitally speaking. *The Chronicle of Higher Education, 54*(30), B14.

Chickering, A. W., & Schlossberg, N. K. (2002). *Getting the most out of college*. Upper Saddle River, NJ: Prentice Hall.

Creamer, D. G. (2000). Use of theory in academic advising. In Gordon, V. N., & Wesley, R. H. (Eds.), *Academic advising: A comprehensive handbook* (pp. 17–24). San Francisco, CA: Jossey-Bass.

Crookston, B. B. (1972). A developmental view of academic advising as teaching. *Journal of College Student Personnel, 13*, 12–17.

Ender, S. C., Winston, R. B., & Miller, T. K. (1984). Academic advising reconsidered. In Winston, R. B., Miller, T. K., Ender, S. C., & Grites, T. J. (Eds.), *Developmental academic advising: Addressing students' educational, career, and personal needs* (pp. 5–34). San Francisco, CA: Jossey-Bass.

Frost, S. H. (1991). *Academic advising for student success: A system of shared responsibility*. ASHE-ERIC Higher Education Report No. 3. Washington, DC: The George Washington University, School of Education and Human Development.

Frost, S. H. (2000). Historical and philosophical foundations for academic advising. In Gordon, V. N., & Habley, W. R. (Eds.), *Academic advising: A comprehensive handbook* (pp. 3–17). San Francisco, CA: Jossey-Bass.

Gaide, S. (2005). Seven steps to meeting the technical needs of online students. *Distance Education Report, 9*(16), 4–5.

Gordon, V. N., & Habley, W. R. (2000). *Academic advising: A comprehensive handbook*. San Francisco, CA: Jossey-Bass.

Gore, P. A. Jr, Leuwerke, W. C., & Krumboltz, J. D. (2002). Time for a paradigm upgrade. *The Counseling Psychologist, 30*, 847–857. doi:10.1177/001100002237758

Granello, P. F. (2000). Historical context. The relationship of computer technologies and counseling. In J. W. Bloom & G. R. Walz (Eds.), *Cybercounseling and cyberlearning: Strategies and resources for the millennium* (pp. 3-1 5). Alexandria, VA: American Counseling Association.

Grites, T. J. (1979). *Academic advising: Getting us through the eighties*. Washington, DC: AAHE-ERIC Higher Education Research Report No. 7.

Habley, W. R. (1988). Introduction and overview. In Habley, W. R. (Ed.), *The status and future of academic advising: Problems and promises* (pp. 1–10). Iowa City, IA: The ACT National Center for the Advancement of Educational Practices.

Habley, W. R. (2004). *The status of academic advising: Findings from the ACT sixth national study*. Manhattan, KS: National Academic Advising Association.

Herring, S. (1999). Interactional coherence in CMC. *Journal of Computer-Mediated Communication, 4*(4). Retrieved from http://jcmc.indiana.edu/vol4/issue4/herring.html.

Howe, N., & Strauss, W. (2000). *Millennials rising: The next great generation*. New York, NY: Vintage Books.

Howe, N., & Strauss, W. (2003). *Millennials go to college: Strategies for a new generation on campus*. American Association of Collegiate Registrars.

Howe, N., & Strauss, W. (2007). *Millennials go to college: Strategies for a new generation on Campus* (2nd ed.). American Association of Collegiate Registrars.

King, M., & Kerr, T. J. (2005). Academic advising. In Upcraft, M. L., Gardner, J. N., & Barefoot, B. O. (Eds.), *Challenging and supporting the first year student: A handbook for improving the first year of college* (pp. 320–338). San Francisco, CA: Jossey-Bass.

King, M. C. (1993). Academic advising, retention and transfer. *New Directions for Colleges*, *21*(2), 21–31. doi:10.1002/cc.36819938204

Laff, N. S. (1994). Reconsidering the developmental view of advising: Have we come a long way? *NACADA Journal*, *14*(2), 46–49.

Light, R. J. (2001). *Making the most of college: Students speak their minds*. Boston, MA: Harvard University Press.

Lipschultz, W., & Musser, T. (2007). *Instant messaging: Powerful flexibility and presence*. Clearinghouse of Academic Advising Resources. Retrieved from http://www.nacada.ksu.edu/clearinghouse/advisingIssues/Instant-Messaging.htm

McQuillen, J. S. (2003). The influence of technology on the initiation of interpersonal relationships. *Education*, *123*, 616.

Melear, K. B. (2003). From in loco parentis to consumerism: A legal analysis of the contractual relationship between institution and student. *NASPA Journal*, *40*(4), 123–148.

Meyer, K. A. (2002). Quality in distance education: Focus on online learning. *Wiley Periodicals*, *29*(4), 67.

Mottarella, K. E., Fritzsche, B. A., & Cerabino, K. C. (2004). What do students want in advising? A policy capturing study. *NACADA Journal*, *24*(1 & 2), 48–6.

Nardi, B. A., Whittaker, S., & Bradner, E. (2000). Interaction and Outeraction: Instant Messaging in action. In *Proceedings of ACM Conference on Computer Supported Cooperative Work* (CSCW 2000), Philadelphia, PA, (pp. 79-88). New York, NY: ACM Press.

National Academic Advising Association. (2008). *Academic advising program: CAS standards and guidelines*. Retrieved from http://www.nacada.ksu.edu/clearinghouse/Research_Related/CASStandardsForAdvising.pdf

National Board for Certified Counselors. (2007). *The practice of Internet counseling* Retrieved from http://www.nbcc.org

Nuss, E. M. (2003). The development of student affairs. In Komives, S. R., & Woodard, D. B. Jr (Eds.), *Student services: A handbook for the profession* (4th ed., pp. 65–88). San Francisco, CA: Jossey-Bass.

O'Banion, T. (1972). An academic advising model. *Junior College Journal*, *42*, 62–69.

Schlossberg, N. K. (1984). *Counseling adults in transition: Linking practice with theory*. New York, NY: Springer.

Smith, M., Cadiz, J., & Burkhalter, B. (2002). Conversation trees and threaded chats. In *Proceedings of the 2002 Conference on Computer Supported Cooperative Work (CSCW)*. New Orleans, LA: ACM Press.

Steele, G. (2005). *Distance advising*. Retrieved from http://www.nacada.ksu.edu/Clearinghouse/AdvisingIssues/adv_distance.htm.

Thelin, J. R. (2003). Historical overview of American higher education. In S. R. Komives, D. B. Woodard Jr., & Associates (Eds.), *Student services: A handbook for the profession* (4$^{TH}$ ed) (pp. 3-22). San Francisco, CA: Jossey-Bass.

Tinto, V. (1993). *Leaving college: Rethinking the causes and cures of student retention*. Chicago, IL: The University of Chicago Press.

Tuttle, K. N. (2000). Academic advising. In Johnsrud, L. K., & Rosser, V. J. (Eds.), *Understanding the work and career paths of midlevel administrators (New directions for higher education no. 111)* (pp. 15–24). San Francisco, CA: Jossey-Bass.

Upcraft, M. L., Gardner, J. N., & Barefoot, B. O. (2005). *Challenging and supporting the first-year student: A handbook for improving the first year of college*. San Francisco, CA: Jossey-Bass.

U.S. Department of Education. Family Educational Rights and Privacy Act. (1974). *Family Educational Rights and Privacy Act (FERPA).* Retrieved from http://www.ed.gov/policy/gen/guid/fpco/ferpa/index.html

U.S. Department of Education, National Center for Education Statistics. (2009). *The condition of education 2009* (NCES 2009-081). *Indicator (Minnesota Mining and Manfuacturing Company)*, 22.

Van Dusen, W. R., Jr. (2004). *FERPA*: *Basic guidelines for faculty and staff a simple step-by-step approach for compliance.* Retrieved from http://www.nacada.ksu.edu/Resources/FERPA-Overview.htm

Werry, C. C. (1996). Linguistic and interactional features of Internet relay chat. In Herring, S. C. (Ed.), *Computer-mediated communication: Linguistic, social and cross-cultural perspectives* (pp. 47–63). Philadelphia, PA: John Benjamins.

Wilkinson, L., & Buboltz, W. C., Jr. (1998). E-mail: Communication of the future*? Proceedings (IR 018 794) at SITE 98: Society for Information Technology & Teacher Education International Conference*, Washington, D.C.

Winston, R. B., Miller, T. R., Erder, S. C., & Grites, T. G. (1994). *Developmental academic advising.* San Francisco, CA: Jossey-Bass.

Yalama, N., & Aydin, C. H. (2004). *Effectiveness of the student support for online learners: The facilitators' point of views.* Retrieved from http://www.cdlr.tamu.edu/dec_2004_proceedings/Yalama.pdf.

# Chapter 6
# Utilizing Virtual Environments for the Creation and Management of an E-Mentoring Initiative

**Pamela M. Golubski**
*Carnegie Mellon University, USA*

## ABSTRACT

*Adjusting to college is difficult regardless if the student is entering higher education immediately after graduating from high school, returning as a re-admit, or an adult entering college after an extended period of time working or raising a family. While colleges offer numerous specialized student support services from tutoring to psychological counseling, most individuals would benefit from added guidance, support, and empowerment from a mentor. While traditional (face-to-face) mentoring is an excellent option, it requires that specific financial, time, schedule, and geographic elements be met. Therefore, an e-mentor initiative might be a viable solution, where all communication interaction is conducted through virtual and Web 2.0 technologies such as Facebook, Instant Message (IM), Skype, Google Groups, Virtual Common Reading Program, and Virtual Reflection Journals.*

## INTRODUCTION

Today, we are all searching for more hours in the day to accomplish all that is essential for the advancement of our careers, personal and professional endeavors, education, and families. On college campuses the essence of success is learning and developing the necessary skills (academic, social, and personal-emotional) to be able to flourish and excel in the world of work upon graduation (Cohorn & Giuliano, 1999). Davis and Humphrey (2000) suggest that the first-year of

DOI: 10.4018/978-1-60960-791-3.ch006

college is a journey of self-definition. This rite of passage brings about important changes in: interpersonal and social adjustment (socialization, and relationships), academic concerns (studying and academic performance), career concerns (interests, abilities, skills, exploration of majors and careers), personal adjustment (locating help when needed, financial decisions, and time management), and commitment to education (value of education, personal success and achievement) (Bishop, Gallagher, & Cohen, 2000). If students were advised on how to successfully maneuver these changes, then the students' chances of experiencing a successful transition will increase and the potential of departure will decrease (Tinto, 1993).

Hence, to aid in the retention, graduation, and future workplace success of students, universities offer many standard, student-centered support services. These include: tutoring, supplemental instruction, writing center/lab, personal counseling, academic, and career advising. These services are optimal in that each offers a student specific support during a time of need. For example, if a student has an upcoming paper due for her College Writing II class, she may visit the writing center to gain some helpful suggestions on how to further develop the topic of her paper or learn the correct way to make citations using APA style. Most support services do not have the man power (staff members), mission statement, objectives, or the time to develop long-lasting influential relationships with students. The student makes an appointment when in need of assistance and in the future returns when faced with similar or another situation.

On the other hand, a mentoring program can provide students with a variety of support services through a matched relationship with the intended purpose of exchanging of ideas, valuable advice, empowering suggestions, best practices, and offer an open line of communication (Floyd, 1993). This relationship can occur between students and alumni, students and faculty or staff members, first-year students and upper-class students (peer), undergraduate students and graduate students, or students and community volunteers or professionals in the workforce. This chapter will focus on pairing current students (traditional and adult learners) with alumni or professionals in the workplace. Fundamentally, mentoring has always been performed in a face-to-face environment, but as finding extra time in one's schedule is a rarity and more than ever, we are all learning how to master multi-tasking and make use of technology in a global, diverse, and ever-changing world. Therefore, moving mentoring to a virtual or online format might be the perfect solution to offer fluidity in relationship development and communication between mentor and mentee.

## HISTORY PERSPECTIVE OF MENTORING

Mentoring has been a viable activity that dates back to early works of literacy and Greek mythology. A mentor was defined as a trusted friend, counselor, or wise teacher (Fénelon, 1699). For example in the mythological story about King Odysseus, who appointed Mentor (friend and counselor to the king) to serve as a teacher, advisor, and friend to the king's son Telemachus (Adams & Scott, 1997). Odysseus intentionally wanted to ensure that someone would be able to provide his son with the skills necessary to ensure he would be competent as the successor of the kingdom (Anderson & Shannon, 1988). Mentor was responsible for all aspects of his son's growth including physical, intellectual, spiritual, social, and administrative development (Crow & Matthews, 1998). As in the story of Telemachus, in ancient Greece it was customary for young males to be matched to a more experienced male in an effort to ensure he learned about being successful in the culture and society in which he belonged. Mentoring has continued to exist and flourish in much of the same format as it did in the early days.

## DEFINING MENTORING

Mentoring is defined as an experienced individual guiding, supporting, role modeling, and empowering a less experienced individual in the areas of academic, personal/emotional (self awareness, self-respect, self-esteem), and/or career development during a time of transition. The easiest definition of mentoring is the act or action(s) taken by a person with life experiences that helps another person learn to grow professionally (Bell, 2002). According to Cohen (1995) there are six behavioral functions of mentoring, (1) empathy, genuine support, trust, and honesty, (2) information and idea sharing regarding academic, personal, and career, (3) exploration of ideas, interests, and abilities, (4) assist with appropriate actions and decision making, (5) sharing of experiences or feelings, and (6) discussion of past and future successes and challenges.

The mentor is simply an individual that has more knowledge, experience, and the willingness to share, guide, and empower an individual with less knowledge and experience. The mentee, protégé, or novice (can be used interchangeably) is defined as the individual who wishes (needs) to gain knowledge, experience, guidance, and support from a more experienced individual.

## TRADITIONAL (FACE-TO-FACE) MENTORING

A traditional mentor program is when a mentor and mentee are matched in an effort to have them develop a one-on-one relationship that occurs through in person meetings and activities. Most comprehensive studies on mentoring were done by using notable, in-person programs like Big Brothers and Big Sisters, which matches children ages 6 through 18 (most from single-parent homes) with adults in the community. Overall the studies found that traditional mentoring program brought about improvement in the mentees attitude toward school, the future, and others (LoSciuto, Rajala, Townsend, & Taylor, 1996; Taylor, LoSciuto, Fox, Hilbert, & Sonkowsky, 1999) and better school attendance, academic competency, and higher grades (Johnson, 1998; LoSciuto, et al., 1996; Tierney & Grossman, 1998; McPartland & Nettles, 1991) when compared to students who were not mentored.

Dubois and Silverthorn (2005) discovered that mentoring had the best outcomes when used in relation to develop a mentee's education and career development. Today formal and informal mentoring programs can be found in corporation, education, and non-profit organizations. The issue as mentioned in the introduction is that colleges are finding it a challenge to match mentors and mentees, given the need to achieve specific time, schedule, and geographical issues.

## E-MENTORING

E-mentoring differs from traditional mentoring in that the relationship does not develop through an in person venue or communication, but through the utilization of virtual and Web 2.0 technologies. In addition, the program is not affected by boundaries such as physical distance (geographical barriers), strict time, and scheduling commitments (Biereme & Merriam, 2002). Therefore, this type of mentoring with its time flexibility and ease of communication has the potential to entice more seasoned or professional individuals to have an interest in guiding, supporting, and empowering college students, especially to those that once shared a similarity to that of the student. For example: same major, high school, family challenge (single mother), fears, insecurities, dreams, or age when they entered college (adult learners).

E-mentoring (electronic) has also been referred to as online, virtual, or cyber mentoring (Kasprisin, Single, Single, & Muller, 2003). The earliest e-mentoring programs came into being in the 1990's with the interaction being through e-mail (Brainard & Ailes-Sengers, 1994). Today with the proliferation of the Internet and Web 2.0, e-mentoring programs are incorporating audio, video, and text. An excellent example of a structured, quality e-mentoring program is MentorNet (http://www.mentornet.net). MentorNet pairs female college students with professional women working in the fields of math, science, engineering, and technology in an effort to retain and further this underrepresented population in the fields. The e-mentoring program utilizes e-mail interaction, e-forums, and virtual resources for mentors and mentees.

## Benefits of E-Mentoring

In the past mentors had to be located in the same geographic location to allow for in-person interaction to occur, which results in a reduced number of available mentors. Therefore, many college mentoring programs, due to lack of mentors, had to restrict programs to certain populations, such as minority students. However, with e-mentoring and the ability to recruit mentors living all over the country or world, colleges can offer more students mentoring opportunities. Mentors can interact with students from the comforts of their own homes/offices during times that are most convenient in their busy schedules. E-mentoring has the additional added benefit of not requiring the mentor and mentee to make plans to commute to a location to meet. The pairs will be afforded the flexibility and freedom to interact as their schedules permit. Interacting through virtual technologies often puts a student who is shy or easily intimidated at ease as opposed to face-to-face interactions (Single & Muller, 1999).

A college budget will also reap a financial benefit when moving from an in-person to an e-mentoring venue. This includes costs associated with the planning and organizing of events that provide an opportunity for pairs to interact, such as social activities, receptions, speakers, or lunch. There are a wide variety of virtual technologies that are cost free and can be utilized in e-mentoring. Finally, e-mentoring programs, after the training portion is complete, are often much easier to manage than traditional program, which frees up time for already over scheduled college staff members.

## Challenges of E-Mentoring

Colleges must remember there are some challenges associated with e-mentoring. The first is that the mentor relationship usually develops more slowly and takes a longer period of time. Second, a mentor/mentee must be comfortable using technology to communicate. There are many people, even in a tech savvy world, who only know how to e-mail and surf the web, and will require training using the various technologies (Ensher, Heun, & Blanchard, 2003). Training others unfamiliar with technology can be a challenge. Training will require that the mentor program director design materials (manuals, podcasts, how to guides, and/or video) to aid in the understanding, set-up, and usage of such technologies prior to the start of the program. Lastly, most virtual and Web 2.0 technologies, with the exception of Skype, lack non-verbal or auditory cues that often add communication clarity and visual stimulation to a relationship (Horowitz, 2004).

# PROGRAM DEVELOPMENT

## Needs Assessment

The first essential step in creating a mentor program is to determine the underlying purpose and outcome objectives. This can be completed by conducting a review of the literature or a quantitative and/or qualitative needs assessment. The needs assessment should gather information by surveying or interviewing students who would potentially participate in the program, as well as alumni or professionals who may volunteer to serve as mentors. The data collected can be statically analyzed or reviewed for reoccurring themes to further ensure that program design has the capabilities of meeting or exceeding the mentor and mentee's needs and expectations. During the needs assessment, there should be a series of questions around technology knowledge, comfort levels, and preferred methods of virtual communication. This information will become especially helpful in further defining your institution's program purpose, objectives, and expectations.

## Design

After completing and compiling the needs assessment, a mission and/or vision statement can be developed to include program objectives and outcomes. After creating a mission statement, the program will need to establish clear and concise expectations of both mentors and mentees so that each party will know what is and is not expected in the relationships. For example this can include the length of the program, the time commitment (virtual interactions occurring how often, weekly, bi-monthly, monthly, etc), the necessary technological needs (securing a Skype or Facebook account), acceptable topics for communication (asking for help or helping students with homework is not an acceptable mentoring function), and any program requirements (journals, reports, evaluations, etc.). The most successful mentoring programs set documented boundaries around the mentoring relationship (Armstrong, 2003). The mentor and mentee should know and agree to what is expected prior to entering the relationship.

Next, a mentor and mentee application should be created that will be used to recruit and match individuals. Mentoring is best if it is offered on a voluntary basis and not a required student support service. The application should include: contact information (address, telephone. e-mail, IM, Skype, and/or Facebook user names), majors/degrees earned, professional employment experience, technological knowledge (allow individuals to rate themselves on different technologies from proficient to no knowledge), days of the week and hours available for virtual communication, personal interests and hobbies, past mentor/mentee experience, mentor matching preferences (specific gender, major, age) and defining the desire to participate in program. Ensher, Heun, and Blanchard (2003) discovered that matching mentors and mentees was best if it was done based on interests as opposed to demographic aspects (gender, sex, and age).

## Evaluation

Minimally, summative data needs to be collected regarding the program outcomes. An evaluation can be created and distributed to mentors and mentees at the conclusion of the program. In keeping with the virtual format, an online survey is best. Foster (2001) determined that most mentoring programs did not formally evaluate the program either during or at the conclusion. However, evaluation is essential and should assess the various aspects of the program including, purpose, quality and benefits, career and skill development and exploration, virtual interactions, building self-confidence for success, guidance provided, lessons learned, and overall satisfaction with the mentoring experience. In addition, a series of open ended questions can be added to gain further information about mentor and mentee's opinions and suggestions for ongoing improvements and adjustments to the program. The evaluation possesses value-added learning in which the primary purpose is to ensure the quality of the mentoring program and the secondary purpose lies in program improvement, modification, and long-lasting infinity.

## RECRUITING MENTOR VOLUNTEERS

It is necessary to formalize a plan on how to recruit mentors. These mentors (peers, faculty and staff members, graduate students, alumni, or community members) must be willing, able, and interested in volunteering their time to the mentoring initiative. According to the latest report released by the United States (U.S.) Department of Labor, Bureau of Labor Statistics (2009), 26.8 percent of the entire U.S. population participated in some form of volunteering (un-paid). The mean number of hours was 52 hours for men and 50 hours for women. Those individuals that were willing to give back through volunteering efforts included the following demographics, women (gender), individuals age 35 to 44 years old (31.5%) and 45 to 54 year olds (30.8%) (age), and Caucasian (28.3%) and Africa American (20.2%) (race), earned a bachelor's degree or higher (42.8%) (education), and were employed part-time or full-time (29.7%) (employment status). Additionally, the vast majority of volunteer hours were given to religious organizations (34.0%) and educational institutions (26.1%) (U.S. Department of Labor, Bureau of Labor Statistics, 2009). Therefore, it is essential to utilize these statistics in order to successfully recruit individuals who will be willing and committed to the mentoring initiative.

In analyzing the above Bureau of Labor statistics, it is evident that alumni and working professionals may be the most successful individuals to recruit to serve as mentors. According to Ross (2003), it is best to recruit mentors that possess a wealth of knowledge, are confident in their careers, and have longevity in a field, which could mean that a seasoned professional might be a better recruit than a recent graduate (alumni). The best viable source to recruit alumni is to work directly with your college's alumni relation office, organization, and/or board. During an economical slump, alumni are often willing to donate time as opposed to money to their alma mater, as a way to feel as though they are giving back. The U.S. Department of Labor, Bureau of Labor Statistics (2009) discovered that 44 percent of volunteers were active in an organization because they were asked or invited to do so by someone in the organization. In order to invite alumni to participate an invitation recruiting mentors can be placed in the alumni newsletter/magazine, website, sent via e-mail or snail mail, or highlighted during alumni events such as homecoming. The invitation should highlight specifics associated with the mentoring initiatives, most importantly the mission, overall objectives, time commitment, expectations, technology utilized, and available training. This ensures that individuals are intrinsically motivated to participate and are made aware upfront of the requirements (Armstrong, 2003).

### Mentor and Mentee Traits

Ross (2003) goes on to highlight traits of a good mentor and mentee. Traits that potentially add to a mentor's success include good interpersonal skills, a strong interest in sharing their knowledge and ideas. A mentor should feel comfortable taking the lead, as students may feel intimidated, at first, in a mentoring relationship due to their lack of educational, career, or professional experience. The mentor has to be willing to encourage the relationship to develop between the mentee.

On the other hand, a good mentee must demonstrate a thirst for knowledge and the desire to learn beyond his/her current level of competence. A mentee should be comfortable in having a relationship with an individual (usually older than them) that is not a family member or a teacher (Ross, 2003).

## VIRTUAL AND WEB 2.0 TECHNOLOGIES USED IN MENTORING

### Web 2.0

The Web 2.0 is the Internet's second generation of innovative applications and networks that use World Wide Web technology and web design to allow users to creative content, share information and knowledge, as well as interact and collaborate with each other (Maloney, 2007). Any users can now write and publish to the Web without possessing any specialized technological or design skills. Mentoring programs can benefit from the Web 2.0 because it encourages an active, participatory role for users and several technologies resemble that of traditional, in-person interactions. The challenge for colleges is to determine how to incorporate the paradigm-altering virtual and Web 2.0 technologies to replicate the traditional (face-to-face) mentoring program. The following free technologies will be addressed as beneficial in virtual mentoring, Facebook, Instant Message (IM), Skype, Google Groups, Virtual Common Reading, and Virtual Reflection Journals. *Facebook*

Facebook is the most popular OSN for college students due to its opt-in social philosophy, whereas students want to be associated and active in various networks as a way to stay connected (Grossman, 2007). A Facebook profile allows the user to create and edit his/her own unique web presence. A user profile can include information such as college major, institution, place of employment, relationship status, interests, activities, hobbies, favorite movies, shows, books, and quotes, birthday, and personal contact information (Mullin, 2006). The site also allows users to upload images, text, video, and sound (Kolek & Saunders, 2008). Once a profile has been created, users can begin to befriend other users, thus creating a social network. The site has the ability to achieve the same objectives of face-to-face communication, such as pleasure, inclusion, escape, relaxation, and social interactions (Adler & Rodman, 2008). Further, Ellison, Steinfield, & Lampe (2007) examined the social systems that formed within Facebook and concluded the site did possess the potential for users to develop social relationships, as well as maintain and build on existing ones. These findings document the viability of using the Facebook for e-mentoring when the purpose is for the mentor and mentee to develop and maintain a relationship.

The first function of Facebook that would benefit an e-mentoring program is to create a private group where mentors and mentees would be invited to join. The group would encourage and allow all participating mentors and mentees to interact and communicate (Farrell, 2006). On the "wall" mentors/mentees could post messages, ask for advice, and share knowledge. For example a mentee might post a question asking "What is one thing you wish you took advantage of when you were in college?" or "What was the most difficult part about going from college to the real world?" and mentors could offer answers to the questions at their convenience, thus students would be gaining a group perspective from a variety of experienced individuals.

The other option would be to make use of threaded discussion/electronic discussion to post and respond to messages on a specific topic. For example a topic thread might be entitled "Summer Internship Advice" and mentors can post some best practices on how mentees can go about securing those, what professional documents they need to design (cover letter, resume, portfolio), how to prepare for an interview, and/or internship openings that might be available at the mentor's organization/company. The discussion format allows participants to easily identify and access topics, as those will be saved and available at any given time. Guy (2002) and Single and Single (2004) determined that electronic discussions had the added benefit of creating community amongst members. The more connected people feel to each other the more willing they will be to share feelings, ideas, and become active in conversation.

## Instant Message

E-mail has been replaced by Instant Messaging (IM) to provide a more realistic conversation medium through real-time communication. IM is a type of Computer Mediated Communication (CMC), where a user can asynchronously share digitally-based information such as text, audio, and video over a network of computers (Internet) (Baron, 2005). IM programs like AOL/AIM Instant Messenger (dashboard.aim.com/aim), Yahoo Messenger (messenger.yahoo.com), Skype (www.skpe.com), Facebook Chat (www.facebook.com), and Microsoft (MSN) Messenger (im.live.com/messenger/im/home) allow users to chat by spontaneously sending messages back and forth. Most of the above IM programs are not compatible with each other, so it is often necessary to establish and advertise what IM program(s) your college's e-mentoring program will utilize (Lipschultz & Musser, 2007). An alternative option might be to suggest that mentors and mentees use programs like Meebo (www.meebo.com) or Trillan (www.trillian.im) that support multiple IM services. These sites allow for one identity to be used across multiple IM programs (Yahoo, AIM, MSN, Bonjour and Skype) and all contacts (users) are collected under one compressive list.

As part of the application process mentors and mentees should have been asked when each would prefer to communicate virtually. The e-mentoring program director should try to match participants based on similarities of available communication days, times, and preferred virtual methods of use. Then after the pairing process the mentor and mentee can establish a fixed IM session (day and time). The pair may agree that this might be every other week on Sunday from 7:00 to 8:00 pm. The IM session should last no longer than 30 to 60 minutes to ensure that each party is not feeling like the mentoring relationship is a timely endeavor. A best practice would be for the college administrator managing the mentoring program to post, perhaps via the Facebook group account wall or threaded discussion, weekly/monthly suggestions of topics that could be discussed during scheduled IM sessions. Offering suggestions will ease any embarrassment or stress that a mentee (student) may face in not knowing what to ask the mentor. It also encourages the mentor to reflect on topics that will be discussed in the future. This practice will help formalize the mentor program and ensure that during IM and other virtual sessions mentors/mentee won't be at a loss of a topic to discuss. If a mentor and mentee feels that after a few sessions of IM they would like the virtual interactions to be more like a one-on-one interaction, with added non-verbal cues, then Skype is the perfect option. *Skype*

Skype is a VoIP (voice over IP) technology that allows users to communicate in asynchronous by text (IM), voice, and/or video over an Internet connection. Skype is free, but requires that a mentor/mentee have a computer, an Internet connection, microphone, and a webcam that supports video. Skype transforms virtual interaction by adding visuals and non-verbal cues. Skype may assist the mentor relationship to flourish and develop because it simulates that of in-person exchanges. As noted in the literature, there are several elements that need to be present to ensure the quality and success of any mentoring initiative, (1) ample communication opportunities for a relationship to develop, (2) an environment that is safe and trusting, and a (3) structure program where participants are aware regarding expectations (Grossman, 1999; Grossman & Teirney, 1998). Skype can accomplish all three in that it offers a free, 24-7 opportunity for mentor and mentee to communicate in real time, in the comforts and safety of their own home, and through the mentor program expectations each participant will know what is required for example that the pair must virtually communicate for at least 90 minutes each month. Another free Web 2.0 technology that is beneficial to an e-mentoring program is Google Groups.*Google Groups*

Google Groups (http://groups.google.com) is a user friendly virtual tool that allows collaborative communication between group members. Google Groups offers members large storage limits and easy customizable group portal pages. Accounts are free and accounts can be public or private. For example a mentoring program that assists first-year students with the transition, acclimation, and integration from high school to college might create a private (closed), group account entitled "mentormeclassof2015".

The first feature of a Google Group that e-mentoring can utilize is the threaded discussion board, similar to that offered by Blackboard, eCollege, or Facebook. This discussion feature allows mentors and mentees to interact with each other by posting and responding to threads (messages). A threaded discussion is easy for users to follow, and has the benefit of fostering interaction, reciprocity, and cooperation among users (Brescia, Swartz, Pearman, Balkin, & Williams, 2004). Online discussions can help mentees better understand skill development, majors, careers, and best practices as mentors and mentees have an opportunity to be active as opposed to passive in the exchange of ideas, concepts, advice, questions, and suggestions (Dillon, 1994; Miller, 1992). Additionally, threaded discussions permit e-mentoring participants to have a shared space where questions or concerns can be posted, answered, and saved in an open forum. The users have the ability to reflect and link ideas and concepts to each other to bring about a complex exchange of ideas, advice, and suggestions (Bonk & Kim, 1998; Sabine & Gilley, 1999). When a topic is introduced it can encourage the entire group (mentors and mentees) it can bring about advanced thinking and generates new virtual conversations.

Google members can upload, share, and access files. For example if a mentor has a summer internship available at her corporation she can upload the posting for the entire group to review, or if a mentor is willing to share a sample of her resume for mentees to view it can be posted. Google groups is also a great location for the mentor program director to post mentor and mentee expectations, handbooks, best practices, training manuals, help sheets, and/or evaluation forms.

Google Groups is especially beneficial for an institution that has limited server space for documents that require extensive amounts of memory such as podcasts, pictures, and video. The site would enable the institutions to host an entire web presence for the e-mentoring program at no cost. The portal can act as a one stop shop where the mentor program director, mentors and mentees could access documents, send an e-mail to an individual or the group, or post a question on the threaded discussion. The best aspect of Google Groups is that the pages allow for a unique blend of communication, interaction, and information sharing.

## Virtual Common Reading Program

A great use of Google Groups might be to add a virtual common reading program to the e-mentoring program. This would act as a group activity where all mentors and mentees could interact to bring about increased feeling of community. First, the program director would choose a book that would be of interest to mentors and mentees alike. An excellent book suggestion for a female e-mentoring program might be *Ask for It,* by Linda Babcock and Sara Laschever (2008) that confers how women can use the power of negotiation to get what they want in life. This book will appeal to mentors and mentees as it not only addresses negotiating in careers (mentees), but in life with spouses and children (mentors).

After a book was chosen, it would be announced and all mentor program participants would be asked to buy the book. A best practice would be to try to secure grant funding that could help fund the virtual reading program such as being able to purchase the book for all program participants.

When books are bought directly from publishers in large quantities there is usually a discounted price available.

After mentees and mentors begin to read the book, they can collectively have virtual conversations about what they are reading. For example each week a different discussion question(s) or exercise(s) might be posted based on the chapter(s) the participants are reading. The pairs can also be encouraged to discuss the book during their individual virtual interactions. The program director can talk to the publisher to determine if the author(s) are available for seminars and workshops. Many publishers, with the popularity of college summer reading programs, have authors who are willing to discuss the book, through a campus visit. With this being a virtual common reader, the author might be more willing to participate in a group discussion since it can be done from his/her own home, as opposed to traveling to a campus to hold an in-person seminar or workshop. As mentioned in the Facebook section, the more connected people feel with each other the more they are willing to open and share (Guy, 2002; Single & Single, 2004) and with the purpose of mentoring as relationship building trust is a important component.

### Virtual Reflection Journals

In an effort to have a mentee reflect on what he/she is learning, a virtual component that might be added to e-mentoring is encouraging or requiring students to keep a virtual reflection journal. There are several free online personal journal sites such as Live Journal (http://www.livejournal.com), E Daily Diary (http://www.edailydiary.com), and My Diary (http://my-diary.org). Journaling is a reflective process that may allow mentees to better assess and identify sustainability of learning through personal expression while developing problem-solving and critical thinking skills (Hiemstra, 2001). Journaling has the added benefit of being able to serve as a record of events or advice that the mentee gained through the mentoring experience. Prawat (1989) determined that journaling can allow mentees to make the connection between newly learned information and application to college and/or the world of work. According to Barth (2001), "by writing about practice, each of us comes to know more about what we do and about what we know"(pp. 68-69), thus e-journaling can support mentees personal growth, synthesis, and reflection on new information. Lastly, Moon (1999) was able to quantify that reflective journals could be used to deepen the quality of learning, better understand one's own learning process, increased active involvement in learning, and enhance self empowerment,

In order to have mentees reflect on their experiences, it might be necessary for the mentor program director to suggest weekly or monthly reflective question. If journaling will be a component of the e-mentoring program then this should be highlighted in the student (mentee) expectations. The expectation must be specific, for example that each mentee is required to login two journal entries a month. The e-journals have an added benefit of serving as a qualitative assessment that can be reviewed at the end of the mentoring experience to better evaluate intrinsic student learning that has occurred and/or challenges associated with the mentoring relationship. Students will also have a personal log of all that they learned and experienced that they can refer back to during their college tenure.

## TRAINING AND MENTOR PROGRAM SUPPORT

Training and support for mentor program participants is crucial for ensuring program success. Most of the training should be aimed at the mentor because a student (mentee) is often hoping or expecting the more experienced person (mentor) to play the leader role in the relationship (Bennett, Tsikalas, Hupert, Meade, & Honey, 1998).

Training should include establishing clear program expectations (Sipe, 1996), for example the process used to match mentors and mentees, defining professional interaction, the length of the mentor program, what virtual technologies will be used, how often interactions are to occur, and the length of those communications. Expectations need to specifically state the purpose of the program and roles of each party. This might mean stating to the mentee that your mentor is not to be used as a tutor to help you with class assignments and projects. A best practice would be to create and distribute a mentor and mentee handbook that covers in detail the mentoring initiative, from mission/purpose to the evaluation process.

When it comes to technology, there needs to be a program in place to train all participants on the virtual and Web 2.0 technologies that will be used for mentoring. This may include showing participants how to create and use a Facebook, Google Group, or Skype account. This can be done by creating a training manual, help sheets, a podcast, or an online tutorial, depending on the program director's technology skills. The mentor application that mentors and mentees completed will offer the program manager some information regarding the technology knowledge of each program participant and the training materials can be designed accordingly.

The area of confidentiality and privacy must be addressed when there will be a vast amount of information sharing. Participants should be aware that even though the Facebook and Google Group accounts are private (closed) that does not mean encryption or fire-wall violations will not occur and information may be viewed by a third party (Cate, McDonald, & Mitrano, 2008). Mentors and mentees should be told explicitly what types of information should never be shared or posted, such as resident hall (dorm) or home addresses.

Lastly, the college should make an effort to provide or reimburse participants for supplies that are an essential component for the mentoring relationship to develop. This might include that mentors/mentees are issued a web camera and/or microphone to further encourage Skype interactions. The web cameras and microphones can be issued and then be required to be returned after the program is complete. If the e-mentoring program will include a virtual common reading selection, the college should try to buy and send the book to mentors and distribute on campus to students (mentees) is an effective way to ensure that everyone has the necessary materials to experience program success. Another option would be to buy the book for mentors and sell the book on campus at a discount to mentees.

There are many available local, state, federal, and corporation grants that provide funding to encourage organizations to start and/or maintain mentoring programs. Many of these grants have the purpose of recruiting and retaining minority or under-represented populations in majors or colleges, such as women in engineering. If your college has a grant, fundraising, development, or corporate giving departments ask for assistance from these experts. If a grant was to be secured, it would act as an excellent source of funding to offset some of the necessary supplies and operation costs of managing a virtual mentoring program.

## FUTURE RESEARCH DIRECTIONS

Significant literature and research studies have been conducted on the benefits of traditional, face-to-face mentoring, but limited literature exists on the effects of e-mentoring. Therefore, the question to answer is if there are significant differences between traditional and virtual mentoring methods in relation to overall benefits, relationship development, and satisfaction. In a technological world, where most students and professionals are using virtual and Web 2.0 technologies on a daily base, it seems that e-mentoring might be a preferred program method. Research studies need to determine what technologies are the most successful in accomplishing the mentoring programs goals and objectives, while building the relationship between mentor and mentee. The research needs to observe the relationship or lack of a relationship that develops during e-mentoring, as well as how that the relationship can be sustained through virtual methods.

In addition, the matching process should be examined to determine if characteristics such as race, gender, occupation, or other factors contribute to the success of e-mentoring program or the mentor/mentee relationship. Finally, unlike the need to meet face-to-face like a traditional mentor program, is it possible that with e-mentoring a mentor can be paired with more than one mentee? This could mean that colleges could offer even more students the option of having a professional mentor during college. However, the overall effects would have to be studied to determine the appropriate mentor to mentee ratio that is feasible to experience e-mentoring success.

## CONCLUSION

In a virtual world, colleges should begin to make use and take advantage of the various technologies available for alternative forms of communication, interaction, and socialization. College students today need additional guidance, support, and advising outside of the college campus, because nationally only 58 percent of students who enter a four-year institution will persist to earn bachelor degrees within six years (U.S. Department of Education, National Center for Education Statistics, 2009). Therefore, colleges must commit to finding alternative options to support and retain students outside of the standard campus support services. E-mentoring might be the solution for colleges to recruit mentors to serve as valuable individuals who can empower and coach the students of today on how to be the successful professional leaders of tomorrow.

## REFERENCES

Adams, H. G., & Scott, S. K. (1997). *The fundamentals of effective mentoring*. Notre Dame, IN: GEM Consortium.

Adler, R. B., & Rodman, G. R. (2008). *Understanding human communication*. New York, NY: Oxford University Press.

Anderson, E. M., & Shannon, A. L. (1988). Toward a conceptualization of mentoring. *Journal of Teacher Education, 39*(1), 38–42. doi:10.1177/002248718803900109

Armstrong, S. (2003). Mentoring program standards for designing a mentoring program that works. *Link & Learn,* 4-6.

Babcock, L., & Laschever, S. (2008). *Ask for it: How women can use the power of negotiation to get what they really want*. New York, NY: Bantam Dell.

Baron, N. S. (2005). Instant messaging by American college students: A case study in computer-mediated communication. *Conference Proceeding from the American Association for the Advancement of Science*, Washington, DC.

Barth, R. S. (2001). *Learning by heart*. San Francisco, CA: Jossey-Bass.

Bell, C. R. (2002). *Managers as mentors: Building partnerships for learning*. San Francisco, CA: Berrett-Koehler Publishers, Inc.

Bennett, D., Tsikalas, K., Hupert, N., Meade, T., & Honey, M. (1998). *The benefits of online mentoring for high school girls: Telementoring for young women in science, engineering, and computing project*. New York, NY: Center for Children and Technology.

Bierema, L. L., & Merriam, S. B. (2002). E-mentoring: Using computer mediated communication to enhance the mentoring process. *Innovative Higher Education, 26*(3), 211–227. doi:10.1023/A:1017921023103

Bishop, J. B., Gallagher, R. P., & Cohen, D. (2000). College students' problems: Status, trends, and research. In Davis, D. C., & Humphrey, K. M. (Eds.), *College counseling: Issues and strategies for a new millennium* (pp. 89–110). Alexandria, VA: American Counseling Association.

Bonk, C., & Kim, K. (1998). Extending sociocultural theory to adult learning. In Smith, M. C., & Pourchot, T. (Eds.), *Adult learning and development: Perspectives from educational psychology* (pp. 67–88). Mahwah, NJ: Lawrence Erlbaum Associates.

Brescia, W. F. Jr, Swartz, J., Pearman, C., Balkin, R., & Williams, D. (2004). Peer teaching in Web based threaded discussions. *Journal of Interactive Online Learning, 3*(2), 1–22.

Brianard, S. G., & Ailes-Sengers, L. (1994). Mentoring female engineering students: A model program at the University of Washington. *Journal of Women and Minorities in Science and Engineering, 1*, 123–135.

Cate, B., McDonald, S. J., & Mitrano, T. (2008, April 4). The law, digitally speaking. *The Chronicle of Higher Education, 54*(30), B14.

Cohen, N. H. (1995). *Mentoring adult learners: A guide for educators and trainers*. Malabat, FL: Krieger Publishing Company.

Cohorn, C. A., & Giuliano, T. A. (1999). Predictors of adjustment and institutional attachment in 1st year college students. *Psi Chi Journal of undergraduate Research, 4*(2), 47-56.

Crow, G. M., & Matthews, L. J. (1998). *Finding one's way*. Thousand Oaks, CA: Corwin Press.

Davis, D. C., & Humphrey, K. M. (2000). *College counseling: Issues and strategies for a new millennium*. Alexandria, VA: American Counseling.

Dillon, J. T. (1994). *Using discussion in the classroom*. Philadelphia, PA: Open University Press.

DuBois, D. L., & Silverthorn, N. (2005). Research methodology. In DuBois, D. L., & Karcher, M. J. (Eds.), *Handbook of youth mentoring* (pp. 44–64). Thousand Oaks, CA: Sage.

Ellison, N. B., Steinfield, C., & Lampe, C. (2007). The benefits of Facebook "friends": Social capital and college students' use of online social network sites. *Journal of Computer-Mediated Communication, 12*(4), 1–4. doi:10.1111/j.1083-6101.2007.00367.x

Enshner, E. A., Heun, C., & Blanchard, A. (2003). Online mentoring and computer-mediated communication: New directions in research. *Journal of Vocational Behavior, 63*, 263–288.

Farrell, E. (2006, September). Judging roommates by their Facebook cover. *The Chronicle of Higher Education, 53*(2), A63.

Fénelon, F. (1699). Telemachus (P. Riley, Ed. & Trans.). In R. Geuss & Q. Skinner (Eds.), *Cambridge texts in the history of political thought*. New York, NY: Cambridge University Press.

Floyd, N. (1993). *Mentoring: Education research consumer guide, 7*. Washington, D.C.: Office of Educational Research and Improvement.

Foster, L. (2001). *Effectiveness of mentor programs: Review of the literature from 1995 to 2000 (California Research Bureau CRB-01-004)*. Sacramento, CA: California State Library.

Grossman, J. B. (Ed.). (1999). *Contemporary issues in mentoring*. Philadelphia, PA: Public/Private Ventures.

Grossman, J. B., & Tierney, P. J. (1998). Does mentoring work: An impact study of the Big Brothers Big Sisters Program. *Evaluation Review, 22*, 402–425. doi:10.1177/0193841X9802200304

Grossman, L. (2007, September 7). Why Facebook is the future. *Time, 170*(10), 54.

Guy, T. C. (2002). E-mentoring: Sharing mentoring relationships the 21st century. In Hansman, C. A. (Ed.), *Critical perspectives on mentoring: Trends and issues* (pp. 27–37). Columbus, OH: ERIC Clearinghouse on Adult, Career and Vocational Education.

Hiemstra, R. (2001). Uses and benefits of journal writing. *New Directions for Adult and Continuing Education*, 19–26. doi:10.1002/ace.17

Horowitz, A. (2004). Are you annoying? *Computerworld, 38*(30), 34–35.

Johnson, A. W. (1998). *An evaluation of the long-term impacts of the sponsor-a-scholar program on student performance. Final report to the Commonwealth Fund.* Princeton, NJ: Mathematica Policy Research Inc.

Kasprisin, C. A., Single, P. B., Single, R. M., & Muller, C. B. (2003). Building a better bridge: Testing e-training to improve e-mentoring programmes in higher education. *Mentoring & Tutoring, 11*, 67–78. doi:10.1080/1361126032000054817

Kolek, E. A., & Saunders, D. (2008). Online disclosure: An empirical examination of undergraduate Facebook profiles. *NASPA Journal, 45*(1), 1–25.

Lipschultz, W., & Musser, T. (2007). *Instant messaging: Powerful flexibility and presence.* Clearinghouse of Academic Advising Resources. Retrieved from http://www.nacada.ksu.edu/clearinghouse/advisingIssues/Instant-Messaging.htm

LoSciuto, L., Rajala, A. K., Townsend, T. N., & Taylor, A. S. (1996). An outcome evaluation of across sges: An intergenerational mentoring approach to drug prevention. *Journal of Adolescent Research, 17*(1), 116–129. doi:10.1177/0743554896111007

Maloney, E. J. (2007, January 5). What the Web 2.0 can teach us about learning. *The Chronicle of Higher Education, 53*(18), B26.

McPartland, J. M., & Nettles, S. M. (1991). Using community adults as advocators or mentors for at-risk middle school students: A two-year evaluation of project RAISE. *American Journal of Education, 12*, 868–586.

Miller, S. (1992). *Creating change: Towards a dialogic pedagogy.* (Report Series 2.18). Albany, NY: National Research Center on Literature Teaching and Learning. (ERIC Document Reproduction Service No. ED 349 582).

Moon, J. (1999). *Reflections in learning and professional development: Theory and practice.* London, UK: Kogan.

Mullin, J. (2006). Facebook and disposition assessment. *Academic Advising Today, 29*(2). Retrieved from http://www.nacada.ksu.edu/AAT/NW29_2.htm

Prawat, R. S. (1989). Promoting access to knowledge, strategy, and disposition in students: A research synthesis. *Review of Educational Research, 59*(1), 1–41.

Ross, K. L. (2003). Seek out the many rewards of mentoring. *The American Institute of Architect,* 1-2.

Sabine, G., & Gilley, D. (1999). Taking it online: A bootstrap approach. *Proceedings of the Mid-South Instructional Technology Conference.* Retrieved from http://www.mtsu.edu/~itconf/proceed99/gilley.htm

Single, P. B., & Muller, C. B. (1999). *Electronic mentoring: Issues to advance research and practice.* Paper presented at the 1999 International Mentoring Association 18 6 Conference, Atlanta, GA. (ERIC Document Reproduction Service No. ED 439683).

Single, P. B., & Single, R. M. (2004). E-mentoring and telementoring: Review of research. In Kochan, F. K., & Pascarelli, J. T. (Eds.), *Technological aspects of mentoring* (pp. 7–27). Greenwich, CT: Information Age Press.

Sipe, C. L. (1996). *Mentoring: A synthesis of P/PV's research*. Philadelphia, PA: Public/Private Ventures.

Taylor, A. S., LoSciuto, L., Fox, M., Hilbert, S. M., & Sonkowsky, M. (1999). The mentoring factor: Evaluation of the across ages' intergenerational approach to drug abuse prevention. *Child and Youth Services*, *20*(1-2), 77–99. doi:10.1300/J024v20n01_07

Tierney, J. P., Grossman, J. B., & Resche, N. L. (1995). *Making a difference: An impact study Big Brothers Big Sisters*. Philadelphia, PA: Public/Private Ventures.

Tinto, V. (1993). *Leaving college: Rethinking the causes and cures of student retention*. Chicago, IL: The University of Chicago Press.

United Stated Department of Education, National Center for Education Statistics. (2009). *The condition of education 2009* (NCES 2009-081). *Indicator (Minnesota Mining and Manfuacturing Company)*, 22.

United States Department of Labor, Bureau of Labor Statistics. (2009). *Volunteering in the United States*, USDL-10-0097. Retrieved from http://www.bls.gov/news.release/volun.nr0.htm

# Chapter 7
# Curriculum Development for Online Learners

**Lesley Farmer**
*California State University Long Beach, USA*

## ABSTRACT

*This chapter focuses on curriculum development issues as they apply to online education. Curriculum and its development are defined and contextualized within online learning environments. The development of online-delivered curriculum is impacted by social forces, the treatment of knowledge, human development, the learning process, technology, and management issues.*

## INTRODUCTION

What do educational institutions want students to learn and know how to do? Student learning outcomes (SLO) define those goals. Usually teachers operationalize those SLOs in terms of curriculum (*what* is to be learned) and behavioral objectives that can be assessed through student outputs such as test performance, research reports, or science lab work. With these outputs in mind, teachers can then determine what content and processing skills students need in order to demonstrate competence. The teaching aspect focuses on *how* students gain that knowledge and skills: through the input of learning activities that set information within a learning environment in which students can actively engage with the material. This process is well described in Wiggins and McTighe's 2001 book *Understanding by Design*.

With these premises, the role of the instructor becomes more the role of a facilitator or change agent, guiding the process more than delivering the content. The newest term for instructional designer is "knowledge engineer." These procedures cross delivery methods, be they face-to-face role-plays to Web-based tutorials. The instruction provides a safe and positive learning climate, structures the setting to facilitate joint planning, assesses the learners' needs and interests in order to identify objectives and craft learning activities, and then implements and assesses the activities. Additionally, instruction and learning should be considered

DOI: 10.4018/978-1-60960-791-3.ch007

as a self-reflective system. Both the instructor and learner bring prior experience. They need to engage with each other and the content at hand. The learner must somehow change, hopefully in a manner that the instructor (or change agent) can discern. This series of thoughts and actions are assessed in order to improve the system. Indeed, throughout instruction, assessment needs to occur: of the process, the product, and the people involved.

This chapter focuses on curriculum development issues as they apply to online education. As such, it addresses social forces, the treatment of knowledge, human development, the learning process, technology, and management.

## CURRICULUM BASES

What are schools teaching students? In the final analysis, the curriculum provides the content that students need to be able to understand and apply so they will be prepared as contributing members of the society. Wiles and Bondi (2011) stated that curriculum may be considered as a cyclic system of development, whereby needs analysis leads to design and implementation, which is evaluated and modified. Wiles and Bondi thus defined curriculum development as "a process where the choices of designing a learning experience for clients (students) are made and then activated through a series of coordinated activities" (p. 2).

Chartock (2000, p. 65) defined curriculum in terms of its orientation, which can be reflected in online environments:

1. teacher-centered (traditional)
2. student-centered (humanistic)
3. subject-centered (academic domains)
4. broad fields (interdisciplinary)
5. technology-based (behavioral)
6. society-based (meeting social needs).

Curriculum and its development can occur on several levels: from an international curriculum, such as media literacy, to a single-incident training about one skill. PK-12 education is the most likely to have a standard curriculum at the state or national level. Professional pre-service curriculum for medicine and teaching are also likely to have standardized student learning outcomes because of licensure requirements. The institutions with which curriculum is affiliated also vary in scope: from a one-person operation to an international consortium. Within each institution, curriculum development needs to address every level of the experience:

- institutional mission and vision: from a comprehensive university to a bartending school
- college: usually broad-based academic domains (such as Liberal Arts) within which departments house separate related programs (such as Languages, Social Sciences)
- program: curriculum for a well-defined, specific academic domain (such as Physical Therapy, French Studies, Educational Administration).
- course: term-long set of sessions of closely-related student outcomes (such as Clinical Electrophysiology, 19th Century French Poets)
- learning activity: a student outcome that is contextualized within a timeframe and learning environment, a teaching approach, relevant resources, and student task that can be assessed
- students: grouped and individual

It should be noted that Posner (1992) asserted that three realities of curriculum exist: the official (what is listed on the books), the operational (what is actually taught), and the hidden. Particularly if curriculum is thought to include the social and emotional learning experiences, hidden agendas that transfer underlying cultural values may result in biased teaching and learning. Online education, by its own existence, communicates certain biases such as the value and privilege of technology, and potentially the lesser status of face-to-face interaction.

Regardless of agenda, curriculum with its specific student outcomes, indicators and standards is usually developed at the program level. Professional accreditation agencies, such as the National Commission for Accreditation of Teacher Education and the Accreditation Board for in an effort to provide high-quality curriculum that attracts top faculty and students, educational institutions often developed curricula that aligned and met those accreditation agencies' standards. At this level, too, enough capacity exists to assess needs in light of desired outcomes and identify effective resources and instruction to insure student success for a substantial level of expertise.

## FOUNDATIONAL FORCES IN CURRICULUM DEVELOPMENT

All curricula and their development need to consider the human context of social forces (society at a whole), knowledge (human ideas and their representation), human development, and learning processes.

### Social Forces

The process of developing, approving, and delivering the curricula, particularly in terms of online education, reflects the social norms of the educational community in specific, and the larger community in terms of societal influences. These social factors exist on several levels, each of which impact online curriculum development.

- *International.* In his seminal 2005 book *A Whole New Mind,* Daniel Pink posited three social trends impacting the economy: abundance (of information and resources), globalization (which impacts allocation of human resources), and technology (which impacts access and processing of information). To remain competitive, people need to focus on creativity that fosters meaning and engagement. As a result, online curriculum development needs to meet the demands of international employers and students. Resources need to be culled from international sources, and made accessible to international learners. Resources and instruction need to address specific language and cultural issues.
- *National.* National standards and accountability issues drive much of United States PK-20 education and its curriculum development. More generically, the national economy impacts curriculum development, not only in terms of preparing future employees and retooling current workers, but also in terms of supporting and sustaining educational institutions and their infrastructures themselves. The increasing diversity of the U. S. population also impacts online education, as globalization issues trickles down to national and local levels.
- *Regional.* At this point, probably the most telling social dichotomy exists between rural and urban settings. The economy also continues to be based on geographic realities: rural agriculture (which depend on having enough land) vs. urban factories (which depend on having enough people). The socio-economic bases differ vastly, thereby impacting educational priorities. The digital divide remains as the "last mile" syndrome continues to constrain technology access to remote homes.
- *State.* Even in light of a gathering swell for national educational standards, state legislation and educational boards generally set

curriculum standards, from content frameworks to college requirements, from preschool to adult education (e.g., regional occupational programs). Technological infrastructures and resource allocation, such as subscription database licensing, are also often regulated at the state level. These state regulations thus mandate, or at least establish the parameters for much of online curriculum development decisions.

- *Local.* Despite social trends and layers of legislation, U.S. education remains a local entity, especially in PK-12 public education. School boards, which make and oversee educational policy and resource allocation, are elected locally and are answerable to the local community. Funding still comes from local pockets, which means that decisions must also be responsive to local priorities. This approach also applies to adult education venues such as public night school, community education, and even local business training. This situation can significantly impact online education, which often originates outside of the locale in which it is delivered. Developers of online curriculum must somehow bridge local needs and broader-based source of resources.

How do social forces play out in online curriculum development? Are students tracked into college preparatory vs. vocational programs, and are those tracks linked to socio-economic status? Does a wide range of online courses enable students to explore career possibilities based on their interests, such as fashion or construction? Does enrollment in advanced classes, be it English or the sciences, reflect the relative proportion of males ad females? Does content itself address socio-economic issues such as sexual identity, health and fitness, and cultural differences?

## Knowledge

What should be taught? Obviously, social forces drive the answer; what knowledge and skills do people need in order to survive and succeed? Social and educational values generally define what is success. They also indicate the goal of education, be it to develop a "well-rounded, educated person" or to insure a responsible and information citizenry that contributes to society. These two sample goals reflect attitudes about the role of education – and of individuals within society. At this point in history, knowledge is generally not considered a good in itself, but assumes value as it is applied (Wiles & Bondi, 2004).

No longer can one expect to know everything or to learn merely what the prior generation learned. Knowledge is not a closed universe, and society is not static. Not only do people now have access to remote resources around the world because of technology, but new knowledge is being generated every hour. Furthermore, knowledge is represented in more formats (such as podcasts and holographs) than ever before. How do educators make sense of all the available information, and organize it into a manageable curriculum, especially since the shape of any body of knowledge impacts how it is perceived and used?

Curriculum development, in preparing for an unknown future that calls for creative innovation and timely response to whatever crises or opportunities that might arise, challenges the hardiest educator. Even though online curriculum leverages technology, it cannot be all-encompassing, especially if it lacks face-to-face interaction. It rather resembles a doughnut with a hole in the center where physical knowledge representations exist.

## Human Development

In the midst of ever-changing knowledge, humanity continues to grow in fairly predictable ways. With its cognitive, affective and kinesthetic domains, the human body grows and develops as it interacts with its environment. Educators need to recognize how humans develop in order to optimize the learning of desired curricula. For instance, a child's concrete operational brain cannot conceptualize abstract calculus. The window of opportunity for deep language acquisition and communication closes by age twelve (Sousa, 2001). While PK-12 education tends to group students developmentally, such practice is not as prevalent in adult education, even though adults develop and change too. This developmental issue can be particularly challenging for online instructors who usually cannot tell the age and developmental stage of their students. Instead, online instructors need to focus on ways to help adults self-monitor their learning, and make appropriate accommodations for those adult development differences through choices in resources and assessments.

In addition, social aspects of human development impact curriculum delivery effectiveness. Social development norms and self-identity experimentation contextualize collaborative learning activities, for instance. In addition, gender-linked development impacts student interaction. For example, with the offset of puberty through adulthood, females tend to under-perform in technology-related tasks when they act in coed settings (Cooper & Weaver, 2003).

Even though online education per se might not be able to identify the stage of the student's developmental stage, it behooves online instructors to develop curriculum that is age or processing appropriate For instance, millenials and senior citizens tend to have different technology attitudes and experiences, and individuals with physical disabilities need to be accommodated in terms of accessing and processing information. At the least, online instructors should consult the relevant educational institution to identify the student population. Then the instructor should design the learning environment such that all students can self-identify their developmental stage and self-regulate their learning through instructor-provided scaffolding.

## Learning Processes

Different educational philosophies emphasize different learning modes. For instance, a behaviorist approach calls for the instructor to structure learning activities to insure desired student responses. Highly structured web tutorials fit this model well. In contrast, a constructivist philosophy would promote a learning environment in which students would choose and explore a variety of resources and co-construct meaning. Again, an online course can be designed with such flexibility in mind. In that respect, online learning can assume a variety of modalities.

Particularly as today's society demonstrates that social equity still does not exist between sexes or across cultures, it becomes imperative that all levels of education try to optimize the learning "playing field." For instance, males are better at retrieving online information, but females understand narrative and expository text better than boys (Smith & Wilhelm, 2002). African American students tend to be more field-dependent learners, and Latinos tend to prefer collaborative learning (Sheets, 2004). At the least, the broader educational community needs to affirm students' learning strengths, provide a broad-based curriculum to accommodate differences in background knowledge and interest, and help students improve in those curricular or learning areas where they are less well developed.

## Decision-Making

For each foundational issue attention should be paid to the decision-maker who makes things happen: legislators, trustees, school boards, superintendents, principals, other administrators, senior staff, and parents. In large educational systems, several spheres of influence may exist, from cross-campus initiative leaders to program coordinators. Do these decision-makers have legitimate power or informal power? Did they get their power based on expertise or on whom they knew (referent power)? How will are they to share their power? Despite societal changes, older males tend to serve in leadership roles, particularly in high schools and post-secondary institutions. What are their attitudes about online education? Further complicating decision-making is the reality that decisions at one level impact those at another (usually from the top down); in some cases, those decision-makers closest to the student may be in a better position to identify and solve curriculum problems, but may be hampered by decisions from those higher up. Probably the most reasonable approach is one of transparent governance and open communication so that the input of all stakeholders is heard and considered.

## A Knowledge Management Model of Curriculum Development Factors

Online learning success rests on a virtual environment that is conducive to learning that is engaged in interacting meaningfully with information and other humans. Such an environment requires the effective allocation and management of material and human resources.

Knowledge management has become a buzz word in today's business world. Increasingly, enterprises realize the importance of intellectual capital. Companies hire individuals with tacit (internal) knowledge, and socialize them within the company so that such knowledge will be made explicit and shared with their employees so that new combinations of ideas can emerge, and then be internalized; dynamic organizations encourage dialogue between tactic and explicit knowledge. This SECI model, developed by Nonaka and Takeuchi (1995), exemplifies the use of curriculum to facilitate learning and improve the organization as a whole. Knowledge management consists of the systematic management of collective information: gathering, organizing, sharing, and analyzing it. By providing on-demand access to managed knowledge, organizations can deal effectively with situations that emerge by drawing upon cumulated experience.

Osborn, Thomas, and Harnack (2005) applied a knowledge management model to educational settings. The following factors need to be considered in the broader online educational sphere as well as within each school setting as curriculum is being developed for online delivery. Specific online implications are noted in italics.

- **General Knowledge:** reading and writing skills; critical thinking skills; ability to learn independently using a wide variety of sources. *Online students need to read and communicate independently. They need to be able to comprehend information in different formats such as written, oral, and visual.*
- **Subject Knowledge:** in-depth, domain-specific knowledge gained from academic preparation and experience (e.g., how does a mathematician think). *Online resources need to explain concepts and best practices. For hands-on learning such as laboratory practice, either simulations need to be provided, or the student needs to physically access local laboratory environments.*
- **Information Literacy:** knowledge and use of information literacy and associated skills; belief in the value, promotion and support of information literacy in teaching and learning. *Online students need to be critical thinkers and collaborative learners. Online resources need to provide choice, and online activities need to leverage collective knowledge.*
- **Cultural Knowledge:** inherited and learned knowledge and values about the dominant culture and other cultures. *Online instructors need to know about their students' cultural norms and expectations. Resources and instruction need to be culturally-sensitive. For instance, topics need to be acceptable to the target audience (e.g., issues of family planning or religion could be problematic). Students*

*may be uncomfortable or ignorant about constructivist learning strategies.*

- **Languages:** attitude about, knowledge of, and use of dominant language and other languages used by the community; understanding of language learning processes; relationship of language to curriculum. *Online instructors should know in which languages students are proficient. Course material may need to be translated, or resources might include non-dominant languages. At the least, online instructors should aim for accessible language use, such as global English with few idioms. Domain-specific glossaries should be provided.*
- **Intellectual Capital:** knowledgeable individuals who have the potential to impact curriculum efforts; attitudes and values of intellectual capital. *Online curriculum development needs to include the input of elearning experts, technicians, adult educators usually, as well as content experts and master teachers. In online courses for adults, student expertise should be leveraged such that the curriculum is co-developed.*
- **Educational Professionalism:** values and practices of teaching and learning related to online-delivered curriculum; ethical code of conduct; active participation within the educational community; ongoing professional development. *Online instructors need to be competent in online instructional design and delivery, and educational institutions need to provide them with needed support to attain such competency through professional development and technical resources.*
- **Educational Collaboration:** communication and joint efforts among stakeholders that impact curriculum. *Curriculum stakeholders, including those with online expertise, need to co-develop online education. Technology should facilitate such collaboration.*
- **Leadership and Management Policies:** structure of decision-making processes, development of student outcomes relative to curriculum; resource allocation practices relative to curriculum. *Sample policies relevant to online education would include infrastructure, funding, hiring/retention of qualified faculty, technical support, accessibility, telecommunication issues, accreditation requirements, assessment, etc.*
- **Educational Policies:** board-approved policies and mandates relative to curriculum; monitoring of resources and services; accountability efforts. *Sample policies relevant to online education would include standards, curriculum review, assessment, admissions and advising, etc.*
- **Legal and Religious Policies:** societally-derived regulations and value systems that impact curriculum (e.g., privacy, sensitive topics). *Sample policies relevant to online education would include intellectual property, privacy and confidentiality, academic honesty, etc.*
- **Knowledge of Communities:** cultural values and practices, socio-political issues, economic issues as they relate to curriculum. *Online instructors need to know students and their affiliated organizations/community in order to provide appropriate curriculum and technical support (e.g., standards for telecommunications).*
- **Partnerships:** mutually-supportive relationships (e.g., suppliers, donors) between the school community and the community at large that impact curriculum. *The educational institution needs to identify and work with telecommunications, target clientele (e.g., industry, human resource development offices), educational counterparts, and social services.*

These factors do not necessarily advance online learning. For example, if policies provide no money for joint planning time or infrastructure, online education will be impeded. Ignorance about online learning or inaction in its support also negatively impacts such instructional delivery modes. While plans and policies are necessary for online curriculum development efforts, they are not sufficient in themselves. Policies should stem from identified needs and values. For policies to be effective, they should be created by all of the stakeholders who are influenced by them. Thus, a policy on student outcomes should include input from faculty, administrators, support personnel such as librarians and counselors, students (including graduates), and relevant community members such as industry and social service representatives. Otherwise, the curriculum stakeholders will not have a sense of ownership for the policy, and may be unwilling to enforce it; the policy will likely be ineffective. Generally speaking, the smaller the distance between the decision maker and the person who implements those decisions, the more likely that such decisions will be implemented. National plans and policies can be extremely difficult to monitor unless a thorough infrastructure is in place to audit local efforts and a strong incentive program (or punitive action) motivates stakeholders.

In short, each of these factors – or stakeholders – needs to become aware of online education's importance and the positive role that it can play in curriculum.

## Administration and Technology

When technology is incorporated throughout educational practice, additional factors beyond good curriculum development and management need to be addressed satisfactorily, primarily by administrators. Without their leadership and support, incorporation of online curriculum is nigh impossible. A good place to start are the International Society for Technology in Education (ISTE) technology standards for administrators, which emphasizes their organizational role.

- *Leadership and vision.* As administrators lead the planning for the educational institution, they set the tone for a culture that is willing to incorporate online curriculum to facilitate student learning. Strategic plans should, therefore, include provisions for technology resources and professional development as well as curricular goals. Administrators need to have a clear vision of technology-infused education, and articulate it convincingly with the entire school community.
- *Learning and teaching.* As instructional leaders, administrators need to spearhead evaluation of appropriate educational technology resources to support online curriculum develop and delivery. They should also facilitate developing online learning environments and professional development that incorporate online experiences.
- *Productivity and professional practice.* Administrators need to stay current about educational technology trends. They need to use technology, particularly telecommunication, to conduct school business with staff, and to facilitate school improvement.
- *Support, management, and operations.* Administrators need to insure that sufficient human and material resources are readily available to implement curricular plans for learning effectively online. Administrators also need to develop policies and procedures to insure appropriate resources and support mechanisms, including time for professional development and planning. To insure sustainability and student improvement, they also need to hire and reward technologically competent staff.
- *Assessment and evaluation.* Administrators should assess online technology's impact,

and also use online technology to assess the school's impact on student learning.
- *Social, legal, and ethical issues.* Administrators are responsible for seeing that their staff comply with legal and ethical guidelines. Policies and procedures should be in place, and implemented, to insure privacy as well as security. Administrators also have to insure that the entire educational community has equitable access to the technology needed.

Because online curriculum is implemented by teachers, administrators should foster online teacher interest and confidence in using online technology in several concrete ways (Cradler, Freeman, Cradler, & McNabb, 2002).

- Provide staff with laptop systems to use at home.
- Provide computers with Internet connectivity in all faculty work areas.
- Provide for a staff listserv or online management system, and use it to communicate school news as well as foster collaborative planning.
- Encourage staff to develop and maintain course and office web pages.
- Provide time for reviewing electronic sources.
- Incorporate technology into staff development activities.
- Encourage and reward staff who incorporate technology into their own professional growth plans.
- Establish a structure for technology mentoring.
- Facilitate just-in-time training.
- Provide opportunities for staff to share best practice in technology-infused teaching and learning.
- Enable staff to explore online learning environments designed by other educational entities.

## The Community's Role

Education is ultimately a community-based endeavor. Even with national curriculum and standards, how curriculum is played out depends on the community's resources and expectations. This impact may seem short-termed as societies become more transient, but it may be equally argued that today's online curriculum may influence the future of people around the globe.

As such, the public sector plays several significant roles in support of online curriculum development (Khoury, 2004).

- *Facilitation:* providing financial and political backing on curriculum initiatives; providing venues for discussing curriculum priorities; advancing information communication infrastructure
- *Regulation:* providing and enforcing information and communication technology (ICT) laws and regulations; accrediting educational institutions; establishing ICT standards and guidelines
- *Use:* bridging educational and economic curriculum applications; identifying and meeting information needs; producing and disseminating information; keeping current in information literacy trends; promoting ICT development and education.

Curriculum developers need to assess the community's material and human resources as a means to enrich students' engagement with the curriculum, both online and as an extension into the physical community. In this respect, service learning provides authentic experiences where students can apply their information literacy skills and can contribute to their community in meaningful ways.

Curriculum developers also need to be aware of community cultural values in order to validate current beliefs and bridge to new understandings. When curriculum practices veer too far from community values and norms, then disconnects occur: between teachers and students, between students and their families, between administrators and community leaders. When educational institutions serve a variety of cultures, which may clash, then administrators and curriculum developers need to focus on identifying overriding common programmatic values and goals that all relevant community members can agree to. Otherwise, students may get mixed messages about the curriculum and its application, and online instruction may be undermined by family values. Little positive learning will occur. On the other hand, education and community can inform each other about novel views about curricular issues, online education and the evolving world, so that both parties can adjust to an unforeseeable future. Otherwise, either will be stuck in the past, unable to survive or compete successfully.

## MANAGING CURRICULUM DEVELOPMENT FOR ONLINE EDUCATION

While curriculum development for online environments is process-oriented, it does not require that the process itself must follow strictly sequentially. Assessment and adjustments should be continual, and prior points may need to be reconsidered in light of new information. Moreover, as these steps are developed, curriculum developers should collaborate with the target participants and the sponsoring agency as appropriate. That is, if a school system mandates that all online educators need training on evaluating digital resources, then the trainer should work with the associated system representative as well as the site teachers. The key is organizational and individual involvement throughout the process so the ultimate learning will be more authentic and impactful. It should also be noted that each step requires assessment and a decision. Furthermore, at any point, the decision may be to stop the process; sometimes the best move is not to move at all. For example, a request for online training for culturally-sensitive ways to treat women with HIV might arise, but face-to-face instruction might be deemed more appropriate. The following steps, for the most part, assume that some kind of professional development activity will need to be provided.

### Assess Needs

Even before any curriculum is planned, a needs assessment should be conducted to identify relevant gaps as well as desired improvements. That is, remediation or other interventions to address a problem may be required. On the other hand, the status quo may be fine, but the educational community wants to enhance itself.

The form of the needs assessment itself may vary. Sometimes targeted groups are asked to identify professional development needs: social service providers, support staff, parents, department chairs, senior citizens, first year teachers, reading specialists. In other cases, the need may be couched in terms of the institution's mission: student outcomes, advancing the learning community, graduation requirements, accreditation, and licensure. Both employees as well as employers should be assessed since the two parties may differ in their perceptions. For instance, online teachers may think that they need tips on cracking down on plagiarism, while the administration may think that teachers need to design more creative, plagiarism-proof assignments. No one constituency can truly see the entire picture, so curriculum developers must try to gather information from these different perspectives. Some of the ways to conduct needs assessments include: observations, surveys and questionnaires, interviews and focus groups, examination of student work, and performance evaluation. Another effective approach is to identify experts / model practitioners, and uncover the factors for success.

As the data are collected, the curriculum developer should also find out the relative importance of the need. For instance, one teacher may think that all students need to learn how to create annotated bibliographies, but no other teacher thinks that it is important. The librarian would probably work with that one teacher instead of including that skill in a standard curriculum. In any case, a decision must be made as to which need to address within the curriculum – and where within that curriculum. In some situations, the deciding factor is priority of the impact, such as accreditation requirements. In other situations, the curriculum may need to be addressed in another way. For instance, online faculty may find that pre-service reading specialists have difficulty in internship settings. Online curriculum might not be the problem; rather, the link between online faculty and field placement needs to be negotiated.

## Identify Learners

Since learners comprise the key factor in any instruction, identifying them is a first step. While learners can self-identify themselves, usually curriculum decision-makers determine the target group. The learner might be one individual, a group, the entire faculty at a school, or a multi-site population. Curriculum developers usually focus on a well-defined group of people, such as pre-service social workers or re-entry mothers. With today's global society, international learners need to be considered. In some cases, curriculum might prepare one company's or industry's employees, while in other cases, educational institutions might go into partnership to provide a comprehensive curriculum for two disparate settings such as Los Angeles and Shanghai.

The identified need usually links the learner and the outcome, one sometimes leading the other. Even if the needs assessment is based on a population's own interests, subgroups may arise with differing priorities. Additionally, a site might structure professional development in terms of job functions (e.g., grade level, academic domain). If the need is based on student outcomes, on the other hand, sometimes the categorization for professional development might still be learner-defined; if the disaggregated data points to first-year students, for instance, then those online instructors who work with that group would be the defining factor, and the outcomes would be refined by those teachers. On the other hand, if the need is defined as increasing student engagement, then specific objectives and appropriate interventions would have to be identified before the appropriate learner set could be determined.

## Identify Outcomes

What are the intended results of the curriculum? The desired outcome is normally considered in terms of a target learner's behavior. In some cases, the outcome focuses on product; in other cases, the outcome may focus on process. Outcomes should also consider affective factors: changes in attitude or social skills. Too often these elements are overlooked, and instructional efforts can be undermined or short-lived as a result. The outcome may well be considered an overarching goal, such as improved student reading. A pre-service student teacher outcome might then be improved skills in teaching strategies. That outcome would need to be refined into several *objectives:* identifying key reading standards within a subject domain for a particular grade level, developing reading diagnostic skills, and determining appropriate interventions to address the deficiencies. Each objective may require a separate online instructional design and delivery.

It should be noted, though, that the outcome itself is just one element within a program's curriculum, which would probably be teaching in elementary school settings. More broadly, that elementary teacher curriculum could comprise one part of a college of education's overall curriculum, which itself would comprise one unit within a university's curriculum: that of preparing post-secondary students to be contributing citizens through a comprehensive set of curricular choices and general education requirements. The curriculum, then, consists of a cluster of related outcomes that describe a competent practitioner. Moreover, each of its sub-elements need to align with the larger curriculum.

How do educational institutions know when students are well-prepared, that they have met the outcome? Today that answer is often "Students meet the standard." The standard, then, identifies "good enough" performance. As standards become pervasive and considered the lynchpin of education, the curriculum is developed to insure that the standards can be met through the course delivery and accompanying learning performances. It sounds simple enough, but the actual picture is more complex. At the very least, the question arises: which standards?

As the education community examines the notion of preparation, they typically think about future employment, citizenship, and personal lives of their students. Certainly the U. S. Department of Labor SCANS report (1991) emphasized the world of work. Increasingly, schools are creating magnet academies to foster specialized expertise, be it hotel management or performing arts. As a result, standards may be couched in terms of employer-friendly language, such as problem solving or effective communication skills. On the positive side, such standards, *if applied equitably to all,* assumes that every student has the capacity to successfully enter the work field. On the negative side, homemaking may be under-valued, for example, which may marginalize females who continue to be more likely to stay at home than males. Another danger, particularly when curriculum has a narrow focus, is that students might not experience a full range of academic and co-curricular possibilities and thus limit their horizons. Additionally, students may associate school only with work, and not realize the inherent joy of learning.

## Identify Indicators

Explicit assessment needs to be addressed early in the curriculum development process because it shapes the instructional approach. Typically, overall program standards are determined, with supporting outcomes. Indicators operationalize those standards. To follow the scenario proposed above, if the desired objective is faculty ability to diagnose reading problems, then some kind of indicator must be identified that can be used to determine if the faculty can demonstrate that skill. Relevant indicators might include: when listening to a student read a text aloud, the teacher notices a reading problem; and the teacher correctly identifies the specific reading deficiency. Once the indicator is determined, then the *assessment* process can be chosen. In the present example, a simulation would be an appropriate method to measure the learner's ability to diagnose a reading deficiency. This planning step facilitates the remaining instructional design since optimum learning tends to occur then all the instructional elements are aligned and reinforced. The scenario also points out the benefit of developing a series of learning activities to build a substantial body of knowledge and experience. When that learning activity occurs online, then the associated assessment must also be doable in that environment; in the above example, the most effective means of measuring that outcome would be a video, which would require that the student have access to that equipment and to the learning environment as well as permissions to videotape the reader.

At the curricular level, regardless of instructional delivery modality, such micro-decisions about assessment are not addressed except as they contribute to the program's overall curriculum assessment. Typically, a program needs to determine if a student meets all the outcomes to graduate from that program, be it as an entering professional (e.g., lawyer, dietician, architect) or as a well-rounded college graduate. To that end, students would need to meet required graduation outcomes, which would be measured through key or signature assessment performances. These assessments are usually imbedded within courses, although exit examinations or portfolios might be incorporated in order to assess cross-course synthesis of knowledge and competencies.

## Identify Pre-Requisite Skills

Knowing the goal and what it looks like helps curriculum developers decide what content to provide so learners can meet that goal. However, curriculum developers must also identify possible pre-requisite skills in order to define the content's parameters. For program development, such skills are usually identified as factors for admission into the program. For online programs, students would need to be technology competent: ability to navigate the Internet, use telecommunications, word process, and other technology skills as applicable to the specific programs, such as engineering. These pre-requisite skills also need to address general education and specific content matter expertise. Usually successful graduation is required for the next higher level of education. Students going into nursing, for example, might be required to have some prior biology and chemistry courses.

## Identify Content

Often, beginning instructors start with this step. By now, it should be obvious that content exists within the context of the organization or collective. As noted above, the pre-requisite skills might drive the content decision as much as the intended goal, and these decisions depend on the larger curriculum picture Even when the topic is identified, such as "alternatives to book reports: different ways to assess student reading comprehension," the number of assessment tools, the depth of detail to describe and experience each assessment method, and the balance between process and product all need to be determined.

Such decisions usually rest with the course instructor; curriculum developers look at the bigger picture in terms of content and student learning assessment. Content to meet program standards is identified, and then organized by course. Sequencing of that content is embedded within course sequencing. Specific readings and other resource materials is then the prevue of the course instructor in most cases.

## Identify the Instructional Format

In the context of curriculum development, "format" refers to a complex set of elements: resources, instructor, method, time frame, sequence, location, grouping, individualization, affective / social factors. These elements are usually the prevue of the instructor. Curriculum developers tend to provide the necessary support for instructors to be able to locate and use the needed resources and instructional strategies. It should be noted that curriculum developers also need to be sure that qualified faculty are available to design and deliver effective instruction.

For online education, curriculum developers need to make sure that an online learning environment is sufficiently supported through stable infrastructure and technical help. Digital resources need to be accessible, and teachers need to be technologically competent as well as comfortable with e-learning instructional strategies.

## Contextualize Curriculum

Curriculum does not exist in a vacuum. It occurs within the larger framework of the learner and of the instructional sponsoring entity. In terms of the learner, the curriculum may facilitate a career-based goal or an informal self-improvement desire. If learning is effective, then the learner changes in some manner. When this change supports or aligns with the learner's environment, then that change is usually welcomed and the learner is positively reinforced. If, however, a misalignment or conflict occurs between the changed learner and the environment, then adjustment of one or both entities will need to occur. For example, a female paraprofessional gains expertise in desktop publishing and decides to pursue a degree in communications. If the family cannot afford for that person to go back to college, or if her spouse is uncomfortable about her taking time away from the family, even in an online environment, then conflict may ensue.

While the educational institution as a whole is not responsible for the external changes that the learner may face, being aware of the impact of change can help instructors when a learner seems stressed. Even if change is positive and supported, learners may need guidance as they start a professional development endeavor. University re-entry learners need to get re-acclimated to the rigors of graduate work with its extensive reading, writing, studying, and project development. An online "back to school" tutorial can help re-orient these students. Particularly with online training, some learners may need extra support as they learn to navigate web-based instruction or other telecommunications efforts. Some learners may not have access to current equipment, and may get frustrated when their system crashes under broadband demands. If the educational institution can support or help problem-solve with the learner, the experience will be more satisfying for both parties.

Online instruction financially impacts the institutions that are developing online curriculum for their own employees in several ways. Obviously, curriculum and instructional design need to be underwritten, and online instructors should be paid. In some cases, particularly in school settings, participating faculty may seek reimbursement for their online participation if done outside school time. Equipment such as laptops may need to be purchased to facilitate content delivery, and the infrastructure has to have the capability of supporting all learners. If substantial online professional development includes lab access, resources may need upgrading and a technician or lab assistant may need to be hired to oversee the facility and coach learners.

## Implement the Plan

Even with careful curriculum development, an online program can still fall on its face without careful management. Poor marketing and communication can result in insufficient numbers of students enrolled in the program's courses. Inadequate admissions processes can result in frustrated students who need significant remediation. Poor professional development of instructors can lead to ineffective use of online learning environments. If Internet connectivity fails during training, the instructor will need to implement a back-up plan, such as anticipated web downloads to burn on CDs. Each step needs to be well planned, with contingent plans in place in case of unanticipated problems.

## Assess the Plan

Each educational level -- learner outcomes, the instructional plan and delivery, and program development and implementation -- need to be assessed in order to build on that experience for future curriculum development. Concurrently, the technology associated with each level also has to be assessed. The measurement instruments should be established during curriculum development from the start to make sure that all efforts are aligned with the desired results. Assessments can be done during planning as well as the learning activity itself: through observation (by an outside observer as well as by the instructor), through survey (done after each portion of the activity, at the end of the entire session, or days later), and through examination of instructor materials (input) and participant work (outcomes). As much as possible, evaluation questions should be posed as neutrally as possible, and should provide opportunity for comment.

## Curriculum Development as a Self-Reflective System

As noted above, assessment does not close the curriculum development circle; it links to the next learning cycle. Even if one decided that the learning experience was terrible and that the concepts learned would never be used again, then such a reaction helps determine what *content* not to teach and what *methods* not to use within that context and audience. More typically, as learners apply their new knowledge and skills, new questions or issues arise that call for further curriculum development.

The instructional design process itself is subject to a cycle of inquiry and self-reflection as part of the larger curriculum development system. As instruction is designed, particularly with the same learner population, the methods can be analyzed in terms of their effectiveness, and improvements in the design factors can be made in order to optimize future instruction. For example, student performance is analyzed, and achievement gaps are identified. The reasons for those gaps are determined, and potentially effective interventions are chosen and tested as curriculum is reviewed. The impact of those changes is then analyzed, thus starting a new cycle.

## CHANGE AND FUTURE TRENDS

Several factors impact current and future curriculum development: globalization and increasing diversity in general, abundance, and technology have already been identified. All of these point to the need for more customization and personalization of curriculum. Personal e-learning space is a growing phenomenon as students pick and choose the learning experiences and curriculum that resonates for them. As a result, curriculum development is becoming more modular and localized.

Web 2.0 has enabled online students to interact more frequently and deeply. Online courses need to facilitate peer collaboration and collective knowledge generation. Such measures require that online instructors share their responsibility and authority with their students, which may conflict with their existing educational philosophies. Furthermore, such collective and constructivist online instructional strategies may also conflict with the cultural norms of some online students.

Lastly, economics will continue to influence curriculum development for online learning. Can institutions support the needed technology, digital resources, and technical expertise? Do students have access to the required technology? On the other hand, online instruction may be calculated to be the most cost-effective way to address the educational needs of underserved populations.

## CONCLUSION

Clearly, online curriculum development requires a flexible mindset and organizational structure. Because information changes constantly, because the world at large changes constantly, the educational community must respond to these dynamics if they hope to have any chance of facilitating student achievement in a global society. Simultaneously, schools serve as institutions of the dominant culture. Therefore, tensions exist between established power and purposeful improvement. As far back as 1991, Thompson synthesized educational trends in that still remain "in transition" in the 21st century:

- school purpose: from selecting the best to ensuring that all students learn
- nature of knowledge: from absolute truths to making meaning
- nature of learning: from passive reception to active engagement
- nature of teaching: from sage on the stage to guide on the side

- curriculum: from a highly structured sequence set of fixed knowledge to a cyclical set of contextualized perspectives
- leadership: from hierarchical authority to transformative empowerment
- assessment: from standardized input points to integrated and outcomes-centered cycled of inquiry.

All the factors in curriculum development need to be continuously audited, assessed and negotiated in order to provide the most efficient online educational experiences to support the curriculum. Curriculum developers need to be aware of these changing dynamics, and serve as a change agent, providing appropriate leadership via professional development, communities of practice, and educational reform efforts.

It should be noted that curriculum developers cannot force change on the rest of the educational community. Even "islands" of online curriculum innovation are not as successful as system-wide approaches to change because the former may not be scalable. These islands usually involve close-knot relationships among a small group of educators: a closed culture. Even though outside funding can help these islands sustain long-term status, the goals and expectations are usually very narrow and specific. Institution wide initiatives, on the other hand, enlist administrative support, leverage larger-scale resources, generate supporting policies, and encourage establish support scalable and sustainable mechanisms. Therefore, curriculum developers should leverage the use of collaboration and distributed leadership to facilitate the conditions for online educational success.

## REFERENCES

Chartock, R. (2000). *Educational foundations: An anthology*. Upper Saddle River, NJ: Merrill.

Cooper, J., & Weaver, K. (2003). *Gender and computers*. Mahwah, NJ: Erlbaum.

Cradler, J., Freeman, M., Cradler, R., & McNabb, M. (2002). Research implications for preparing teachers to use technology. *Learning and Leading with Technology*, *30*(1), 50–53.

Khoury, R. (2004). *National ICT priorities*. Paper presented at ICT Lebanon 20004: The Arab Technology for Development Conference, Beirut.

Nonaka, I., & Takeuchi, H. (1995). *The knowledge-creating company*. New York, NY: Oxford University Press.

Osborn, M., Thomas, E., & Hartnack, D. (2005). An evolving model of knowledge management in education and the South African reality. In Lee, S. (Eds.), *Information leadership in a culture of change: IASL reports* (pp. 1–15). Erie, PA: International Association of School Librarianship.

Pink, D. (2005). *A whole new mind*. New York, NY: Riverhead Books.

Posner, G. (1992). *Analyzing the curriculum*. New York, NY: McGraw-Hill.

Sheets, R. (2004). *Diversity pedagogy*. Boston, MA: Allyn & Bacon.

Smith, M., & Wilhelm, J. (2002). *Reading don't fix no Chevys: Literacy in the lives of young men*. Portsmouth, NH: Heinemann.

Sousa, D. (2001). *How the brain learns* (2nd ed.). Thouand Oaks, CA: Corwin Press.

Thompson, J. (1991, May). Resource-based learning can be the backbone of reform improvement. *NASSP Bulletin*, 24–28. doi:10.1177/019263659107553506

U. S. Department of Labor. (1991). *Secretary's Commission on Achieving Necessary Skills*. Washington, DC: Government Printing Office.

Wiggins, G., & McTighe, J. (2001). *Understanding by design*. Englewood Cliffs, NJ: Prentice Hall.

Wiles, J., & Bondi, J. (2011). *Curriculum development* (8th ed.). Upper Saddle River, NJ: Pearson Education.

Wright, H. (2000). Nailing jell-o to the wall. *Educational Researcher*, *29*(5), 4–13.

# Chapter 8
# Gender Issues in Online Education

**Lesley Farmer**
*California State University Long Beach, USA*

## ABSTRACT

*Women constitute the majority of U.S. online learners, an environment that can cloak gender issues. Nevertheless, people bring their experiences and attitudes to the educational table, and gender remains a significant factor that online educators need to consider. This chapter focuses on the biological and social aspects of gendered learning and self-identity as they apply to online learning, particularly in Western societies. Gender-sensitive instructional design and technology incorporation strategies are provided to support gender-equitable engagement in online education.*

## INTRODUCTION

At this point in history, women constitute the majority of online learners. Moreover, the online learning environment can, to a degree, cloak gender issues. Nevertheless, people bring their experiences and attitudes to the educational table, and gender remains a significant factor that online educators need to consider.

Learning is a result of the interaction of an individual and his or her environment, in which context change in behavior or attitude change. As such, both biological and social factors are involved. One's sex comprises the "nature" part of the interaction, and one's gender reflects the "nurture" impact of society. Both elements need to be considered when addressing gender issues in learning.

This chapter focuses on the biological and social aspects of gendered learning and self-identity as they apply to online learning.

DOI: 10.4018/978-1-60960-791-3.ch008

## BIOLOGICAL-BASED LEARNING

Gender differences in learning start with the brain; even in the womb, male brains are larger and more rigid than girls. Male right brains, where abstract thinking and sequencing dominate, are thicker than girls, although girls tend to have thicker left brains, which impact image and holistic thinking. Girls' brain hemispheres are more connected than boys so their brain is more coordinated (Sousa, 2001). When crises occur, the lower part of boys' brains dominate: fight or flight; in contrast, girls' upper thinking brain dominates in such cases, which may explain why girls tend to take fewer risks (Moir & Jessel, 1991).

Learning demonstrates sexual developmental differences. While some differences even out over time, having initial advantages in specific modalities of perception and processing can impact later learning. In infancy, boys are less bothered by loud noises than girls, who prefer soft tones and singing; on the other hand, girls have better hearing and are able to distinguish emotional nuances. Developmentally, girls develop their language skills earlier, and boys flex their already greater muscle more (Gurian & Henley, 2001). Similarly, boys play out their emotions through action while girls use words; for this reason, boys tend to prefer icon prompts while girls prefer textual ones in software (Cooper & Weaver, 2003). Unfortunately, because girls tend not to play with spatially manipulated toys as much as boys, they are less prepared to succeed later with mechanical and spatial challenges (Moir & Jessel, 1991). In terms of emotional development, even as early as the primary grades, boys are better able than girls to separate emotion from reason. On the other hand, by sixth grade, boys are more likely to take aggressive action to solve problems. Interestingly, primary boys are more rule-bound than their female peers; by their teenage years, though, boys rebel more against those rules than do girls (Gurian & Henley, 2001). Recognizing these early differences, online instruction can leverage these differences by motivating youngsters through gender-specific comfortable modalities to present new content, and presenting familiar subject matter through less-practiced learning modalities; in this way, students strengthen less developed approaches to learning.

In adolescence, development is significantly gender-linked. While biology continues to play a role in differentiation, by this point, the psychological and social factors take on a much greater importance. Even the timing of the onset of puberty is viewed differently by boys and girls. Early male maturers tend to gain more power and popularity while females who mature at an earlier age tend to be self-conscious and uncomfortable with such physical changes. In particular, girls tend to lose their "voice," confidence and self-esteem in early adolescence as they try to relate to peers and their own morphing bodies. Appearance becomes more important to them, and societal messages often reinforce rigid expectations for females; not surprisingly, two-thirds of girls have a negative body image (Orenstein, 1994; Pipher, 1994). Interestingly, athletic girls have higher esteem than their non-athletic peers, but in co-ed sports those same female athletes lose their self-confidence (American Association of University Women, 1992). Thus, bodily changes can impact learning as girls vie for social acceptance more than academic prowess, and thus cut themselves out of challenging courses that appear to be male-dominated, such as engineering. In the process, girls do not learn those sets of skills as well as males (Knight, 1997). It should be noted that this phenomenon is culturally contextualized; where rites of passage empower both boys and girls, self-deprecation is observed less often. Likewise, in cultures where gender roles are more defined and validated, such esteem "dips" are less pronounced; for instance, African American girls gain social power in adolescence, and Latina's quincenera rite validates womanhood. Nevertheless, those same roles can limit girls' potential if they do not fit the norm (American Association of University

Women, 1992). In that respect, online learning can provide some comfort for girls because that they do not have to spend as much time worrying about their body image. In fact, online learning provides a venue for cross-gender role-playing; especially with the use of avatars, boys and girls can experience how people treat each sex. Girls may feel more empowered or see the consequences of aggressive behavior while boys may find that they are better treated as girls or that they may feel uncomfortable being "hit upon."

Other cognitive learning styles preferences rise from these biological and social differences, which can impact online learning. For example, in Western societies girls tend to approach problem-solving cautiously and reflectively while boys take greater risks and act more impulsively. Thus, online instruction can benefit girls who may need more time to think rather than respond immediately. Girls tend to be more field-dependent, concrete learners; that is, they contextualize meaning. This behavior favors case studies and service learning, which can be substantive parts of online learning. On the other hand, boys' ability to separate emotion from reason and to be more field-independent because of their split brain hemispheres, favors abstract reasoning and traditional teaching strategies. Girls also appreciate processes while boys favor product. Even girls' worldview often differs from boys': time is considered fluid, measured in terms of relationships rather than in objective units; power is limitless rather than zero-sum; leadership is based on facilitation rather than power; individuals are more important than rules; and the world is to be lived with, not exploited (Miller, 1976). These attitudes should be identified according to cultural norms, and should be leveraged when designing online instruction: encouraging study buddies, structuring group pages, assigning small collaborative group projects, having students lead online discussions, having students assume online identities to explore different points of view, and incorporating service learning as a way to test abstract concepts and share real-life experiences that link with the curriculum.

The affective domain also needs to be considered when discussing learning, and this too has a sex-linked biological basis. Key in effect is motivation, which jumpstarts learning. Pintrich and Linnenbrink (2002) posit four components of motivation: self-efficacy, attribute theory, locus of motivation, and achievement goal theory. Girls tend to under-estimate their self-efficacy. Moreover, girls tend to blame themselves for their failures while boys tend to blame others; in contrast, successful girls think they are lucky while boys who achieve pat themselves on their back. (American Association of University Women, 1992). Girls' intrinsic motivation is more likely to be based in interpersonal factors than for boys, which complements achievement goal theory, in which boys are more performance-oriented while girls are mastery-oriented. Being aware of students' self-perceptions and interests, both within school and outside, can help online educators look for ways to provide intriguing learning activities that foster intellectual risk-taking in a safe environment.

## GENDERED SCHOOLING

These biological differences impact schooling. In most American education, girls work harder, are more motivated, make better grades and are more satisfied with school than are boys. Martin (2002) found that boys exhibit significantly less cognitive engagement and less concentration than girls, although boys can fixate on an activity to the exclusion of other demands. On the other hand, boys are less stressed and fearful than girls about learning, and may more a more playful attitude about learning, which can motivate them and help them achieve, although they are less concerned about grades than are girls (Scherer, 2002). Furthermore, boys are less comfortable with rules and authority than girls, and are more apt to think that their teacher does not like them (Black, 1995). Online learning can help level the playing field by providing simulations that encourage self-paced risk-taking exploration within strict parameters, which addresses both sexes' abilities and needs.

Gender differences in school behavior start from the first year. In examining how American children interact in playground games, Pellegrini et al. (2002) found that boys played a greater variety of games, especially chase and ball games, and that girls played more verbal games. Facility in playing games was an accurate predictor of boys' social competence, and both sexes' adjustment to first grade. Girls develop earlier than boys, so their bodies can process stimuli meaningfully at a younger grade. It takes boys longer to learn, yet they have shorter attention spans and need more teacher time than girls. Gender-linked subject matter, linked to kinds of reasoning, already surfaces by third grade. For example, because beginning reading requires both sides of the brain, girls are, again, at an advantage. On the other hand, by third grade, reasoning math skills showcase boys' natural lead (Gurian & Henley, 2001). Learning disabilities start early too as boys are more likely to be hyperactive and need reading remediation. Moreover, more boys are held back in grades more than girls. Online instruction, particularly in the form of serious games, benefits both sexes because of self-pacing features and exposure to different subjects and learning styles.

Puberty accentuates other gender-linked learning issues. In the U.S., Girls' IQ scores drop off during middle school, although they rise again in high school. Nevertheless, girls are routinely discouraged from registering for advanced courses in male-associated domains such as the hard sciences; those girls who persist in taking these courses often find themselves a distinct minority and may feel out of place. Even the stereotype of male dominance or achievement in such courses can impact how well girls perform because they – and their teachers – unconsciously play out the "predestined" attributions (Brownlow, Jacobi, & Rogers, 2000). This biased thinking seriously impact girls' pursuit (or non-pursuit) of technology-related subjects. This biased thinking is played out in gaming, in which boys excel in coed settings. Interestingly, girl gamers perform better than boys in low-stakes single-sex settings, although they perceive that they are not as capable as boys, mainly due to female attribution behavior (Gargittai & Shafer, 2006). Nevertheless, online learning environments could prove to be an effective way to offset coed perceptions, particularly when learners are given timely feedback (Cooper & Weaver, 2003).

Because learning is largely a social process, the emotional lives of adolescents needs to be acknowledged and leveraged to bring out the best in each gender – and build up their less-utilized traits. Indeed, the American New Boys Movement has focused on the plight of adolescent boys, noting how society has constrained boys' psychological options (e.g., boys don't cry, boys should hide their feelings, etc.) (Smith & Wilhelm, 2002). Boys tend to pursue power while girls pursue a comfortable environment. Additionally, boys' social hierarchies tend to be stable while girls' are fluid. Girls are more likely to be depressed, but boys are more likely to successfully commit suicide. Still, teens look for experiences that create intense feelings (Park, 2004). Thus, collaborative skills take on more nuanced meaning in adolescence. Additionally, personal coping skills need to be explicitly taught in order to help students overcome their personal frustrations so they can focus on academic endeavors. In that respect, online social networking provides a relatively safe environment for males to express their emotions. In fact, youth sometimes over-estimate their sense of anonymity, and share more than they should

As young women enter college in the U.S., they continue to experience gendered expectations, particularly in the hard sciences, where they find that their high school transcript limits their academic horizons. Calculus tends to serve as an academic gatekeeper, so if students without that background have to take remedial courses, which lengthens their college time and discourages them from majoring in technology and related domains. Even when females choose those majors, they find themselves as minorities in a male-dominated environment, including their instructor. Too often females tend to feel intimidated or lose self-confidence about their abilities; some put in extra effort to keep up or surpass their male peers, only to find that the stress of high competition is not worth the effort and so change majors (Lips, 2007).

## SOCIETAL CHANGES

As implied above, societal expectations carry as much weight as nature in learning. Social development has continued to start with the family, grow to include neighbors and relatives, and then include community and larger entities. Within the last half century, societal expectations about females and males have been tested repeatedly; today's youth grow up in a different social climate than their parents or grandparents, by and large. Many businesses reflect "flatter" bureaucratic hierarchies, and deal with organizational well-being as much as the bottom line. The glass ceiling has become more permeable, and career options have increased for both males and females. Both sexes can self-realize their full potential to a greater extent.

These societal changes can impact the learning environment, particularly as students and faculty may be up to four generations apart in age and gendered expectations. For example, in the fifties, women were expected to stay at home and raise their children, while the Pill helped bring about the sexual revolution of the 1970s, and feminist studies gained favor in the latter part of the twentieth century. On the other hand, a senior professor might have grown up with a mother who worked in a factory during World War II and passed on an expectation of female empowerment. In any case, when generations mix, their gendered expectations and needs may conflict, so the push for a more inclusive and gender-equitable school culture can face complications along the way.

Overall, today's males and females reflect a wide range of interests and learning styles. Individual differences overrule sex-linked traits. Perhaps because the United States has become more pluralistic, lifestyles have become less stable, and social messages have diversified, young people's personal experiences are more varied. On one hand, television and other forms of instantaneous communication have helped spread common cultural experiences such as *The Simpsons* and *American Idol.* On the other hand, stereotypical images and expectations are communicated daily in the mass media and in daily life. Particularly when students are stressed or uncertain about themselves, they are more likely to regress to stereotypical behavior. In brief, as individuals try to find their identities within society, they experience the dynamic between personal uniqueness and social acceptance, both of which involve sexual issues. As a result of these dynamics, gendered roles and expectations are not easily explained or designated in many parts of the United States. The negotiations involved in finding a mutual ground of understanding and cooperation provides a positive model for students.

## GENDER ISSUES AND TECHNOLOGY USE

The technology picture relative to gender has changed and become more nuanced over the years. Technology in some format has become almost ubiquitous, so people have opportunities to use it. At this point in time, women constitute the majority of online learners and Internet users. However, they are more likely than men to have computer anxiety, and remain seriously under-represented in technology careers. Females have the ability to use technology, but remain more selective in its use. While many factors account for differences in how learners use technology, such as socioeconomics and personality, on the whole, males and females have exhibited distinctive behaviors relative to technology. For example, girls are more likely than boys to use technology for email, word processing and schoolwork; boys use it more for gaming (U. S. Department of Education, 2004).

Brunner (1997) identified several sex-linked differences in technology use. Females tend to see technology as a tool that has meaning as it enables them to achieve some goal, while males see technology as a powerful machine to control. Females value technology for its social facilitation, while males tend to have more of a relationship between themselves and the technology itself. For females, technology use improves with accuracy and reflection; for males, technology use improves with risk-taking. This picture has changed to some degree, though not systematically, as girls have had increasing access at home and more opportunities to use technology. Nevertheless, the percentage of women in the U. S. information technology (IT) industry declined by eighteen percent between 1994 and 2006, comprising barely a quarter of IT workers (U. S. Department of Labor, 2006). As such, knowing the socially-constructed issues underlying attitudes towards technology helps online educators address possible gender inequities.

## DEVELOPMENTAL ISSUES

In childhood, girls and boys have similar attitudes towards technology, and are likely to use technology similarly. In terms of egame genres, Fromme (2003) noted that boys preferred action and fighting games, sport games and platform games, while girls preferred logic and puzzle games (20 percent). However, when youth are required to play different kinds of games, both boys and girls preferred adventure games overall, as Van Eck (2006) discovered in his study of fifth and sixth graders. According to the 2000 report of the American Association of University Women, if girls do not use computers by sixth grade, they are likely never to pursue science or technology. Therefore, if schools delay incorporation of technology until middle school, technology literacy may be too late for some girls. Particularly since parents are more likely to purchase computers for boys than for girls, education's role in technology access is critical (Hackbarth, 2001).

When puberty sets in, attitudes about technology become sex-linked. Males tend to spend more time using technology, while females' use drops (Christensen, Knezek, & Overall, 2005). In their 2000 study of girls and technology, the American Association of University Women showed that girls' self-confidence also drops, and they take fewer technology-related courses than boys (sometimes because academic counselors themselves exhibit gendered attitudes about technology careers). As technology becomes more complex, it assumes a male-dominated connotation that girls may avoid in an effort to appear more feminine to get social acceptance. Sadly, girls often do not realize the long-term implications if they prematurely cut off technology options.

Egaming practices showcases these differences. Game-based learning begins with failure; students must build skills and knowledge over time by accessing new information, evaluating circumstances, and through practice (Gee, 2007). These challenges can significantly impact girls' performance because girls are less likely to take risks, are more likely than boys to avoid situations where they might fail, and sometimes exhibit learned helplessness both within and outside the gaming environment (Brosnan, 1998; Orenstein, 1994). In her 2008 research about girls and gaming, Forssell found that girls who do not have immediate success are more likely to abandon egames, unlike males, and non-gamer girls are the most likely to dismiss games. On the other hand, expert gamers show no significant gender difference in behavior. In other words, girls have a lower technology frustration level, so online educators need to make sure that girls have early successful experiences using technology.

The social life of technology is often a completely different story. Ninety-six percent of Internet user 9- to 17-years old do online social networking such as FaceBook and blogging. Almost half of them visit such sites daily. Girls are the majority participants, and tend to use these sites to reinforce existing human relationships. In fact, over 90% of girls use social networking as a way to keep in touch with friends they see frequently. In contrast, boys are more likely than girls to use social networking to flirt and find new friends. (Lenhart & Madden, 2007).

These gender differences relative to technology use continue through college and beyond where females use technology to make connections in contrast to males who use technology to demonstrate competence. Many adult women still consider technology as The Other, something that has to be dealt with rather than enjoyed and controlled (Harris, 1999). Only within the last few years have women led technology corporations; traditionally, females have had to deal with a very male culture in technical fields, which sometimes undervalued family time or social relationships. Fortunately, Millennial women are finding their way into technology-based companies and holding their own; these go-getter twenty-somethings have strong self-images, and know how to combine technology aptitude with feminine sensibilities. They are creating fun, supportive software and web sites that demonstrate girl tech power, and they are mentoring their younger "sisters."

## MILLENNIAL ATTITUDES

As millennials, females have always lived in a digital world, watched cable television, clicked digital cameras, played on Gameboys, and "owned" virtual pets (Beloit College, 2007). Japanese teenage girls exemplify "techno-cultural suppleness": the ability to find emerging technology and then mold it to their own uses, sporting colorful cell phones so that can connect with mail bears and toddler samurai, taking photos with blinking light digital cameras that incorporate MP3 players, wearing tiny pick MiniDisc players with clip-on remotes (Mann, 2001). Technology is not a separate world, but almost serves as electronic wallpaper in their lives. As such, girls might not even realize the extent to which they rely on technology, even in the most isolated areas. Girls are digital natives, but just as someone who lives in the United States might not speak English, today's young women might not speak "techie." IMing does not equate with efficient online searching or digital data analysis. In short, today's young women regard technology as one aspect of their lives, but not a central interest or concern.

While differences between females and males are significant, overall more variation exists within each sex, particularly in this age. Additionally, as boys and girls mature and grow older, they have even more in common. Other factors -- individual, cultural, and situational -- largely shape who we are. What seems clear is that gendered education has to be exposed, and strategies to acknowledge such practices and offer gender-equitable learning activities need to be implemented, based on librarians' and other educators' own gender awareness and knowledge. Ultimately, though, learners have the most need to see how gender impacts their own self-perception and learning; by embracing their own gender and understanding their counterparts' approach, *all* students can learn more effectively.

## GENDERED ONLINE BEHAVIOR

Theoretically, online education mitigates the power of gender, age, and socio-economic status. Nevertheless, inequities exist relative to online behavior, both in terms of technology literacy as well as instructor bias. The majority of online learners in the U.S. are re-entry females who choose this learning environment because of its flexibility and convenience. However, online courses generally are not designed in light of gender, which negates the needs and contributions of each sex. With these realities, online educators need to become aware of gendered online behavior in order to provide more effective learning opportunities.

In a 1995 study of distance education for U.S. nurses, who were mainly female, Ross and her colleagues found that 80 percent of the students had difficulty connecting to the university server, and three-quarters had persistent serious problems using conferencing software. Part of their problem arose from lack of prior online access and experience, which disadvantaged them in comparison to males' situations.

In a study of gender differences and distance education in the U.S., Marley (2007) found that females made more effort and commitment relative to technology, and were more likely to ask for help. Nevertheless, males spent more time on computers and had more positive attitudes about digital libraries.

Large (2005) synthesized several studies about web-based information-seeking behaviors, which provide significant insights about gendered attitudes towards and use of technology. Females tend to use more words, spend more time viewing retrieved web pages, and jump between pages less quickly than males. On the other hand, males are more apt to ask questions and communicate more, while females tend to use vaguer speech (McGrath, 2004). In addition, males are more put off by a text-heavy web page. Females are more likely to assume that Internet content is credible, and girls are more likely than boys to spend time with a parent searching the Net.

The result is that a wide spectrum is represented in online learning environments, from technophobic to technorati so that the greatest challenge may be training older faculty to incorporate technology authentically into online learning activities – and to learn in concert with their students.

## GENDER-SENSITIVE DESIGN FOR ONLINE EDUCATION

Gallini (2001) provides a useful model to describe how to design gender-sensitive online learning environments. She posits three domains: background, design, and impact. Background deals with the instructor's and student's beliefs, and instructional goals. Design deals with type of technology, degree of technology integration, degree of online task structure, and online technology tools. Impact is student-centered; it includes learning assessments, interaction, student engagement, and collaborative learning.

## BACKGROUND

Clearly, how females learn needs to be considered when designing online instruction. In recent decades, more attention has been paid to females' ways of knowing in the U.S., which are based on Gilligan (1982) and Belenky et al. (1986). Belenky and her colleagues noted that women: 1) keep silent about their knowledge; 2) listen to others' voices, known as received knowledge; 3) listen to their inner voice, known as subjective knowledge; 4) look for separate and connected knowledge, known as procedural knowledge; and 5) integrate different points of view contextually, known as constructed knowledge. Feminist scholarship has also come into its own, paying more attention to underlying populist points of view, contextual reality, and issues of social justice that help students question the status quo and gather more data in order to develop a fuller understanding.

At the very least, instructional design needs to strive for inclusivity. The online learning environment needs to be a safe place where students can take educational risks as they explore their environment and themselves. Some indicators include:

- a sense of inclusion where everyone is respected, and everyone participates according to skill and interest
- a sense of community where everyone plays an important role and is interdependent
- a holistic attitude where behaviors, thoughts and feelings are intertwined and valued, and the curriculum reflects the whole person
- a sense of authenticity where instruction and assessment related to multi-faced performance, and learning connects each person meaningfully with her/himself and the world.

It should be noted that online instructors also need to examine their own educational philosophies and instructional style. They may find that they have to do some soul-searching and personal change as they identify and address possible prejudices or discomfort. Considering that students have to do this same kind of self-examination as they encounter different types of instruction, it seems fair that instructors engage in such intellectual self-reflection as well.

Particularly for adult education, online educators should conduct a needs assessment to determine learner characteristics, needs, and probable gaps in knowledge in order to design instruction that optimizes meaningful and efficient learning. Furthermore, educator and learner goals need to be negotiated so that all stakeholders can feel ownership in the learning process and can satisfy their own personal and professional needs. This approach requires that the online instructor needs to build in opportunities for input and flexibility. Usually, this process can be accomplished by establishing clear outcomes, which can be added to, key resources within which students can have choices and add content, and key assessments within which students have choices for demonstrating competence. As long as student goals and contributions align with and support the course, then these accommodations can be reasonably implemented. In any case, educators need to learn about the population they serve: their backgrounds, their interests, their needs, and their resources. Such tasks can be difficult in online environments without explicitly asking for such information in non-threatening ways.

At this point, the curriculum has been determined. Nevertheless, instructors should make sure that the curriculum is relevant for students. Does it reflect both sexes' interests and needs. What perspectives are included? Does the curriculum address different types of knowledge -- declarative, experiential, procedural, and contextual – that have meaning for both sexes? (Hubbell, 2010).

## STUDENT IMPACT

According to Shannon (2002), the most effective education melds active engagement, project-based learning, attention to individual needs, technology, and authentic assessment. A useful model for online learning that leverages females' ways of knowing and facilitates inclusive learning is an online learning community. Basically, an online learning community consists of a group of people with common values and learning goals. A learning community usually has a social dimension that fosters interdependence, although its raison-d'être is professional development. Carney (1999) defines a learning community as "a place where student learners are made to feel that their prior knowledge, the knowledge that they are acquiring, and the skills that they are learning to acquire future knowledge are all tied together" (p. 53).

### Active Engagement

One of the main attributes of learning communities is the concept of active engagement: between individuals, and between humans and materials. Students need to engage in their learning both cognitively and emotions so they can understand new information in terms of their individual contexts.

Online learning environments can optimize such interaction because it provides tools for interaction outside of class time in any locale. Instructors should provide training materials that are intellectually stimulating and emotionally engaging (e.g., novel problems and solutions, personable narratives that apply principles to real world settings). Likewise, authentic tasks, preferably with real world connections, should constitute the learning activities used to enable students to practice and demonstrate competency.

In terms of online experience, students – and instructional design – tend to progress through a number of stages of interaction and learning. Salmon (2000) provides a useful framework for identifying these stages. The italicized suggestions explain how online instructors can use technology to optimize each stage.

1. **Access and motivation**. The instructor sets up the online entity (locating or establishing it), and informs learners who choose to access it. *The instructor can welcome students via video or audio clip, and include images that activate the learner's curiosity. Instructors should also assure students that the learning environment is confidential and safe.*
2. **Online socialization.** The instructor provides opportunities and venues for students to communicate and get to know each other virtually. This interaction might be purely social rather than academically based. *The course can include a home page feature where students can share something about themselves, including pictures. A "water cooler" or "café" corner can provide a sanctioned area for personal chatting.*
3. **Information exchange.** Participants, including the instructor, offer and share information, and value that interchange. *A variety of communication channels (e.g., threaded discussions, instant messaging, group pages) can facilitate information sharing. A rich collection of materials and links to relevant resources can jump-start learning. Instructors should provide advance organizes and scaffold learning for those students in need. Students should be encouraged to contribute information or good resources found to add to the training body of knowledge.*
4. **Knowledge construction.** Participants, particularly learners, express ideas and give feedback that helps to generate knowledge. *Instructors should provide group pages, web 2.0 tools (e.g., wikis and blogs) and other conferencing features. Instructors should assign group projects, and support public problem-solving.*
5. **Development.** Learners assume responsibility for their learning, and need little guidance from the instructor. *Instructors should give timely, specific feedback—and encourage others to critically review and ask advice from peers.*

Wenger, McDermott and Snyder (2002) defend the notion of a range of involvement. They assert that most learning communities consist of 10-15 percent core members who often assume leadership roles, 15-20 percent activate members, a majority of peripheral members on the sidelines, and non-members who may lurk learning communities. The researchers contend that each set of individuals contributes to the learning community, and derives benefits that may, in turn, contribute to the members' other learning communities as well as to themselves. While most instructors wants high-level interactivity among all learners, this idea of different levels of participation recognizes individuals' learning preferences. Furthermore, learners may well be applying their new found knowledge to the professional settings to which they belong outside of the course, which can improve the profession as a whole.

## Assessment

At the course level, assessing student work on a formative basis helps instructors diagnose student process and gaps in learning. This information can be used to modify course delivery as well as provide feedback for students so they can make their own adjustments in learning approaches. Students can also self-assess their experiences and learning. When shared, these reflections can be used to help students understand concepts through contextualization and generate knowledge. Reflections can also be reviewed by colleagues to provide peer coaching. Instructors can analyze student self-assessments to identify individual and class trends in understanding and application. Moreover, instructors can triangulate the assessments to determine student self-efficacy.

In an online environment, students and instructors can interact more often, and preserve their thinking processes more easily. Work can be posted and shared quickly and efficiently, and feedback can be given in a more timely manner. Technology can facilitate self-reflection and metacognitive processing. Online course management systems can capture and organize assessments for more effective analysis. As a result, assessment can be ongoing and more effective in online learning environments. When females realize that their actions impact the course, then they can feel more empowered.

Obviously, any assessment needs to align with the course outcomes, and needs to acknowledge the students' existing knowledge base. For instance, if students are required to create a podcast to demonstrate the ability to tell a story, the instructor must make sure that the student knows that technology; otherwise, the assessment will be measuring a different skill. If the story is short, voicemail message could serve as an appropriate alternative means to measure storytelling. If podcasting is an explicit outcome, then the instructor needs to train students in using that technology. Because females may be more wary of technology than males, instructors need to make sure that all students are given adequate support to be successful with the required technology, be it via web tutorials, tech coaches, or online help desks.

Secondly, instructors should use several assessments throughout the course in order to measure specific skills and knowledge, and to triangulate assessment data. For instance, to demonstrate competence in social work students might analyze a case study, conduct a critical observation, and develop an intervention. If students do not perform well in one of the above assessments, then the instructor can determine if the problem lies in the quality and degree of knowledge (e.g., a differential between comprehending extant information and capturing information) or in expressing knowledge (e.g., a differential between writing essays and recording case notes). Because males and females may differ in types of knowledge or communication styles, providing multiple measures offers more inclusivity and gender sensitivity.

Thirdly, instructors should provide alternative means to demonstrate competence. For instance, students might be able to choose from three comparable case scenarios to analyze factors, or they can choose different communication channels to demonstrate knowledge (e.g., essay, oral presentation, or wiki). Logically, it makes sense that outcomes can be met in several ways. This acknowledgment is not only good instruction but it is also a valuable lesson for students to learn. Here are several gender-sensitive assessment methods that work well in online learning environments.

- **Content analysis** enables students to determine key concepts and leverage different perspectives to discern significant patterns. Ideally, students should be able to have a reasonable time frame, such as one-two days so students can have time to process and balance the academic demand with other life demands.

- **Text document creation** such as brochures, white papers, and annotated bibliographies privilege students (typically women) with good organization and writing skills. If organization is not part of the outcome, instructors might help students by providing a graphic organizer so that learners can focus on content rather than language.
- **Image document creation** such as comics, photo journal, or concept map requires visual literacy and, in some cases, equipment (e.g., to take photos). Instructors may need to think about equitable ways to assess content knowledge. If the outcome involves understanding visual knowledge representation "grammar," then instruction and practice of these visual concepts need to be incorporated into the online material.
- **Multimedia document creation** such as podcasts, videos, and presentation (e.g., PowerPoint, Keynote) usually require technical skill as well as conceptual knowledge. These products can leverage females' ability to cross media formats and synthesize complex information, but they can also disadvantage students (mainly females) who have less technology experience.
- **Interviews** leverage students' verbal ability. If the assessment prompt requires that the student respond "on their feet," then the weight of that assessment should not be too high stakes because it could compromise the students' ability to perform accurately; students under stress may react negatively. On the other hand, individual interviews can make students feel more comfortable than a focus group because they do not have to perform in front of others.
- **Performance assessment** usually involves critical observation of student behavior. In online environments this can be done via video conferencing or by videotaping the performance in situo. Some students may feel uncomfortable being videotaping; however, if the instructor can insure confidentiality, students may feel less stress. Additionally, since females value concrete and contextualized learning, performing in natural or working settings gives females an opportunity to apply knowledge in meaningful settings.

## Technology Design

Online learning environments can optimize learning because it provides access to information and tools for interaction outside of class time in any locale. On the other hand, technology can seem very abstract and remote, because it is often text-oriented. Therefore, online educators need to design features that that minimize technology limitations and optimize technology possibilities. Within the parameter of online instruction, several choices exist relative to online tools and the structure of the online instruction. Those choices should emerge from instructional decisions about student impact: the desired actions should drive the technology. Matching technology to the activity is vital. Web 2.0 tools greatly expand the possibilities for interactivity, which is especially important for American female learners.

- **Threaded discussions** archive individual contributions and responses chronologically and by subject.
- **Blogs** (web logs) enable individuals to write about their experiences chronologically, and others can comment on the entries.
- **Wikis** (quick-edit web pages) facilitate joint production of web pages that reflect collaborative knowledge.
- **Multimedia** programs such as Voicethread enable users to develop and share online group albums.
- **Image sharing** programs such as Flickr enable users to upload and share photos

and other images; these items can be combined into albums that reflect content matter knowledge.

- **Online chats** enable individuals to discuss ideas in real times. Some chat programs include features that allow documents and web pages to be viewed in common.
- **Web-based conferencing** incorporates text, image and sound to more closely approximate physical interaction.
- **Virtual environments** (objective-oriented online encironemtns0 enable individuals to interact virtually using avatars. Virtual environments usually include ways for applications to be embedded and documents to be stored.

Asynchronous online communication also helps level the playing field of learning. In the typical classroom, some students talk more than others for a variety of reasons: knowledge of the topic, verbal ability, more risk-taking behavior, extroversion vs. introversion, cultural/social norms and expectations, language/vocabulary knowledge. Second language learners and women, in particular, benefit from this type of participation because they can self-pace and control their contributions. Additionally, students with physical disabilities can use assistive technology to permit them to communicate with others: the hearing impaired certainly benefit, and the visually impaired can use software to read aloud documents and input student ideas via speech recognition programs. In addition, discussion has the potential to be deeper and more honest, particularly if the course is set up so that no "outsider" can access their writing.

Another set of educational technology consists of learning objects: self-sustaining educational modules that can be used independently or embedded within a course. Learning objects can take several forms:

- **Animations** use moving images to show a process or tell a story
- **Simulations** model a process, and enable students to test contributing variables
- **Case studies** provide concrete examples of a concept or practice
- **Drill and practice** exercises help learners practice skills, such as mathematics or language
- **Presentations** complement lectures
- **Reference** materials provide factual information
- **Tutorials** explain concepts through structured experiences
- **Assessment tools** measure competence

Instructors can use learning objects to introduce and reinforce concepts as well as provide extra practice for students as they need it. Learning objects are particularly good for courses that include a broad spectrum of student expertise because they can help students fill in knowledge gaps on their own; instructors list appropriate learning objects to help students "get up to speed" on their own time. Because students self-choose to use learning objects, they do not have to self-disclose to the class about their lack of prior knowledge, and they gain more control of their learning, both of which can help females who lack self-confidence.

An essential element of online technology is communication. Different tools match different instructional functions.

- **Announcements** enable instructors to post timely information.
- **Emails** provide instant information to individuals, a selected set of students, a designated group, or the entire group. To promote collaborative learning, instructors should permit students to email each other.
- **Discussion boards** enable students and instructors to share documents and comments. Typically, instructors post a prompt for student to respond to. Students can also critique or add to another student's work. This practice increases student interaction,

and enables students to learn more about a particular topic. For instance, Students in one course had to create a thematic webliography (i.e., bibliography of web sites). Each student chose a unique topic so that the entire group could then produce a wide range of webliographies that they could use in their own work settings. Discussion board can also be used to clarify questions or to provide a venue for virtual socializing.

- **Group pages** facilitate collaborative projects. Students can exchange files and discuss among themselves without other students seeing their work. Generally, the instructor is a member of each group in order to oversee student efforts and intervene when appropriate.
- **Synchronous online chat** enables a class to meet virtually and can serve as an online office hour communication channel.

In terms of assignments, online instructional design should determine supportive resources, exemplars and assessment instruments. Content and assignments should be explained and contextualized to help students link coursework to their daily lives. To facilitate a sense of a learning community, online instructors can ask students to submit work in a shared learning space so that peers can compare work, comment on it, and build collective intelligence. This approach also reinforces the concept of investment: each student contributes intellectual capital, and has access to the intellectual capital of many others. To counter the concern that students who submit their work early might be disadvantaged, instructors can permit their students to revise their work if posted early; they can receive additional feedback, which results in improved work. As a corollary, student work is less likely to be submitted late. Timely and specific feedback about student efforts is particularly important to females.

Typically, course management systems provide the structure for course delivery. For those instructors who develop courses more loosely and students who like flexibility, the structure sometimes feels binding – and for others it made course development easier to do: rather like filling in the blanks. The "one-stop" course access does provide efficient student access to course information and material such as syllabi, lecture notes, presentations, readings, and websites as well as student work; certainly students should be able to contribute to the body of knowledge in online learning environments. On the other hand, having all instruction conducted online requires that instructors give very clear directions and explanations since face-to-face gestures and negotiations are nigh impossible (even using web conferencing). To address possible misunderstanding, a "Clarifying questions" discussion forum can be used to share concerns; this mechanism also provides a venue for students to offer suggestions and support.

Another aspect of course delivery is the pedagogy (or andragogy) involved. Online learning environments should be designed so they may be explored according to the students' needs and interests. Sequential-access and random-access approach work equally well. The incorporation of hyperlinks introduces another dimension so students may "drill down" to the extent they wish or need, limited more by their own time or interest constraints rather than the constraints of the presentation of the information.

## RECOMMENDATIONS

Online instructors needs to pro-actively support gender-equitable engagement in online education by encouraging intellectual risk-taking and a playful spirit as well as supporting values of relationships, collaboration, social concerns, creativity, communication, and growing independence. Here are some beginning ways to provide an engaging and inclusive online learning environment.

1. Model and talk about effective use of technology for academic and personal applications.
2. Provide online female role models and mentors.
3. Provide opportunities for learners to customize and personalize their online learning space.
4. Provide opportunities for online communication and mutual support for both content matter and technology
5. Balance competition and collaboration.
6. Emphasize collaborative technology projects, particularly utilizing web 2.0 interactive tools.
7. Include content that interests both and either sex.
8. Integrate service learning and other ways to link online learning with every day life.
9. Offer female-only technology training.
10. Have students create electronic publications and other products that are the result of collective intelligence.

## CONCLUSION

Distance education, particularly in an online environment, may seem to offer a socially neutral learning situation. However, this environment that can cloak gender issues. People bring their experiences and attitudes to the educational table, starting with biological factors that can be further underlined through culturally-specific social messages. Thus gender remains a significant factor that online educators need to consider. Gender-sensitive instructional design and technology can result in enclusive practices that can optimize learning not only for both sexes, but also for persons in different cultures and individuals with special needs.

## REFERENCES

American Association of University Women. (1992). *Shortchanging girls, shortchanging America*. Washington, DC: American Association of University Women.

American Association of University Women. (2000). *Tech-savvy: Educating girls in the new computer age*. Washington, DC: American Association of University Women.

Belenky, M., Clinchy, B., Rule Golberger, N., & Mattuck Tarule, J. (1986). *Women's ways of knowing: The development of self, voice, and mind*. New York, NY: Basic Books.

Beloit College. (2009). *Mindset lists*. Beloit, WI: Beloit College. Retrieved from http://www.beloit.edu/mindset/2013.php

Black, G. (1995). *CSMpact for education: Do boys and girls experience education differently?* Rochester, NY: Harris Interactive.

Brosnan, M. (1998). The impact of psychological gender, gender-related perceptions, significant others, and the introduction of technology upon computer anxiety in students. *Journal of Educational Computing Research*, *18*, 63–78. doi:10.2190/LVHH-EPGB-AE7J-WEV8

Brownlow, S., Jacobi, T., & Rogers, M. (2000). Science anxiety as a function of gender and experience. *Sex Roles*, *18*, 63–78.

Carney, J. (1999). How classrooms as cultures influence entire schools. *Primary Voices K-6*, *7*(3), 53.

Christensen, R., Knezek, G., & Overall, T. (2005). Transition points for the gender gap in computer enjoyment. *Journal of Research on Technology in Education*, *38*(1), 23–37.

Cooper, J., & Weaver, K. (2003). *Gender and computers: Understanding the digital divide*. Nawah, NJ: Erlbaum.

Csikszentmihaly, M. (1998). *Finding flow: The psychology of engagement with everyday life*. New York, NY: Basic Books.

Forssell, K. (2008). Girls, games, and getting interested in technology. In K. McFerrin, et al. (Eds.), *Proceedings of Society for Information Technology and Teacher Education International Conference 2008* (pp. 991-996). Chesapeake, VA: American Association of Computer Education.

Fromme, J. (2003). Computer games as a part of children's culture. *Game Studies, 3*(1). Retrieved from http://www.gamestudies.org/0301/fromme/

Gallini, J. (2001). A framework for the design of research in technology-mediated learning environments: A sociocultural perspective. *Educational Technology*, *41*(2), 15–21.

Gee, J. (2007). *What video games have to teach us about learning and literacy* (2nd ed.). Palgrave, UK: Macmillan.

Gilligan, C. (1982). *In a different voice*. Cambridge, MA: Harvard University Press.

Gurian, M., & Henley, P. (2001). *Boys and girls learn differently! A guide for teachers and parents*. San Francisco, CA: Jossey-Bass.

Hackbarth, S. (2001). Changes in primary students' computer literacy as a function of classroom use and gender. *TechTrends*, *45*(4), 19–27. doi:10.1007/BF02784821

Hubbell, E. (2010). Using McREL's knowledge taxonomy for edtech professional development. *Learning and Leading with Technology*, 20–23.

Knight, H. (1997, May 7). Study finds few signs of an academic gender gap. *Los Angeles Times, A1*, 33.

Knowles, M. (1990). *The adult learner* (4th ed.). Houston, TX: Gulf Publishing.

Large, A. (2005). Children, teenagers, and the Web. In Cronin, B. (Ed.), *Annual review of information science and technology* (pp. 347–392). Medford, NJ: Information Today.

Lehrman, S. (1997). Woman. *Stanford Today*, *25*(3), 47–51.

Lenhart, A., & Madden, M. (2007). *Social networking websites and teens: An overview.* Washington, DC: Pew Internet & American Life Project. Retrieved from http://www.pewinternet.org/Reports/2007/Social-Networking-Websites-and-Teens.aspx

Levinson, D. (1978). *The seasons of a man's life*. New York, NY: Knopf.

Lips, H. (2007). Gender and possible selves. *New Directions for Adult and Continuing Education*, *114*, 51–59. doi:10.1002/ace.256

Mann, C. (2001, August). Why 14-year-old Japanese girls rule the world. *Yahoo! Internet Life*, 99-103.

Martin, A. (2002). *Improving the educational outcomes of boys*. Canberra, Australia: Department of Education. Retrieved from www.decs.act.gov.au/publicat/pdf/Ed_Outcomes_Boys.pdf

Miller, J. B. (1976). *Toward a new psychology of women*. Boston, MA: Beacon Press.

Moir, A., & Jessel, D. (1991). *Brain sex*. New York, NY: Dell.

Orenstein, P. (1994). *School-girls*. New York, NY: Doubleday.

Park, A. (2004). What makes teens tick? *Time*, *163*(19), 56–65.

Pellegrini, A., Kato, L., Blatchford, L., & Baines, E. (2002). A short-term longitudinal study of children's playground games across the first year of school. *American Educational Research Journal*, *39*(4), 991–105. doi:10.3102/00028312039004991

Philbin, M., & Meier, E. (1995). A survey of gender and learning styles. *Sex Roles*, *32*(7-8), 485–494. doi:10.1007/BF01544184

Pintrich, P., & Linenbrink, E. (2002). Motivation as an enabler for academic success. *School Psychology Review*, *31*(3), 313–327.

Pipher, M. (1994). *Reviving Ophelia: Saving the selves of adolescent girls*. New York, NY: Putnam.

Salmon, G. (2000). *E-moderation: The key to teaching and learning online*. London, UK: Kogan Page.

Scherer, M. (2002). Do students care about learning? *Educational Leadership*, *60*(1), 12–17.

Shannon, D. (2002). The education and competencies of school library media specialists: A review of the literature. *School Library Media Research, 5*. Retrieved from http://www.ala.org/ala/mgrps/divs/aasl/aaslpubsandjournals/slmrb/slmrcontents/volume52002/shannon.cfm

Smith, M., & Wilhelm, J. (2002). *Reading don't fix no Chevys: Literacy in the lives of young men*. Portsmouth, NH: Heinemann.

Sousa, D. (2001). *How the brain learns* (2nd ed.). Thousand Oaks, CA: Corwin Press.

U. S. Department of Education. (2004). *Toward a golden age in American education*. Washington, DC: U. S. Department of Education.

Van Eck, R. (2008). COTS in the classroom: A teacher's guide to integrating commercial off-the-shelf (COTS) games. In Ferdig, R. (Ed.), *Handbook of research on effective electronic gaming in education* (pp. 1143–1165). Hershey, PA: Idea Group.

Wenger, E., McDermott, R., & Snyder, W. (2002). *Cultivating communities of practice*. Cambridge, MA: Harvard University Press.

# Chapter 9
# Instructional Methods for Online Learners

**Judith Parker**
*Columbia University, USA*

## ABSTRACT

*While a plethora of instructional methods are documented and utilized in educational and training programs, some are more appropriate for the online learner than others. This chapter will examine these selected methods: lecturing, discussion, action-learning, experiential learning, and active learning. Each of these will be discussed in its own right and then considered in the context of online learning. Examples of these methods and student comments are included as well as a view into future possibilities.*

## INTRODUCTION

Instructional methods have been a mainstay of discussions among educational professionals and students alike. What methods are best for certain subjects? What methods are best for selected student populations? Whether the focus is on content or students, the opinions are diverse and research studies abound. While theorists and practitioners alike can argue supporting evidence for our own ideas, Stephen Brookfield (2006) gets to the heart of the matter with his statement that "skillful teaching boils down to whatever helps students learn" (p. xvii). But what is that? How do we find out what really helps students learn? Is there one answer to this question or multiple possibilities? Is the answer different if the course is online? Let's begin by clarifying the elements of our topic of instructional methods by defining, describing and examining examples of various methodologies. In the spirit of adult education, we will critically reflect on our assumptions about them and on the effectiveness of their implementation remembering Brookfield's (2006) definition that "critical reflection is the process by which we research the assumptions informing our practice by viewing these through four complementary lenses – the lense of students' eyes, colleagues' perceptions, literature and our own autobiography" (p. 26).

DOI: 10.4018/978-1-60960-791-3.ch009

## ESSENTIALS OF EFFECTIVE INSTRUCTIONAL METHODS

Effective implementation of instructional methods for online learners depends on four elements: good instructional design by the instructor, web/computer expertise of the learner, information technology infrastructure of the organization and adult learning principles. Good instructional design demands that the selection of instructional methods be based on a foundation of organizational, group, and individual needs. Substantial effort must be dedicated to uncovering these needs before any decisions about the design of training are made. Students in the Staff Development and Training course that the author teaches are required to submit a profile of the organization, perform a needs assessment and report on the conclusion as a preparation for documenting their decisions about the training design and methods. They are usually surprised at the amount of work that goes into these initial phases of the assignment and often argue about being necessity. They become impatient, wanting to get to the content of the training. However, their end of project reflections reveal that they realized the importance of the work when it came to decision making about the content and methodology and were often surprised at the new insights uncovered by their work.

If the design is to include online activities, an additional layer of knowledge about the organization, group and individuals are required. Can the organization's information technology infrastructure support any new software requirements and increased activity load on its servers? Are the informational technology personnel available to support software/hardware and the learners? Will the organizational culture support the online activities? Are students computer savvy enough to utilize the online components? Technology must be transparent; technology cannot mask learning. If the organization has multiple sites, do all sites have high speed access and if international locations, do all countries have the infrastructure necessary to support online activities? Later in this chapter, we will explore an example of a leadership development project involving eight Asian countries in which this was a key consideration.

A clue to the importance of connectivity can be seen in the abundance of advertising about 3G, 4G and fiber optic networks and shaded maps for emphasis. If an organization's key manufacturing location falls between the shaded areas of the map, any learning plan involving online components could be in trouble.

Adult learning theories provide the additional essential element for consideration. Malcolm Knowles introduced the term "andragogy" in the United States. It's source was a European colleague who defined it as the "art and science of helping adults learn" (Merriam, Caffarella, & Baumgartner, 2007, p. 84). Knowles (2005) presented six core andragogical principles as a foundation for new theories and a guide for practice: "the learner's need to know, self-directed learning, prior experience of the learner, readiness to learn, orientation to learning and problem solving, and motivation to learn" (p. 183). Illeris (2004) considers adult learning to comprise three distinct dimensions: cognitive, emotional and social. His model of an inverted triangle places the two psychological poles, Piaget's cognition and Freud's emotion, at the two corners at the top of the triangle and society at the lower vertex but he stresses that "all three dimensions are always integrated parts of the learning process and in practice do not exist as separate functions"(p. 20). After consideration of these four elements, SMART objectives can be formulated. Piskurich (2006) describes good objectives as being Specific, Measurable, Action-oriented, Reasonable, and Timely. These objectives become the foundation for moving forward with method selection.

### Categories of Instructional Methods

In considering topics for inclusion in this chapter, I started with a list of personal favorites. Further research yielded an exhaustive list of methods for consideration. Silberman's (2006) list includes active learning methods such as demonstration, case study, guided teaching, group inquiry, information search, study group, jigsaw learning, tournament learning, role playing, simulations, observation, mental imagery. Nilson (2003) offers lecture, discussion, case method and experiential learning while Brookfield (2006) focuses on lectures and discussions.

Piskurich (2006) suggests that there are "only a half dozen or so general training delivery methods to choose from" (p. 93). Of these he focuses on instructor-led classrooms, on-the-job-training, self-instruction and technology-based training. He notes that "many of the most successful training processes combine delivery systems" (p. 97), a concept often termed blended learning. Brookfield (2006) warns that "one of the traps that advocates of discussion method often fall into is that of setting up a false dichotomy between lecturing and discussion" (p. 98). This warning should be expanded to include building false silos around any one method. However in order to bring some sense of order to this chapter, the author will investigate her favorite methods and student reflections on them.

## Lecturing

The term lecture often brings to mind a less than engaging experience. However, we can probably also remember a few lectures that were amazing educational experiences. The fact is that lecturing is an essential method of instruction. Brookfield (2006) offers a positive hopeful image by dedicating an entire chapter to "lecturing creatively". He also proposes that lecturing should be the method of choice to achieve some specific objectives such as "to establish the broad outline of a body of material,...to explain with frequent examples, concepts that are hard for learners to understand,... to model intellectual attitudes and behaviors you wish to encourage in students,...to encourage learners interest in a topic (pp. 100-101).

Nilson notes that several studies have indicated that "the lecture is as effective as any other method in conveying factual knowledge" (p. 93). However she continues that the lecture falls short of more student-centered methods such as discussion if the objectives of the training include criteria such as "attitude change, development of thinking and problem solving skills, transfer of knowledge to new situations, student satisfaction with the course, motivation for further learning, and post-course retention of knowledge" (p. 93). Examining the objectives referred to earlier in the chapter will allow for decision making about effective methodology. If the objectives that Nilson mentions above are the goal of the training then the discussion method might be a good choice and should be examined.

## Discussion

Palloff and Pratt (1999) reinforce Nilson's comments on objectives by suggesting that "Key to the learning process are the interactions among students themselves, the interactions between faculty and students, and the collaboration in learning that results from these interaction" (p. 5).

Brookfield (2006) suggests three categories of reasons to use discussion: intellectual, emotional, and sociopolitical. Intellectual purposes include "to engage students in exploring a diversity of perspectives, to increase students' awareness of and tolerance for ambiguity and complexity, to help students recognize and investigate their assumptions, to increase intellectual agility and openness, to develop the capacity for the clear communication of ideas and meaning, to develop skills of synthesis and integration" (pp.119-121). Emotional purposes include "to help students become connected to a topic, to show respect for students' experiences" (pp. 121-122). Sociopolitical purposes include "to encourage attentive respectful listening, to help students learn the processes and habits of democratic discourse, to affirm students as co-creators of knowledge" (pp. 122-124).

While discussion is often viewed as more egalitarian than the lecture method, Brookfield and Preskill (1999) warn that " putting students into circles and telling them to speak to each other rather than to you does not alter the fundamental power dynamics in the classroom" (p. 37). They counsel that "In our experience, generating the conditions for critical and democratic conversation takes considerable time" (p. 37) and in the author's experience, considerable energy. But the effort is well worth it if we agree with Cranton (2006) who emphasizes the importance of empowering the student by interactions in the learning environment and being aware of power relationships. These discussions can be a vehicle for building learning communities. "The creation of a learning community supports and encourages knowledge acquisition. It creates a sense of excitement about learning together and renews the passion involved with exploring new realms in education" (Palloff & Pratt, 1999, p. 163).

## Action Learning

Action learning was pioneered by Rag Ravens (1982), a Cambridge physicist, who believed that "learning was best derived from mutual reflection on real issues, where the owner of the problem would ultimately have to do something about it, assisted by discoveries made with others" (Kesby, 2008, p. 27). Kesby describes action learning as a "dynamic process and a powerful problem-solving tool" (p. 26) It involves working on real work opportunities, problems, tasks and projects and encompasses a learning cycle of action, reflection, theorisation and application. Mezirow (2000) emphasizes that there are three components that are essential to action learning: action, critical reflection, and building one's own theories. Mumford (1997) adds that the learners are expected to try out new behaviors, to reflect critically on their experiences, to distil some generalisable principles and to try the principles in other similar contexts. This learning cycle is very similar to the problem solving process that managers use in their daily practices. Marsick and Watkins (1999) clarify the difference between action learning and action research. "People take action while they are learning, and bring the results of their experiments to the group for discussion, as would happen in an action research project. Unlike action research, however, equal (and sometimes more) attention is paid to the personal learning than to problem solving" (p. 120). An example of an action learning project involving online learning is included later in this chapter.

## Experiential Learning

The importance of experience to learning has been noted by several educators. "Experience is, according to Dewey, not primarily associated with knowledge but with human beings' lives and living. In Dewey's terms, living is the continuous interaction between individuals and their environments" (Elkjaer, 2009, p. 74). Wenger (2009) expands on this idea. "What if we adopted a different perspective, one that placed learning in the context of our lived experience of participation in the world? What if we assumed that learning is as much a part of our human nature as eating, or sleeping, that it is both life-sustaining and inevitable, and that – given a chance – we are quite good at it? And what if, in addition, we assumed that learning is, in its essence, a fundamentally social phenomenon, reflecting our own deeply social nature as human beings capable of knowing?" (pp. 209-210).

Experience plays an important part in learning both as a foundation on which to build future learning and as a method by which to learn. Knowles (2005) cites "prior experience of the learner" (p. 183) as one of his six key principles of andragogy. This is especially evident in a graduate course on "Staff Development and Training", in which students bring experience from internships, employment and from their involvement in diverse organizations. Yet their major project for the course is the experience of developing a training module for a real organization. They must develop a profile of the organization, experience the data gathering necessary to assess the needs of the organization, and document their decisions leading to the training module development. Their final assignment is to submit a reflection on the entire experience and the learning achieved from the process as well as the final project. Elkjaer (2009) summarizes the process by noting that "Dewey's future-oriented and experimental concept of learning serves as a comprehensive and contemporary theory of learning that emphasizes creativity and innovation" (p. 88).

### Active Learning

Nilson (2003) profiles the students as learning best when they are actively engaged, when learning evokes emotional not just intellectual involvement. While discussion is one way of engaging students in their learning, active learning provides yet another method. Silberman (2006) characterizes active learning as a way in which "learning activities are designed so that the participants acquire knowledge and skill, rather than merely receive them" (p. 1). He suggests that the methods that are consistent with the principles of active learning are designed to "increase participation, enliven learning, deepen retention, encourage application" (p.10). As noted above, Silberman (2006) dedicates an entire volume to the implementation of active learning techniques such as demonstration, case study, guided teaching, group inquiry, information search, study group, jigsaw learning, tournament learning, role playing, simulations, observation, mental imagery. The author cites Silberman's text as a recommended text for her Staff Development and Training course for only those with some background in good instructional design. This is the result of a personal history of seeing too many corporate trainers whose programs are a constant string of activities with little attention to learning. However, with the knowledge and experience of good instructional design as a foundation, active learening techniques can help create an engaging learning environment. Palloff and Pratt (1999) emphasize that learning is an active process in which both the learner and the instructor must participate.

## INSTRUCTIONAL METHODS IN AN ONLINE LEARNING ENVIRONMENT

Prompted by different environments, populations with unique requirements or advances in technology, instructors have always explored new instructional methods to enhance learning. But only a few methodologies have evoked an adjective to describe them: Silberman's active learning, Raven's action learning, Mezirow's transformational learning and of course elearning and online learning. While many of these adjectives are used almost exclusively by the teaching and learning community, elearning and online learning have become part of the global mainstream vocabulary. So it seems useful to explore how the onset of online learning has impacted instructional methods. Classroom lectures have morphed into webinars (synchronous) and websites (asynchronous). Class discussions have expanded their scope with chat rooms (synchronous) as well as asynchronous threaded discussions, Wiki's and Bloggs. The reality of experiential learning has been enhanced with the virtual landscape of Second Life. Active learning includes online activities with simulation and social networking. Action learning can take advantage of enhanced online communication and access to remote resources. Multimedia resources no longer are limited to physical media but extend to Youtube, videos on websites and a plethora of text, animations, and virtual resources.

Applying Illeris' model to online learning would seem to particularly emphasize the emotional and social dimensions. The author's experience with adult learners attempting an online course for the first time is that they approach it with a great deal of emotion and often judge its effectiveness as much on how they felt about the experience as how much content they learned. The emerging application of social networks speaks to Illeris' social dimensions.

Brookfield (2006) relates his own experiences of his students citing parallels between his classroom activities and their online experiences. He realized that "online teaching was not necessarily qualitatively different from its face-to-face counterpart" (p. 192) and that e-learning guides addressed the same issues of how to engage students, account for different learning styles, etc as those speaking to teachers in face-to-face classrooms. Therefore, we will explore the selected methodologies previously discussed in this chapter in light of online learning. For adult learners, Malcolm Knowles (2005) sees technology as providing learning opportunities in the "andragogical tradition" (p. 237) and as consistent with the adult learning idea of self-directedness.

## Lecturing Online

As a new professional decades ago, I attended a workshop on the use of new technology in education. Its focus was the use on the then new overhead projector (yes, that big bulky piece of equipment that sits on a cart collecting dust in many classroom corners), its effective use in the classroom and the preparation of transparencies with text and graphics. Over time, this technology has morphed into the use of power point presentations with embedded video and website links. Shea-Schultz and Fogarty (2002) note that "old technologies are changing: classroom walls are rearranging" (p. 169). Examples can be found as Silberman (2006) describes a typical virtual classroom as including "tools for synchronous delivery like chat rooms and online whiteboards. They also include asynchronous tools like discussion boards and email that students can use at a time that is convenient for them (p. 199). Technology brings resources into the classroom and links to resources outside of it. More technological sounding labels such as "smart boards" and "smart classrooms" beg the question of whether all this has produced smarter students.

Moving into an online environment, it is still important to consider Brookfield's advice in the previous section on what learning objectives can best be met with lecturing. From a remote location, how can the instructor best deliver material, explain concepts, model behavior and encourage interest. In a traditional classroom model, the student might be asked by the instructor to read some material, the student might hear the content from the instructor with the instructor's voice and personal interpretation, see content in a Powerpoint or on a whiteboard, will probably take notes on points relevant to the student and finally review the material. Online learning should attempt to simulate as many of these student focused activities as possible. Offering the student a printed transcript of a lecture does not even come close to achieving this. An hour long "talking head" video of the instructor might be one step forward as might the voice of the instructor over a Powerpoint presentation. Yet most of us have seen or been subjected to these under the title of online learning. So let's take Brookfield's advice about "creative lecturing" and examine a few examples from different venues.

Parker (1996) profiles the efforts of a large multinational corporation would often arrange for world experts in a technology relevant to the company to travel to the headquarters to present two to three day seminars. Often employees from remote technical centers would request that the seminar be videoconferenced to their site. The Global Technical Education Manager, attempted to put their request in perspective by asking them to remember the longest professionally produced Hollywood movie they had ever seen. It usually evoked a response of 2+ hours and an admission that they were loosing interest at that point. I then asked them to imagine sitting in front of a small monitor for several days watching a talking head on seriously technical subjects without the improvements of a Hollywood producer and director. The analogy usually made the point of the ineffectiveness of this idea. However the following primarily lecture models were successfully developed to achieve similar objectives.

In one example, a technical expert traditionally taught a classroom based course using lecture and working groups. To offer this course to a global audience, the instructor recorded his lectures for distribution globally. At that time he installed a videoconference unit on his home computer for group discussions. This step could easily be replaced with today's webconferencing technology. The scenario for course delivery was as follows. A small group of technical employees in any one location requested the course from the headquarters location. They were given access to the recorded lectures, a workbook of instructions and a schedule of working group discussions with the instructor. The group was responsible for viewing the recording, having discussions in their home language, and doing the follow-up work on their project before the scheduled on line meeting with instructor. While the scheduled meeting was intended to keep the course moving forward, the learning group was free to contact the instructor at any time to arrange a meeting to ask questions or report progress.

Another example involves imaging technology with most of the expertise at the headquarters, pockets of expertise in several global locations and a need for the information at a manufacturing site. As mentioned previously, the lecture method itself tends to set up a power structure between the lecturer and the students. An additional layer of power usually exists between employees at a large organization's headquarters location and those in remote locations. This variation of the lecture model allowed for the expertise from the headquarters laboratory to be distributed to remote locations but empowered and showcased the expertise of employees at the remote locations. Two hour long sessions once a week for several weeks were scheduled to accommodate the workday in the locations in Europe and the U.S. This was sufficient time for a substantive lecture followed by questions and answers. It also was sensitive to the exhausting effort of the employees for whom English was a second language. The European locations were encouraged to scheduled additional time for their group at their location in their home language. Any additional questions that resulted could be emailed to the instructor for that session. Each week, the lecturer could be at the headquarters or one of the remote locations. In addition a manufacturing location heard about the course and asked to participate as students only. So a total of four locations across the globe participated in a classroom lecture.

While large organizations still utilize videoconference sites, the above models can be easily replicated by smaller organizations using webconferencing software, a webcam and or computer projector at each location. While many programs offer voice over the internet, more sophisticated webconferencing software provides a computer screen with a whiteboard, voice and video capabilities. The following is an example of this in an academic setting. A small specialized graduate school had potential students in numerous locations. Initially a larger group of students existed in one location and videoconferenced classes were provided to that location. Eventually these numbers dwindled. About the same time that requests for the courses came from individuals or small groups in other locations, the technology for webconferencing capabilities began to emerge. The main classroom was equipped with a computer, projector, and screen which is almost standard for today's Powerpoint classroom environment. In addition, two webcams were added to the computer. One was focused on the instructor and the other on the classroom. While the instructor was lecturing, any notes were on the screens whiteboard visible to the class and on the remote student's computer. If a student in the classroom asked a question, the webcam focused on the class was activated. If the remote student asked a question, that webcam projected the remote student's image on the screen. Students reported the development of a sense of a learning community that included the remote students.

In the more formal part of the elearning world, Silberman (2006) lists webcasts and webinars as lecture equivalents. He defines a webcast as "typically based on one-way communication, with a lecturer speaking from prepared notes and slides to a widely dispersed audience" (p. 195). While this has the limitations of a synchronous learning event, some webcasts are taped and made available online offering the flexibility of an asynchronous event. Webinars are more interactive and might be more appropriately considered under the discussion section of this chapter. Silberman (2006) defines it as a "more interactive version of a webcast (p. 196) usually characterized by application sharing between the trainer and the participants" (p. 196).

New online tools provide creative options for lecture. In an attempt to maximize this sense of connectedness, the author's teaching assistant in an online course this semester experimented with a program she had used called "Crazy Talk". The teaching assistant's voice was overlaid on an animated character as a more personal way to introduce students to the course and its requirements. We will be assessing the effectiveness of this experiment later in the course. Methods such as this are continually emerging and the adult educator must be willing to experiment with those that seem appropriate to the content and the students in a particular course.

## Online Discussions

Just as classroom discussions are often used to reinforce lecture content or facilitate the development of new understandings by student discussion, online discussions can take many forms. Previously in this chapter, the author cited Brookfield's (2006) argument that the reasons for discussions could be classified into intellectual, emotional, and sociopolitical and his and Preskill's (1999) noting the importance of setting up the appropriate climate for "critical and democratic conversation" (p. 37). Continually improving commercial learning management systems add additional methods for synchronous and asynchronous discussion with little attention to setting up the environment. Even generally available sites to set up wiki's and bloggs offer the space but not the guidance for these to be used effectively to build a learning community.

In an online learning environment, the warning of Brookfield and Preskill still ring true. Just setting up a thread for a discussion or a space for a blog will not ensure a good discussion. Brookfield (2006) devotes two chapters of his text on being a skillful teacher to discussion techniques. While they specifically address face-to-face discussions, many of them can be adapted to an online environment. Wenger (2009) challenges us to view "... learning as social participation" (p. 210). This section will include several examples of online classroom discussions in various venues.

An online discussion can be used to reinforce lecture content or as a convenient way to "cover" a class in the event of a conflict with a professional conference. It is important to select a topic that will engage students in discussion. The class can be divided into small groups for a synchronous discussion or kept as a complete class for asynchronous threaded discussions. An entire class is usually too cumbersome and chaotic in a synchronous discussion. For the small synchronous discussions, the group must record the discussion for review by the instructor at a later time. For asynchronous discussions, the students are given the guidelines that they must post one substantive response about the topic, read several postings of other students, and respond to at least two of the other student's postings. Student feedback usually involves the realization that this is more work than sitting in a classroom. They also note that they feel like they are held accountable for their discussions since the instructor can see who is speaking and what is said when the text is reviewed. But their comments also show that they value the experience.

With regard to synchronous text chat discussions, one student noted that "the best part lies in my realization toward the end of the chat that a synchronous professional discussion isn't too difficult a thing for me. This is my first time to do a real one with international professionals. As a non-native speaker, I was very self-conscious and afraid I'd lose face before this highly learned group who seem to have a better and deeper understanding of all the theories we're learning. But the 2-hours went by fast and I felt more and more comfortable, even not nervous when it's my turn."

With regard to asynchronous online communication, two students offered these insights:

- "Everybody could get a chance to express his own ideas. Moreover, the discussion board online gives us a further opportunity to share ideas with all of the class. It has been developed into a real learning forum. Everybody chose their favorite articles about learning and training in their fields, and then shared their own ideas on the 'blackboard', thus evokes a real open discussion. This learning style makes me feel that I can learn anytime anywhere from so many people of diverse fields. By posting, reading, and replying online, our learning location has burst out of the limited classroom and lecture time boundary, thus it has given us an authentic flexibility and motivation to learn."
- "I like posting my summary, opinion, and how the readings related to my life on the discussion board, and then writing a response to someone else's summary. It allowed me to think about what I was reading, as well as view other students' opinions."

The value of these online discussions is seen by numerous organizations that deliver online course. For example the American Museum of Natural History has a series of online seminars with rich science content for each week's topics. But students' participation in weekly online discussions is required to fulfill the objectives of the course. Students are graded on the content of their discussions but also on their enabling the dialogue throughout the entire week of that topic's discussion by responding to different students on different days. Since most of these students are pre-service or in-service teachers, these discussions could also provide the beginning of a foundation for developing learning communities or communities of practice. Wenger (2009) notes that "Communities of practice are an integral part of our daily lives. They are so informal and so pervasive that they rarely come into explicit focus, but for the same reasons they are also quite familiar. We all belong to communities of practice. At home, at work, at school, in our hobbies – we belong to several communities of practice at any given time" (Wenger, p. 212).

## Action Learning Online

Discussions are also an integral part of well defined instructional methods such as action learning. Yiu and Parker (2005) selected this method for a leadership development program for technical managers of a large multinational corporation operating in Australia, China, Hong Kong, India, Korea, Philippines, Singapore, Taiwan, and Thailand. The company's major laboratories were in the U.S. with Neuss, Germany as the hub for research and development activities in Europe and Sagamihara, Japan as the hub of research and development activities in the Asia Pacific area. Each region had additional technical centers with the focus of this project being the 10 technical centers located across the Asian region being managed by nationals from their respective countries. While most of the laboratory work involves technical service, manufacturing support and product modification, an increasing amount of technology development is conducted outside the United States. The program sheds light on the process of creating on-going learning networks within a global company spanning across Europe (Switzerland), North America (USA), and Asia. This project involved the three essential components of action learning: action, critical reflection, and the building of one's own theories as outlined by Mezirow (1990) however, for the group of highly results oriented engineers who had become managers of their technical centers, the critical reflection element was the most difficult. Since building new knowledge is a recognized result of Web 2.0, these new technologies could play an important role in building one's own theories. This project was a model of blended learning methods involving the participants in an annual workshop, online and on phone team meetings.

## Experiential Learning Online

As noted earlier in this chapter, Dewey was an early proponent of the value of experience in learning. Technology can facilitate documenting experiences and the learning associated with it. Electronic journals and portfolios are just two examples. One student commented that "it is helpful to be able to use the discussion board as a record of both my own and the class's learning". Online experiences can also be offered using simulations or by posting videos created to illustrate a topic.

The Staff Development course that is referred to above in the Experiential Learning section is taught both online and on campus during different semesters. The assignments are identical but instead of reporting on each segment of the assignment in person, online students must post their assignments online for feedback from the instructor and eventually post their training module for others in the class to view and comment. Usher (2009) suggests that preconditions exist if experiential learning is to be successful. These are "creating sufficient student security and self-confidence…and at least an outline theoretical framework from which to examine and understand student experience" (p. 182). Creating such an environment may be particularly challenging in an online environment. One student commented, "I found a couple methods valuable to my learning. The training module was a great way of applying what we learned. Since it was broken down into steps, it allowed me to get feedback on each part as I went along, as well as made the process of creating the module easier to do."

## Active Learning Online

Discussions can serve as an integral part of an online course to achieve specific course objectives. One specific project in an introductory graduate level course involved the student's developing their own personal philosophy of adult learning. After being exposed to the foundational theories numerous schools of thought in adult learning, students were asked to write a draft of their personal philosophy. Students were assigned to small groups depending on their area of experience or interest such as business, high education, K-12, non-profit, health care, etc. Each group was given a "group page" in the learning management system that was only available to their group members. The goal was to develop a learning community among these like-minded individuals and a safe space for them to share and explore their own philosophies. The individuals were to post their draft philosophy in the shared space in their group page. They were to read each other's philosophy papers taking notes on questions or comments they would make to the individual. The small group of 4 – 6 individuals was then to schedule a time for an online synchronous discussion. Students all have access to the "collaboration" text chat function available within the learning management system but were told they could select other online tools that their group might have available. For example, this past spring a group decided to use the web conferencing software Adobe Connect to have a voice discussion using webcams. Allowing for options and student decision making is a valuable tool within online learning. Students uncomfortable with webconferencing were not forced to use it but students who were anxious to experiment were encouraged to do so. During the online discussion they are to take turns discussing and questioning each member's philosophy paper. It is suggested that individuals in the group volunteer for roles of facilitator and timekeeper to keep the discussion moving and to ensure that enough time is available for every student. After the chat they are to submit a revised philosophy paper to the instructor as well as a reflection on the process.

Some students' comments from the reflections follow.

- "The process of responding to skilled questions posed by co-group members allowed me to consider and deeply reflect on my actions with respect to learning and how it is applied at the workplace. The methodology used for this course integrates technology with a pedagogy practice that supports the deeper, more reflective self-directed activity thus, emphasizing on constructivist teaching."
- "A community emerged during the chat session as the group members experienced a sense of personal relatedness."
- "Since my partner is from different culture, industry and gender from mine, I learnt a lot of new perspectives."
- "The chat session personalized e-learning, which can sometimes seem cold and robotic. It provided an interactive, personal channel through which numerous learning and experiences could be shared."

Farmer (2010) notes that "with today's changing technology, communication methods are now available for sophisticated interactive learning: among students, educators, and resources. Web 2.0, egaming, videoconferencing, and course management systems exemplify these delivery systems that incorporate learning activities" (p. 186). Farmer (2010) adds that e-gaming is a "new form of instructional strategy that enables learners to explore issues within a prescribed virtual environment, often interacting with other players" (p. 179). While this appears to combine educational and recreational components, she cautions that e-gaming protocols need to be intuitive so as not to intrude on the content of the learning.

It is also possible to adapt active learning activities normally used in the classroom so they can be utilized online. For example, directions can be given for students to engage non-course participants in activities. The author has done this in an online class. Students report back and reflect on the results. As previously noted in a quote from Wenger (2009), "learning is, in its essence, a fundamentally social phenomenon…" (p. 210). So Web 2.0 should provide numerous opportunities for online social engagement and active learning.

## FUTURE DIRECTIONS

Student projects provide the author with a continuous window into the future. Each semester, project assignments are produced with more technological sophistication than the previous semester. Recent assignments included the following projects. Avatars on a New York bus discussing the important of critical reflection in adult learning. A blogg on food preparation was an application of self-directedness. Short self-recorded videos on adult development were embedded in a Facebook page that was developed as a course project. These resulted from an assignment in which students ranked their choice of an adult learning topic for the project. Based on their priority, they were assigned to a group with the instruction that the group was to introduce the others in the class to their selected topic in a creative manner. They were encouraged to use the talents of those in the group but were assured that their grade would depend on the quality not glitzy techniques employed.

A colleague at an international training company alerted me to the fact that they have an APP for online coaching to supplement their classroom based workshops. As mobile devices become more commonplace, instructional methods are expanding to adapt to the need for instant answers and advice.

The continuous challenge is to ensure that the use of new technologies are grounded in adult learning theory and sound instructional design techniques. So it is not surprising that an organization such as "Quality Matters" (QM) has emerged. Their website describes it as a "nationally recognized, faculty-centered, peer review process designed to certify the quality of online courses and online components. Colleges and universities across the country use the tools in developing, maintaining and reviewing their online courses and in training their faculty." (www.qualitymatters.org 2006) It is further described as an organization focused on "Inter-Institutional Quality Assurance in Online Learning". The organization has created a rubric of forty specific elements distributed across eight broad standards, by which to evaluate the design of online and hybrid courses. These include: "course overview and introduction, learning objectives, assessment and measurement, resources and materials, learner engagement, course technology, learner support, and accessibility." (www.qualitymatters.org 2006).

But it is good to remember the words of Shea-Schultz and Fogarty (2002) who suggest that "e-learning is an art, not a science (p. 168). Merriam (2008) notes two main shifts in adult learning. One shift is from the individual learner to the learner within the various contexts in which learning takes place. This new perspective considers "learning as part of the system's cultural and historical norms…(and) how physical space and spatiality encourages or inhibits learning" (p.94). The second shift is from learning as a purely cognitive activity to a multidimensional phenomenon. This is often considered to be a more holistic approach in which "learning is construed as a much broader activity involving the body, the emotions, and the spirit as well as the mind" (p.95). Web 2.0 and other online tools would certainly offer valuable tools to deal with both of these situations.

## CONCLUSION

Methods prompted by learning management systems such as Blackboard, ecollege, Moodle or university developed LMS offer opportunities for presenting material, whole class or small group document sharing and text chatting. Piskurich (2006) provides some pragmatic advice that instructional design decisions should be made based on "what's right for the content, the learners, the time available for both design and implementation, and the cultural and technology environment of the company" (p. 98). This seems like wise advice no matter what the organization.

Shea-Schultz and Fogarty (2002) put the topic in perspective. "The e in e-learning wasn't short for electronic or electric. It was for entropy, which is defined as (1) the capacity of a system to undergo spontaneous change and (2) a measure of the randomness, disorder, or chaos in a system" (p. 1). Accepting the reality of this statement will allow us the freedom to critically reflect on our options and enjoy the opportunity for spontaneity and creativity. Good instructional methods linked to sound objectives will produce effective learning with or without technology and whether in the classroom or online.

## REFERENCES

Brookfield, S. (2006). *The skillful teacher*. San Francisco, CA: Jossey-Bass.

Brookfield, S., & Preskill, S. (1999). *Discussion as a way of teaching*. San Francisco, CA: Jossey-Bass.

Cranton, P. (2006). *Understanding and promoting transformative learning*. San Francisco, CA: John Wiley & Sons.

Elkjaer, R. (2009). Pragmatism: A learning theory for the future. In Illeris, K. (Ed.), *Contemporary theories of learning: Learning theorists... in their own words* (pp. 74–89). New York, NY: Routledge.

Farmer, L. (2010). Innovative instructional strategies with the use of technology for adult learners. In Wang, V. (Ed.), *Integrating adult learning and technologies for effective education* (pp. 170–188). Hershey, PA: IGI Global.

Kesby, D. (2008). Exploring the power of action learning. *Knowledge Management Review, 11*(5), 26–30.

Knowles, M., Holton, E., & Swanson, R. (2005). *The adult learner* (6th ed.). Burlington, MA: Elsevier.

Marsick, V., & Watkins, K. (1999). *Facilitating learning organizations*. Brookfield, VT: Gower.

Merriam, S., Caffarella, R., & Baumgartner, L. (2007). *Learning in adulthood: A comprehensive guide* (3rd ed.). San Francisco, CA: John Wiley & Sons.

Mezirow, J. (2000). *Learning as transformation*. San Francisco, CA: Jossey-Bass.

Mumford, A. (1997). Action learning as a vehicle for learning. In Mumford, A. (Ed.), *Action learning at work* (pp. 3–24). Hampshire, UK: Gower.

Nilson, L. B. (2003). *Teaching at its best*. San Francisco, CA: Anker Publishing.

Palloff, R., & Pratt, K. (1999). *Building learning communities in cyberspace*. San Francisco, CA: Jossey-Bass.

Parker, J. (1996). *Integrating technology into delivery methods for global technical education. Compendium on uses of distance learning technologies in engineering education*. American Society for Engineering Education.

Parker, J. (2009). The online adult learner: profiles and practices. In Wang, V. (Ed.), *Handbook of research on e-learning applications for career and technical education: Technologies for vocational training* (pp. 737–746). Hershey, PA: IGI Publishing. doi:10.4018/978-1-60566-739-3.ch056

Piskurich, G. (2006). *Rapid instructional design*. San Francisco, CA: John Wiley & Sons.

Quality Matters. (2006). *Inter-institutional quality assurance in online learning*. Retrieved from www.qualitymatters.com

Ravens, R. (1982). *The origin and growth of action learning*. London, UK: Chartwell Bratt.

Shea-Schultz, H., & Fogarty, J. (2002). *Online learning today: Strategies that work*. San Francisco, CA: Berrett-Koehler Publishers.

Silberman, M. (2006). *Active training*. San Francisco, CA: John Wiley & Sons.

Usher, R. (2009). Experience, pedagogy, and social practices. In Illeris, K. (Ed.), *Contemporary theories of learning: Learning theorists... in their own works* (pp. 169–183). New York, NY: Routledge.

Wenger, E. (2009). A social theory of learning. In Illeris, K. (Ed.), *Contemporary theories of learning: Learning theorists... in their own words* (pp. 209–218). New York, NY: Routledge.

Yiu, L., & Parker, J. (2005). Cyber action learning and virtual project teams for leadership and management development. In Jacobs, R. L., & Osman-Gani, A. M. (Eds.), *Workplace training & learning: Cases from cross-cultural perspectives* (pp. 1–14). New York, NY: Pearson/Prentice Hall.

# Chapter 10
# Comparing Traditional Teaching with Andragogical Teaching via Web 2.0 Technologies

**Judith Parker**
*Columbia University, USA*

## ABSTRACT

*The social networking and knowledge development features of Web 2.0 have offered new opportunities and challenges for teaching. This chapter will explore how these have impacted instructional methods utilized in both traditional and andragogical teaching in both face-to-face and virtual classrooms. It will include case studies as well as student comments.*

## INTRODUCTION

The introduction of new technology has always caused instructors to revisit their teaching methods with an eye to integrating the newest ideas. Both pedagogy and andragogy have been influenced by technology. Since the advent of the internet, new capabilities in presentation, communication, and collaboration have grown at an increasing rate. The recent introduction of Web 2.0's features has extended the voice and face of online connections. This chapter will explore the impact of those features on teaching in both an instructor focused (traditional) and student focused (andragogical) learning environment. Brunner (2009) sets the tone for this dichotomy by describing "two strikingly divergent conceptions about how mind works. The first of these was the hypothesis that mind could be conceived as a computational device. The other was the proposal that mind is both constituted by and realized in the use of human culture" (p. 159). He explains that "The first or computational view is concerned with information processing: how finite, coded, unambiguous information about the world is inscribed, sorted,

DOI: 10.4018/978-1-60960-791-3.ch010

stored, collated, retrieved, and generally managed by the computational device. The process of knowing is often messier and more fraught with ambiguity than such a view allows" (pp. 159-160). He further clarifies that "The second is "culturalism" which suggests that "mind could not exist save for culture. Culture in this sense is superorganic. But it shapes the minds of individuals as well. Its individual expression inheres in meaning making, assigning meanings to things in different settings on particular occasions" (p. 160). His view of the mind as a computational device is consistent with the practice of instructor focused traditional teaching. His second view is a more holistic picture of the student shaped by culture and not just absorbing facts but making meaning of them within the student's reality consistent with the practice of andragogy.

## Web 2.0 Technologies

Rhoades, Friedel, and Morgan define Web 2.0 as that second generation of the World Wide Web that "aims to enhance creativity, information sharing, collaboration and functionality of the web" (p. 25). Farmer (2009) describes Web 2.0 technology as a place where "knowledge is collaboratively built and shared" (p. 272). Farmer (2010) also notes that "rather than one-way communication, Web 2.0 applications enable people to participate in two-way active communication to create information" (p. 178).

Chmielewski and Guynn report in the March 10, 2010 Los Angeles Times that 111.8 million people signed on to Facebook and 66.7 million signed on to MySpace in the U.S. alone in February, 2010. While these numbers represent a 5% decrease for MySpace, they represent a 95% increase for Facebook over the past year. They also note that Facebook users average 267 minutes per month on the site which MySpace users average 130 minutes. These statistics are clear evidence that online social networking is an integral part of many people's lives.

However, Web 2.0 has become yet another of those numbered terms in the technology vocabulary. There are Windows 7 and 3G and 4G networks. The Blackboard Learning Management System versions seem to move forward by a whole number or at least by a decimal each academic year. The numbering schemes seem an indication of the fast paced changing landscape of technology. It is a constant reminder that something preceded the current version but also cautions not to become too comfortable with it because the next upgrade is lurking around the corner. So before Web 3.0 becomes a reality, it might be useful to examine how Web 2.0 developed.

Belfiore (2009) reports that the roots of Web 2.0 can be found in the Eisenhower administration's establishment of the National Aeronautics and Space Administration (NASA) and the Advanced Research Projects Agency (ARPA) in 1957 in response to the Soviet Union's launch of Sputnik, the world's first artificial satellite. According to Shea-Schultz and Fogarty (2002), for over two decades, this network was the "province of academic institutions, scientists, and government employees engaged in research and communications" (p. 7) allowing them to share data between their remote computers. In 1989, the development of World Wide Web standards" (p. 8) led to the widespread utilization of this web based communication.

Shea-Schultz and Fogarty (2002) report that the next major advancement for the web occurred in 1992 as a result of two events. The Mosaic browser allowed graphics to be embedded in text and the U.S. government made the web available for commercial use. In addition, the "rise of increasingly powerful, yet reasonably priced, personal computers fueled by silicon microchip processors" (p. 9) made the hardware increasingly available. This was the beginning of a trend of increased access and processing power and decreased hardware size that has continued until today. Only a few decades ago computers filled large rooms and communication between them and humans was cumbersome with magnetic tapes and punch cards. Developing technology made possible desktop models, then laptops, then net-books, then handheld devices. These ubiquitous miniature communication devices provide almost constant connectivity. Fueled with Web 2.0 features, they have the possibility of having a dramatic impact on both traditional and andragogical teaching. This impact will be discussed later in this chapter. While technology seems to be characterized by the rapid increase of its numbering system, education is committed to maintaining the dichotomy between pedagogy and andragogy, between traditional and adult teaching and learning described earlier by Brunner

## Traditional Teaching

The traditional teaching model is extensively described in the previous chapter under the topic of the lecture method. It generates visions of large lecture halls with hierarchical relationships and impersonal communication between instructor and student. "Traditional teaching pedagogy was designed to transmit codified or written knowledge to young generations within the paradigm of general standardized industrial production and mass consumption" (Ahedo, 2010, p. 239). It is a classic example of Freire's (2006) "banking model" of education in which the knowledge holder imparts precious knowledge to the knowledge seeker. "Education thus becomes an act of depositing, in which the students are the depositories and the teacher is the depositor. Instead of communicating, the teacher issues communiqués and makes deposits which the students patiently receive, memorize, and repeat. This is the 'banking' concept of education, in which the scope of action allowed to the students extends only as far as receiving, filling, and storing the deposits" (Freire, 2006, p. 72).

While many of these images appear to be negative, Brookfield (2006) reminds us that to achieve certain learning objectives, lecturing is the best method and dedicates an entire chapter to "creative lecturing" (p. 97). Kegan (2009) offers broad insights of traditional and modern that have parallels to the comparison of traditional and andragogical teaching. He suggests that "The self-authoring mind is equipped, essentially, to meet the challenges of modernism. Unlike traditionalism, in which a fairly homogeneous set of definitions of how one should live is consistently promulgated by the cohesive arrangements, models, and codes of the community or tribe, modernism is characterized by ever-proliferating pluralism, multiplicity, and competition for our loyalty to a given way of living" (pp. 51-52). His description of modernism appears to be leading to issues of post-modernism which will be addressed later.

## Andragogical Teaching

While our current concept of andragogy is often connected to Malcolm Knowles, Lee (2009) reminds us that andragogy is rooted in the works of "Socrates, Plato, Aristotle, Renaissance thinkers, via the French thinkers of the Enlightenment, the encyclopedic materialist's of the Russian revolutionary Democrats" (p. 28). Lee continues to explain that Plato's educational ideas were the basis for a German educator, Alexander Kapp, to coin the word "andragogy" in 1833 The term reappeared in several European countries in the 1920's and was finally popularized in North America by Malcolm Knowles.

Knowles (2005) teaching model is characterized by six core andragogical principles: "the learner's need to know, self-directed learning, prior experience of the learner, readiness to learn, orientation to learning and problem solving, and motivation to learn" (p.183). He traces the historical development of learning theories from Dewey of the early 1900's to Brookfield and Mezirow today. He lists 61 propounders and 33 interpreters who have influenced the development of learning theories over the past century. He notes that Dewey's belief that experience was always the starting point of an educational process, not the end result continues to be a topic of discussion in adult education. Critical reflection is often claimed to be a distinctive characteristic both of adult learning and of adult education practice-on itself. It is described by Brookfield (1986) as "reflecting on the assumptions underlying our and others' ideas and actions, and contemplating alternative ways of thinking and living" (p. x). This description is consistent with Brunner's previously stated explanation of how the mind works.

Illeris (2004) developed a theory that considers adult learning to comprise three dimensions: cognitive, emotional and social. His inverted triangle model places the two psychological poles, Piaget's cognition and Freud's emotion, at the two corners at the top of the model and society at the lower vertex but he stresses that "all three dimensions are always integrated parts of the learning process and in practice do not exist as separate functions" (p. 20). All three dimensions can be supported by the concept of a learning community. Palloff and Pratt (1999) describe a learning community as creating "a sense of excitement about learning together and renews the passion involved with exploring new realms in education" (p. 163). This concept will be explored in the context of an online learning community later in this chapter.

Kegan (2009) expresses it this way. "'Informative learning' involves a kind of leading in or filling of the form. Transformative learning puts the form itself at risk of change (and not just change but increased capacity" (p. 42). Farmer (2010) suggests that "just as Web 2.0 acknowledges and builds on each person's knowledge base, so too does adult education" (p. 178). All of the authors cited above provide various views of andragogy, however a few core themes exist throughout. Andragogical teaching is learner centered and personal. It acknowledges the previous knowledge and experiences of the individual and focuses on building on that foundation. This is in sharp contrast to the traditional teaching focus on the information transferred from the instructor to the student. Now, these ideas about the traditional and andragogical model will be examined in the context of Web 2.0.

## THE INFLUENCES OF WEB 2.0 ON TEACHING

### The Influence of Web 2.0

With powerful handheld devices, connectivity to other individuals and to information is a 24/7 possibility. The social and the educational possibilities are a reality. Herrington (2010) characterizes today's students as the "net generation" and "participatory learners" who need "participatory technologies" (p. 10). But Herrington (2010) also notes that "mobile technologies and emerging technologies of 'participatory culture' on the Web comprise powerful cognitive tools for authentic learning environments" (p. 8). He continues to explain that "authentic learning provides authentic contexts, tasks, collaborative construction of knowledge, authentic assessment" (p. 18). Berger (2009) delineates some features of Web 2.0 as "streaming video and audio, more sophisticated databases, evolved social networking sites, and improved networking applications" (p. 228). He also notes that "information will be more readily available to learners and instructors, and can be used to suit more learning styles" (p. 228).

Several authors address this new culture that provides a new idea of space and society. Loader (1998) notes that numerous social scientists share the notion that "society is being transformed by a revolution in information technology which is creating an entirely new social structure" (p. 4). Hakken (1999) suggests that the @ symbol used to indicate an electronic domain in an email address, also indicates the social space to which one is connected but he advises that "we must come to terms with an accelerated decoupling of space from place (p. 215). White and Bridwell (2004) concur by suggesting that new technology is "significantly altering the social role of learning" and that distance learning is only an intermediate step toward a "telelearning environment" in which distance and location become arbitrary (p. 287). However, the availability of new technologies and a new sense of space and time do not ensure effective utilization. Whether the teaching is traditional or andragogical, care must be taken to focus on the instructional objectives and select the tools that are appropriate to maximize learning. While the title of this chapter focuses on teaching, the suggestion and warnings about instructional technologies and instructional methods from Chapter 9 must be considered.

Loader (1998) announces that "the emergence of the new information and communications technologies such as the Internet are said to herald the coming of the "information society": a new social and economic paradigm restructuring the traditional dimensions of time and space within which we live, work, and interact" (p. 3). This new social paradigm changes our entire sense of space and time. Sitting with an individual or group of colleagues in a room has been replaced by typing on a computer keyboard or on any of the numerous hand held internet accessible devices, reading text on a screen, or listening to voices on a phone. Instead of feeling the presence of other collaborators, participants are connected by voice or text and might be easily distracted by daily tasks.

Often, Web 2.0 is described using vocabulary from a previous era. It is often discussed as being infused into courses or selected as just another methodology. Web 2.0 effectively has changed the entire landscape for learning because it has altered the communication norms for society as a whole.

## Web 2.0 and Traditional Teaching

Within the image of traditional teaching described earlier in this chapter, it might initially appear that Web 2.0 has little place in this instructor dominated methodology. However, the social nature and knowledge building features of Web 2.0 can have significant impact on the content delivered, the delivery methodology, and the student-teacher relationship itself within this traditional setting.

As instructors prepare their lectures, they search for the latest research and advances in their specialty. Content is enriched by the instructor's access to information and colleagues. Previously the instructor was burdened with visits to archives and libraries and limited to local experts and practitioners. But information communication technology has had a huge impact on this effort. Michael Moe (2000), in a publication entitled "The Knowledge Web" refers to the "richness" and the "reach" of the Internet (p. 3). In academic circles, this richness or depth of information becomes obvious in the plethora of digitized reports, texts, and publications from government agencies, academic institutions and private enterprises that are available online. The reach or breadth of the sources of information is obvious in the access to digital libraries across the planet. Moe (2000) also notes the importance of improved bandwidth for speedy access and comments that "cable companies, telco's, satellite/wireless companies and ISP's are locked in an epic battle over standards, protocols, open access and kilobits per second" (p. 63). This leads one to believe that this competition will result in even increased downloading speeds and easier access.

Web tools not only provide instructors with access to the latest publications but the social networking features of Web 2.0 provide them access to colleagues globally who are at the forefront of their research. Increasingly sophisticated web browsers, university websites and the social networking sites of Web 2.0 facilitate this process. And once located, communication can be facilitated by phone, email, and web-conferencing to name just a few possibilities.

Through collaborative tools, new knowledge can be collectively built and shared. The frequently cited Wikipedia is a well known example. The accuracy of the content may be questionable but the opportunity for collaboration and building a knowledge base is amazing. The results of these collaborations will enhance the quality of lectures and provide the instructor with tools for creative lectures. Alheit (2009) noted that "The communication and interaction networks of the IT age, which have long since permeated, extended and modified the realms of conventional industrial production and the character of classical services and administrations, remain dependent – more so than traditional forms of knowledge in the past – on the individual user. The latter's personal options in respect to the new, virtual markets – his/her contacts, productive inputs and consumer habits in the Internet – are what create the future forms of knowledge. The knowledge of the information society is *doing knowledge*, a kind of lifestyle that determines the structures of society far beyond the purely occupational domain and lends them a dynamic of ever-shorter cycles" (p. 119).

Traditionally this communication took the form of a paper presented at a professional conference or publication in a scholarly journal. Rhoades, Friedel and Morgan (2009) cite the lag time from data analysis until the publication in a journal as being eliminated by several open source journals that allow researchers to share findings quickly with mass audiences. They also mention how the traditional workshops, seminars and conferences are being supplemented by online communities of practice web sites. While the peer review process has always required communication between colleagues, today that communication is facilitated by a number of new developments in the area of information communication technology. Global communication is easy and free using Skype. Information can be broadcast to groups in real time using podcasts and asynchronously by a post on Youtube, wiki's or bloggs. The emergence of computer mediated communication (CMC) as a field of study suggests the level of impact that technology has had on communication. Just as the body of knowledge surrounding adult education has developed over almost a century to define that field, the literature on CMC is beginning to define this new field. The intersection of the field of CMC and adult education might be the topic of future studies. Rhoades, Friedel and Morgan (2009) define collaboration as "the process of shared creation: two or more individuals with complementary skills interacting to create a shared understanding that none had previously possessed or could have come to on their own (p. 24). The collaboration among members of a discipline has always existed in the form of face-to-face meetings and conferences or written communication. But information communication technology has added several new dimensions to this process and in fact has changed our social paradigm.

Web 2.0 provides numerous tools for enhancing a lecture. While the lecture itself is instructor focused, most would agree that lecture content might be reinforced and explored more deeply if followed by a discussion. This often doesn't happen because there is no time built into the schedule or the environment such as a large lecture hall is not conducive to discussion. However, students can be assigned to small online groups for followup discussion on lecture material. Learning management systems have previously afforded these opportunities but with the social networking advantage of Web 2.0, the freedom to set up synchronous webchats or asynchronous threaded discussions is available to everyone in the class without requiring instructor involvement. Now students can even take the initiative of setting up their own wiki's or blogs for study groups.

The once instructor focused course can become a rich learning experience in which students are engaged. If the lecture content is delivered online, the same discussion format can be used. One student involved in such a discussion offered the following comment. "I was enamored with the power of this medium. In my opinion, the on-line synchronous communication came closest to simulating a traditional classroom context within the distance-learning framework. It gave me a sense of jointly occupying a temporary space (similar to a class room) and created the illusion of physical proximity and group cohesion through spontaneous conversation and sharing. At the same time it eliminated space restrictions—all four of us gathered from numerous locations, Carol from as far as the UK, to meet and discuss the topic in a real-time environment." In this new societal paradigm, a new sense of community emerges. The adult education vocabulary around "learning communities" and "communities of practice" has been around for a few decades but their meaning has evolved with the new sense of space provided by information communication technology. Paloff and Pratt (1999) remind us that the words "community and communicate have the same root, communicare, which means to share" (p. 25). Now that sharing takes place outside of shared physical space.

While earlier tools required a high level of technological expertise, Web 2.0 tools are often easy to use. Farmer (2010) lists some examples of Web 2.0 tools useful to teaching and learning. Just a sampling include "audacity" for recording and editing audio files, "Google Docs" for sharing and editing documents, and "ning" for sharing groups, links, documents and videos.

With large amounts of information available to students as well as instructors, the student-teacher relationship can be altered. Many of the impacts of Web 2.0 mentioned above alter the student instructor relationship as well. No longer is the instructor the possessor of knowledge and the student the receiver. Multitasking students can access resources in today's wireless classrooms and interject useful information into a classroom setting.

## Web 2.0 and Andragogical Teaching

As indicated in the previous chapter, many instructional methods involve not only communication between instructor and student but also between students themselves. The social networking capabilities of Web 2.0 with its wiki's and blogs and Facebook and Myspace can be an asset in facilitating these methods and support the collaborative aspects of andragogical teaching learning. Farmer (2009) notes that "adding this broad-based authoring set of tools to the educational concept of constructivism results in student-centered curriculum" (p. 272). She notes that "learners will shop around for a widening variety of learning opportunities that best meet their needs" (p. 274). Malcolm Knowles (2005) considers technology as consistent with his adult learning principle of self-directedness and as providing learning opportunities in the "andragogical tradition" (p. 237).

In an andragogical model where more student participation is expected, assignments can be structured to include social engagement. Since the author teaches graduate courses in adult learning and leadership, her intent is to model good andragogical practices. Therefore the previous chapter includes several examples of the andragogical model in the context of instructional methods for online learners. An additional example is an assignment in which the students are asked to select two journal articles about staff development and training. One student provided insights on the assignment. "The discussion conducted here is very involving; everybody could get a chance to express his own ideas. Moreover, the discussion board online gives us a further opportunity to share ideas with all of the class. It has been developed into a real learning forum. Everybody chose their favorite articles about learning and training in their fields, and then shared their own ideas on the "blackboard", thus evokes a real open discussion. This learning style makes me feel that I can learn anytime anywhere from so many people of diverse fields. By posting, reading, and replying online, our learning location has burst out of the limited classroom and lecture time boundary, thus it has given us an authentic flexibility and motivation to learn."

Web 2.0 also alters the way in which students perceive course requirements. One student commented in an evaluation of online course: "This course is even more demanding than face to face courses. You must stay on top of the reading." But she also observed that she "Got to hear from all of my classmates, and hear from them in depth, whereas face to face, only the talkers get heard. Here, everyone had a voice – a deep voice." Another student commented: "The conversations were not superficial interactions but purposeful, focused and useful. The instructions preceding the chat in terms of reading position papers, preparing questions followed by chat on each paper allowed all group members an equal opportunity to have their "voices" heard, making the chat more effective. Setting up small groups of 4 students, rather than a whole class, allowed each one the time and opportunity to participate and understand each other's situations more closely and attentively. The archived feature of the chat that automatically creates transcripts of discussions make it useful for rereading and future reference."

One methodology that has developed in the environment of andragogy is action learning which involves working on real work opportunities, problems, tasks and projects and encompassing a learning cycle of *action, reflection, theorisation and application.* An example exists in a pre-web 2.0 action learning project with twelve technical center managers in 8 Asian countries. During his 14 month cycle of the action learning model, learners are expected to try out new behaviors, to reflect critically on their experiences, to distil some generalizable principles and to try it out in other similar contexts. While Web 2.0 offers expanded opportunities for collaboration, earlier internet capability and even phone conferencing were utilized to achieve the same goals. Much of what was learned in this environment is applicable to Web 2.0 technology and will be considered later in this chapter.

The project required that each manager participate in two groups offering the opportunities and challenges of cross boundary and cross cultural communication. Based on the results of their pre-work learning styles inventory, the participants were assigned to project teams and learning groups. Each manager was assigned to one of three country project groups for Taiwan, India and Singapore. They worked in a peer group on a real management related project and were asked to formulate recommendations based on research and data analysis. The three project titles were: How to manage the growth of the laboratories within Asia including the delegation of responsibilities, and the evolving roles of supervisor and manager. How to accelerate the technical investment by leveraging resources since the growth of the lab oratory is traditionally restricted to a portion of growth in sales but labs need to grow faster in order to catch the fast growing market in Asia. How to accelerate the technical competency of employees and build a technology base in the region in a cost-effective way. Electronic forums were created for group discussions and for capturing the knowledge created and exchanged among the forum members. Regular group meetings were held via video or audio communication channels. Today's Web 2.0 knowledge building capabilities would greatly enhance this process.

Managers were also assigned to a reflection group consisting of representatives of each country specific project. This group discussed issues related to group dynamics and shared feedback with other group members. They met by phone conference or video conference depending on availability in their respective locations. Today's Web 2.0 technologies would also have greatly facilitated these activities. While this project had the advantage of a 3 day workshop held in Korea to facilitate team building, introduce the project and relevant content and formulate the planning process for the project, the remainder of the project was virtual. Project teams met on line to discuss the work regarding their learning/consulting project with the support and input from the instructors. At the end of the project a compendium of project reports was published and distributed to each participant, country business head and the vice presidents responsible for the Asia region and the international laboratory operations. A closing ceremony, a virtual graduation by phoneconferencing, was held at the end with class photos, certificates, and executive speeches. This ceremony would have been more effective using today's webconferencing technology allowing each member to be visually present for the ceremony.

Since the concept of a virtual classroom was new to the participants, it was necessary to model the experience after a more familiar real classroom. "The following parallels need to be considered. The Dimensions: Thousands of miles wide by thousands of miles long by thousands of miles high. The Chalkboard: Fax machines, computer files, email, phone lines, telephones, and videoconferencing facilities. Sitting in the classroom: typing on a computer keyboard, reading a computer screen, listening to voices on the phone, watching a monitor" (Yiu & Parker, 2005). This process utilized adult learning theory in the course design and delivery. The action learning model provided an excellent framework for learning in a business climate that mandated pragmatic focused learning.

In reflections on their action learning project described earlier in this chapter, Yiu and Parker (1995) noted a number of challenges faced by their project and learning that could influence future work. Examples of issues that made the teamwork process more challenging consisted of the following:

- Time lag in communication. Team meetings, if not held through video or audio conferencing, tended not to be held in real time. This resulted in a slower tempo of communication often interspersed with long gaps. This required the teams to be highly self-regulated and self-directed in order to stay on course.
- Proximity for collaboration. While some researchers consider that people are not likely to collaborate very often if they are more than 50 feet apart, this needs further investigation in online learning venues in light of the growing comfort level with online communication.
- Competing priorities. The group action research projects required a substantive amount of time commitment from the team members. Since these projects were not part of the routine work of these Asian technical managers, competing priorities at times pushed the team project low down on the priority list. Face-to face priorities seem to have higher priority than virtual ones.
- Physical links. Due to the uneven access to multiple media in different countries, the physical links amongst the virtual teams also differ. Locations with video-conferencing facilities provided some of the teams greater physical contacts with each other. These physical contacts, even though only through video channels, helped to reduce the perceived distance from each other. This still exists within countries, even within the U.S.
- Bonding and trust. A shared sense of purpose is essential to sustain the cross-border virtual teams. Task interdependence provided some motivation to collaborate for most of the teams. Trust is a very important element of any effective team. The lack of daily face-to-face time, which offers opportunities to quickly clear the air, can heighten misunderstandings or create communication barriers within the virtual teams. The need to share high trust within the virtual teams was of significant importance due to the different cultural backgrounds of its members.
- Cultural diversity. Each team consisted of three members of three different cultural and national backgrounds. This cultural diversity influenced the teams' approach in dealing with leadership issue, in expressing disagreements, and in managing common tasks. Even within the same country,

regional and organizational differences impact team effectiveness.

While this action learning project was an example of a hybrid design the advice is applicable to any project involving an online component. Since Web 2.0 focuses on social networking, its applicability to teams and especially virtual teams is important to consider.

Networks, by definition, are based on personal contacts and resource exchanges. While a regional headquarters represents the formal administrative and decision-making channels, the informal channels need to be created between people in the field and their respective colleagues across country subsidiaries and with the headquarters. Without these informal boarder-crossing networks, it would be relatively difficult to achieve any desired regional synergy. While each project had specific business objectives, the development of such regional networks were considered to be one of the significant outcomes of this learning project. Recognising that virtual teams will be one of the most vital forms communication for future organisation, this project allowed participants to experience this virtual process while integrating the results into the actual work environments and exploring ways in making this new form of network function effectively and efficiently. These teams have become increasingly important in today's business and academic climates and rely on the functions provided by Web 2.0.

## Comparing or Combining?

Most colleges with programs for adult learners, distinguish traditional students from adult students. Malcolm Knowles reinforced this dichotomy with his focus on adult education (andragogy) vs pedagogy. A recent conference attended by the author was titled "Serving the Adult Learner". While different support services might be required for the two groups of learners, should teaching be different based on age?

The language of instructional technology, online learning, distance education, challenges the teacher and the learner to cross boundaries of social class, national borders, and Web 2.0 offers tools for collaborating and new knowledge development yet educational language still delineates two categories of learners therefore implying the need for two categories of teaching. Would it be more correct and useful to consider a continuum model with strict instructor dominated lecture at one end and student dominated/instructor guided experiential instruction at the other? Depending on content, course objectives and teacher and learner comfort level, a teaching/learning strategy at the appropriate location on the continuum might be selected. (See Table 1.)

If the question is whether to use traditional or andragogical teaching methods, the answer is yes. Brookfield (2006) reminds us that the three core assumptions of skillful teaching apply equally to all forms of teaching. "Good teaching is whatever helps students learn, good teaching is critically reflective, and the most important knowledge teachers need to do good worwk is how students experience their learning" (pp. 196-197). Considering the individual student and the organizational culture, one should select the most effective methodology from the menu of choices along the continuum. In the spirit of postmodernism, a model that eliminates boundaries and embraces the "e" in entropy might be best. Remember the quote introduced in Chapter 9 from Shea-Schultz and Fogarty (2002). "The e in e-learning wasn't short for electronic or electric. It was for entropy, which is defined as (1) the capacity of a system to undergo spontaneous change and (2) a measure

*Table 1.*

| | |
|---|---|
| Instructor Dominated (95%) | Instructor Guided (5%) |
| Student Dominated (5%) | Student Focused (95%) |

of the randomness, disorder, or chaos in a system" (p. 1). It challenges us to find opportunities in fluidity and fractals. As more options are added to the Web 2.0 toolkit, the menu of teaching methods should expand. Brookfield (2006) emphasizes the importance of "credibility and authenticity in teachers" (p. 197) as equally important in any setting.

## FUTURE TRENDS

The future will surely include traditional internet connectivity, Web 2.0 and beyond. It will expand the connectivity between those of eastern and western thought. As the walls of our virtual classrooms expand, several authors offer advice and thoughts for reflection. For example, it is important that we consider how our primarily western developed thoughts on andragogy will be accepted globally. Wang and King (2009) remind us that "the theory of andragogy boils down to a democratic style and method which is characterized by negotiating curricular priorities with adult learners, involving learners in planning the process, giving out learning contracts, and so forth. In some situations where adult learners are inexperienced with subject matter and do not have independent learning styles or in situations where culture or subculture does not allow the use of andragogy, adult educators become frustrated" (p. 22). They continue with the example that "to teach adult learners in Asia is to follow wise men's sayings such as those of Confucius and a detailed formula prescribed by higher authorities" (p. 22). Will we need to develop a more inclusive definition for andragogy.

Lave (2009) notes that "Knowledgeability is routinely in a state of change rather than stasis, in the medium of socially, culturally, and historically ongoing systems of activity, involving people who are related in multiple and heterogeneous ways, whose social locations, interests, reasons, and subjective possibilities are different, and who improvise struggles in situated ways with each other over the value of particular definitions of the situations, in both immediate and comprehensive terms, and for whom the production of failure is as much a part of routine collective activity as the production of average ordinary knowledgeability" (p. 207).

Walther and Ramirez (2010) recount today's social networking sites such as Facebook and MySpace and their role in establishing large social networks that "help individuals maintain a larger number of ties than people can typically maintain without such technology" but believe that "the greatest utility of social networking systems has yet to be explored" (pp. 278-79). This is consistent with the 2 main shifts in the focus of adult learning noted by Merriam's (2007) in Chapter 9. One shift considers "learning as part of the system's cultural and historical norm (and) how physical space and spatiality encourages or inhibits learning" (p.94). The second shift is from learning as a purely cognitive activity to a multidimensional phenomenon. This is a more holistic approach in which "learning is construed as a much broader activity involving the body, the emotions, and the spirit as well as the mind" (p. 95). Kasworm and Londoner (2000) offer useful advice in suggesting that it is important "to accept and embrace the possibilities of technology" (p. 225).

The blurring between traditional and andragogical teaching takes on new meaning as time progresses. For example, the Quality Matters (2006) website reports that one researcher, one researcher found that the millennial generation of students appeared to have greater recall and recognition when content was in the form of a visual presentation via computer (such as a slideshow) rather than other visual learning environments or traditional lecture". Was the computer presentation now traditional for this group?

Alheit (2009) summarizes it effectively. "In the process, the nature of education and learning is dramatically changed. They no longer entail the communication and dissemination of fixed bodies of knowledge, values or skills, but rather a kind of knowledge osmosis' for ensuring what must now be a permanent and continuous exchange between individual knowledge production and organized knowledge management. The idea of lifelong learning, and especially self-managed learning, seems highly predestined for this process – as a framework concept at least" (p. 119).

There might be a lesson in a report from researchers at Teachers College/Columbia University (2007) titled "From English language Learners to Emergent Bilinguals" rather than the traditional idea of English Language Learners or English as a Second Language. They note "linguistic interdependence" as the "notion that two languages bolster each other and the students' ability to acquire knowledge" (p. 18). The lesson might be to consider emergent bi-learning ideas and to consider that traditional and adult learning support each other. It might be useful to take the best methodologies from each of the two worlds and enhance their effectiveness using Web 2.0..

## CONCLUSION

Separating traditional and andragogical teaching is useful for the sake of analysis and discussion. However in most real or virtual classrooms, they exist as complementary methods to achieve a goal. Chapter 9 emphasized the important role of objectives as the foundation for decision making about the selection of instructional methods. Andragogical and traditional are broad categories each of which encompasses several instructional methods. While a dichotomy is established between the traditional and online classrooms's yet hybrid courses are becoming more the norm. Online activities are becoming an integral part of classroom based courses. The methods generally considered as characteristic of each are becoming part of all effective teaching. The best practices of each should be considered as models for all effective teaching and learning.

## REFERENCES


Ahedo, M. (2010). Comparing the principles of adult learning with traditional pedagogical teaching in relation to the use of technology. In Wang, V. (Ed.), *Integrating adult learning and technologies for effective education* (pp. 238–254). Hershey, PA: IGI Global.

Alheit, P. (2009). Biographical learning–within the new lifelong learning discourse. In K. Illeris, (Ed.), *Contemporary theories of learning: Learning theorists... in their own words* (pp. 1 16-128). New York, NY: Routledge.

Belfiore, M. (2009). *The department of mad scientists*. New York, NY: HarperCollins.

Brookfield, S. (1986). *Understanding and facilitating adult learning*. San Francisco, CA: Jossey-Bass.

Brookfield, S. (2006). *The skillful teacher*. San Francisco, CA: Jossey-Bass.

Bruner, J. (2009). Culture, mind, and education. In Illeris, K. (Ed.), *Contemporary theories of learning: Learning theorists... in their own words* (pp. 159–168). New York: Routledge.

Chmielewski, D. C., & Guynn, J. (March 10, 2010). MySpace looks to the past for its future. *Los Angeles Times,* B1-B3.

Department of Development and External Affairs. (2007). Calling a rose by its other name. In *2007 annual report of Teachers College/Columbia University*. New York, NY: Teachers College/ Columbia University.

Farmer, L. (2009). Career and technical education technology: Three decades in review and technological trends in the future. In Wang, V. (Ed.), *Definitive readings in the history, philosophy, practice and theories of career and technical education* (pp. 259–278). Hershey, PA: IGI Global.

Farmer, L. (2010). Innovative instructional strategies with the use of technology for adult learners. In Wang, V. (Ed.), *Integrating adult learning and technologies for effective education* (pp. 170–188). Hershey, PA: IGI Global.

Freire, P. (2006). *Pedagogy of the oppressed.* New York, NY: Continuum.

Hakken, D. (1999). *Cyborgs@cyberspace*. New York, NY: Routledge.

Herrington, J., Reeves, T., & Oliver, R. (2010). *A guide to authentic e-learning*. NY: Routledge.

Illeris, K. (2004). *The three dimensions of learning*. Malabar, FL: Krieger.

Kasworm, C. D., & Londoner, C. A. (2000). Adult learning and technology. In Wilson, A. L., & Hayes, E. (Eds.), *Handbook of adult and continuing education* (pp. 224–242). San Francisco: John Wiley & Sons.

Kegan, R. (2009). What "form" transforms? A constructive-developmental approach to transformative learning. In Illeris, K. (Ed.), *Contemporary theories of learning: Learning theorists ... in their own words* (pp. 35–52). New York, NY: Routledge.

Knowles, M., Holton, E., & Swanson, R. (2005). *The adult learner* (6th ed.). Burlington, MA: Elsevier.

Lau, L. (2000). *Distance learning technologies: Issues, trends and opportunities*. Hershey, PA: Idea Group Publishing.

Lave, J. (2009). The practice of learning. In Illeris, K. (Ed.), *Contemporary theories of learning: Learning theorists ... in their own words* (pp. 200–208). New York, NY: Routledge.

Lee, K. (2009). Philosopher or philistine? In Wang, V. (Ed.), *Assessing and evaluating adult learning in career and technical education* (pp. 27–51). Hershey, PA: IGI Global.

Loader, B. (1998). *Cyberspace divide*. New York, NY: Routledge. doi:10.4324/9780203169537

Merriam, S., Caffarella, R., & Baumgartner, L. (2007). *Learning in adulthood: A comprehensive guide*. San Francisco, CA: John Wiley & Sons.

Moe, M. (2000). *The knowledge Web*. Beverly Hills, CA: Knowledge Enterprises Group.

Palloff, R., & Pratt, K. (1999). *Building learning communities in cyberspace*. San Francisco, CA: Jossey-Bass.

Quality Matters. (2006). *Home page information*. Retrieved from www.qualitymatters.com

Rhoades, E., Friedel, C., & Morgan, A. (2009). Can Web 2.0 improve our collaboration? *Techniques, 83*(9), 24–27.

Shea-Schultz, H., & Fogarty, J. (2002). *Online learning today: Strategies that work*. San Francisco, CA: Berrett-Koehler Publishers.

Silberman, M. (2006). *Active training*. San Francisco, CA: John Wiley & Sons.

Walther, J., & Ramirez, A. (2010). New technologies and new directions in online relating. In Smith, S., & Wilson, S. (Eds.), *New directions in interpersonal communication research* (pp. 264–284). Thousand Oaks, CA: Sage.

Wang, V., & King, K. (2010). Transformative learning and ancient Asian educational perspectives. In Wang, V. (Ed.), *Assessing and evaluating adult learning in career and technical education* (pp. 13–26). Hershey, PA: IGI Global.

White, B. A., & Bridwell, C. (2004). Distance learning techniques. In Galbraith, M. (Ed.), *Adult learning methods: A guide for effective instruction* (pp. 273–288). Malabar, FL: Krieger.

Yiu, L., & Parker, J. (2005). Cyber action learning and virtual project teams for leadership and management development. In Jacobs, R. L., & Osman-Gani, A. M. (Eds.), *Workplace training & learning: cases from cross-cultural perspectives* (pp. 1–14). New York, NY: Pearson/Prentice Hall.

# Chapter 11
# Age Issues in Online Teaching

**Lesley Farmer**
*California State University Long Beach, USA*

## ABSTRACT

*Age impacts online instructional design and delivery in two ways: developmental/biological and social/cultural. Developmental and generational issues are detailed as they impact e-learning. Attitudes towards technology and its social use are explained in light of age. Because the online community reflects lifelong learning, it behooves online educators to factor in age when developing and delivering online instruction.*

## INTRODUCTION

Online teaching differs from face-to-face instruction in terms of physicality. Teachers and students are not in the same space at the same time. For that reason, the senses have less information to base decisions about information; a disconnect occurs as gestures are less able to be interpreted, for instance, even in video conferencing venues. Theoretically, when instruction exists without any images or sounds of teachers or students, the impacts of age is minimalized; people are less likely to impose their preconceived notions of generations in the educational setting. With that assumption made, some instructors may think that online courses can be standardized for a global audience.

However, such an assumption is false. People bring their backgrounds and experiences to their online learning situation, and interpret the course in light of their existing mental schema. In comparison to face-to-face interactions, it may be more difficult for teachers and students to ascertain the basis for individuals' contributions and responses in the online environment. With less information about the individual available, misinterpretations may actually increase in number. For example, if an e-learner asserts that birth control is bad, it helps to understand that person's statement if it is known that the learner is a twenty-year old Black male rather than a sixty-year old Latino.

DOI: 10.4018/978-1-60960-791-3.ch011

Age impacts online instructional design and delivery in two ways: developmental/biological and social/cultural. As the brain develops, it processes and communicates information in different ways. Furthermore, the time period in which individuals live shapes their online experience. Therefore, as the online community reflects lifelong learning, it behooves online educators to factor in age when developing and delivering online instruction.

## CHILD DEVELOPMENT AND ONLINE TEACHING

Learning changes with physical development, even at the pre-natal stage as billions of neurons are formed and connected (Sousa, 2001). That interconnectivity activity continues unabated until puberty when the brain determines which connections should be permanent. Other windows of learning opportunity also occur in childhood. For instance, children's ability to learn motor skills peaks at age six. The window for developing emotional control is the first two and a half years. The window for language acquisition closely largely by age eleven.

The question is not if children *should* learn with technology; today's students are technology natives (Kaiser Family Foundation, 1999). As far back as 1994 it was determined that the average age that children started using computers was between 18 and 24 months old (Casey, 1997). By the time a child is seven, their learning style is pretty much set, so even kindergartners should have learning experiences using technology in order to feel more self-confident about using digital skills. Since individuals with abstract sequential learning style preferences, which style is more often exhibited by males, tend to like computers more than individuals with other learning style preferences, early success with computers also can take advantage of the brain's early malleability (Ames, 2003).

Rather the issue is *how* children use technology, specifically e-learning, particularly in early grades. The Northwest Regional Education Lab (Van Scoter & Ellis, 2001) offers useful guidelines for technology use in light of child development factors. For example, to meet children's social and emotional development needs, one computer should be used by two students in a learning structure that insures that both students have hands-on experience and opportunities to talk about their efforts, including in online conversations. The American Association for the Advancement of Science (1999) found that more peer teaching and helping occurs when students use computers; with web 2.0 tools, this peer interaction can occur in cyberspace. In terms of language development, students should play with reading-rich digital resources and be encouraged to talk about their processes while using technology in order to develop more complex speech and reading fluency; again, social networking can broaden the basis for language use. To address motor development, word processing – if done using smaller keyboards – can actually be easier for some children than physically forming letters. Of course, computer use should be brief for little ones in order to prevent obesity and vision problems. Usually a combination of on-computer and off-computer activity within a learning activity yields the best academic and social results (The American Association for the Advancement of Science, 1999).

## ADOLESCENT DEVELOPMENT

This generation of adolescents is probably the most diverse in terms of ethnicities, backgrounds and experiences. Nevertheless, some psychological conditions resonate for most teenagers today. In their study of teenagers, Girl Scouts (2002) found the following common characteristics.

- Teens want to be a part of a group and develop friendships.
- Teens need to feel safe to express their questions and opinions, and need help dealing with stress.
- Teens feel pressured by others to conform and to succeed.
- Teens want a feeling of accomplishment, but they also want to have fun.
- Teens like to learn by doing and by connecting with other same-sex peers and adults who are teen-savvy.
- Teens want flexibility and choice in their lives, and they want to plan with adults to make things happen.

Each teenager is unique, yet all teens share certain developmental tasks to insure successful transition into adulthood as well as positive experiences in adolescence. On the most basic level, teens need to move towards independence, deal with the future, address sexuality issues, and develop personal values and direction. The nonpartisan children's research organization Child Trends classifies desirable youth development outcomes into four major categories: educational achievement and cognitive attainment, health and safety, social and emotional development, and self-sufficiency. The Harvard Center for Health Communication (Simpson, 2001) posits ten tasks for adolescents:

- get adjusted to physical bodily changes and emotions
- think abstractly
- develop a more complex perspective
- develop more rigorous decision-making and problem-solving techniques
- develop personal moral and value systems
- understand and express emotion
- develop close and supportive friendships
- develop a self-identity
- assume more responsibility
- negotiate offspring-parent relationships.

To this list James (1974) adds a number of adolescent needs that may seem diametrically opposed: to be needed and to need, to belong and to be separate, to be physically active and to be still, to have intensity and risk and have routine, to get facts and imaginative stimuli.

Phelan, Davidson, and Yu (1998) examined adolescent transition in terms of "borders" that have to be negotiated in their worlds:

- socio-cultural: cultural differences between family and school
- socio-economic: economic differences between family and peers
- psycho-social: emotions that distract from learning
- linguistics: communication differences between family and peers
- gender: expectation differences between boys and girls
- heterosexist: conflicts in worldview about sexuality
- structural: school environment features that impede learning, etc.

In studying youth, Besharov (1999) found that as teens grow up, about a third of them feel disconnected from institutes (e.g., school) or people (e.g., peers, families, community) at least six months, with at least 50% of Latino and African American males exhibiting these signs although ethnicity in itself has no significant effort on how teens respond to these factors. However, youth who feel disconnected for three or more years suffer long-term social and financial problems.

Those developmental tasks and needs represent most teenagers' realities, behaviors that are usually successfully fulfilled over time. However, the approaches that teens use to address these tasks changes differ significantly in early, middle and late adolescence, as noted by the American Academy of Child and Adolescent Psychiatry (2003). Implications for online learning are noted in italics.

- In middle school years, ages 12 to 14, early teenagers are somewhat self-conscious, struggling with their own sense of identity and "normalcy" while trying to fit in as they transition to middle school. They fluctuate between a need to rely on parents and on friends, and see parents for their flaws. They often act out of emotion so may be moody. They are growing rapidly and unevenly, so they may be physically awkward, restless and tired. In general, they are eager to explore the world around them. Living mainly in the concrete "now," these early teenagers testing adult rules, and may start experimenting with risky behaviors. Girls usually are more mature than boys at this age. *Online instructors tend to find that girls take online instruction more seriously than boys, and are more likely to follow the instructor's directions. Instruction also needs to be highly structured, particularly since boys may need more organizational skills, yet flexible enough to provide students with opportunities for self-choice* (Farmer, 2007).
- Beginning high schoolers, ages 14 to17, alternate between poor self-esteem and high self-expectations as they experience rites of passage. They may seem overly critical of their own appearance and of their parents. They search actively for peer acceptance and group identity, and yet feel sad about their loss of closeness with their parents. They are starting to develop career goals, and are exploring their sexuality. *Online instruction should incorporate social interactive features and collaborative learning opportunities. Fortunately, online instruction can mitigate the influence of negative body-image and can facilitate gender role-play within a safe environment.*
- Older teenagers, ages 17 to 19, have a more realistic self-concept and stabler personality. They are able to think independently and abstractly. They take pride in their own work, and are able to delay gratification and make reasonable compromises. They feel stress, and look for skills to help them survive day to day as well as to prepare for an uncertain future. They are making serious post-secondary educational and career decisions, and are considering serious sexual relationships. They also accept social institutions and cultural traditions. *Online instruction should link academic subject matter to everyday realities, and encourage learners to apply course concepts to community-based contexts. Online instruction also enables older teens to assume more responsibility for their own learning, including choices in document usage and allocation of time for online experiences.*

Obviously, attitudes and behaviors vary among individual teenagers, but the progression of steps cross most cultures. Moreover, most teenagers manage to grow up without too much difficulty. As long as teens learn how to be productive, are able to navigate through difficulty, stay healthy, have health relationships, and get involved in communities, they will succeed. (Gambone, Klem, & Connell, 2002) Still, personal and societal problems can disrupt adolescent growth. When these issues are hard to avoid, such as rural isolation or endemic poverty, then persistent problems can impact adult success if teens do not know how to cope. Symptoms of stress and difficulties include personality changes, low self-esteem, social problems, disconnectedness, academic problems, withdrawal, and avoidance (Williams-Boyd, 2003).

Online teaching has the potential of helping teens deal with developmental issues.

- Teens can have access to educational opportunities that are not available locally, particularly in low-income areas. Sometimes school itself is not safe for the teen, so online instruction might be less stressful than face-to-face instruction.
- Teens can network with people outside their immediate surroundings to cross socio-economic borders, which can offer new social connections, timely interventions, and opportunities for personal growth.
- Teens can feel more self-confident and less distracted because they do not have to deal with confrontations that arise from physical differences (e.g., sex, body image, disabilities) and possible language barriers. Online learning offers more anonymity.
- Teens can feel more independent and in control of their education as they negotiate their online learning environment, especially if they can self-pace their online learning.
- Teens can take more intellectual risks because they do not have to deal with physically-based social norms and prejudice. They can even take social risks, experimenting with different persona to see how people react to them online without physical consequences (to some extent).

Today's teens have grown up in the midst of the digital society. Because of such technological ubiquity, teens expect that information should be convenient and available all the time; for this reason, portable devices are favored by them. Teens use technology for entertainment (especially gaming for boys), finding personal information, and creating content and sharing it (Rainie, 2006). Likewise, they are likely to interact with a variety of information sources simultaneously (Abram & Luther, 2004). Basically, teens choose their form of media based on the type of activity: phones for immediate personal contact, television for news, video games for escape. It should also be noted teens do not use media homogeneously.

Adults have mixed attitudes about online education for teenagers. Teachers complain about student plagiarism and cut-and-paste essays. Routinely, adults talk about their fear of youngsters cruising pornographic sites and having online sex – or being preyed upon by molesters. Some fear that students will lack social skills if they learn mainly online, although social networking can mitigate such propensities. The 2007 National School Boards Association surveys of parents, however, contradict these dour attitudes. Generally, parents think that the Internet is safe and useful for education; they also think that their children are careful about interacting with strangers, and they monitor their children's use to some extent.

Teens at the fringe of technology typically lack assets of external support, empowerment, expectations, and use of time (Chatman, 1996). They are disconnected not only from technology but from other aspects of live. To make the situation more serious, studies show that at-risk behaviors tend to cluster so that teenagers display multiple symptoms of dysfunctional behaviors. Generally, teens on the technology fringes are also on the educational and societal fringes. They tend not to have the safety nets *over a substantial period of time* to help them resolve "outside" crises successfully. To further explain this situation, one can use the analogy of being "broke" to being poor: the former is short-term, the latter is a substantive condition. For these reasons, online education is essential for those people who are least likely to have access to it. Therefore, special effort needs to be made by educational institutions to provide such access and explain to these "fringer" teens why technology benefits them.

## MILLENNIALS

The newest adults, the millennial generation born since 1980, exhibit a unique set of characteristics, largely the result of societal and cultural changes. Globalization has led to fewer cultural distinctions, greater interaction, and a greater common language (often based on music and television) (Ousley, 2006). While they seem to have a sense of entitlement and appear egocentric, they are very social and more tolerant than past generations. While they can be surface-oriented, they seek active involvement. Likewise, while their attention may seem short at times, they can also spend hours on some activity of their own choosing. Nevertheless, they highly value authenticity and directness, and want to make a difference in society. Although they can be very conventional in their thinking and need a sense of security, they also tend to be greater risk-takers and more creatively expressive (McLester, 2007).

Millennial learners tend to multitask and learn by doing (Carlson, 2005). They expect to be able to make choices and customize their learning. They tend to learn by doing, and want immediate results; they are also less fearful of failure. In terms of information-seeking, millennials are not intent on looking for the right answer; in fact, they tend to perceive all information as being equal. Likewise, the format of information makes little difference to them in terms of credibility. They expect instant information, and feel comfortable during several tasks simultaneously, yet experience information overload (McLester, 2007). They are high communicators, although their formal knowledge of grammar and speaking may not be well developed. In fact, for most millennials, their overall scholastic goal is "good enough" learning and intellectual "skimming", partly because they feel overstressed and partly because schools themselves do not teach deep learning engagement (Carlson, 2005).

In terms of technology, millennials are considered the first generation of digital natives. The Internet, cell phones, faxes, bar codes high-definition television, and virtual reality have always been around. Indeed, because of the ubiquity of multimedia, millennials tend to use more modalities and think less linearly. A 2005 study by the Kaiser Family Foundation found that youth spend an average of almost six and a half hours daily using media, and in 2003, the Internet surpassed television as the media of choice among teens (Harris Interactive & Teenage Research Unlimited, 2003). When EDUCAUSE surveyed incoming college freshmen in 2006, they discovered that over 98 percent owned computers, and about three-quarters owned a portable music or video storage/player device. They spent an average of eighteen hours weekly online, principally for communicating (Salaway, Caruso, & Nelson, 2007). In 2003 Harris Interactive and Teen Research Unlimited marketers classified millennial media/technology users into six cluster groups:

- Hubs (15%): heaviest Internet users; they want the latest information
- Chic Geeks (16%): rebellious, urban, early technology adaptors with a wide social network; they seek the newest trends
- Miss Insulars (18%): tech fringers; they check if information is accurate
- Alter-ego.coms (14%): heavy Internet users but unconfident; they prefer life online
- IQ Crew (15%): highly educated loners: they want practical information
- Now Crowd (22%): social, suburban heavy media users; they want immediate information

Of course, just because this generation has been surrounded by technology does not mean that they are tech-savvy, and many do not see a need to be so. Males tend to over-rate their technology prowess while females tend to under-rate their ability.

Again, the principle of "good enough" applies to technological use, which also reflects a "need-to-know" assessment and ongoing prioritization of time management. Incoming college freshmen self-report that they know enough technology to do what they need to do, and they tend to think of technology in terms of the context: personal versus academic. Nevertheless, students think that their teachers should become more tech-savvy, and that any student technology knowledge limitations for schoolwork should be remedied by teacher instruction (Salaway, Caruso, & Nelson, 2007).

These experiences with technology color their expectations about online learning. Millennials may need to be taught the difference between social networking for personal reasons and academic discourse. In some cases, personal use of technology might be mentally "siloed" from academic use. In other cases, searching techniques for personal information gathering (e.g., Googling) might be over-generalized when conducting research so that subscription databases might be ignored. Indeed, so many technology strategies in online education exist that it is possible that millennials may assume that they know "all about technology" only to find that they have gaping holes in their technology knowledge bank. Nevertheless, most millennials have little fear of technology so they can presumably explore and learn the technology needed in order to access and manipulate any needed online information.

## HOW ADULTS LEARN

Interestingly, earlier centuries considered children as miniature adults, and taught them through example; children mimicked adults. The idea of *pedagogy* marked a consciousness about the unique aspects of children and the way they learn. Ironically, *andragogy*, the science of adult education, is a late 20th century concept. In fact, many universities still refer to the act of instruction in higher education as pedagogy, which does not recognize the special attributes of adult learners. This reality is especially ironic since the typical online learner is a re-entry, part-time adult (National Center for Educational Statistics, 2002).

Building on growing research about lifelong human development, andragogy pioneer Malcolm Knowles (1990) leveraged the idea of adult self-concept and responsibility to explain the needs of adult learners. Those factors need to be considered when designing instruction for this population.

- *Self-direction.* Adults want to be treated as responsible, self-directed learners. They want to be in control of their learning. Therefore, online instructors should develop a learning environment that provides adults choices in what they learn, how they learn, and how they demonstrate their learning.
- *Experience.* Adults have extensive and diverse experiences, which help them to construct meaning from learning activities. Online instructors should help adult learners identify what they already know, and then build on that knowledge in an online community of learners, each contributing to the group's body of knowledge. In addition, experienced adults build up high expectations, so instructors should be responsive to those demands; in online environments, adults may expect immediate communication so instructors need to give reasonable expectations such as 24-hour response time. Instructors should also realize that adult learners may have experienced negative learning situations, so they have to overcome those negative connotations. This issue happens particularly in light of technology ignorance or past technology failure.
- *Motivation.* Adults are motivated internally: by job needs, personal desire, and

self-esteem. Whenever possible, online instruction should be developed in response to adult interests and needs, and should be offered as an elective. In this scenario, the participants are willing, committed learners, thus offering a positive atmosphere. Particularly since some adults feel threatened by technology, the more that they can *choose* that format rather than have it forced upon them, the more likely they are to succeed.

- *Readiness.* Adults learn when they see a need to learn in order to cope with their lives or improve them. As with motivation, readiness should dictate the creation of learning opportunities. Additionally, learning activities should be contextualized so adults see how it fits into their daily experience; therefore, online instructors should provide opportunities for adult learners to link online content through interactive community-based guest speaker sessions and reflect on their own ways of incorporation through blogs. It should also be noted that online instructors need to incorporate methods of dealing with change especially since that technology-based learning may be unexpected and uncomfortable.
- *Need to know.* Adults need to know what they are going to learn and why they are learning it before they commit to the learning. Therefore, online instructors should have their courses set up on the first day, noting the learning outcomes and benefits of each learning activity.
- *Timing.* Adults have many demands for their time, so need to fit learning within the framework of the rest of their lives. Online instructors need to provide reasonable deadlines and provide a structure that allows for self-pacing.
- *Practical.* Adults appreciate immediate and close transfer of learning and practical instruction. Hands-on, concrete learning activities that are domain-specific work well with adults; therefore, online learning should include opportunities for learners to reality-check online content by testing it in real-world situations.
- *Social.* Adults want their social needs to be met as well as their academic, intellectual needs. Moreover, adults learn through shared knowledge construction. Online instructors should provide interactive structures and opportunities for adult learners to share their thoughts, such as web-based conferencing, discussion threads, blogs, and wikis. By offering these outlets, instructors find that learners are more satisfied with the course and learn more as well. On the negative side, adults may have trouble taking criticism, so instructors need to be sensitive to adult discomfort and make sure that their comments are accessible only to classmates.

Additionally, adults develop cognitively and psychologically throughout their lives. The immediate issues of a thirty-year old, for instance, usually differ from the issues of a sixty-year old. This factor becomes critical in professional development where an entire faculty or professional group is participating. Illustrative examples need to cross generational experiences. Adult development sage Erik Erikson (1980) ascertained a unique set of issues that a person needs to address at each point in life. Beyond adolescence, he identified three stages:

- Young adulthood deals with love: intimacy vs. isolation.
- Adulthood focuses on care: generativity vs. stagnation.

- Old age deals with wisdom: integrity vs. despair.

Psychologist Daniel Levinson (1978) studied men's interaction between their inner life and external events, and identified their development as "seasons in a man's life." Building on Erikson's stages, Levinson detailed three eras. Each stage includes seasons of upheaval and change as well as seasons of stability and synthesis. Implications for online learning follow in italics.

- Early adult: 22-28 years old entering the adult world, 28-33 transitioning between old life structures and new life challenges, 33-40 settling down. *These learners are likely to be tech-savvy or willing to explore new options. Online instructors should emphasize the benefits of skill-building to optimize career options.*
- Middle adult: 40-45 mid-life transition, 45-50 entering middle adulthood, 50-55 transitioning as in early adulthood, 55-60 culmination and peaking of middle adulthood. *Online instructors can show adults how technology can provide them with balance in their lives, both by being more productive as well as using technology for personal growth.*
- Late adult: 60-65 late adult transition, 65 onwards old age. *Older adults can mentor younger learners using web 2.0 tools. These adults are likely to have less hand dexterity, but can use assistive technology if needed. Their cognitive processes may be slower, but the self-pacing aspects of online learning can actually be more comfortable than strict class time learning, particularly if the online course incorporates easy-to-use options for socializing.*

## GENERATIONAL DIFFERENCES

When one also considers the age of an individual within the context of an era, such as reaching adulthood in the 1940s as opposed to reaching it in the 1970s, then the picture becomes even more complex. Each generation exhibits trends of behaviors and expectations. While individual differences trumps any generalization, some patterns do emerge (Hicks & Hicks, 1999).

- Gen Xers (1966-1980) are individualistic career nomads. Self-starting and resourceful, they seek autonomy and purpose.
- Baby Boomers (1946-1965) are the counter-culture turned mainstream, hard-working citizens who still carry a torch for ideals. Continuing to be competitive (because of their numbers), they seek public recognition before it is too late.
- Traditionalists (born 1945 and before) are retiring after loyal service to a single employer, if possible. They tend to be patriotic (partially because of WWII experience) and conforming in behavior.

Nor do these developmental issues take into consideration cultural differences. Each culture has its own rites of passages and adult roles, which may be determined by age, gender, and life situation. When ethnicities are set in different cultures, such as a sixty-year old Chinese woman in a rural village in Western China as opposed to another sixty-year old Chinese woman in a Los Angeles corporate office. Most basic of all, personality, can vary wildly among most groups of individuals.

As the need for continuous education becomes more evident and life spans lengthen, it is possible that four generations of adults may be learning together. Therefore, online instructors need to balance the universal with the particular. To address a diverse group of adult learners, online instructors need to establish a common goal and some common values. They need to provide choices for their learners to personalize their experiences, and elicit from them appropriate examples as well as offer universal illustrations that can resonate for everyone. Online instructors should incorporate social opportunities to help younger adult feel that they belong, to help adults mentor their younger peers, and to enable older learners to share their knowledge. Online communities of learners offer an effective means to implement this model. Additionally, online instructors need to acknowledge differences in processing time as people age. Older learners may need repeated instruction or slower pacing, so online instruction may actually be more effective for them than strict face-to-face sessions.

## ATTITUDES ABOUT TECHNOLOGY

What are the attitudes of adults today toward technology? Today's adults are probably the last generation of electronic immigrants; a generation ago few K-12 schools offered digital technology courses or provided Internet access for students. In 2002 the National Science Foundation conducted an in-depth study of U. S. public attitudes and understanding about science and technology. Here are some of their findings.

- About ninety percent of adults stated that they were interested in new technologies. Those with more science and math education reported higher interest.
- Fewer than fifteen percent felt well informed about the use of new technologies, and about a third thought they were poorly informed. Furthermore, people feel less informed now than before.
- Most adults learn about the newest technology development via television.
- Adults who have home access to the Internet are more positive about technology and know more about science.
- Adults hold stereotypical images about scientists and technology professionals.

It should be noted that having gadgets does not equate to positive technology attitude or competency. A recent survey by the Pew Internet & American Life Project (Horrigan, 2007) found that some people use just a few technology tools, but are very productive and pleased with them; likewise, other people have cell phones, PDAs and other equipment but feel overwhelmed by -- and dissatisfied with – technology as a whole.

Because digital technology is a fairly recent experience for most adults, usually after their initial formal education journey, online instructors may need to explicitly help adults accept technology as a learning tool in order to use it as a means to learn content matter. For some adults, online learning may be out of the question because in their minds the technology itself poses a barrier to learning; if they cannot accept the online environment, adult learners will not be able to have physical and intellectual access to the information itself.

Several models trace adult acceptance of technology and innovation, recognizing the affective domain. Rogers' seminal research on the diffusion of innovation (1962) focused on the individual within the organization. The four factors involved in diffusion included the innovation (new idea, practice, or object), communication channel, time (both decision-making and adoption processes), and the social system. Individuals bring their personality and social characteristics, as well as their perceived need for the innovation as they learn about the innovation, couched within social system norms. As individuals decide whether to accept or reject the innovation; they perceive the innovation's characteristics, including its

- relative advantage over other available tools
- compatibility with social practice
- complexity or ease to learn
- triability before having to commit to it
- observability of its benefits.

Based on these acceptance stages Rogers identified five categories of technology adopters:

- innovators, who see technology's potential and take risks to incorporate it
- early adopters, who model successful integration of technology
- early majority, who think carefully before incorporating technology, and usually do not collaborate
- late majority, who are influenced by peers and external incentives
- laggards, who resist change and have few resources to support change.

A related concerns based adoption model (Hall & Loucks, 1979) posited that people progressed from self concern (awareness, informational, personal) to task concerns (management) to impact concerns (consequence, collaboration, renewal). Nevertheless, the affective domain is an active element throughout the stages since adults' attitudes about impact colors their learning style and collaborative efforts.

Educators need to take these issues into consideration when designing online instruction, differentiating activities to recognize adults' level of acceptance. For instance, learners should be able to demonstrate competence in a variety of ways, choosing a familiar technology approach so that they can focus on the content rather than the technology itself.

## SOCIAL ASPECTS OF TECHNOLOGY USE

Individual technology use is often connected with a collaborative phenomenon, which raises the point about socio-technical systems thinking. This philosophy stipulates that technology in itself has little meaning; it gains its value in socially constructed environments and human interdependence (Pasmore & Sherwood, 1978).

One of the most widely known and researched theoretical bases, Davis's 1989 Technology Acceptance Model (TAM) identified four affective factors that predict intent to use technology: perceived usefulness, perceived ease of use, attitude toward using technology, and subjective norm. The latter factor indicates the degree to which peers and other people around the individual encourage technology acceptance. In that respect, Davis's work recognizes that other people's beliefs impacts one's own attitude and willingness to accept new technologies, even if personally uncomfortable with change in general. In that respect, incorporating web 2.0 features into online instruction can facilitate social acceptance of technology and ease stress that may be experienced in early online learning.

Karahanna, Straub and Chervany (1999) found an interesting connection between individuals and groups relative to pre-and post-adoption attitudes about information technology. Potential technology *adoption* intent was based on normative pressures while technology *user* intent was based their personal attitude. Likewise, pre-adoption attitude drew on a wider spectrum of attitudes about change and innovation (Rogers, 1995) than continuing users, who focused on perceived technology usefulness and on personal improved status. Therefore, instructors need to provide socially-based rationales and incentives for online learning experiences. To that end, online instructors can leverage the wide range of experiences of their students so that veteran online learners can assure new online learners that the benefits of this learning environment outweigh possible disadvantages, thus creating a norm of technology tolerance and acceptance.

Building on TAM, Dennis, Venkatesh and Ramesh (2003) focused on the adoption of collaborative technology. They hypothesized that an individual's belief in the relative usefulness of technology to improve task performance or to attain personal goals would determine their acceptance of that technology. In testing 349 Finns' use of short message services, the researchers found that self-efficacy (perceived ease of use) and immediacy in communicating with others (perceived usefulness) correlated positively with the services' use.

Ajzen and Fishbein (1980) also investigated the affective domain relative to technology acceptance, noting both personal belief systems and response to subjective social norms. Their theory of reasoned action asserted that individual's attitudes about the consequences of behaviors (the extent of success and the value of the outcome) and the influence of others (both in terms of their belief about the outcome and the motivation to comply to other's expectations) led to intent of behavior, such as the use of technology.

It should be noted that the technical ability of encouraging peers (or others in the organization) can negatively impact the affective domain of novice technology users. Wilson, Ryder, McCahan, and Sherry (1996) found that these users resisted accepting and using technology because they felt intimidated and challenged by the 'techno gurus,' and did not value learning strange technical language. Recalling the concerns based adoption model (Hall and Loucks, 1979), these people were at the personal stage of concern where they felt uncertain about the task or their ability to do the tasks.

Bjørn-Andersen, Eason, and Robey (1986) further asserted that technology acceptance depended on the affective aspects of control and enhancement, whereby a feeling of less personal control increased resistance while a sense of self-improvement and contributing facilitated adoption. This issue of control within an organization was addressed in Gould and Lewis's 1985 principles for user-centered instructional systems design; they asserted that early focus be given to users and actual tasks, and that design should be a participatory set of activities incorporating user testing and feedback. Rogers (1962) also advocated broad program development participation and user modification of specific design features. Similarly, Sherry (1998) found that close collaboration between design teams and users led to high local use and adaptation.

These social factors meld well with andragogy, which advocates jointly-constructed education. Applied to online learning environments, adult learners should be encouraged to suggest relevant content and contribute to the collective intelligence of the learning community. Web 2.0 tools should be used to facilitate social interaction and mutual support learning teams.

## CONCLUSION

Learning with technology may be considered from two different standpoints: attitudes toward technology and use of technology to do tasks. The former includes the factors of affinity, confidence, lack of anxiety, and perceived usefulness (Loyd & Gressard, 1986). Another way to approach online learning is in terms of the resources and tools that are available for students that would not be otherwise possible. Technology provides more access to resources, particularly in terms of global information, and it motivates students because of its novelty and multimedia choices.

It should be noted that learner expectations relative to technology have changed over the years. To what extent do today's Millenials differ from prior generations? A more salient question might be: how does the world differ? A key factor is technology. The proverbial Digital Divide is largely a generational issue now, between youth and their elders; if young people want to get their hands on a computer, they can find a way. As Abram and Luther (2004) contend, today's youth were "born with the chip." This same phenomenon impacts learning since youth, in particular, find themselves as technical experts to their parents and teachers; the days of hierarchical transmission of sanctioned knowledge may soon become extinct. Intuitively, this new generation learns experientially, and favors higher-level thinking over facts and rote learning. Indeed, the cutting edge technology user may well be the 14-year old Japanese girl. They have "what William Gibson calls a techno-cultural suppleness – a willingness to grab something new and use it for their own ends" (Mann, 2001, p. 101).

These changes impact education, if for no other reason than students expect to use technology in school. Thus, the greatest challenge may be training older faculty to incorporate technology authentically into learning activities – and to learn in concert with their students. Both in terms of learning approaches as well as technological acceptance and use, Learners' developmental stages need to be considered when designing and implementing online instruction.

Gurian and Henley (2001) surveyed successful teachers about developmentally appropriate educational measures that can facilitate equitable learning. Some of the tips that are applicable to online education are as follows.

**Kindergarten**:

1. Foster experiential learning through hands-on learning environments (e.g., object-based manipulatives, puzzles, games).
2. Have children use digital cameras to capture positive behavior and learning.
3. Channel children's energy positively
4. Let children express their feelings; use emoticons to identify and express moods.

**Elementary grades**:

1. Encourage kinesthetic learning, including whole-body movement and engagement.
2. Provide opportunities for a variety of positive online learning experiences that use competitive, cooperative, and individual effort.
3. Provide many, varied writing experiences.
4. Encourage storytelling.
5. Be sensitive to children who do not act in stereotypical gendered ways, and accept their differences.

**Middle school**:

1. Express high expectations both academically and socially.
2. Provide positive rite-of-passage experiences.
3. Facilitate one-on-one mentoring using social networking.
4. Teach social and tension coping skills.
5. Ensure equitable computer access and training.
6. Balance sedentary and active learning experiences.

**High school**:

1. Incorporate service learning.
2. Help students learn and practice communication and negotiation skills.
3. Encourage and facilitate intellectual risk-taking.
4. Facilitate online one-on-one mentors, and introduce adult role models reflecting a wide variety of interests and skills (e.g., male nurses, women engineers, single fathers, women sky-divers).

**Adult education**:

1. Involve learners in instructional design and implementation.
2. Create a professional learning community structure that offers practical contexts.
3. Provide opportunities for socializing and its role in collective intelligence.
4. Provide choice in content resources and methods of demonstrating competence.
5. Design the course to facilitate self-pacing and self-monitoring.

## REFERENCES


Abram, S., & Luther, J. (2004). Born with the chip. *Library Journal, 129*(8), 34–37.

Ajzen, I., & Fishbein, M. (1980). *Understanding attitudes and predicting social behavior*. Englewood Cliffs, NJ: Prentice-Hall.

American Academy of Child and Adolescent Psychiatry. (2003). *Facts for families*. Washington, DC: American Academy of Child and Adolescent Psychiatry. Retrieved from http://www.aacap.org

American Association for the Advancement of Science. (1999). *Dialogue on early childhood science, mathematics, and technology education*. Washington, DC: American Association for the Advancement of Science.

Ames, P. (2003). The role of learning style in university students' computer attitudes: Implications relative to the effectiveness of computer-focused and computer-facilitated instruction. (Doctoral dissertation, The Claremont Graduate University, 2003). *ProQuest Dissertations and Theses* (AAT 3093249).

Besharov, D. (Ed.). (1999). *America's disconnected youth*. Washington, DC: CWLA Press.

Bjørn-Andersen, N., Eason, K., & Robey, D. (Eds.). (1986). *Managing computer impact: An international study of management and organizations*. Norwood, NJ: Ablex.

Carlson, S. (2005). The next generation goes to college. *The Chronicle of Higher Education, 52*(7), A34–A37.

Casey, J. (1997). *Early literacy: The empowerment of technology*. Englewood, CO: Libraries Unlimited.

Chatman, E. (1996). The impoverished lifeworld of outsiders. *Journal of the American Society for Information Science American Society for Information Science, 47*, 193–206. doi:10.1002/(SICI)1097-4571(199603)47:3<193::AID-ASI3>3.0.CO;2-T

Davis, F. (1989). Perceived usefulness, perceived ease of use, and user acceptance of information technology. *Management Information Systems Quarterly, 13*(3), 319–339. doi:10.2307/249008

Dennis, A., Venkatesh, V., & Ranesh, V. (2003, March 4). *Adoption of collaboration technologies: Integrating technology acceptance and collaboration*. Bloomington, IN: Rob Kling Center for Social Informatics.

Erikson, E. (1980). *Identity and the life cycle*. New York, NY: Norton.

Farmer, L. (2007). Developmental social-emotional behavior and information literacy. In Nahl, D., & Bilal, D. (Eds.), *Information and emotion: The emergent affective paradigm in information behavior research and theory* (pp. 99–120). Medford, NJ: Information Today.

Gambone, M., Klem, A. L., & Connell, J. (2002). *Finding out what matters for youth*. Philadelphia, PA: Youth Development Strategies.

Girl Scout Research Institute. (2002). *The community connection: Volunteer trends in a changing world*. New York, NY: Girl Scouts of the U.S.A.

Gould, J., & Lewis, C. (1985). Designing for usability: Key principles and what designers think. *Communications of the ACM, 29*(3), 300–311. doi:10.1145/3166.3170

Gurian, M., & Henley, P. (2001). *Boys and girls learn differently! A guide for teachers and parents*. San Francisco, CA: Jossey-Bass.

Hall, G., & Loucks, S. (1979). *Implementing innovations in schools: A concerns-based approach.* Austin, TX: Research and Development Center for Teacher Education, University of Texas.

Harris Interactive and Teenage Research Unlimited. (2003). *Born to be wired.* Sunnyvale, CA: Yahoo.

Hicks, R., & Hicks, K. (1999). *Boomers, xers and other strangers*. Wheaton, IL: Tyndale House.

Horrigan, J. (2007). *A typology of information and communication technology users.* Washington, DC: Pew Internet and American Life Project. Retrieved from http://pewinternet.rg/pdfs/PIP_ICT_Typology.pdf

James, C. (1974). *Beyond custom*. New York, NY: Agathon Press.

Kaiser Family Foundation. (2005). *Generation M.* Menlo Park, CA: Kaiser Family Foundation.

Karahanna, E., Straub, D., & Chervany, N. (1999). Information technology adoption across time: A cross-sectional comparison of pre-adoption and post-adoption beliefs. *Management Information Systems Quarterly, 23*(2), 183–213. doi:10.2307/249751

Knowles, M. (1990). *The adult learner* (4th ed.). Houston, TX: Gulf Publishing.

Levinson, D. (1978). *The seasons of a man's life*. New York, NY: Knopf.

Loyd, B., & Gressard, C. (1984). The effects of sex, age, and computer experience on computer attitudes. *AEDS Journal, 18*(2), 67–77.

Mann, C. (2001, August). Why 14-year-old Japanese girls rule the world. *Yahoo! Internet Life,* 99-103.

McLester, S. (2007). Technology literacy and the MySpace generation. *Technology & Learning, 27*(8), 17–22.

National Center for Educational Statistics. (2002). *Distance education at degree-granting postsecondary institutions: 2000-2001*. Washington, DC: U.S Department of Education, National Center for Educational Statistics.

National School Boards Association. (2007). *Creating and connecting*. Washington, DC: National School Boards Association.

National Science Foundation. (2003). *NSF's program for gender equity in science, technology, engineering and mathematics*. Washington, DC: National Science Foundation.

Ousley, M. (2006). Hope for a more equitable society. *Journal of College & Character, 7*(4), 1–10.

Pasmore, W., & Sherwood, J. (Eds.). (1978). *Sociotechnical systems: A sourcebook*. San Diego, CA: University Associates.

Phelan, P., Davidson, A., & Yu, Y. (1998). *Adolescents' worlds: Negotiating family, peers, and school*. New York, NY: Teachers College Press.

Rainie, L. (2006). *Digital natives.* Washington, DC: Pew Internet and American Life Project. Retrieved from http://www.pewinternet.org/PPF/r/71/presentation_display.asp

Rogers, E. (1962). *Diffusion of innovations*. New York, NY: Free Press.

Salaway, G., Curuseo, J., & Nelson, M. (2007). *The ECAR study of undergraduate students and information technology, 2007*. Boulder, CO: EDUCAUSE.

Sherry, L. (1998). An integrated technology adoption and diffusion model. *International Journal of Educational Telecommunications, 4*(2/3), 113–145.

Simpson, R. (2001). *Raising teens: Development, relationships, and culture* (9th ed.). Boston, MA: Harvard Center for Health Communication.

Sousa, D. (2001). *How the brain learns* (2nd ed.). Thousand Oaks, CA: Corwin Press.

Van Scoter, J., & Ellis, D. (2001). *Technology in early childhood*. Portland, OR: Northwest Regional Education Laboratory.

Williams-Boyd, P. (Ed.). (2003). *Middle grades education*. Santa Barbara, CA: ABC-CLIO.

Wilson, B., Ryder, M., McCahan, J., & Sherry, L. (1996). *Cultural assimilation of the Internet*. Paper presented at the AECT InCITE '96 Conference, Indianapolis, IN.

# Chapter 12
# Engaging Traditional Learning and Adult Learning via Information Technologies

**Judith Parker**
*Columbia University, USA*

## ABSTRACT

*Student engagement is a key factor in learning whether it involves traditional or adult learners. While the role of the teacher may differ, it is primarily the responsibility of the teacher to engage the student by fostering a positive student-teacher relationship and supportive classroom culture conducive to engagement. Discovering a methodology that is effective with individual students can be challenging, but Information Technology provides a plethora of new tools to assist in achieving this goal. This chapter will illustrate the importance of engagement, provide several examples in various venues and investigate the role of Information Technology in this process.*

## INTRODUCTION

This chapter will build on the themes of traditional learning, adult learning and information technology from previous chapters but the theme of "engaging" adds a new and important dimension to the discussion. Good educational practice engages students. Information technologies have the capability to enrich that engagement or block it.

The responsibility for engaging the student is primarily that of the teacher who must create an environment that fosters a positive student-teacher relationship and that supports a classroom culture conducive to engagement. These two responsibilities can be compared to two general models for interaction. The concept of gravity can be explained by two different models proposed

DOI: 10.4018/978-1-60960-791-3.ch012

by two physicists. Isaac Newton's explanation envisioned two distinct objects in the universe. The gravitational force between them depended on the mass of each object and the distance between them. Albert Einstein's explanation involved a continuum of space. Any object in space distorts the space. A second object's motion through the space was affected by the distortion of the space.

An analogy can be made to the teacher-learner relationship in which it is assumed that one object is the instructor and the other is the student. The Newtonian analogy considers the individual interaction between a student and an instructor in which each has an equal role in the process and responsibility for the outcome. This parallels an adult learning model or andragogy. The analogy to Einstein's view sees the instructor as warping the space/time of the real or virtual classroom by setting up an environment conducive to learning. The effect is the attraction (engagement) of the student. This chapter will discuss both methods of engagement for both traditional and adult learning and then the influence of information technologies.

## LEARNING

Research on the cognitive functions of the human brain have provided insights into the learning process and as such have informed the development of learning theories, inventories and the effective use of instructional technology. In a recent article in *Science*, Schneps, Griswold, Finkelstein, McLeod, and Schrag (May 28, 2010) explain that there is a disconnect between the linear traditional instructional methodology and the more haphazard process by which people really learn. They report that "our knowledge builds from conflicting ideas that we weigh, one against the other, so that the understanding that emerges is the weighted sum of probabilistic beliefs" (p. 1119). Yet, they point out that "all too often instruction assumes that students build knowledge sequentially, from one prerequisite idea to the next, in a linear, hierarchical manner that mirrors the design of traditional textbooks and lectures" (p. 1119).

Jarvis (2009) notes that "as a psychologist I recognized that all the psychological models of learning were flawed, including Kolb's well-known learning cycle, in as much as they omitted the social and the interaction" (p. 23). However, Merriam, Caffarella, and Baumgarten (2007) note that learning styles inventories have "proved useful in helping learners and instructors alike become aware of their personal learning styles and their strengths and weaknesses as learners and teachers" (p. 409). They note that Kolb's Learning Styles Inventory is the "most often used instrument to assess learning styles in adult education and classified learning styles into four different categories: accommodators, divergers, convergers, and assimilators" (p. 408). Honey and Mumford (1989) developed a learning styles inventory based on Kolb's learning styles. Their four styles were labeled activist, reflector, theorist and pragmatist. They were motivated by the conviction that "people should be helped to learn effectively rather than be exposed to inappropriate learning experiences, or be given learning experiences without learning how to use their learning strengths" (p. 1). After they guide the learner through scoring the inventory, they then provide suggestions for the learner on selecting learning activities that would be consistent with their preferred style as well as suggesting how the learner might improve each style for which they had a lower score. Merriam, Caffarela, and Baumgarten (2007) also note that the Myers-Briggs Type Indicator is the "most often used measure to assess learning styles based on psychological type preferences" (p. 408). But, they also note that "learning styles may be in part culturally based" (p. 408).

Lee (2009) notes three approaches for learners: didactic, Socratic, and facilitative. The didactic is synonymous with lecture in which the instructor controls both the direction and content of the learning. In the Socratic approach, the instructor directs the learner by using a series of questions.

The facilitative method requires that instructors limit their roles to create an environment in which learning can occur.

At the end of the day, after all the analysis, how this is put into practice is the most important. Brookfield (2006) advises what "skillful teaching boils down to whatever helps students learn, that the best teachers adapt a critically reflective stance towards their practice, and that the most important knowledge we need to do good work is an awareness of how students are experiencing their learning and our teaching" (p. xvii). These three core principles place power in the hands of the teacher but can also be used to empower the student.

## Traditional Learning and the Teacher-Student Relationship

Whether the objective of the learning involves content knowledge or skills, in the traditional setting, the instructor is the source of that knowledge or skills and imparts it to the student by lectures or demonstrations. A hierarchical structure exists with the teacher in the power position over the student. Brookfield (2006) dedicates an entire chapter of his book to "dealing with the politics of teaching" (p. 235). He defines a political process as "one in which someone attempts to persuade, direct, or coerce someone else into devoting scarce resources into a particular activity" (p. 236) and notes that "teachers are people who constantly try to influence learners into devoting their resources – their money (in the form of tuition), their energy, their time – into studying a particular subject or developing a particular skill. As they pursue these objectives, they exercise power to organize the classroom a certain way." (p. 236). This power manifests itself in the teacher-student relationship which directly impacts learning. In many academic and organizational settings, this relationship can provide very positive results. Sequences of courses require a strict adherence to specific topics. Specific skill sets are required for many jobs.

## Traditional Learning with the Teacher Setting the Environment

In this model the teacher functions primarily in a facilitator role. Schneps, Griswold, Finkelstein, McLeod, and Schrag (May 28, 2010) note that "while the traditional approach to instruction presents ideas in a linear progression, we make sense of this material through a process that is much more malleable and fluid and is subject to many more influences that we currently understand or acknowledge. This process of nonlinear reasoning, inherent in science, mirrors how the human brain makes meaning from sensory inputs" (p. 1119). These influences could be managed by the instructor to support learning.

Brookfield (2006) reminds us that the three core assumptions of skillful teaching apply equally to all forms of teaching. "Good teaching is whatever helps students learn, good teaching is critically reflective, and the most important knowledge teachers need to do good work is how students experience their learning" (pp. 196-197). Focusing on the third of these assumptions provides an insight into the teacher's role in setting the environment for learning. Later in this chapter, methods for discovering how the student is experiencing learning will be discussed.

## Adult Learning and the Teacher-Student Relationship

Adult learning is characterized by Knowles (2005) six core andragogical principles: "the learner's need to know, self-directed learning, prior experience of the learner, readiness to learn, orientation to learning and problem solving, and motivation to learn" (p.183). This last principle of motivation will be the focus of Chapter 13. However, all of these impose a responsibility on the instructor to gain knowledge about the students in the classroom.

Some of that knowledge might be viewed in light of predetermined categories. Lee (2009) segments learners by age and warns that "catering for all of their needs and ensuring they are all engaged is a challenge which is only now beginning to be researched. How this will be achieved in an ever decreasing time-span is yet to be determined" (p. 46). In one case he distinguishes "traditional learners", those focusing on "tradition, the antiquated (the past in general), the exotic, the sacred, the unusual, and the place of the local rather than the general or universal" from "traditional learners" from the "post-modern learners" who are "consumed with their own lives and less concerned with old loyalties" (p. 41) and suggests ways for adult educators to engage these different learners. However, he further suggests that further research is needed to be able to engage learners in 4 distinct categories: traditionalists (1925-43); Baby Boomers (1943-64); Generation X (1965-80), Generation Y (after 1980). He suggests that because these groups have been influenced by different significant world events, they will have different needs and interests. (p. 45). He adds another layer of complexity by suggesting that "as the technology and environment changes so will the needs and composition of the adult learners" (p. 46).

In addition to this knowledge about the student and content knowledge, the teacher also brings a professional persona to the classroom which can influence learning. Brookfield (2006) notes two factors as creditability and authenticity and notes that students value these two characteristics in teachers. Indicators of teachers' credibility include their expertise, experience, and rationale for classroom decisions and conviction. Common indicators of authenticity are congruence between words and actions, full disclosure of expectations and assumptions that guide practice, responsiveness of teaching to students' learning and personhood. Cranton and Carusetta (2004) expresses similar ideas in suggesting that authenticity has four parts: "being genuine, showing consistency between values and actions, relating to others in such a way as to encourage their authenticity, and living a critical life" (p. 7). They also reinforce the importance of authenticity and connect it to transformative learning.

Schneps, Griswold, Finkelstein, McLeod, and Schrag (May 28, 2010) note that "our brains appear to be wired so as to resolve ambiguity – actively filling in detail with information that is peripherally observed – to build an understanding that is consistent with our experience" (p.1120). The challenge of using these as a foundation for a teacher-student relationship in order to engage the learners using information technologies will be discussed later in this chapter.

## Adult Learning with the Teacher Setting the Environment

In an adult learning venue, an important role of the teacher is to create the environment for learning but also to continue to ensure that that environment remains positive through the entire course. Brookfield (2006) suggests using the Critical Incident Questionnaire to continually monitor the classroom environment and "gives you a running commentary on the emotional tenor of each class you deal with" (p. 41). He suggests using it at the end of each class or each week as appropriate. A few simple questions request that students focus on specific events or incidents that "engaging, distancing, confusing, or helpful" (p. 42). Responses can be read by the instructor and discussed at the next class. It is not only a feedback tool for the instructor but engages the student in their own learning and reflective practice about its success.

Illeris (2009) emphasizes the complexity of the classroom climate by noting that "all three learning dimensions must be taken into account, that the question of relevant learning types must be included, that possible defense or resistance must be considered and that internal as well as external learning conditions must also be dealt with" (p. 18). He focuses on the importance of both internal and external learning conditions. Intelligence, including Gardner's idea of multiple intelligences, and learning styles are examples of internal conditions. External conditions include the "features of the immediate learning situation and learning space and more general cultural and societal conditions" (p. 17).

Kling and Courtright (2004) continue this theme but include two models contrasting conceptions of the internet. The "standard model" is described as one that "allows people to engage in many of the activities that they have traditionally performed offline, including conversation, work, commerce, hobbies, meetings, worship, reading, and learning, yet without the usual constraints of space and time" (p. 92). The "socio-technical model" features environments that are "populated by many different kinds of spaces, each structured both socially and technically" (p. 95). These include websites with information, those that support more open communication, online games, and electronic forums. Both can be useful in engaging learning.

Usher, R. (2009) focuses on the importance of environment especially in experiential learning. "As a pedagogy, experiential learning has the capacity to unsettle the established order and hence has a transformative potential" (p. 175). Therefore there are "...necessary preconditions for experiential learning" which include "creating sufficient student security and self-confidence... and at least an outline theoretical framework from which to examine and understand student experience" (p 182).

Whether in the classroom or online, this focus on communication, the environment and community must be given careful consideration. Barab, Kling, and Gray (2004) emphasize that "someone external cannot simply impose a pre-designed community onto a group, but rather community is something that must evolve from within a group around their particular needs and for purposes that they value as meaningful" (p. 5). Kling and Courtright (2004) consider that "the casual use of the term community to characterize groups that are engaged in learning, or groups that participate in e-forums, is seriously misguided. As we shall see, developing a group into a community is a major accomplishment that requires special processes and practices, and the experience is often both frustrating and satisfying for many of the participants" (p. 91).

## ISSUES AND EXAMPLES OF ENGAGING LEARNING VIA INFORMATION TECHNOLOGY

### Information Technologies

Information technology is used to access information, disseminate information in the classroom and on-line in both the traditional and andragogical tradition. The emergence of information technology has spawned entirely new departments which have become integral parts of the infrastructure of every institution whether academic or business or non-profit. Information technology has changed how data is recorded and analyzed and stored. It has changed how ideas are communicated from formal written messages where vocabulary and style were important to today's instant messaging environment with a cryptic style focused on speed of creation and transmission. All of these features have impacted traditional learning and adult learning. A previous chapter recounts how technological advances allowed information technology hardware to become smaller and smaller. This miniaturization and relatively low cost have promoted the quick, instantaneous but abbreviated communication that allows the instructor and the student to share new information with peers and with each other.

## Engaging Learning

Learner engagement might at first glance seem like an ultimate goal that might be mostly unachievable. It could be compared to Maslow's "self-actualization" at the very peak of his hierarchical triangle. But if engagement is examined in light of the familiar classroom setting, students can be categorized as attending, participating or engaged. Most instructors have had experience with all three categories and can easily identify them when they see them. The attending student is there, nothing more and nothing less. Attendance might be mandatory for the job or the course is a prerequisite for a program or degree. The participating student answers questions, completes assignments, fulfils the minimum requirements to "pass" the course or receive a completion certificate. The engaged learner asks insightful questions, searches for additional information, attends extra activities, and participates fully in discussions and building a sense of community within the classroom. Although referring to an online situation, Conrad's (2004) description is applicable to any environment. He notes that "engaged learning stimulates learners to actively participate in the learning situation, and thus gain the most knowledge from being a member of an online community" (p.7).

Engagement can be purely intellectual or it can be transformational. Mezirow (2009) explains that "Transformative learning theory as I have conceptualized it, holds that cultures enable or inhibit the realization of common human interests – the ways adults realize common learning capabilities. Transformative learning is a rational, metacognitive process of reassessing reasons that support problematic meaning perspectives or frames of reference, including those representing such contextual cultural factors as ideology, religion, politics, class, race, gender and others. It is the process by which adults learn how to think critically for themselves rather than take assumptions supporting a point of view for granted" (p. 103). At its best, engaging learning would be transformational. This engagement can happen either because the topic is engaging or the methodology is engaging. Both of these will be discussed below with examples of each in various venues.

## Engaging Learning through Engaging Topics

An example of engaging learning through an engaging topic can be found in a new course developed by the instructor titled Astronomy in Action: Observing and analyzing light from the night sky. This course was especially designed for the non-science major who wants to explore and experience real astronomical observations. By collaborating with a local Amateur Astronomical Association, the college physics department was able to offer this course as a blend of on campus classroom lectures and labs with use of the astronomy association's telescopes and spectrometer at their observatory located minutes from campus. This course was scheduled for 10 weeks to allow for several weeks of classroom time at the beginning and end of the course and several weeks for observing time and independent/group research in the middle. Topics included the history, nature and properties of light, the use of reflection and refraction in telescopes, spectral analysis to determine the temperature, chemical composition of objects in the sky, planets, stars and nebula. The study was supported by laboratory experiments on stellar spectra and night sky observing. The course design was intended to be very self-directed. Students would do a literature review on the specific telescope(s) to be used, the spectrometer to be used, and the objects to be studied. The observatory research included a schedule of 4 nights at off campus observatory (this will allow for 2 nights of observing and data collection with alternate rain/cloud days), calibrate spectrometer, take spectra, analyze spectra. Students would then prepare a report/

presentation to include introduction, literature review, methodology, analysis, results. Weather will affect the schedule. The software to graph the data will require some learning. What we observe depends on what is visible at this time of year. Just as action learning uses a real problem as the engaging element, this astronomy course uses interesting topics and opportunities for hands on experimentation. This engaging topic assumes that the research component will be engaging but it requires a comfort with the ambiguity by the students and instructor.

A very different yet equally important example is the graduate Staff Development course taught by the author. While some students are clearly at the attendance and barely participating stage, many are engaged because they see the applicability of their learning in their work. When the course is taught online, it is particularly populated by working adult students who are engaged because they feel a need for the information and experience of learning about and developing a training module. In many cases, the result of their class assignment, their training module, is actually used in their workplace so it demonstrates an increased skill developed in the course.

## Engaging Learning Methodology Case Study

While organizational culture is often cited as important for an effective training program, so is departmental culture within that organization. This culture of a strong learning ethic can be evidenced in a number of ways. At 3M, this culture had been developing for more than a decade when the group responsible for the education and development of the company's laboratory employees were reassigned from the corporate human resources department to become part of the company's research and development organization. This provided a unique opportunity to leverage the climate of creativity and innovation that had long been a hallmark of the R & D group in order to develop the creative and innovative global technical education programs. Strong sponsorship from the international research and development vice-president created the environment conducive to integrating new methodologies including technology into learning. Some of the learning activities that emerged are highlighted in this and other chapters by this author.

Often, engaging students in something that someone else has created can be challenging. One strategy for engaging learners is to provide them with the opportunity to be involved in the creation of the learning project. An example of such a project was a training program developed at 3M for Global Technical Service employees (Parker, 1997) within the department described above. The course objective was to train approximately 1,700 3M technical service employees around the globe in their role in the technical service function. Employees needed to receive a consistent message about their roles and their careers. The employees worked in very diverse situations. Some worked in a laboratory or technical center while others were in locations removed geographically from any corporate facilities. Some employees had easier access to a computer than others. Employees had a wide range of facility with the English language.

The use of interactive multimedia with a companion workbook was selected as the best mode of delivery to address these issues. However employees globally were engaged in every aspect of the course development. The course was developed by partnering with a multimedia organization in the U.K. which gave the project an instant international flavor rather than something developed at the headquarters in the U.S. and shipped around the world. Having a vendor with expertise in both curriculum development and technology was essential as was their openness to understanding the culture of the organization. Once the content was organized, examples of best technical services practices were identified and filmed in various locations around the world. The strategy was to use existing 3M video assets when available and to film real 3M employees telling their stories and best practices during their technical service careers. Photos from Neuss, Germany; video from Bracknell, U.K. and St. Paul, MN were utilized. 3M employees were interviewed in St. Paul, Antwerp, and Neuss. These factors added to the global feel of the course and employees were able to identify colleagues outside of the headquarters throughout the course. The objective was that students/employees would connect with their own culture in at least one of the modules of the course. The intent was also to provide the foundation for a learning community within the geographical regions and also internationally. The workbook was based on the work of the Technical Service chapter of the European Technical Managers council and supported this international flavor by including a list of every 3M employee who participated in the course by name and location.

The use of a Compact Disc Interactive with its stand-alone plug-in-and-play hardware provided the best hardware solution. Portable CD-I players were purchased and placed in technical centers and technical libraries around the globe (St. Paul, MN; Austin, TX; England; Neuss, Hamburg, and Borken, Germany; Belgium; Italy, France, Australia, New Zealand, Singapore, Philippines, Taiwan, China, Hong Kong, Korea, India, Thailand, Mexico, Argentina, Brazil, Chile, Columbia, Costa Rica, Puerto Rico, Venezuela, and South Africa). Some countries purchased one or more additional units. Employees in countries without a technical center borrow the portable players.

Careful attention was paid to the course introduction, registration, and completion to promote a sense of inclusion and foster engagement throughout the process. The course was announced at the Asia Technical Managers Meeting in March and at the European Technical Managers council in June. In July, a mailing was sent to all 3M U.S. technical employees and to the mailing lists of the technical managers in Europe and Asia with a course description and registration details. To register, employees were to complete and fax a registration form to the Technical Development Department in St. Paul, MN. And designate a particular month that they would like to take the course. Registrants immediately received a faxed acknowledgement of the receipt of the registration and were told that a workbook and additional course information would be mailed about a week before the month indicated on the registration.

Near the end of every month, all the registrants for the following month were entered on a class list with their name, contact information, city and country. A class list, a course workbook, and a country-specific letter with instructions about the course and location of the CD-I player and course discs were sent to each registrant. Assignments throughout the course encourage employees to contact another employee on the class list and "discuss" by phone or email the suggested topics related to the course content. Experienced technical service employees who have completed the course can volunteer to be mentors. Approximately twice a year, they are assigned eight to ten students for a month and asked to contact them, introduce themselves as a mentor for the course, and volunteer to answer any questions. These class lists and assignments are intended to create a global class across international boundaries.

Upon course completion, employees complete and returned course evaluations to the headquarters. Employees sign in to the course with their employee number each time they take a section of the course. The CD-I hardware kept track of their pre-and post-text scores from each disc and which sections they completed. A completion diploma disc was mailed to employees when they successfully completed the course.

From a project management perspective, many strategies worked successfully. Announcements were published and distributed widely so everyone had equal access to information. But employees were encouraged to register to ensure that several people were participating in the course at each location but not too many so they are frustrated at the unavailability of hardware. New information about the course such as awards, student comments, statistics, etc., was continually published so there was continued awareness. Remote management is very similar whether development is taking place across town or across oceans – the communication distance is just a little longer. The project management included a combination of meetings, fax, phone calls, emails, and large file distribution between locations. Whatever information technology was available at that location was used to promote engagement throughout the course.

The project was successful enough that a second training project using the same methodologies was planned to focus on toxicology issues around the globe. The course was intended to ensure that 3M employees consider and react appropriately to toxicology issues at every stage in the life-cycle of a product from conception to disposal. It included sections on the mission and history of Toxicology Services and its role in adding value to the product and in government advocacy. Again, 3M case studies from around the globe were used to illustrate the use of material safety data sheets, global labeling, and risk assessment and foster a sense of engagement by employees at every location. The registration procedure was the same as that for the "Innovation Formula" but the audience was actually broader. The course was necessary for every technical employee within 3M, not just technical service, but also was intended to be a tool for sales and marketing when working with customers and government officials.

## Engaging Learning in the Corporate Classroom

While lecturing is often viewed as less than engaging, the case has been made in previous chapters for its necessity and often its being the preferred methodology for achieving an educational objective. Lecturing can and must be engaging. While the fact that there is no learning without engagement appears obvious, however instructors are often so eager to get to the content that little effort is focused on the engagement. As a technical development manager at 3M, the author was often faced with the challenge of engaging learners in very technical subjects. The motivation for the learner was often that the visiting instructor was a recognized expert in his or her technical field so the knowledge learned would be state of the art. However, a colleague in the sales training department was very aware of the engagement issue. One day, he was defending his department's use of what might be viewed as excessive active learning in all his sales training programs. Realizing that this was often criticized by others, his insightful defense was that if he didn't have his audience's attention, it was useless to attempt to deliver any content. He understood that for a group of high energy sales people, keeping them active and engaged was essential to learning.

## Engaging Learning in Higher Education

As mentioned above, students might be classified as attending, participating, or engaged in a learning activity. Often they enter the classroom, whether real or virtual, with the attitude that would label them with one of these classifications. If the objective of the instructor is to have as many students as possible at the engaged level by the first moment of class, some preparation is necessary. Using the email feature in a learning management system, the instructor emails all enrolled students about a week before the beginning of the class. The email begins with a light hearted statement that if they are enjoying the last precious days of their summer vacation or between semester break, then they should read no further, not open the attachment and enjoy. They are then told to log into the course on the first official day of the semester. The next paragraph begins with the note that if however they are anxious about the course requirements or want to order their textbook early, the syllabus is attached. They are encouraged to email any questions or concerns. The objective is to be proactive in engaging the student in the class community yet to be respectful of the fact that for working adults, this may be their only break with family or just to relax. Another welcoming and informational email is sent the first day of the course to engage any late registrants and those who had chosen to ignore the earlier email.

Engagement can also be accomplished by allowing the students to participate in the decision making. Students in both the graduate courses that the author teaches both online and on campus are allowed to make decisions about their grade and their activities. In the Staff Development course, one assignment requires students to select, read and post a summary and reflection on two journal articles related to staff development in an area in which they are interested. While most of the course reading is in a required text, this allows the student to investigate staff development in business, health care, higher education, etc. In the Introduction to Adult and Continuing Education course, the students have several core assignments that must be completed. In addition they must do one or two papers. Submitting two quality papers will ensure them a grade of A or B. Submitting one quality paper will ensure them a grade of B or C. Busy students who are confident about their grade on other assignments will frequently opt for one quality paper. They feel empowered and the instructor is not reading two mediocre papers which would have resulted in a grade of B for the student as well. When either of these courses is taught online, students have the option of substituting any of their threaded discussions about the assigned readings with a text chat or web-conferencing discussion. Students become engaged because they must take the initiative to contact others in the class who might want to join them as well as set up the logistics of the synchronous activity.

In the spirit of authenticity discussed above, it is important for the instructor to role model what is being taught about adult learning theory and practice. The instructor's role in setting the climate of the classroom is extremely important here. If creativity is to be encouraged, a safe environment must be established to encourage the student to try some new technology or incorporate one of Brookfield's discussion techniques into a training module. The spirit of learning should be emphasized as more important than perfection.

## Role of Information Technologies in Engagement

In the case of several of the students in an online graduate level course, they reveal that they are taking an online course in order to experience an online course. This is encouraged by the instructor because it is important that professionals in human resource fields have the experience in order to reflect on it and make informed decisions in the future. But as engaging as information technology can be to some, it can set up barriers to others. In an end of course survey, one student admitted almost apologetically that one important lesson from the course was that she never wanted to do that again. This was a valuable insight that would inform her decision making for her and possibly others in the future. It is important not to be an advocate of the use of any form of informational technology just as it is not advisable to be an advocate of any particular methodology like lecture or discussion. As has been emphasized previously, the decision of what methodology should be used should be linked to the course objectives. The comfort level of the instructor and students should also be considered.

Within the past year, an astronomy student proudly displayed his "droid" with a star chart "app" which allowed him to point the "droid" in any direction and the GPS feature of his droid allowed the screen to display the portion of the sky with constellation, planets, etc. He noted the obvious advantage over the computer software we had been using in the classroom which required purchasing the software, setting the location of the observer as well as the observer's date and time. Not to mention having to drag the laptop around the outdoors. Actually a student this past semester reported that he had in fact done just that. In search of a dark sky devoid of light pollution, he took his laptop to a park location adjacent to his property for better viewing of the sky but then had to explain his adventure to the park police after a neighbor called and reported that he could see some guy with an laptop screen glowing in the dark who was walking around in the park in back of his property glancing consistently between the laptop and the sky.

Another example is evident in an online course offered by a museum which utilizes Google Maps to model solar system distances onto the earth's surface. Students use an online calculator from another museum website to facilitate their calculations and then plot the locations on a U.S. map using the scaled distances. Their hometown is the location of the Sun and the planets are positioned at the appropriate locations. The scaled distances reinforce the vast scale of our solar system and provide a model for similar exercises. Many of the students in this course are pre or in service teachers so not only do they become engaged in the activity but they are able to adapt the ideas from this assignment to their own classrooms. Since other aspects of this course involve video, it is useful to note that Schneps, Griswold, Finkelstein, McLeod, and Schrag (May 28, 2010) describe a video project of the Science Media Group at the Harvard-Smithsonian Center for Astrophysics which is "investigating how to make effective use of video-based materials to convey difficult ideas in science" (p. 1119). They note that their project is fueled by the "explosive growth" in the number of online courses and the need to produce materials that are effective in this venue. These are only a few examples of information technology's role in enhancing engaging learning. The future will likely offer more creative examples.

The Quality Matters website reports that Rovae and Jordan (2004) investigated the sense of community felt by 68 graduate students enrolled in a traditional, a fully online, and a hybrid course. They found that students in the hybrid course felt a stronger sense of community than students in the other two learning formats, An ever expanding list of virtual locations and tools are emerging to facilitate these hybrid courses. Some platforms such as Eluminate or Adobe-connect allow a whitescreen for presentation during a webconferencing as well as space for discussion. Is the concept of face-to-face instruction expanding to include faces on a computer screen interacting as if they were in a classroom?

## FUTURE TRENDS

Blumenfeld notes that "there is both an art and a science in examining what lies ahead. Such an exploration of future possibilities is integral to our modern consciousness. Any critical look at future projections, however, demands that one knows who is making predictions and what their motives are" (p. 11). He also notes that the visionary director of the Media Lab at Massachusetts Institute of Technology "stresses that the world of tomorrow means connectivity, or immediate access in communications. He is very much aware that futurologists can be led astray when they rely too heavily on technology and not enough on human values" (p. 21).

Barab, Kling, and Gray (2004) suggest that "we are currently in an exciting time in which pedagogical theory and technological advances have created an opportunity to design innovative and powerful environments to support learning" (p. 13). However, they caution that it is important to remain "optimistic and visionary while at the same time avoiding hyperbole and unsubstantiated assumptions" (p. 13). In that cautionary tone, the Quality Matters' (2009) website provides a rubric for evaluating the quality of an online course that includes a section on learner engagement. It delineates four items with relative point values that warrant attention. 1. The learning activities promote the achievement of the stated learning objectives. (3 points) 2. Learning activities foster instructor-student, content-student, and if appropriate to the course, student-student interaction. (3 points) 3. Clear standards are set for instructor responsiveness and availability (turn-around time for email, grad posting, etc.). (2 points) 4. The requirements for student interaction are clearly articulated. (2 points) This total of 10 points for learner engagement is out of a total of 85 points in the total rubric. Other categories include Course overview and introduction, Learning objectives, Assessment and measurement, Resources and materials, Course technology, Learner support, and Accessibility. To put this in perspective, it is important to know that to meet the Quality Matters requirements, an online course must earn 72 out of the 85 possible points which indicates their perception of the value of learner engagement in effective online learning.

For specific examples of what is appearing on the horizon, Farmer (2010) lists some technologies that will impact adult learning. Using "cloud computing", learners will be able to access learning objects anytime, anywhere, any way and store their own work on multi-purpose servers. She notes that while the "Semantic Web" is becoming more accurate and multi-lingual and should "advance global learning dramatically" (p. 102). Talking computers would reduce the need for written literacy and require a focus on oral communication. She also predicts that learning will become more customized with "push" technologies pushing information to the user.

## CONCLUSION

While considering the role of "apps" and "avatars" in engaging both traditional and adult learning is important, returning to the issues addressed at the beginning of this chapter are equally important. Brookfield (2006) describes the reality of today's classrooms. "These days, no college teacher can avoid teaching in a hybrid manner, combining electronic and face-to-face communication. The only question remaining is the degree to which electronic communication is integrated into course activities" (p. 191). The numerous examples in this chapter not only illustrate this point but indicate that the statement should be expanded to "no instructor" no matter what the venue. They also illustrate the importance of paying attention to the changing roles and relationships between instructors and students and the classroom culture in engaging learning.

## REFERENCES

Barab, S., Kling, R., & Gray, J. (2004). *Designing for virtual communities in the service of learning*. Cambridge, UK: Cambridge University Press.

Blumenfeld, Y. (1999). *Scanning the future*. New York, NY: Thames & Hudson.

Brookfield, S. (2006). *The skillful teacher*. San Francisco, CA: Jossey-Bass.

Conrad, R., & Donaldson, J. (2004). *Engaging the online learner*. San Francisco, CA: John Wiley & Sons.

Cranton, P., & Carusetta, E. (2004). Perspectives on authenticity in teaching. *Adult Education Quarterly*, *55*(1), 5–22. doi:10.1177/0741713604268894

Farmer, L. (2010). New perspectives of andragogy in relation to the use of technology. In Wang, V. (Ed.), *Assessing and evaluating adult learning in career and technical education* (pp. 87–106). Hershey, PA: IGI Global.

Farmer, L. (2010). Career and technical education technology: Three decades in review and technological trends in the future. In Wang, V. (Ed.), *Definitive readings in the history, philosophy, practice and theories of career and technical education* (pp. 259–278). Hershey, PA: IGI Global.

Honey, P., & Mumford, A. (1989). *Capitalizing on your learning style. King of Prussia.* PA: Organization Design and Development, Inc.

Illeris, K. (2009). A comprehensive understanding of human learning. In Illeris, K. (Ed.), *Contemporary theories of learning: learning theorists... in their own words* (pp. 7–20). New York, NY: Routledge.

Jarvis, P. (2009). Learning to be a person in society: Learning to be me. In Illeris, K. (Ed.), *Contemporary theories of learning: learning theorists...in their own words* (pp. 21–34). New York, NY: Routledge.

Kling, R., & Courtright, C. (2004). Group behavior and learning in electronic forums. In Barab, S., Kling, R., & Gray, J. (Eds.), *Designing for virtual communities in the service of learning* (pp. 91–119). Cambridge, UK: Cambridge University Press.

Knowles, M., Holton, E., & Swanson, R. (2005). *The adult learner* (6th ed.). Burlington, MA: Elsevier.

Lee, K. (2010). Philosopher or Philistine? In Wang, V. (Ed.), *Assessing and evaluating adult learning in career and technical education* (pp. 27–52). Hershey, PA: IGI Global.

Merriam, S., Caffarella, R., & Baumgartner, L. (2007). *Learning in adulthood: A comprehensive guide* (3rd ed.). San Francisco, CA: John Wiley & Sons.

Mezirow, J. (2009). An overview of transformative learning. In Illeris, K. (Ed.), *Contemporary theories of learning: Learning theorists... in their own words* (pp. 90–105). New York, NY: Routledge.

Parker, J. (1997) *Open learning without frontiers– open learning across international boundaries.* Presented at Session B6 of The Open Learning for Business Conference in Birmingham, England on September 24, 1997.

Quality Matters. (2006). *Homepage information.* Retrieved from www.qualitymatters.com

Rovani, A. P., & Jordan, H. M. (2004). Blended learning and sense of community: A comparative analysis with traditional and fully online graduate courses. *International Review of Research in Open and Distance Learning*, *5*(2), 1–13.

Schneps, M., Griswold, A., Finkelstein, N., McLeod, M., & Schrag, D. (2010, May 28). Using video to build learning contexts online. *Science*, *328*, 1119–1120. doi:10.1126/science.1186934

Usher, R. (2009). Experience, pedagogy, and social practices. In Illeris, K. (Ed.), *Contemporary theories of learning: Learning theorists... in their own words* (pp. 169–183). New York, NY: Routledge.

# Chapter 13
# Encouraging Student Motivation in Distance Education

**Judith Parker**
*Columbia University, USA*

## ABSTRACT

*While motivating students to enroll, participate, and complete any learning activity has always been a challenge, distance education adds a new dimension of complexity to the problem. This chapter will explore the development of distance education and the internal and external motivational factors that need to be considered when attempting to encourage student motivation in distance education.*

## INTRODUCTION

The term distance education has become synonymous with on line learning in today's technology focused world. But is has a long history of providing courses and directing learning in situations where the instructor and learner are not co-located. The image of today's students attempting to learn from their hand held devices in short intervals between meetings or riding on public transportation may be new, but the issues of motivation are not. Influenced by a plethora of external and internal motivational factors, the learner distanced from the instructor has always had to prioritize life's responsibilities and struggle to keep their remote responsibility from falling to the bottom of the list behind pressing face-to-face issues.

While Chapter 12 addressed the importance of engaging students to affect learning, it assumes that they are already motivated to learn. Therefore this chapter gets to the heart of the learning issues: what motivates them to enroll (commit to learning) and what motivates them to continue their commitment throughout the duration of the course or learning activity.

DOI: 10.4018/978-1-60960-791-3.ch013

## DISTANCE EDUCATION

Distance education presents issues inherent in any interaction between persons at a distance. It is also important to realize that distance education existed in many forms before the advent of computers. Merriam, Caffarella & Baumgartner (2007) explain that "the defining characteristic of all forms and generations of distance education is the separation of student and teacher in time or space. What in the literature is often termed first-generation distance education consisted of print-based correspondence courses, a form still in existence. How many generations follow differs by author; but the simplest model has the second generation being broadcast and television technologies, followed by the third generation of information technologies of which web-based courses are a part. (pp. 39-40). Conrad (2005) adds to these categories by suggesting that this third generation is "distinguished by an increased degree of learner control and flexibility, interactive communication and group-oriented processes" (p. 445). This would certainly imply the inclusion of Web 2.0 technologies with their social networking strengths. Lau (2000) views history from a slightly different prospective and offers a more restrictive definition of distance learning. She notes that "distance learning was pioneered at Stanford University more than 30 years ago to meet the increasing demand for high-tech engineers and computer scientists at Silicon Valley" (p. i).

Merriam, Caffarella, and Baumgartner (2007) suggest that "online learning is a form of distance education, which has a long history of serving adults who otherwise would not have access to continuing and higher education" (p. 39). There are numerous reasons why these adults might not have access but Li and Irby (2008) describe one group of them as "busy working people, often on shift who want to advance their career, frequent travelers, those who physically find it difficult to attend college and parents who want to or have to spend more time at home with their children" (p. 451). There is likely a connection between this profile information noted by these two authors and the information reported by Piskurich and others on retention.

Piskurich (2006) cites statistics that indicate that 60 – 80% drop out of elearning courses. Li and Irby (2008) also mention the low rate of retention but add concerns for lower student performance and the need for enhanced specific skills such as writing, communication, time management, organization, and the ability to work independently.

In spite of these issues, distance education opportunities in both the continuing education arena and rigorously academic programs have thrived. Lau (2000) reports that "today, nontraditional bachelor and master's distance learning programs are offered by more than 150 accredited academic institutions in this country (p. i). This number has likely risen since Lau's writing so it is worth investigating the motivating factors that bring students to these programs. Most authors distinguish between factors internal to the individual learner and those that are external.

### Motivational Factors

The subject of motivation has attracted the attention of numerous theorists and researches over the past decades. Kolb (1984) developed a theory that was consistent with that of humanistic educators who viewed learning as a highly personal endeavor and motivation as intrinsic, emanating from the learner. Merriam, Caffarella, and Baumgartner (2007) explain that "from a learning theory perspective, humanism emphasizes that perceptions are centered in experience, and it also emphasizes the freedom and responsibility to become what one is capable of becoming. These tenets underlie much of adult learning theory that stresses the self-directedness of adults and the value of experience in the learning process" (p. 282). Both self-directedness and experience are essential components of Knowles theories of andragogy. Knowles (1980) suggested that "individuals are motivated to engage in learning to the extent that they feel a need to learn and perceive a personal goal that learning will help to achieve" (p. 56). He defined an "educational need" as "something people ought to learn for their own good, for the good of an organization, or for the good of society (p. 88). Knowles continued to suggest what would cause an adult to feel this need. "The urge for growth is an especially strong motivation for learning, since education is, by definition, growth in knowledge, understanding, skills, attitudes, and appreciation" (1980, p. 85). Although his philosophy paralleled Kolb's in the assertion that this motivation is intrinsic, he suggested that feeling a need is an important factor.

Merriam, Caffarella, and Baumgartner (2007) note that Maslow addressed needs on a broader scale by defining a theory of human motivation based on a hierarchy of human needs: physiological needs (hunger and thirst), safety (security and protection), belongingness, esteem, and self-actualization (a person's desire to become all that he or she is capable of becoming). Of these five, he categorized four as deficiency motives and only self-actualization as a growth motive. "For Maslow self-actualization is the goal of learning, and educators should strive to bring this about" (p. 282). Since studies showed each of these needs peaking at a different age, the effect these needs had in influencing motives for participation in education may also have been age-dependent.

This seems consistent with the idea of "life-span psychology" introduced by Illeris (2004) which delineates 4 phases that relate to learning: childhood, youth, adulthood, and mature adulthood. While the first two are obvious, he distinguishes adulthood from mature adulthood in terms of motivators for learning. He defines the adult phase as "traditionally been marked by a kind of ambition that implies a striving to realize more or less clear life aims relating to family, career, interests or something else – but in late modernity this representation is also on its way to being overlaid by the continual societal changes, the unpredictability of the future, the conditioning of the market mechanism and the unending succession of apparent choices" (p. 217). He defines a "life turn" as a psychological phenomenon concerning the perception and acknowledgement that the remaining time in one's life is not unlimited. He suggests that this is often brought on by a life event such as retirement, children leaving home, etc. He distinguishes it from adulthood by explaining that adulthood is dominated by a sense of "purposefulness" while in mature adulthood "people spend their time on things they perceive as quality activities, such as cultural of social activities, helping others, their partner, if they have one, their children, grandchildren, or disadvantaged groups they are involved with". Mature adulthood is "without aura of necessity or external incentive which often forms the basis for learning in earlier adulthood" (p. 223).

An examination of the abundance of information on studies on the topic of adult motivation for learning revealed patterns that suggest that results of studies were often a restatement of Maslow's needs. In 1961, Cyril Houle published the results of his in-depth interview study on the subject of motivation in his book "The Inquiring Mind". He characterized adult learners as belonging to three categories based on their motivation: "goal-oriented learners" who were motivated to achieve specific objectives; "activity-oriented learners" motivated by the social nature of the learning activity; and "learning-oriented learners who engaged in learning for its own sake (Brookfield, 1984, p. 36). The goal-oriented learners were motivated by a goal in any one of the four top human needs in Maslow's scale. The activity-oriented learners were motivated by the need for belongingness, and the learning –oriented learners were motivated by a search for self-actualization.

David McClelland developed a theory of "achievement motivation" which he characterized as the "result of a conflict between a hope of success (approach motivation) and a fear of failure (avoidance motivation)" or as a "competition against a standard of excellence" (Weiner, 1992, p. 201). McClelland's hypothesis was that "achievement motivation is in part responsible for the economic growth of societies" since the individual was the "promoter of his own career and agent of his own progress". Therefore McClelland's goal was to develop achievement motivation in adults in business through an Achievement Motivation Development Course. He defined three essentials of his course as the instructors "warmth" (acceptance of the individual and his decisions), a "retreat setting" to "define the training as an experience apart" and the "heightening of participants' sense that they are joining a new reference group" (McClelland, 1961, p. 281). These three motivations will be discussed later in this chapter in light of distance education and educational technology.

In addition to the internal factors discussed above, individuals are influenced by a number of external factors. Barry Morstain, and John Smart, using a multivariate analysis of group differences, to study motivational factors and found that their study indicated that "individual differences such as sex, age, and socioeconomic status are only weakly associated with motivational orientation factors" (Darkenwald & Merriam, 1982, p. 134). They did, however, identify six motivational factors: social relationships, external expectations (pressures), social welfare (altruistic concern for other people), professional advancement, escape/ stimulation; and cognitive interest (knowledge for it s own sake).

McClusky's Theory of margins is grounded in the notion that adulthood is a time of growth, change, and integration in which one constantly seeks balance between the amount of energy needed and the amount available. This balance is conceptualized as a ratio between the "load" (L) of life, which dissipates energy, and the "power" (P) of life, which allows one to deal with the load. "Margin in life" is the ratio of load to power: more power means a greater margin to participate in learning. (Merriam, Caffarella, & Baumgartner, 2007, p. 93)

Of Illeris' (2004) three dimensions of learning, cognitive, emotional, social, the emotional dimension involves "psychological energy, transmitted by feelings, emotions, attitudes and motivation which both mobilize and at the same time are conditions that may be influenced and developed through learning" (p. 18). He suggests that "all learning includes three simultaneous and integrated dimensions: a cognitive content dimension, an emotional, psychodynamic, attitudinal and motivational dimension and a social and societal dimension" (p. 25).

Parker (1992) summarized the findings of studies over a twenty year period and listed the following as factors influencing participants' motivation to learn: cost, lack of time, inconvenient time, lack of information, job responsibilities, home responsibilities, interest in subject, confidence, relevance, procedural problems, lack of quality, no benefit, not personal priority, personal problems. The list spans the categories of internal and external motivators mentioned earlier. If the list is examined in light of distance education, only a few factors would change in their influence. If the distance education program is asynchronous, the issue of inconvenient time would be eliminated. Or if the online course was asynchronous, it might be easier to juggle job or home responsibilities. On the negative front, the students' confidence in studying alone or using technology could impact their motivation.

Parker's (1992) study of reentry adult learners in a formal technical education program offers some insights. The study utilized critical incidents, questionnaires and interviews to focus on those factors that reentry students perceived as facilitators or barriers to their academic progress in their technical degree programs and the relationship between these factors. The critical incident responses revealed data on the student's previous math and science background and the impact of the family on their success. The students' value systems ranked among the most significant and most positive factors in motivating them to return to college and complete their degree program. The unanimous reason could be paraphrased by the following response of one of the students, "I'm doing it for me". One student commented that completing a degree was "something I wanted to do and I just set goals for myself". On site, convenient classes were identified as important to success. The course workload was identified as the most negative factor in two of the methodologies used and the degree completion time appeared in the top three rankings of all three data sets. Family responsibility was the only sociocultural factor that appeared in the top three rankings which the value system and self-confidence were the only psychosocial factors that were prominent. Students credited the instructor's characteristics and instructional methodology with helping them achieve self-confidence in extremely difficult courses. The following comment is characteristic of those throughout the students' interviews. "I worked very hard at it but with having him as a teacher, it really made it possible for me to do Calculus". Another student commented on the collaborative relationship with their instructor and described the experience as a "give-and-take of knowledge and skills and experience". A number of these motivational factors will be considered more closely in the context of distance education in the following section.

## DISTANCE EDUCATION AND STUDENT MOTIVATION

### Motivation to Enroll: An Academic Setting

Merriam, Caffarella, and Baumgartner (2007) suggest that "there is little double that there is a strong link between the motivation to participate in a learning activity and an adult's life experiences and developmental issues. From studies of participation and motivation that document that adult roles, especially that of the worker, are prime motivators for learning, to Mezirow's (1991) process of perspective transformation that is precipitated by a "disorienting dilemma" – that is, one's familiar patterns of coping with life events prove ineffective – learning in adulthood is a function of social roles and developmental issues (p. 426).

In an academic setting, several motivational factors can come into play. In a graduate institution, students may be motivated by the acquisition of increased skills and the credentials of an advanced degree. However, many of the factors previously listed make this difficult or impossible. Distance education in the form of online courses offer increased opportunities. Parker (2009) reviewed nearly a decade of pre and post course surveys and reflections about the students' motivation for taking an online course. These findings are summarized below.

- From past experience, they loved learning online
- They had no experience with online learning but were curious about how they would react to the course and how it could help them with current responsibilities
- They were interested in the course content and the fact that it was offered online was superfluous to their decision to enroll.

However the richness of the findings can be found in the student responses. Students' perceptions of what constituted a positive past online experiences were very different.

- One student's reflection on a past online course led him to comment that he "really enjoyed the flexibility and the communication between the professor and students. I actually felt I was more participatory in that class than in a real time course." The social aspect of the learning was of obvious importance.

- Another student commented "I feel that I am able to express myself more effectively when I have more time to think about the issues and questions. I know that I will be able to contribute more to the class and to the discussions." The student's need for time to reflect and process the information could important.
- Students' positive experiences often included comments about the flexibility of online learning fitting into a particular lifestyle or geographic location. Comments included: "I live in China with my family…" "I will be working at a summer camp this summer…" "I'll be on vacation for two of the weeks and this enables me to take a course over the summer and draw a little closer to completing my degree."

Students have participated from China, Japan, Korea, Taiwan, Pakistan, England, India, Iceland, Bosnia-Herzegovina, Canada, South Africa and 16 states. While the motivators for each student were very personal, the end result was a richness of the discussion which would be limited if it only included people who could travel to campus.

Students in this graduate course have many commonalities with other adult online learners; they want real life applications and value the opportunity for experiential learning and reflection. However, they are unique in that they are not only interested in the content being taught but in analyzing the actual methodology in terms of its effectiveness in their own field of practice. So their curiosity as a motivating factor might be unique to this group of students however this curiosity makes their reflections particularly rich with data. As online courses have become more prolific in academic and organizational settings over the years, there has definitely been an increase in the number of students who openly express that their motivation for enrolling in an online course is curiosity about its effectiveness and their comfort level with the methodology. Student comments in answer to: "Why are you taking this course" in the pre-course survey indicate a growing awareness of and concern about ineffective staff training in their organizations. One student's summary was "our professional development offerings are a joke". These concerns are across survey categories of business, K-12, higher education and non-profit as well as health care, religious education and government. There has also been an increase in cross registration from students in graduate programs in business, engineering and public health. This curiosity about online learning experiences is evident on many levels.

- One student working for a national non-profit stated that "we keep considering online mediums. I thought it might be helpful if I took a course online myself to see to what extent I found it as useful as a face-to-face class".
- Another saw the value in experiential learning. "I am intrigued to experience taking a class online because I have never done so before and it seems that on-line learning may be an important (and increasingly common) delivery system for education/training. Therefore, the experiential piece is important to my personal understanding of what online learning is."
- While one student admits that with her hectic summer schedule, "an on-line course should be a natural fit", she adds that "I'm quite anxious about what its effectiveness might be".
- Several students admitted to the role of critical reflective practitioners. One suggested, "I am very skeptical of how universities will use it and how it will affect education. I want to experience it to learn the potential benefits but also to sharpen my critique as an educator."

So while curiosity is the obvious motivator, they are curious because they want to have a positive impact and a voice in improving existing programs or beginning new one. The third category noted above is of interest because the content and the need to know factor was the motivator to take the course and the methodology neither motivated nor deterred them.

Parker (2009) noted that in contrast, students taking the same course on campus had three very different reasons why they preferred on campus classes: personal preferences, personal experience, and friends' personal experiences. One indicated that she had never participated in an on-line course before and was a bit skeptical and another just indicated that she preferred the interaction of a face-to-face course. One shared that he had tried an online course but "did not have the discipline" to successfully complete it. Yet another noted that "friends have found that such classes lack the personal engagement that is needed to learn most effectively" However, in the most recent semester, one third of the on line course participants indicated that this was their first online class.

In considering what might motivate a student to participate in a distance learning activity, Fahy and Ally (2005) note a relationship between Kolb's learning styles discussed in Chapter 12 and students comfort in an online environment. "Convergers, in this study, may be disposed to greater participation, finding online interaction (and online communities) attractive, while other styles find the requirement to interact regularly less useful, even toilsome." Their finding that "convergers seemed most engaged with the online network was consistent with theoretical expectations" (p. 17). They also found that "accommodators appeared to be most comfortable in the online environment" (p. 18). Clearly the factors that motivate people to initially enroll in a distance education class are varied. But once they make that commitment, keeping them enrolled is another issue. As noted earlier, retention statistics in distance learning courses have been traditionally low. However as indicated in Chapter 12, new technology offers increasing opportunities to engage students in learning in both a traditional and andragogical environment. This engagement would be a positive step in motivating them to continue in the course and succeed.

## Motivation to Enroll: A Corporate Case Study

While working adults who are participating in distance education courses experience some of the same issues as those in an academic setting, they also have some unique experiences. Parker (1989) reported how this is illustrated in a corporate environment. She chronicles the development of 3M's technical development program and the influence that the corporate culture had on increased demand for more flexible learning activities. The underlying motivation for the employees was to meet the corporate requirements so they might advance their careers. The integration of technical development into the career of every technical employee worldwide created an increased demand for courses that would accommodate flexible schedules and overcome location barriers. These adult learners in St. Paul, MN and Austin, TX research locations, as well as U.S. manufacturing plants and outside U.S. technical centers were also anxious for courses that fit their individual learning styles.

3M initially began to meet these employee needs by initiating a paper and pencil technical development self student program of about 20 courses available to employees nationwide. After several years, this curriculum was expanded to about 150 courses and offered to 3M technical employees worldwide. As technology advanced in the educational area, computer based training (CBT) courses were added to the self study program and both CBT and Interactive Video Disc (IVD) courses were available in a learning center in St. Paul. An increasing number of technical employees were selecting courses offered in a CBT and IVD format in a learning center environment.

To address the issues surrounding the use of CBT and IVD in corporate education, two committees were formed. One focused on the authoring and evaluation of existing courseware in the use of computers and selected software packages and produced a guide to authoring and evaluating CBT. The second committee focuses on the integration of CBT into existing development programs in the technical, management, and employee development areas. Emerging technology was becoming a mainstay in the education arena and was successfully providing an additional mechanism for delivering quality education adaptive to the individualized schedules and learning styles of 3M's workforce. While courses were available in traditional classroom semester length and special short courses, microwave/satellite delivered graduate level courses and self study courses, statistics indicated self study including CBT and IVD to be the fastest growing area in technical development.

## Motivation to Succeed

While the motivation to enroll in a course may have little to do with the instructor, the motivation to succeed is very much the instructor's responsibility. Silberman (2006) offers six suggestions for motivating participants into any planned exercise but they can also be useful in motivating students to participate and continue in an extended learning activity. He suggests that the instructor "explain the objectives, sell the benefits, convey enthusiasm, connect the activity to previous activities, share personal feelings with participants, express confidence in participants" (p. 265). These six ideas will be examined in the context of a larger learning activity.

- Learning objectives should set the tone for the entire course. While they are often printed on a course syllabus or the front page of a workbook, they are often not given the emphasis they deserve in order to ensure that everyone has the same expectations from the course. It is important not to assume that the participants know the instructor's objectives
- Benefits might seem obvious to the instructor but may not be so to the participant. An explanation of what benefits the participants will derive from the training whether on the job or in personal growth will be a motivator
- An instructor's enthusiasm for the course will likely be internalized by the students. If the instructor is not excited about and engaged in the topic and activities, it is unlikely that he or she will be able to motivate the students to do so.
- Subject matter for an entire course or a specific topic or activity cannot be seen as isolated. They must be obviously connected to other content within the course, previous courses, or activities outside the course.
- While this connects to the benefits, the instructor's personal stories about why he or she or others have found this content or activity to be valuable helps to make the point very specific
- Participants often have varied histories of success or failure with certain subject matter content or a type of activity. Telling the participants that you feel confident that they are ready for the new challenge can be an valued assurance.

Illeris (2004) suggests that "it is basically characteristic that adults learn what they want and have very little inclination to acquire something they do not want, i.e. something they do not perceive as meaningful for their own life goals, of which they are aware in varying degrees of clarity. A rule of thumb for understanding adults' learning would state that adults learn what they want to learn and what is meaningful for them to learn, adults draw on the resources they already have in their learning, adults take as much responsibility for their learning as they want to take (if they are allowed to) (pp. 219-220). He comments on internal motivators by noting that "as a consequence of this, rather than having various more or less unconnected motives as the foundation for their educational and learning activities, adults have more coherent strategies relating to goals that are normally fairly clear and known to the individual" (p. 220). Tennant (2009) suggests that postmodernism collapses the binary opposition and "treats the 'subject' and the 'social' as jointly produced through discursive practices" (p. 152). He also offers this warning. "Existing adult education technologies, in the name of promoting autonomy and freedom, can be accomplices in the process of subjugation." (p. 158).

Knowles' assumptions about adult learner's "self concept, experience, readiness to learn, problem-centered focus, and internal motivation" (Merriam, Caffarella, & Baumgartner, 2007, p. 104) offer additional insights into how the instructor may motivate the student throughout the course. Some of these like internal motivation or readiness to learn may be outside the control of the instructor. However, the instructor can play an important role in promoting the learner's self concept, valuing the learner's experience, and providing problem-centered activities. Tennant (2009) suggests that "existing adult education technologies, in the name of promoting autonomy and freedom, can be accomplices in the process of subjugation" (p. 158).

Considering these ideas along with those previously mentioned in the section earlier in this chapter about motivation can lead to very practical ideas for motivating students participating in distance education. Some examples are presented here from the author's experience with distance education. The underlying idea is that engagement is a strategy for motivating. Whether considering Illeris' social dimension of learning or Maslow's need to belong, engaging the student continually and purposefully at the onset and continually throughout the course is at the heart of this strategy.

The tone for engagement must be set at the beginning of the course. Chapter 12 suggests some of these ideas. In addition to introductory emails, the first assignment for students in an online class is to post an introduction about themselves. It is made clear that they are free to disclose as much or as little about their personal life as they wish. Some write a few sentences which others reveal details about their family, work and hobbies. As students read each others introductions they find common interests or ideas and begin a dialogue in the threaded discussion. One interesting example occurred a few years ago. A Chinese student was taking the online course from China and posted that she was active in soccer. An American student taking the course from New York noted her passion for the sport as well. Throughout the dialogue the Chinese student noted that she came to New York each summer for an intensive 6 weeks as a part of her degree program. The students set a date to meet in New York the following summer.

Besides engagement that occurs between students, the instructor has an important role to play. She also replies quickly to each posting by a student and tries to connect with some personal aspect of the posting. Since the instructor has traveled extensively in Europe and Asia, just the mention that she remembers Singapore being full of beautiful flowers during a business trip or that she presented a paper at a conference in London makes a personal connection with a learner at a distance. The connection can be work related or a favorite instructional video. This initial engagement can be a motivating factor in providing a comfortable online space for the student during the course.

The survey feature in a learning management system can also be a useful tool. Another week one assignment is for students to complete the online survey. It asks demographic questions as well as information about students' motives for taking an online course. The statistics that are collected and a summary of the short answers are shared with the students. This provides a profile of the participants who are part of this learning community for the duration of the course. Students see what countries are represented, what fields of practice or interest are represented and how many first time online learners are in the course. The objective is to promote a sense of community and belonging at the onset of the course. Students in an online course lack the visual connection often made by looking around the classroom the first day of class so attention must be paid to providing an alternative way to connect with other learners. While students at this point in the course have passed the point of being motivated to enroll in the online course, they are often still apprehensive about the expectations and fear they will be the only one with no online course experience. While this course has been taught online for almost a decade and while the number of online learning opportunities universally has increased exponentially, each semester's course has at least three to four first time online learners. Knowing this, it is possible for the instructor to be especially vigilant about following their progress and offering assistance throughout the course.

Course assignments are a mix of individual and group work. For the first group assignment, students are assigned to a group with others in their same field of practice or interest. Students know that others in the group share their same vocabulary and experiences in a particular field such as business, high education, K-12, non-profit, health care, etc. This not only helps to build community but also provides a comfort level for initial discussions. Since the students in this group will be encountering new adult learning vocabulary and theories, this foundational comfort is key to their success.

Continued and timely attention to interactions with students is essential throughout the course. While everyone uses emails, when that email contains an assignment that must meet a deadline and be graded, this familiar action from a computer or hand held device can become stressful. As soon as a student emails an assignment, the instructor acknowledges receipt. Often it is just that, a quick reply saying "just acknowledging receipt – feedback in a few days" or a simple "received your email – you forgot the attachment". It eliminates the stress of the student wondering if the email arrived and it eliminates the string of follow up emails from students asking if the instructor received the assignment. Of course timely constructive feedback as promised in the cryptic acknowledgement email is essential.

In a classroom, the instructor and other students will notice if a student is missing and often the student will email an excuse for the absence. In a distance learning course, this weekly check-in is missing. It requires the instructor to be proactive is emailing a note about a missed class or late assignment. This can be the motivating factor that will bring the student back on track. Without this attention, missing one deadline by a few days is easily prolonged into a week or more and it is impossible for a student to catch up with the assignments. After about a decade of teaching the same courses online and on campus, the instructor has observed that the online course offering always has several "incompletes" at the end of the semester while the on campus class seldom has any. For busy adult learners, it is easy for the distance education requirements to slip to the end of their list of priorities.

Conrad and Donaldson (2004) stress the importance of engaging the learner and the challenge of creating "exhilarating learning experiences when you lack verbal and visual cues" (p.16) available in the traditional classroom. Carr and Ponton (2003) see that "creating collegial environments conducive to autonomous learning is the quintessential goal of the facilitator of learning in the asynchronous e-learning platform." (p.151) "Key to the learning process are the interactions among students themselves, the interactions between faculty and students, and the collaboration in learning that results from these interaction." (Palloff & Pratt, 1999, p. 5) Cranton (2006) emphasizes the importance of empowering the student by interactions in the learning environment and being aware of power relationships. "The creation of a learning community supports and encourages knowledge acquisition. It creates a sense of excitement about learning together and renews the passion involved with exploring new realms in education." (Palloff & Pratt, 1999, p. 163)

## FUTURE TRENDS

Distance education will likely continue to plan an important role in future learning. Advancing technologies have changed and will continue to alter the way in which that distance is traveled. The transition from mailed workbooks to emailed assignments to interactive online sites has impacted the interaction between instructor and learners and between the learners themselves. New technologies continue to increase the opportunities for encouraging student motivation.

In considering McClelland's (1961) definition of three essentials of his course mentioned earlier in this chapter, how they would play out in distance education might be interesting to consider. How would the instructors "warmth" (acceptance of the individual and his decisions) be communicated online? If a "retreat setting" to "define the training as an experience apart" was seen as essential to learning, what is the role of the ubiquitous handheld devices in learning? Could technology actually have a positive influence on the "heightening of participants' sense that they are joining a new reference group"? (p. 281). Web 2.0 could play an integral part in the establishment of and the fostering of their "new reference group".

Blumenfeld (1999) notes that "studying our possible futures can not only enhance our ability to understand what is happening in a wider historical context but can also imbue our consequent acts with a greater awareness and a feeling of participation. Expanding the perceived range of what I call "plausibilities" is enormously challenging because in so doing we can ultimately affect the outcomes. Through these pieces you may participate on many different levels in the creative process of imagining a better world" (p. 7).

As new technologies allow for distances to be crossed faster and easier, Sandmann, Reischmann, and Kim (2007) see a role for asynchronous e learning in broadening and deepening the global perspectives of the learner. However they also caution that educators need to recognize differences in motivations and expectations of learners in different cultures. They also noted marked differences in the participation patterns of students from different cultures.

White and Bridwell (2004) see the 21st century as an "age of convergence" (p. 287) between networks and within networks demonstrating a multiplier effect and integration. They also suggest that new technology is "significantly altering the social role of learning" and that distance learning is only an intermediate step toward a "telelearning environment" in which distance and location become arbitrary. (p. 287)

Barab, Kling, and Gray (2004) see this as an "exciting time in which pedagogical theory and technological advances have created an opportunity to design innovative and powerful environments to support learning" (p.13). However, Nilson (2003) makes an important point in mentioning that she expects the low-tech instructional tools such as the black or white board or overhead projector to be around for years while the high tech tools will become obsolete very quickly. This may indicate that the paper and pencil, snail mailed distance learning courses might also be a part of the future of distance education.

## CONCLUSION

While many studies have been completed and many theories developed around motivating the learner and distance education, a number of issues still need to be addressed. Lau (2000) notes that "according to the United states Distance Learning Association (USDLA), an organization committed to promoting and developing distance learning, there were no significant differences in effectiveness between distance learning and the traditional learning techniques (p. i). However, this would assume that the comparison was between students who were equally motivated to learn.

Merriam, Caffarella, and Baumgartner (2007) offer these ideas for consideration. "Online learning presents both opportunities and challenges to adult educators. As we have seen, online learning occurs in formal, nonformal, and informal settings. What we as adult educators need to think about is how the Internet is facilitating adult learning in all three settings and how we can maximize its potential. At the same time, online learning presents challenges particularly with regard to access, even in the information-rich, technologically advanced United States" (p. 42). While this chapter has offered numerous examples of distance education and motivating factors, it is important to note that encouraging student motivation may look very different if the education setting is formal, nonformal or informal.

## REFERENCES


Barab, S., Kling, R., & Gray, J. (2004). *Designing for virtual communities in the service of learning*. Cambridge, UK: Cambridge University Press.

Blumenfeld, Y. (1999). *Scanning the future*. New York, NY: Thames & Hudson.

Brookfield, S. (2006). *The skillful teacher*. San Francisco, CA: John Wiley & Sons.

Conrad, D. (2005). Onine learning. In English, L. M. (Ed.), *International encyclopedia of adult education* (pp. 442–446). New York, NY: Palgrave Macmillan.

Fahy, P. J., & Ally, M. (2005). Student learning style and asynchronous computer-mediated conferencing (CMC) interaction. *American Journal of Distance Education*, *19*(1), 5–22. doi:10.1207/s15389286ajde1901_2

Illeris, K. (2004). *The three dimensions of learning*. Malabar, FL: Krieger Publishing.

Knowles, M. (1980). *The making of an adult educator*. San Francisco, CA: Jossey-Bass.

Knowles, M., Holton, E., & Swanson, R. (2005). *The adult learner* (6th ed.). Burlington, MA: Elsevier.

Kolb, D. (1984). *Experiential learning*. NJ: Prentice-Hall.

Lau, L. (2000). *Distance learning technologies: Issues, trends and opportunities*. Hershey, PA: Idea Group Publishing.

Li, C., & Irby, B. (2008). An overview of online education: Attractiveness, benefits, challenges, concerns and recommendations. *College Student Journal*, *42*(2), 449–458.

McClelland, D. C. (1961). *The achieving society*. New York, NY: D. Van Nostrand.

Merriam, S., Caffarella, R., & Baumgartner, L. (2007). *Learning in adulthood: A comprehensive guide* (3rd ed.). San Francisco, CA: John Wiley & Sons.

Nilson, L. B. (2003). *Teaching at its best*. San Francisco, CA: Anker Publishing.

Palloff, R., & Pratt, K. (1999). *Building learning communities in cyberspace*. San Francisco, CA: Jossey-Bass.

Parker, J. (1989). Individualized instruction in CEE at 3M: From paper and pencil to personal computer. In L. Grayson & J. Biedenbach (Eds.), *American Society for Engineering Education 1989 College Industry Education Conference: Partners in Education* (p. 4). Lincoln, NE: University of Nebraska.

Parker, J. (1992). *Employees pursuing technical baccalaureate degrees: Success factors*. New York, NY: Teachers College/Columbia University.

Parker, J. (2009). The online adult learner: profiles and practices. In Wang, V. (Ed.), *Handbook of research on e-learning applications for career and technical education: Technologies for vocational training* (pp. 737–746). Hershey, PA: IGI Global. doi:10.4018/978-1-60566-739-3.ch056

Piskurich, G. (2006). *Rapid instructional design*. San Francisco, CA: John Wiley & Sons.

Sandman, L. R., Reischmann, J., & Kim, Y. S. (2007). Emerging adult educators' experiences in an international on-line forum. *Convergence*, *40*(1/2), 25–40.

Silberman, M. (2006). *Active training*. San Francisco, CA: John Wiley & Sons.

Tennant, M. (2009). Lifelong learning as a technology of self. In Illeris, K. (Ed.), *Contemporary theories of learning: Learning theorists... in their own words* (pp. 147–158). New York, NY: Routledge.

Weiner, B. (1992). *Human motivation*. London, UK: Sage Publications.

Wenger, E. (1998). *Communities of practice: learning, meaning and identity*. Cambridge, UK: Cambridge University Press.

Wenger, E. (2009). A social theory of learning. In Illeris, K. (Ed.), *Contemporary theories of learning: Learning theorists... in their own words* (pp. 209–218). New York, NY: Routledge.

White, B. A., & Bridwell, C. (2004). Distance learning techniques. In Galbraith, M. (Ed.), *Adult learning methods: A guide for effective instruction* (pp. 273–288). Malabar, FL: Krieger.

Yiu, L., & Parker, J. (2005). Cyber action learning and virtual project teams for leadership and management development. In Jacobs, R. L., & Osman-Gani, A. M. (Eds.), *Workplace training & learning: Cases from cross-cultural perspectives* (pp. 1–14). New York, NY: Pearson/Prentice Hall.

# Chapter 14
# Online Knowledge Dictator or Learning Facilitator

**Victor C.X. Wang**
*California State University Long Beach, USA*

## ABSTRACT

*While online knowledge dictators are determined by certain teaching/learning situations, Rogers' (1969) five well-accepted hypotheses suggest that teachers be learning facilitators to focus on what is happening in the learners. To help teachers become learning facilitators, this chapter specifies what exactly teachers can do in both the traditional classroom and online teaching/learning settings. The chapter also examines what other factors may contribute to this dichotomy of online knowledge dictators and learning facilitators. To compare and contrast this dichotomy, cultural backgrounds in relation to learning are also discussed to increase the readers' background in order to better understand the argument made in this chapter.*

## INTRODUCTION

Learning takes place anywhere, any time. To say that individuals learn 24/7 is not an exaggeration. As people live and breathe, they learn. Three reasons people learn are that they want to manipulate and control the environment, predict observable physical and social events, and take appropriate actions (Cranton, 2010, p. 5). There are many ways to view learning. Some scholars view learning in terms of behavioral changes. As long as learners have changed their behaviors, they have learned. If learners have changed their attitudes, they have learned. Likewise, if learners can think differently, they have learned. Yet, to some other scholars, learning is also a social activity. Learners learn when they engage with knowledge in social contexts (Jarvis, Holford, & Griffin, 1998). In fact, learning as a social activity is nothing new. Consider this anonymous Chinese saying advocated 2000 years ago: "If I am *walking* with two other *men*, each of them will serve as my *teacher*"[emphasis mine]. Individuals also

DOI: 10.4018/978-1-60960-791-3.ch014

learn when they engage with things or with other people's beliefs. No one questions that people acquire knowledge through the sense of sight, the sense of hearing, the sense of touch, the sense of smell, the sense of taste. The more senses people use, the better they learn. Constructivist scholars believe that individuals learn by making sense of experiences or by giving meaning to the world in which we live and work. People learn informally and through formal education or training. People also learn in many other ways: watching television, reading newspapers, conducting research, family emergencies and play tennis. What matters is the learning experience and how people learn. People do learn differently.

Very broadly, some learners are visual learners, some learners are auditory learners, and others may be tactile learners (Dunn, 1984; Friedman, 1984). In addition, some learners are global, meaning that they must take in the whole picture first before going into the details regarding learning of any kind. There are also field dependent learners and field independent learners. field dependent learners want to depend on others for their expertise before engaging in learning anything. At the turn of the 20th century, American researchers such as Watson studied animals and successfully advanced behaviorism. Based on behaviorism, researchers know more about how children learn. According to Piaget's (1967) research, researchers know more specifically about the education of children. It was not until the 1970s that researchers began to pay more attention to how adults learn. Knowles (1970, 1984) made the distinction between the education of adults and the education of children in the early 1970s. At the time, how many scholars believed in this dichotomy? The debate over this dichotomy slowly advanced into the 21st century, which is characterized as the "electronic education." The other name for electronic education could be called online education or online learning in the new century. As scholars continue to debate over the dichotomy, researchers have realized that children and adults do learn differently. Learners, young or old, do acquire knowledge through the same senses, although children may possess more sharper senses given their ages. However, the context in which adults learn is drastically different from the context in which children learn (Wang, 2007/2008).

Why do adults require online learning? Is such a context better than the traditional four-walled classroom setting where they have more interaction with their course instructors? The primary reason is that adults are capable of teaching themselves in the virtual environment given their prior experience, which can be served as the best resources for learning. Is this to say that children cannot learn online? Children are more technology savvy. Many of them can multitask, which means they can do many things while learning online. All the aforementioned information or knowledge about learners' learning styles, ways of approaching knowledge, or learning contexts is vitally important to those who educate children or help adults learn. Based on learners' ways of acquiring knowledge, educators must prescribe their appropriate teaching styles. It is commonly argued that educators' teaching may facilitate or inhibit learning. Positively used, one's teaching will surely facilitate learning. Negatively used, teaching online will stifle learning. More importantly, according to Rogers (1951, 1961, 1969), educators cannot teach another person directly. Learning must instead be facilitated. This hypothesis has proven to be true in the realm of teaching and learning. When applied to teaching online, Rogers' hypothesis has great educational implications to educators. If applied appropriately, educators become online learning facilitators. If applied negatively, educators become online knowledge dictators.

The objective of this chapter is to discuss whether online knowledge dictator will stifle learning or learning facilitators will facilitate learning. What led to this dichotomy? Why is it so important to educators who are engaged in teaching online? These are two of the questions this chapter seeks to answer. We also intend to shed some light on what educators can do in the virtual environment to help learners learn.

## BACKGROUND

The debate concerning online knowledge dictator or learning facilitator stems from the work of the educational psychologist, Carl Rogers who popularized student-centered approach to education. ***Carl Rogers*** (January 8, 1902 – February 4, 1987) was an influential American psychologist and among the founders of the humanistic approach to psychology. Rogers is widely considered to be one of the founding fathers of psychotherapy research and was honored for his pioneering research with the Award for Distinguished Scientific Contributions by the American Psychological Association in 1956. Rogers was found to be the sixth most eminent psychologist of the 20th century and second, among clinicians, only to Sigmund Freud. His student-centered approach to education was also interpreted as client-centered therapy in counseling. His books regarding teaching and learning have been widely cited in the field of education.

To Rogers, client-centered therapy parallels student-centered teaching. Student-centered teaching indicates that teachers are no longer knowledge dictators, or information presenters. Instead, teachers are learning facilitators who do everything they can to make students' learning easier. Prior to Rogers' developing student-centered approach to education, teachers were considered pedagogues, which means teachers are dictators of knowledge. Teachers represented knowledge. Education was considered top down. In other words, teachers were assigned full responsibility for making all decisions about what will be learned, how it will be learned, when it will be learned, and if it has been learned. It is teacher-directed education, leaving to the learner only the submissive role of following a teacher's instructions (Knowles, Holton, & Swanson, 2005, pp. 61-62).

In the past, it seemed to be the only model that teachers followed in terms of educating and training learners. Then Rogers advanced five "basic hypotheses." These basic hypotheses really made sense to teachers and learners. His first hypothesis was as follows: We cannot teach another person directly; we can only facilitate his learning. He explains this hypothesis as this: "every individual exists in a continually changing world of experience of which he is the center and the learner reacts to the field as it is experience and perceived" (as cited in Knowles, Holton, & Swanson, 2005, p. 49). Evidently, this hypothesis requires teachers to focus on what is happening in the learner instead of focusing on what the teacher does. In other words, what is happening in the learner is of primary importance. What the teacher does is of secondary importance. It is out of the scope of this chapter to discuss Rogers' four other hypotheses, but they are listed here for your reference:

- Second hypothesis: A person learns significantly only those things that he perceives as being involved in the maintenance of, or enhancement of, the structure of self.
- Third and fourth hypotheses grouped together: Experience that, if assimilated, would involve a change in the organization of self, tends to be resisted through denial or distortion of symbolization, and the structure and organization of self appear to become more rigid under threats and to relax its boundaries when completely free from threat.
- Fifth hypothesis: The educational situation that most effectively promotes significant learning is one in which (1) threat to the self of the learner is reduced to a minimum and (2) differentiated perception of the field is facilitated. (as cited in Knowles, Holton, & Swanson, 2005, p. 50)

It is believed that Knowles considered Rogers his personal mentor, and it was Knowles who further popularized student-centered approach to education. The following was written by Knowles to encourage teachers to be learning facilitators instead of knowledge dictators:

Finally, I found myself performing a different set of functions that required a different set of skills. Instead of performing the function of content planner and transmitter, which required primarily presentation skills, I was performing the function of process designer and manager, which required relationship building, needs assessment, involvement of students in planning, linking students to learning resources, and encouraging student initiative. (1998, p. 201)

As an educator, Knowles devoted his whole life to encouraging teachers to be learning facilitators based on Rogers' seminal hypotheses. For other hypotheses, please refer to Rogers' books. Concepts in teaching and learning are just like people's dearly held ideologies that are hard to change. Teachers were so used to being knowledge dictators for centuries. For teachers, learning to be a learning facilitator is easier said than done. Later, Knowles developed a seven-step process that requires teachers to

- Set a cooperative learning climate.
- Create mechanisms for mutual learning.
- Arrange for a diagnosis of learner needs and interests.
- Enable the formulation of learning objectives based on the diagnosed needs and interests.
- Design sequential activities for achieving the objectives.
- Execute the design by selecting methods, materials, and resources.
- Evaluate the quality of the learning experience while rediagnosing needs for further learning. (Bash, 2003, as cited in Carlso, 1989, pp. 5-6)

It is important for teachers to understand the difference between knowledge dictators and learning facilitators. The two schools of thought are just like applicable theories or philosophies for decision making for teachers regarding what to teach and, above all, how to teach in the traditional classroom settings, as well as the virtual environments. Initially as soon as teachers began to teach online, most teachers were knowledge dictators, dumping their courses onto the computer screen, utilizing programmed instruction characterized by behaviorism or a liberal education philosophy. Later, as more adult educators began to use andragogy to deliver their online courses, teachers focused more on problem solving models or constructivist models or even the theory of transformative learning (the center of which is learners' critical reflection; still closely related to Rogers' student-centered approach to education). Knowles's facilitating approach or his seven-step process (formula) did create a large following among teachers and trainers in the field of education. Also, the differences between online knowledge dictators and learning facilitators signifies the differences between the education of children and the education of adults. Above all, they require educators to adopt and adapt these two predominant instructional approaches in the online teaching and learning environment.

## ONLINE KNOWLEDGE DICTATORS OR LEARNING FACILITATORS: WHY IS THIS DICHOTOMY IMPORTANT?

The world is full of confrontations between people, groups, and nations who think, feel, and act differently (Hofstede & Hofstede, 2005, p. 2). It is true that teachers teach differently. In the American culture, teachers are encouraged to become learning facilitators due to the prominent work advanced by Rogers and Knowles. Teachers firmly believe in the student-centered approach to education translated from Rogers' client-centered therapy. In the adult education field, teachers and practitioners are strongly against teachers' being knowledge facilitators. Based on Rogers' five basic hypotheses and research conducted by other prominent researchers, teachers in English speaking countries generally believe that effective learning is likely to take place in teaching environments with the following characteristics (Biggs, 1996, pp. 45-46, as cited in Jarvis, Holford, & Griffin, 1998):

- Teaching methods are varied, emphasizing student activity, self-regulation and student-centeredness, with much cooperative and other group work.
- Content is presented in a meaningful context.
- Classes are small.
- Classroom climate is warm.
- High cognitive level outcomes are expected and addressed in assessment.
- Assessment is classroom-based and conducted in a non-threatening atmosphere.

When we think deeper about these teaching environments, we realize that teachers focus on what is happening in the learners, not on what teachers do in the classroom settings. Teachers in the American culture are strongly against top-down education. They are committed to the democratic process of teaching, which means they do not want to be solely information presenters. They want to be learning facilitators, linking students to the learning resources. In adult education, learners are considered equals of their course instructors. Every learner is treated with dignity and respect in the American culture. Because classes are small, enough individual attention can be given to everyone. When it comes to assessment, high cognitive level outcomes are expected. The ideal is the use of the higher order thinking skills of Bloom's Taxonomy (1956) characterized by analysis, synthesis and evaluation.

In general, Western teachers (e.g., American teachers) may frown upon memorization and rote learning that are most often used by knowledge dictators in Confucius-Heritage countries. Western teachers may argue that many East Asian education systems must be producing low-quality learning. Their teachers teach to tests and place more emphasis on the lower order thinking skills of Bloom's Taxonomy. Eventually, learners will become docile learners high on scores, low on real abilities (Ross, 1992). Typically, teachers in these East Asian countries (or Confucius-Heritage countries) are expected to be performers (Chen, 1981; Paine, 1992), and learners are expected to be good listeners. Teachers are considered to be authority figures, people between students' parents and God. Any disruptive behavior on the part of the learners is indicative of disrespect of their course instructors and these learners are "punished" by their course instructors or political behavior instructors.

What teachers in East Asian countries do is against Rogers' first hypothesis. Teachers are not focusing on what is happening in the learners. Instead, they are focusing on what they do as instructors in the classroom settings. Evidently, now we know when to be knowledge dictators and when to be learning facilitators. Our larger social environments pre-determine what kind of roles we need to play as course instructors. The safe advice for all teachers can be: When in Rome, do as the Romans do. However, researchers concluded recently that high scores could not be achieved through mere rote learning or memorization (Jarvis, Holford, & Griffin, 1998). We often hear that those learners from East Asian countries obtain very high scores or even perfect scores on TOELF or GRE that have shocked even native speakers of English. Some high school students from China who have never been to English speaking countries have obtained near-perfect scores on TOEFL or GRE. After successful graduate school studies, some of these learners become scientists, engineers or educators in the United States. After these learners are admitted into American universities, they quickly adapt to American learning facilitators although they are so used to knowledge dictators in their home countries. Regarding the debate on rote learning, memorization versus Western high cognitive learning, Biggs (1996) and his associates concluded based on their investigation:

- East Asian teachers believe that rote learning characterized by repetitive learning or memorization provides a basis to be creative with while Western educators believe that exploration should precede the development of skills.
- To East Asian teachers, repetition is a strategy for deep rather than surface learning. Western teachers are wrong in insisting that rote learning is mechanistic and without thought. When learners repeat something, they do use all their senses to rethink it.
- Although there is not much interaction between course instructors and learners in the classroom settings in East Asian countries, teachers in these countries allow for more interaction with learners outside class.
- While Westerners attribute success and failure to ability or the lack of it, East Asian students see effort or lack of effort as the primary factor.
- Although learners respond relatively poorly to teacher-led instruction in class, the majority of East Asian students do engage in collaboration with other learners after class. (pp. 75-76)

Even if teachers practice their teaching in the same country (e.g., the United States), there are times when they can be knowledge dictators or learning facilitators. In general, teachers should conform to Rogers' (1969) hypotheses regarding teaching. If we consider his hypotheses to be true, then teachers are expected to do the following in order to be learning facilitators:

- The facilitator has much to do with setting the initial mood or climate of the group or class experience.
- The facilitator helps to elicit and clarify the purpose of the individuals in the class as well as the more general purpose of the group.
- The facilitator relies upon the desire of each student to implement those purposes, which have meaning for him as the motivational force behind significant learning.
- The facilitator endeavors to organize and make easily available the widest possible range of resources for learning. Writing, materials, psychological aids, persons, equipment, trips, audio-visual.
- The facilitator regards himself/herself as a flexible resource to be used by the group.
- In response to expressions in the classroom group, the facilitator accepts both intellectual content and the emotionalized attitudes.
- As the acceptant classroom climate becomes established, the facilitator is able increasingly to become a participant learners.
- The facilitator takes the initiative in sharing himself/herself with the group—his feelings and his thoughts.
- Throughout the classroom experience, the facilitator remains alert to the expressions indicative of deep or strong feelings.
- In his/her functioning as a facilitator of learning, the facilitator endeavors to recognize and accept his/her own limitations.

Knowles (1970, 1984, 1998) took Rogers' hypotheses even further by suggesting the following to teachers in order for teachers to become learning facilitators:

- At the very beginning of a semester, learning facilitators are expected to negotiate course syllabi with their learners regarding what to learn, how to learn, why to learn or if anything can be learned. He believes shared control of learning will result in more effective learning on the part of the learners. Again, the focus is on the learners.

- Knowles believes in giving out learning contracts. Learners normally take responsibility for their own learning. Because of this, learners should abide by the learning contracts.
- Needs assessment should be used to determine the gap between the present level of learners and the desired level of learners so that the right instruction can be provided.
- Both Knowles and Rogers believe in learner self-evaluation. Evaluation by course instructors is of secondary.

Being a learning facilitator can be successful in many teaching and learning settings. Sometimes, being a knowledge dictator can also be successful especially when we take into consideration learners' learning styles, learning preferences etc. Even highly mature learners can be field-dependent learners, which means they tend to depend on their course instructors to be information presenters. Some learners may be labeled as auditory learners, which means they prefer to be all ears in a classroom settings. Then, instructors probably need to lecture much in order to accommodate learners' learning preference. In some situations where learners are mandated to be listeners, learning facilitators must be knowledge dictators.

When learners are not experienced with a certain subject matter, they depend on their instructors to be knowledge presenters. Perhaps, the safest advice on when to be a knowledge dictator and when to be a learning facilitator is to follow Grow (1991) stages in learning autonomy. To Grow, most learners do go through stages of learning and teachers' roles (Grow, 1991 as cited in Wang, 2007, p. 146) need to be situational in order to meet learners' learning needs. See Grow's stages in learning autonomy below:

A teacher is a leader; a leader is a teacher. As a leader, a teacher needs to know how to lead their learners in the realm of learning. Naturally, teachers are expected to know what kinds roles they need to play in the classroom settings. When learners are from East Asian countries, clearly, they may expect instructors to be knowledge dictators. Likewise, Western learners may expect their teachers to be learning facilitators. Assessing learners' needs should be the first step in order to be successful in any teaching and learning settings. The dichotomy of knowledge dictator and learning facilitator is important simply because it helps teachers make sound and meaningful decisions as to what kind of correct roles they can play in their classroom settings. Learners will be disappointed if course instructors assume the wrong roles.

In the virtual environment, it is even more important for instructors to know exactly what roles they need to play. Learners and instructors are separated by the physical distance and time. However, learners can easily tell what kind of roles online course instructors can play. The minute instructors begin to emphasize problem-solving models, constructivist approaches to learning, or critical reflection skills, learners know for sure

*Table 1. Grow's (1991)Stages in Learning Autonomy*

| Stage | Learner | Educator | Methods |
|---|---|---|---|
| Stage 1 | Dependent | Coach | Coaching with immediate feedback, drill; Informational lecture |
| Stage 2 | Interested | Motivator | Inspiring lecture plus guided discussions; goal Setting |
| Stage 3 | Involved | Facilitator | Discussion facilitated by teacher who Participates as equal |
| Stage 4 | Self-directed | Consultant | Internship, dissertation, self-study |

that course instructors are trying to be learning facilitators. By emphasizing problem-solving models, constructivist approaches or critical reflection skills, instructors most likely to emphasize high cognitive assessment of learning. This means learners are encouraged to engage in higher order thinking skills of Bloom's Taxonomy. On the contrary, if instructors use more terms such as knowledge, comprehension or application, learners know immediately that instructors aspire to be knowledge dictators. These terms may appear anywhere from announcements, discussion boards, learning resources to course assignments. If instructors are committed to programmed instruction, learners know for sure that instructors aspire to be knowledge dictators. It is vitally important for learners to know their instructors' teaching styles in the virtual environment. Then, based on learners' learning styles, preferences or time constraint, learners can adapt to their instructors' teaching style or simply request that course instructors change their instructional roles to adapt to learners' learning preferences.

In the virtual environment, interaction via technologies should be made as dynamic as in the traditional classroom settings. The dichotomy of knowledge dictator and learning facilitator should help predetermine this dynamic interaction in the virtual classroom. Once again, we caution, there are rules to follow regarding how to "dump our courses onto the computer screens." Without following these rules, teachers will fail to be facilitators.. Failure to follow these rules will frustrate our learners. Eventually, learners may give instructors a name, that is, "disorganized."

## FUTURE RESEARCH DIRECTIONS

Online education is relatively new in the 21st century. Teachers are still in the mode of experimenting with the idea of delivering courses via Web 2.0 technologies. Regardless of learners' preferred learning styles, teachers have their preferred teaching styles. Some senior faculty still refuse to change their preferred teaching styles when they have to deliver their courses online. Some school administrators may lack of any knowledge regarding online teaching and learning. Many educators are not familiar with the work by Rogers or Knowles, let alone the dichotomy of online knowledge dictators and learning facilitators. Given the aforementioned situations, researchers will continue to investigate this meaningful dichotomy. Also, Rogers' five basic hypotheses concerning student-centered approach to education represent only one dimension of teaching and learning.

There are other factors that also help predetermine teachers' teaching preferences online. For example, one's philosophies and experience may predetermine one's teaching preferences. Online knowledge dictators do not become knowledge dictators overnight. Their teaching preference has to do with their former education and training. If their former educators instill in the current teaching philosophies such as liberal, behaviorist philosophies, these current teachers are most likely to adopt the role of online knowledge dictators facilitators? To liberal education instructors, to teach means to develop the intellectual power of the mind of the learners and their teaching method must be that teachers are knowledge dictators, imparting knowledge to learners. If teaching philosophies such as humanistic and progressive philosophies, these current teachers are most likely to adopt the role of learning facilitators.

Therefore, another trend can be that researchers examine educators' teaching philosophies in order to determine what roles teachers can play in the online environment. We are not writing to say that the online knowledge dictator is superior to the learning facilitator or vice versa. Although Rogers' five hypotheses have been well accepted, online knowledge dictator still has its place in education. This is true especially when learners are field-dependent learners and are inexperience with a subject matter, teachers need to be knowledge dictators, making sure that the correct information is presented to learners. However, when learners are motivated enough to learn on their own, teachers do need to conform to Rogers' teachings on becoming learning facilitators.

Perhaps, researchers in the new century may continue to experiment with Grow's learning stage autonomy in relation to the dichotomy. Some learners like to be told what to learn and how to learn. Younger learners can belong to this group of learners. This means these learners may prefer knowledge dictators to learning facilitators. Some mature learners may not like to be told what to learn and how to learn. They may want to negotiate with their course instructors regarding what to learn and how to learn. When this happens, learners clearly prefer learning facilitators to knowledge dictators. Technology provides one access point to knowledge. Learning facilitators may take advantage of technology to link learners to learning resources. We all agree that we all learn from technology, with technology and technology can even be a subject matter for learners. The next possible trend can be that researchers look into the possibility whether technology as a subject matter predetermine one's teaching styles or preferences.

## CONCLUSION

In this chapter, we (authors) have demonstrated that there exists the dichotomy of online knowledge dictators and learning facilitators. Due to Rogers' well accepted hypotheses, we cannot teach another individual directly, we (educators) have to facilitate his/her learning. However, certain teaching situations may require teachers to be knowledge dictators. We (authors) have demonstrated that in order to be learning facilitators based on Rogers' hypotheses, there are things instructors need to in a classroom setting or in an online teaching/learning environment. Knowles also prescribed a seven step process or formula to learning facilitators. He shared with us his instructional role of a learning facilitator instead of an information transmitter. The dichotomy of online knowledge dictator and learning facilitator has to do with the distinction made by Knowles (1970, 1984) between the education of children and the education of adults in the 1970s.

Now we (educators) seem to agree that this distinction even applies to adult learners only due to different teaching and learning situations. In a sense, both the dichotomy and the distinction by Knowles are revolutionary because they help teachers adopt and adapt proper instructional roles in the traditional classroom and online teaching/learning settings. Without properly adopting appropriate instructional roles, instructors are most likely to frustrate learners who already possess certain learning preferences. To teach traditional age learners or to help mature learners learn with information communication technologies, the very first thing for instructors to do is to familiarize themselves with this dichotomy. The goal is to adopt and adapt one instructional role to fit the learning preferences of the learners online. Once again, the dichotomy represents only one dimension of the teaching and learning process or transaction. There are more instructional roles that teachers can adopt and adapt. For example, Grow's learning stage autonomy represents another dimension. Some researchers try to borrow concepts from management and leadership. Situational leadership styles have been addressed in the teaching and learning process. Then "flexibility" in teaching approaches may represent another dimension. Although teaching philosophies are not the focus of this chapter, they can predetermine one's teaching approaches, either student-centered or teacher-directed approaches to education.

## REFERENCES

Bash, L. (2003). *Adult learners in the academy*. Bolton, MA: Anker.

Biggs, J. (1996). Western misconceptions of the Confucian-heritage learning culture. In Watkins, D., & Biggs, J. (Eds.), *The Chinese learner* (pp. 46–47). Hong Kong: University of Hong Kong Comparative Education Research Center.

Bloom, B. S. (Ed.). (1956). *Taxonomy of educational objectives*. London, UK: Longman.

Carlson, R. (1989). Malcolm Knowles: Apostle of andragogy. *Vitae Scholasticae, 8*, 1.

Chen, T. H. (1981). *Chinese education since 1949: Academic and revolutionary models*. New York, NY: Pergamon Press.

Cranton, P. (2010). Working towards self-evaluation. In Wang, V. C. X. (Ed.), *Assessing and evaluating adult learning in career and technical education* (pp. 1–11). Hangzhou, China & Hershey, PA: ZUP and Information Science Reference. doi:10.4018/978-1-61520-745-9.ch001

Dunn, R. (1984). Learning styles: State of the science. *Theory into Practice, 23*(1), 10–19. doi:10.1080/00405848409543084

Friedman, P., & Alley, R. (1984). Learning/teaching styles: Applying the principles. *Theory into Practice, 23*(1), 77–81. doi:10.1080/00405848409543093

Grow, G. O. (1991). Teaching learners to be self-directed. *Adult Education Quarterly, 41*(3), 125–149. doi:10.1177/0001848191041003001

Hofstede, G., & Hofstede, G. J. (2005). *Cultures and organizations: Software of the mind*. New York, NY: McGraw-Hill.

Jarvis, P., Holford, J., & Griffin, C. (1998). *The theory and practice of learning*. London, UK: Kogan Page.

Knowles, M. S. (1970). *The modern practice of adult education: Andragogy versus pedagogy*. New York, NY: Association Press.

Knowles, M. S. (1984). *Andragogy in action*. San Francisco, CA: Jossey-Bass.

Knowles, M. S., Holton, E., & Swanson, A. (1998). *The adult learner*. Houston, TX: Gulf Publishing Company.

Knowles, M. S., Holton, E., & Swanson, A. (2005). *The adult learner* (6th ed.). Boston, MA: Elsevier Butterworth Heinemann.

Paine, L. (1992). Teaching and modernization in contemporary China. In Hayhoe, R. (Ed.), *Education and modernization: The Chinese experience* (pp. 183–209). New York, NY: Pergamon Press.

Piaget, J. (1967). The mental development of the child. In Elkind, D. (Ed.), *Six psychological studies by Piaget*. New York, NY: Random House.

Rogers, C. R. (1951). *Client-centered therapy*. Boston, MA: Houghton-Mifflin.

Rogers, C. R. (1961). *On become a person*. Boston, MA: Houghton-Mifflin.

Rogers, C. R. (1969). *Freedom to learn*. Columbus, OH: Merrill.

Ross, H. (1992). Foreign languages education as a barometer of modernization. In Hayhoe, R. (Ed.), *Education and modernization: The Chinese experience* (pp. 239–254). New York, NY: Pergamon Press.

Wang, V. C. X. (2007). Chinese knowledge transmitters or Western learning facilitators: Adult teaching methods compared. In King, K. P., & Wang, V. C. X. (Eds.), *Comparative adult education around the globe: International portraits and readings of the history, practice, philosophy, and theories of adult learning* (pp. 114–137). Hangzhou, China: Zheijian University Press.

Wang, V. C. X. (2007/2008). *Facilitating adult learning: A comprehensive guide for successful instruction* (rev. ed.). Boston, MA: Pearson Education.

# Chapter 15
# Addressing Cultures in Online Teaching

**Lesley Farmer**
*California State University Long Beach, USA*

## ABSTRACT

*In online environments, identifying and addressing different cultures can be challenging, but differences exist as increasingly diverse student populations interact with resources and humans. Making cultural factors explicit can lead to deeper understanding; students can discover how culture informs knowledge. This chapter focuses on key elements of culture and online teaching: students, teachers, curriculum, and the learning environment. Each element interacts, and has cultural implications.*

## INTRODUCTION

In today's digital world, awareness of different cultures and interaction among them have risen dramatically. This globalization has also impacted education. Online technology has become a commonplace form of curriculum delivery, and students are crossing political and cultural lines to participate in educational experiences. This cross-cultural phenomenon occurs especially in professional development because many economic sectors either deal with clientele representing different cultures or the employees themselves work and come from a variety of cultures. To that end, therefore, educational venues must also address cross-cultural issues, either in terms of their students or in terms of culturally-relevant content.

In an online environment, identifying and addressing different cultures is more challenging than in face-to-face learning environments. It can be easy to brush aside cultural differences, but they exist, nevertheless, as students interact with resources and humans. Making cultural factors explicit can lead to deeper understanding, and online learning environments, because they tend to minimize physical cues, can actually address

DOI: 10.4018/978-1-60960-791-3.ch015

these differences clearly and transparently. In the process, students can discover how culture informs knowledge.

This chapter focuses on key elements of culture and online teaching: students, teachers, curriculum, and the learning environment. Each element interacts, and has cultural implications.

## THE BIG PICTURE: THE CULTURAL CONTEXT

Regardless of the scale, when people form together into stable groups with sustained shared value/belief systems and normative expectations/behaviors, they comprise a culture. UNESCO (2002) defines culture as: "the set of distinctive spiritual, material, intellectual and emotional features of society or a social group, and that it encompasses, in addition to art and literature, lifestyles, ways of living together, value systems, traditions and beliefs" (p. 1). An individual may belong to several cultures: family, worksite, neighborhood, race, profession, social club, political party, country. Likewise, a group may belong to several cultures; chemists may be members of a site staff, a union, an industry, a state organization, a national organization, and an international organization. Some of these cultures may overlap or even contradict, in which case, the individual or group must either live with the disequilibrium or resolve the conflict (i.e., reject one or the other, reject both, or incorporate parts of each). A culture may also be measured in terms of how cohesive it is in terms of inside and outside pressures; if conflict arises from outside its borders, do members stay within the culture or switch allegiance to the other culture?

## REPRESENTATIVE CULTURES AND SUBCULTURES

Cultures are well-defined, sustained groups of people with common norms, expectations and values, which can be distinguished from other culture groups. Subcultures are more specialized groups that still belong to the larger group and its norm, but have more specific characteristics. For example, Latinos can be considered a culture, but Puerto Ricans differ significantly from Peruvians, and homeland Puerto Ricans differ from New York born Puerto Ricans (subculture within a subculture). Such differentiations are important to note because too often generalizations are made about a culture (or even mega-culture such as Asians), which have little validity on a subcultural level or case-by-case basis. One might use the analogy of food, such as "All Asian food uses soy sauce," to demonstrate the feebleness of such generalizations. Particularly when a course has just one student of a certain culture, that student might be called upon to represent that entire culture, which can be a very frustrating – and sometimes condescending – experience for that individual.

Nevertheless, race and ethnicity impact educational achievement and social status, even in the 21st century. The Educational Test Service asserted that "educational inequalities begin at birth" (Viadero, 2003, p.1) because of lower birth weight and other health factors. Blacks and Latinos are less likely to be read to by their parent(s), and are more apt to learn in overcrowded classrooms from inexperienced teachers. Additionally, they are more likely to move, and change schools, which means that they have to renegotiate social relationships. Native American teens are often separated from their families and tribes as they go to distant schools for high school education. As youth get older, disparencies in academic success increase so that minority teens experience greater difficulty keeping up with their Anglo peers. Minority populations may be able to overcome their disadvantages with maturity, but they also realize that they have much catching up to do, and may feel frustrated as their own cultural advantages are not recognized or leveraged for society's good as a whole.

It is also important to look beyond students themselves and examine conditions in the schools they attend. Bowker (2003) reported that students who drop out cite several school-related problems: failure or inability to get along with teachers, dislike of school, inability to get along with other students, boredom, feelings of not belonging, and suspension. According to Caine and Caine (1997), students who are confronted with racist threats on a regular basis often lose a positive sense of cultural identity and begin a process of downshifting, which eventually leads to dropping out. Similarly, Irvine (1990) suggested that when there is a cultural incongruity between the school and the student, miscommunication and confrontation often occur among students, teachers, and families, resulting in hostility, alienation, and eventual dropping out.

On one hand, online instruction can ameliorate physical cultural conflicts. However, the digital divide colors this picture as physical access to online education may have some cultural associations. At this point in time, age and educational level are much better predictors than race in terms of Internet access and use (Pew Internet and American Life Project, 2009), but historically, socio-economic factors impacted the likelihood of access to digital technology and ownership of computers so that today's minority adult population remains disadvantaged because of less technology experience growing up, even in schools that should have provided equitable opportunities.

Several representative cultures are described below. In the process, each culture holds beliefs about, and practices normative behaviors relative to, education and technology, which impacts online teaching. It should be noted that these generalizations do not account for all attitudes and behaviors, since each person has unique characteristics and experiences.

## African Americans / Blacks

African American, or Black, families cover a broad spectrum of expectations and experiences. The Black community as a whole has a strong sense of social relationships and personal distinctiveness. Black, as a rule, use language expressively, and complement speech with nuanced body language. They tend to respond to issues holistically, and use internal cues to solve problems. They appreciate novelty and freedom, and have a keen sense of justice.

For several socio-economic reasons, African Americans are over-represented among the urban poor where the economic gap is widening. Overcrowding and crime impact family life and personal development. Part of teen development involves risk-taking, but in dangerous neighborhoods, such behavior can have serious consequences. Murder is the number one cause of death among African American youth, and teen suicide tripled between 1960 and 1988. With societal prejudice against Black teenage males in particular, these young men have a harder time getting jobs and sustaining strong families. Tatum (2003) asserts that Black males need a safe environment in which to search for meaning in their lives and the means to challenge status quo, analyze society, and improve it.

The Black community expects schools to provide their children with a good education (Josey & DeLoach, 2000). Nevertheless, peer acceptance can take precedence over academic achievement among Black male teens, especially if white power predominates the educational scene. In searching 20$^{th}$ century African American adult education, Johnson-Bailey (2002) found that instruction historically often emphasized assimilation so that Blacks would maintain their traditional social role rather than advance. Blacks also saw education as a way for their unique cultural heritage to survive; African-American studies exemplify this objective. A third educational agenda was education for resistance, instructing Blacks in the use of political and economic power. However, curriculum tended to be controlled by whites, and integration efforts sometimes resulted in downplaying African-American distinctive culture, both factors undermining Black educational power.

Technology can provide a means to empower African Americans; access to online information is an "alternative to conventional teacher-directed on-site paradigm; informational justice is a human rights issue" (Josey & DeLoach, 2000, p. 601). In an editorial in *Black Enterprise* (March, 1998), Muhammad asserted that Blacks have opportunities to access the Internet: "The only thing holding us back is our own foresight." Economically secure African Americans own computers, and use technology at work and at home to the same extent as other ethnicities. However, poor Blacks have fewer computers than poor whites. Several reasons may account for this difference: less community-based investment or public funding for connectivity infrastructure, lack of knowledge about technology and its benefits, little Internet content that address their needs, distrust of government and big business interaction with technology. Fortunately, this racial gap has shrunk over time so that in 2009 the difference in Internet use by whites and Blacks was just six percent, and Blacks outpaced whites in wireless Internet use by seven percent (Pew Internet and American Life Project, 2009). In terms of Internet content participation, Blacks are significantly more represented (47 percent) than whites (36 percent) or Latinos (33 percent) (Pew Internet and American Life Project, 2010); this trend could bode well for participatory online courses.

## Latinos

Latinos comprise a variety of subgroups, from Californian land-grant descendants to recent Haitian refugees. Rice (2007) painted the following picture about this population. Two-thirds were born in the U. S., and three-quarters speak Spanish at home. Latinos constitute the fastest growing ethnicity in the United States, and are younger than the general population. Most Latinos speak Spanish and develop self-pride from being part of the family. They tend to have less education, and a quarter of them live in poverty. Puerto Rican families have a high rate of divorce and female heads-of-households: about the same as African Americans. This situation is the result of overcrowded urban living conditions, need for women to work, and adjustments in immigrating.

Focusing on one Latino subculture, Rice (2007) reported that almost 75% of Mexican-Americans live a segregated life in urban barrios. Many Mexican American children do not start school with the same advantages of other students for several reasons: they might not be exposed to rich cognitive experiences, parents might not have much formal schooling, parents might not speak English at home, and free and open conversation might be discouraged in authoritarian environments. In school, teachers might not be able to speak Spanish, and they may react negatively to Spanish being spoken by students.

Adolescence can be even more stressful for Mexican Americans, according to Moller (2001). These teens are particularly worried about family issues: illness, crime, alcohol abuse, moving, and unemployment. Additionally, the tight family structure can discourage independence, especially for girls. Oldest sons are sometimes indulged and given greater freedom, but not expected to achieve academically. Risk-taking is not encouraged; rather, youth are told to be careful and not shame the family, so they may be less competitive than their Anglo peers. Latino tends tend to get married earlier than other ethnicities, and drop out of education earlier, and get lower-paying jobs.

Family values play a large role in educational participation and achievement. Males tend to be given preferential educational support, although Latinas perceive that education is one effective way to gain socio-economic status (Colon & Sanchez, 2010). Indeed, as Latinos attend college, they realize that education not only helps them individually but also helps the family because of expanded socio-economic opportunities (Becerra, 2010). Immigration status and acculturation also impact educational choices and experiences. For instance, tear of deportation affects education as families may be afraid to enroll their children in school. In that respect, online education that does not require registration may be attractive to learners who want to maintain their anonymity while pursuing knowledge. Language barriers constitute a major barrier to education as well. Most information about education, including applications and financial options, are provided just in English (in the United States) so those families who are not well acculturated, and have few English-speaking network connections, are less likely to know how to navigate the educational world (Becerra, 2010). Online education, in that respect, may ameliorate language barriers as Spanish online resources expand and online translation tools improve.

Latinos have lower computer ownership, have less access to the Internet, and use computers to a lesser extent than other ethnicities because of economic limitations, less education, and immigrant status (Luevano-Molina, 2001, p.134). This picture has improved in the last decade so that now almost two-thirds of Latinos use the Internet regularly (Livingston, Parker, & Fox, 2009), a ten percent increase in just two years. Furthermore, the greatest increase in use occurred among low-income and low-educated Latinos. Broadband access also grew significantly from 2006 to 2008, with a 75 percent penetration for Internet users, more than any other ethnic group.

## Native Americans

Native Americans have the highest birth rate, highest death rate, and shortest life expectancy of any ethnic group in the U. S. They have one of the highest unemployment rates, lowest income levels, and overall low standards of living. Furthermore, they suffer from hunger and malnutrition more than other ethnic groups (Rice, 1998, p. 72). Their leading illness is middle ear disease, resulting in hearing loss, which impacts learning how to read as well as other academic skills (Rice, 1998, p. 73). In that respect, online course delivery can provide a more equitable educational experience.

According to a study conducted by Strand and Peacock (2002), American and Alaskan Indian students have to manage the often-conflicting cultures of Anglo educational expectations and family values. This situation is particularly troubling in instances where boarding school separate students from their families. Many students feel despair, and the suicide rate among this teenage population is 2.5 times higher than the combined rate of all the other ethnicities. Resilient youth tend to think of themselves as bicultural, taking the positive aspects of each environment (Strand & Peacock, 2002). Although the drop-out rate has improved for Native Americans, it remains higher than any other ethnic group in the United States. In her analysis of drop-out students, Fernandes (2008) found that the main reasons for leaving included family factors, community economic status, student disengagement, and the school system. Students with a strong ethnic identity were more likely to be academically successful.

Morris and Meinrath (2009) investigated new media technology and Internet use by Native Americans. They discovered First Nation homelands are often isolated, which impedes Internet connectivity. Wireless connectivity, when available, is usually too expensive for these families. On the other hand, when physical access to the Internet exists, Native Americans prove to be technologically savvy. They are building tribal-centric online content as well as their own broadband highways when no one else will.

## Immigrants

In the United States there are 32 million immigrants, about a tenth of the population, mainly due to globalization, poverty, and political unrest. About a half are women. Because of mass media, immigrants tend to be more knowledgeable about the U. S. than prior generations. Yet the dominant culture in the U. S. tends to display a xenophobic attitude, even though almost everyone's family immigrated to the states at some time. As a result, asserted conflicts with immigrants arise in terms of race, language, jobs, and cross-generations (Luevano-Molina, 2001).

Foreign-born are more likely to be poor. About a fifth of foreign-born without a U. S. citizen parent live below the poverty line, and a quarter of non-citizens are poor as compared to 11.4% of naturalized citizens (Zuvekas, 1999, p. 3) Moreover, culture shock can lead to depression and a sense of isolation. Immigrants between the ages of 12 and 24 are particularly vulnerable to attempting suicide. (Zuvekas, 1999) Those immigrants who cannot speak English have less access to health and other social services. In some non-U.S. cultures, health issues are not discussed, and preventative medical treatment or Western medicine is not pursued. It should be noted that English language learner (ELL) immigrants more likely to want Internet information in their primary language than those who were born in the United States.

Acculturation is particularly difficult for teens because they want to feel like they belong, but are torn between two or more cultures. Their peers may consider them foreigners and outsiders; their own parents may think that they are abandoning family values. Not only does each ethnic group have its own identity, but those immigrants who came as refugees have an additional identity to confront and may have to overcome tragic experiences. It should also be noted that refugee teens may well be more educated and sophisticated than their parents, which upsets the traditional authority of elders and reverses roles of responsibility.

As immigrants deal with at least two significant cultures, their own and the U. S. dominant Anglo, they make decisions as to how to balance their allegiances.

- They may stay with their primary culture, withdrawing from the dominant one; they choose to remain social outsiders.
- They may reject their original culture, and whole-heartedly embrace the Anglo dominant culture, and thus become over-acculturated. Family stress may well rise as a result.
- They may assume most of the values of the dominant culture, and maintain the trappings of their original culture, thus making them mainstreamed.
- They may reject both cultures, and thus become marginalized.
- They may accept both cultures, drawing the strengths from each, and thus become bicultural.

Educational experiences can be problematic for immigrant teens because of first-country differences in practices and values. Not only might immigrants lack knowledge about these institutions and their benefits, but they may also harbor negative attitudes towards government. They also tend to lack guidance in their use since they might not be members of mainstream social groups. Literacy efforts may also suffer, not only because of language differences, but also because U. S. education tends to favor English-only instruction. Moreover, in some countries, reading is not considered very important. What with immigrant families focusing on survival and acculturation, education and technology usually take a back seat (Constantino, 1998).

## English Language Learners

English language learners (ELL) may be subdivided into two categories: those born abroad and those born in the U.S. In both cases, there are several roadblocks to education, particularly online formats: socio-political differences, economic conditions; xenophobia, anti-bilingual education, prejudicial institutional culture; lack of teacher knowledge about ELL, orthographical differences; and different cultural values relative to reading (Grant & Wong, 2003).

If they are out of the social loop, ELLs are less likely to have experienced technology and so are unlikely to see its benefits. Even if they used technology in their first county, it may seem hard to find or costly to access technology in their new country, resulting in lower technology usage by ELLs. Increasingly effective online translation programs can mitigate language barriers so ELLs can locate documents and their original language and get at least approximate translations, assuming that they are literate in their first language. However, for ELL readers of non-Roman language systems, English-only software, Internet browsers, and even Roman alphabet keyboards can be particularly daunting.

## Culture Impact on Learning

Culture plays a significant role in community attitudes towards education, which informs online instruction and practice. Suefert (2002) identified a number of learning system dimensions that can be culturally profiled.

- *Educational epistemology:* to pass on knowledge, to preserve the status quo, to socialize, to prepare workers, to help students self-actualize
- *Pedagogical epistemology:* instructivism to constructivist
- *Underlying psychology:* behavioral to cognitive
- *Goal orientation:* sharply focused to unfocused, short-term vs. long-term, individualistic vs. society
- *Experimental value:* abstract to concrete
- *Role of instructor:* Master lecturer to egalitarian facilitator, interpreter to questioner
- *Value of errors:* errorless learning to learning from experience
- *Motivation:* extrinsic to intrinsic
- *Structure:* high to low
- *Accommodation of individual differences:* none to multi-faceted
- *Learning control:* none to unrestricted
- *User activity:* rote to generative
- *Cooperative learning:* none to integral

For instance, if a cultural norm about the role of the instructor is to tell students what is right and true, then independent critical evaluation of information might be discouraged. If a culture values independent thinking and competitiveness, then collaborative research might be considered cheating. If the culture believes in a highly-structure educational experience, then students may feel lost in loosely defined or student-defined projects.

Just as the meaning and value of education are cultural contextualized, so too are the conditions for online education. Online instructional designers need to examine the cultural landscape in order to discern – and align with – shared values and expectations. Ignorance or denial of cultural norms will spell disaster for online learning. If the most influential culture shares the goals and strategies of the online curriculum, then the online instructor has a natural "in." If the culture is strong, then the path to success is even better paved. On the other hand, a strong culture that discounts online education and has a closed attitude can pose challenges. A culture that undervalues online education may be won over if they have a more accepting nature – and can be persuaded by an overlapping stronger culture to join in the overarching goal.

Hofstede's 1980 model of cultural dimensions provides a useful framework for examining culturally-sensitive learning. Implications for online teaching are noted in italics.

- **Power distance.** What is the degree of equality between people? How equitable is the power distribution as defined from low-status people? In low-power distance societies, status is less important. *Power distance impacts teacher-student relations. In high-power distance cultures, the teacher is omnipotent, and the student never questions the teacher; conversely in low-power distance cultures, little hierarchy exists so that teacher and student are considered co-learners with equal status.*

- **Individualism vs. collectivism**. People in individualistic societies tend to belong to several groups, each of which is loosely-knit, while collectivist societies tend to have a few, well-defined groups who are highly loyal. In-group refers to a collective in which members are highly interdependent and have a sense of common fate; groups to which they do not belong are out-groups. *Learners and teachers have preconceived attitudes about individual vs. cooperative efforts. In the U.S., individual effort is usually promoted, while in Indian culture, the caste is the central identity.*
- **Masculinity**. To what degree are genders differentiated? Are traditional gendered roles supported in terms of achievement, control and power? How are women valued relative to men? *In instruction, males in some cultures might be more competitive or need more praise. Some educational roles are sex-linked in some cultures; only males can be doctors and only women can be nurses.*
- **Uncertainty avoidance**. How tolerant is society of uncertainty and ambiguity? Are different options acceptable or are strict rules the norm? *How structured should learning activities be? Does assessment ask for one right answer or does it encourage new answers? Do learning activities focus on accuracy or on different perspectives? In the traditional Chinese culture, students are expected to parrot back the single right answer. In some theocratic societies, dogma is absolute and to be obeyed without question. In contrast, parts of the U.S. culture encourage open-mindedness and intellectual exploration such as in scientific research.*
- **Long-term vs. short-term orientation**. Long-term values include perseverance and thrift; short-term values include respect for tradition (keeping the status quo) and social "face." Do people think it is useful and feasible to plan for the distant future, or is day-to-day life so unpredictable that such long-term attitudes are considered foolish? *To what degree is intellectual exploration encouraged and supported? Generally, a short-term orientation would foster obedience to the teacher and face-saving interventions.*

More specifically, different cultures tend to reinforce different learning styles. For example, collective societies tend to reinforce field dependent and non-linear learning where the specific location and people present determine the meaning of a concept. In contrast, other cultures emphasize essential truths or step-by-step learning. Instructors need to start a unit by giving the Big Picture, and they provide such learners with more guidance along the way (Chen & Macredie, 2002).

The impact of culture may be further analyzed using Biggs' 1978 3P model of teaching and learning. Presage deals with experiences before learning takes place. This includes learning characteristics, prior knowledge and experience. Process occurs during learning and concerns learning conditions and activities. Product focuses on the outcomes of learning such as assessments, application, and context. Thus, learner experiences are interdependent with situational elements such as teaching factors (such as style, institutional procedures, and assessment) and the learning environment (such as learning activities and social climate). Biggs also differentiates surface approaches to learning (reproducing information), deep approaches (thorough understanding), and achievement orientation (that is, focus on grades). Biggs, Kember, and Leung (2001) emphasized the importance of identifying which factors are universal and which are culturally-defined. Most significant are those practices that are imposed as if universal such as outlining a report, that actually reflect specific cultural norms, particularly those of the United States; learners outside that culture may feel discounted or under-prepared.

## CULTURE IMPACT RELATIVE TO ONLINE LEARNING

Joo (1999) identified several cultural issues that emerged with classroom use of the Internet. Resource content matter may be culturally-sensitive, such as religious practices, or may perpetrate stereotypes. Writing style degree of formality may differ between cultures; an informal tone online may be uncomfortable for some learners. Web design norms differ between cultures along several dimensions: color theme and use, layout, and content sequencing (e.g., right to left in Semitic languages).

Bentley, Tinney, and Chica (2005) reviewed studies on cross-cultural Internet-based learning, and found the following value differentials.

- **Technical infrastructure**. All the online educational stakeholders (institution, instructors, students) need to have electricity stability, Internet connectivity, and broadband capacity to some extent.
- **Educational culture**. Culture-specific values may run into conflict when learners from several cultures enroll in the same course. Even if online education is provided to just one culture, that population might not value virtual instruction or the methods used to examine subject matter.
- **Local versus global context.** Some courses might emphasize local perspectives while others may aim for global or universal concepts. Usually basic, factual information can be handled across cultures. In contrast, "soft" skills and specific interactive services might need to be taught face-to-face locally.
- **Learning style.** E-learning can incorporate individualized and collaborative work. Instructors need to determine what kind of learning matches the desired student outcome as well as what approach fits with existing cultural practices.
- **Social context.** Learners who need contextualized content might be disadvantaged in globalized e-learning environments.

Building on culturally-contextualized learning, McMahon and Bruce (2002) noted several cultural factors that impact online teaching, as noted in italics.

- **Language**. Students use native or primary language skills of reading and writing differently than secondary languages; usually, the latter is more formal and standardized while the former is more varied and nuanced. *Online instructors should explicitly introduce subject-specific vocabulary and relevant idiomatic knowledge (such as the use of sports terminology in U.S. corporate business environments).*
- **Educational philosophy and experiences**. The role of education varies among cultures, and can be especially problematic for immigrants or international students who participate in online courses originating in another culture. Curriculum and instruction practices vary between cultures, and can be very frustrating when the instructor's culture differs from the students'. Likewise, student academic behavior norms might differ from the institution's or instructor's expectations. *Online instructors need to provide clear expectations about student engagement and work habits from the beginning. Even students who hold rigid views about education prefer upfront directions rather than trying to ferret out the instructor's tacit philosophy.*
- **Gender issues**. Culturally-defined educational, career, and workplace expectations and norms may be sex-linked. *Online learning environments may mitigate highly differentiated gender roles, but factors such as the instructor's sex may impact student engagement; for instance, Arabic*

*males may downplay a female teacher's expertise. Usually students will accept the instructor's status if strong credentials are provided or if the instructor has been "vetted" by the educational institution (that is, power by association).*

- **Age-linked cultural norms**. Generation-specific roles and expectations vary across cultures; in some cases, those norms are highly developed while in other cultures, demarcations are fuzzy at best. Norms and expectations are also impacted by global and social realities, such as technology advances that digital natives experience first hand more than older generations; in such cases, older students may need to rely on younger teachers, which may be culturally uncomfortable. *Online environments tend to mask ages unless students self-disclose their ages via sharing past experiences. Online instructors may choose to downplay age factors, or they might leverage age as a socially-relevant part of the educational experience.*
- **Knowledge of content.** Social patterns for transmitting information differ across cultures; some emphasize orality while others value the written word. Similarly, the institutional disseminators may vary, from a single personality to a church or a public library. Cultural expectations and norms may also be discipline-specific, such as research scientist communities vs. artistic colonies. On the other hand, community needs and practices largely determine local agricultural economy, while international agribusiness may use a standardized corporate model. *Online instructors should try to find out what students know about subject matter at the beginning of the course as well as the source of knowledge. Both cognitive and affective domains should be considered, particularly for cultures that emphasize the social construct of knowledge.*

In general, when content matter is culturally neutral, online instructors can introduce learning activities that might be more culturally defined so that students can gain experience in different ways of learning without it overloading their cognitive burden. For instance, students who might be more comfortable with rote learning or individual study habits might learn facts by using a collaborative jigsaw exercise. On the other hand, when the content matter is culturally sensitive, such as marriage practices, culturally-neutral learning approaches such as compare-contrast essays might be more appropriate than oral debates.

## ONLINE INSTRUCTORS' CULTURAL COMPETENCY

Just as students bring their cultural assumptions and behaviors to the online learning environment, so too do online instructors. As curriculum experts and learning facilitators, online instructors need to become culturally competent so they can manage student interaction as well as provide relevant learning experiences.

To this end, online instructors need to self-examine their own cultural values, assumptions, expectations, and norms. Everyone has cultural prejudices, which color personal perceptions about the surrounding world. Identifying and owning up to those prejudices can help instructors interact more authentically with their students and avoid possible misunderstandings.

As online instructors work in cross-cultural settings, or at the very least work with learners from different cultures, they should strive for cultural competence. Kalyanpur and Harry (1999) list several benchmarks that note progress in becoming culturally competent. Possible actions for online instructors to take are italicized.

- **Cultural knowledge.** One becomes familiar with cultural characteristics, history, behaviors and values of people of another cultural group. *If the online instructor knows that a substantial percentage of students belong to a specific culture, he can read about that culture.*
- **Cultural awareness.** One understands another culture and changing attitudes about culture; one remains open flexible when relating to people of another culture. *Online instructors realize that cultural differences exist, and that they can impact how students participate online. Instructors try to meet students halfway rather than acting in an authoritarian or dogmatic way.*
- **Cultural sensitivity.** One realizes that cultural similarities and differences exist, without assigning relative value to those differences. *Online instructors recognize that students might participate in different ways, and prefer different types of learning experiences. Instructors try not to privilege any one way to gain or assess knowledge, but instead provide choices in ways to acquire and demonstrate student competency.*
- **Cultural competence.** One develops a congruent set of behaviors, attitudes and policies to enable one to work effectively in cross-cultural situations. *Online instructors should develop a repertoire of instructional design strategies, instructional practices, and assessment modes that respect the cultures of each student.*
- **Cultural proficiency.** One develops a way of being to successfully interact with others who are different from him or herself. *Online instructors fully internalize culturally-sensitive, effective educational and personal practices that respect and empower each student while making them feel safe and self-confident.*

## CULTURALLY-SENSITIVE CURRICULUM

The curriculum identifies what students are supposed to learn: what they should know and be able to do. Because knowledge itself is culturally-contextualized, curriculum automatically contains certain cultural assumptions and perspectives. It makes sense that the curriculum to be delivered online should explicitly address cultural aspects. As noted before, all curriculum reflects educational philosophies and cultural values. At the very least, educational decision-makers determine the nature of the curriculum, which reflects what they value enough that they want students to learn and apply that information in their personal or professional lives.

Using McREL's knowledge taxonomy, Hubbell (2010) posited four types of knowledge --- declarative, procedural, contextual, experiential -- each of which has cultural implications.

Declarative knowledge addresses what learners need to know. This kind of knowledge tends to be factual and less culturally-sensitive. However, some declarative knowledge may differ from culture to culture, such as writing systems or appropriate ways to dress.

Procedural knowledge explains how to use knowledge or perform a skill. In some cases, processes are culturally-neutral, such as the process of word processing. Other procedures may well be culturally defined, such as interviewing techniques. Online instructors need to determine what procedures are universal, and which aspects may be modified because of cultural norms. Students can also share cultural differences relative to procedural knowledge, which would recognize the cultural expertise of each student.

Contextual knowledge helps learners know when to use knowledge or a skill. For example, a spreadsheet would be useful when making predictions based on numerical manipulations such as budgets. Contextual knowledge is more apt to be culturally-sensitive when "soft skills" are involved, such as determining at what point to ask about domestic child discipline practices, which might be considered a private matter or a possible "face" threatening situation.

Experiential knowledge identifies the reason that specific knowledge is important. For instance, testing a patient's blood is important because it provides important clues as to the person's health and possible disease symptoms. This practice, though, might not be valued in some cultures; in fact, drawing blood might be taboo. Thus, knowing how a discipline is practiced within a culture can impact what curriculum will be included.

Just as education is culturally contextualized, so too are the conditions for cultural-sensitive online curriculum. As online instructors seek support for a culturally-sensitive curriculum, they need to examine the cultural landscape in order to discern – and align with – shared values and expectations. Ignorance or denial of cultural norms will spell disaster for cross-cultural initiatives. If the most influential culture shares the goals and strategies of cultural sensitivity, then the online instructor has a natural "in." If the culture is strong, then the path to success is even better paved. On the other hand, a strong culture that discounts cultural sensitivity and has a closed attitude can pose challenges. A culture that undervalues cultural sensitivity may be won over if they can be persuaded by an overlapping stronger culture to join in the overarching goal. Ideally, culturally-sensitive online education should be explicitly addressed and integrated throughout the organization rather than isolated in an online course or two. Certainly, online instructors can make little cultural headway if their institutions do not support such an agenda.

## UNIVERSAL INSTRUCTIONAL DESIGN

In the global society, people come into contact with other cultures more frequently and deeply. In some cases, those interactions may be characterized as clashes. Misunderstandings occur because of tacit assumptions and cultural perceptions. Thus, the need for understanding different cultures is more important than ever. Domer and Gorman (2006) offer several useful suggestions, which largely apply to all types of learning settings.

### Student-Teacher Relations

Learners from high power-distance cultures expect formal, hierarchical relationships with their teachers; in such cultures, the teacher has high status and his judgment should never be questioned by students. To ease their stress in more egalitarian or constructivist courses, online instructors can clearly and explicitly define their roles, and work with students to make clear decisions about learning expectations. Personal acknowledgment rituals and relationships can also counterbalance power distance formality (Gurubatham, 2005). They can also tell students the appropriate term of address to use (e.g., Mrs. Ramirez, Mrs. R, Paula). Students who are shy about asking for help should have several options available: confidential email, intermediation by a course student representative/spokesperson, peer assistance, referrals to resources such as online tutorials. Online instructors can pre-emptively help this situation by frequently checking for understanding (e.g., short online quizzes and quick writes) and giving all students immediate feedback.

The affective aspect of student-teacher relations impacts academic achievement. For instance, non-cognitive variables accounted for about a quarter of the variance in grade point averages for African Americans at predominately white universities; at black universities, non-cognitive variables accounted for about 18 percent of grade average variation (Lockett & Harrell, 2003). The authors concluded that the relationship between students and faculty influence self-confidence and self-efficacy. Even though online learning might mitigate such differences in perception, language use in written and oral communication may indicate a person's cultural background, and might influence some party's perceptions either of the instructor or the interaction.

## Topics of Discussion

Online instructors should be aware of possible taboo subjects. This issue might emerge in health issues where gendered practices might inhibit practice, such as attitudes towards family planning in cultures where males are expected to make such decisions or are praised for impregnating women. Online instructors would do well to consult their peers in relevant countries to find out ahead of time what topics might be sensitive to their learners. Accommodations for alternative topics, resources, or ways of learning should be provided so as to not disadvantage affected learners. In almost all cases, connecting course concepts with real world context and applications helps all learners, not just field dependent ones.

## Choice of Resources

In most cases, online instructors choose the material to be covered in a lesson, or they select in collaboration with other educational stakeholders. That selection or filtering process may reflect cultural bias that might disadvantage some international students; specific ideas might be supported and other omitted, thus shutting down opposing viewpoints. Even a simple factor of choosing examples reflecting only urban practice might ignore the needs of students working in rural areas. At the least, online instructors should enable students to choose from a wide spectrum of reading materials reflecting a variety of perspectives. It should be noted that students tend to find and understand web-based information more quickly when the content is created by designers from their own cultures (Faiola & Matei, 2005). Alternatively, online instructors should permit students to seek self-relevant sources. This latter approach might trouble classroom teachers who want to control students' reading materials, which, in itself, reflects a certain cultural value. Likewise, in some cultures, such as China, students typically read only what the instructor chooses, so self-determination of materials can be uncomfortable for them at first.

## Learner Participation

Again, clear expectations and course norms from the first contact help reduce learner confusion and distress. If the student population includes a mix of cultures, then a corresponding combination of individual and collaborative activities would be appropriate. Likewise, a mix of cooperative and competitive activities allows learners from different backgrounds to excel at different points. Alternatively, online instructors can provide students with options to do work independently or with others. To accommodate learners from collective cultures, online instructors may need to initiate discussion or start groups off when introducing problem-based learning; step-by-step guidelines also facilitate field dependent learners. Web 2.0 technology should also be incorporated in order to provide learners with opportunities to interact with each other, collaborate, and produce creative work for authentic audiences. In any case, the e-learning environment should be safe and comfortable for all learners.

## Learning Activities

Probably the best solution for culturally-sensitive activities is inclusive instructional design that accommodates *all* students. Here are some other specific suggestions. Some students are not used to self-directed learning. Rather than telling students the answer, the online instructor can model the process required to find it. Students may be accustomed to rote learning facts, rather than applying skills; online instructors can help students apply general principles to a variety of research situations. Students might not be used to critically evaluating information; online instructors can provide checklists or criteria for students to use in evaluating sources. Many students are only interested in what is needed to pass exams (achievement orientation); online instructors can emphasize the importance of knowledge and skills for lifelong success as well as immediate career advancement.

### Assessment

Culture impacts student performance in several ways. In terms of language, even simple tasks such as following directions can disadvantage some students. Some of the measures that can be taken to mitigate cultural discrepancies include: giving shorter tests and recall items rather than tasks that require sophisticated language and literacy skills (Teresi, et al., 2001), provide accurate translations in those cases where language ability is not the element being tested, provide bilingual glossaries, consider the option of having students demonstrate their skill kinesthetically (e.g., video recording their performance or having a local expert verify their ability). In any case, content should outweigh presentation. Additionally, online instructors need to make sure that the test is not culturally biased, that is, one cultural group does not outperform others systemically. Bias usually occurs when cultural knowledge is assumed (e.g., use of bidets, knowledge of July 4, eating habits). Images too may have culturally-defined meanings or connotations (for example, owls connote different attributes in different cultures). The easiest approach is to check with students via non-test activities about their understanding of textual and visual information.

## CULTURE-SENSITIVE INSTRUCTIONAL DESIGN

Learning occurs in a setting, be it physical or virtual, and involves people (peers and instructor), curriculum (content information and resources) and instructional design. Within that environment, learners interact with the content and individuals. An e-learning environment incorporates technology as a communications and storage vehicle. Furthermore, just as with face-to-face instruction, online instruction needs to integrate differentiation to accommodate diverse learners. Particularly since some online instruction is set before any users access it, variations need to be considered ahead of time. Regardless of content, the student population is increasingly diversified in cultural background and experience. All too often, cultural sensitivity is overlooked when designing curriculum and delivery. Not only should online instructors be aware of the impact of culture in their instruction, but they should leverage those cultural differences to provide a richer educational experience.

In researching cross-cultural e-learning, Edmundson (2007) developed a two-pronged approach in her cultural adaptation process (CAP) model of instructional design accommodation in order to address cultural differences both between the instructor and students as well as among the student population. One prong focuses on the learner, and the other prong analyzes the course. Edmundson posits a four-step process, aligned with the complexity of the content.

1. Evaluate the content along a continuum from simple, core information (such as basic procedures and products) to complex knowledge and soft skills (such as project management and conflict resolution. The e-learning delivery dimension can range from one-way lectures and handouts to social networking
2. Identify instructional methods and activities along the spectrum from objectivist/rote to constructivist-cognitive/high context communication.
3. Identify cross-cultural dimensions relative to learning.

   a. Cooperative learning: from unsupported to integral
   b. Origin of motivation: from extrinsic to intrinsic
   c. Learner control: from non-existent to unrestricted
   d. Teacher role: from didactic to facilitative
   e. Value of errors: from errorless learning to learning from experience
4. Identify culturally-contextualized e-learner preferences.
   a. User activity: from multiple access methods to the same content to learner-generative processing
   b. Experiential value: from abstract to concrete
   c. Accommodating individual differences: from non-existent to multi-faceted

In e-learning environments, the degree of cooperative learning and the origin of motivation are particularly culturally-sensitive, and need to be addressed when designing instruction.

For basic, objective learner outcomes in low-context cultural norms, materials just need to be translated, typically using global English with simple grammar and standard phrases. Examples should try to be culturally neutral, such as climate and mathematics. The only cultural dimension that may impact e-learning would be orientation to time so culture-sensitive accommodations for synchronicity and sequencing need to be made.

With increasing complexity and culture sensitivity, courses need localization where resources and examples reflect the daily life and cultural context of the target learner. Sometimes learners, particularly adults, can locate or generate such examples. The burden is on the instructor to determine if the learners' selections are relevant and appropriate.

Further complexity and socially-constructed courses can be modularized, with culture-specific learning objects. When cultural soft skills constitute the central learning outcome, it is probably best for that culture to originate the instruction design and delivery, even for e-learning environments.

## CONNECTING LEARNING TO THE LARGER ENVIRONMENT

Online learning does not exist in a virtual vacuum. Online instructors of diverse students need to help those learners navigate within the educational and their family cultures successfully. These skills might include learning social expectations and norms, identifying the cultural assumptions being made about presented (and missing) content, and communicating in socially acceptable ways (e.g., avoiding jargon, understanding social space). For instance, "school" talk might be more formal than discussions at home. At school, females might be taught to speak up but at home be expected to be passively quiet.

As learners straddle two (or more) cultures, they need to interpret information in light of differing perspectives, and negotiate the relevant application of such information to their daily life. Particularly if the school ethos contradicts familial values, learners might artificially separate those two worlds, try to integrate the two, or reject one set of values. In advising library staff, McMahon and Bruce (2002) recommended that they take care to respect each student's cultural stance while noting the importance of learning about the social climate to be experienced as a potential employee. Along with this advice, online instructors would do well to contextualize content in terms of students' local reality or at least build on those realities as students need to assimilate new cultural understandings

In an e-learning environment, technology significantly impacts student learning, and also is subject to cultural influence. For instance, learners might have different degrees of access due to cultural attitudes about technology, socially-constructed gender role expectations, and socio-economic values. World experience and knowledge impacts learners' ability to locate and evaluate online information. Even social attitudes about language acquisition and attitudes about English can impact online use. Online instructors should find out their students' technology realities, and try to provide accessible learning activities for all, or at least make accommodations for online students who have technical constraints. For example, documents might be saved in.rtf format, video clips can be transcribed, and students can be given choices of resources to use.

## CONCLUSION

As laudatory as culturally-sensitive online teaching efforts appear, they require a flexible mindset and organizational structure. Because information and information literacy changes constantly, because the world at large changes constantly, the entire educational enterprise must respond to these dynamics if they hope to have any chance of facilitating student achievement. Simultaneously, these institutions usually reflect the dominant culture. Therefore, tensions exist between established power and purposeful improvement. Some of the current trends in education anticipated by Thompson in 1991 are still coming to fruition in multicultural settings:

- educational purpose: from selecting the best to ensuring that all students learn
- nature of knowledge: from absolute truths to making meaning
- nature of learning: from passive reception to active engagement
- nature of teaching: from sage on the stage to guide on the side
- curriculum: from a highly structured sequence set of fixed knowledge to a cyclical set of contextualized perspectives
- leadership: from hierarchical authority to transformative empowerment
- assessment: from standardized input points to integrated and outcomes-centered cycled of inquiry.

These patterns are not absolutes that online educators can count on. Rather, they point out options that can be called upon when discussing online education options.

All the conditions for culturally-sensitive online education – curriculum, resources, learning environment, intellectual capital, leadership, community, plans and policies– need to be continuously audited, assessed and negotiated in order to provide the most efficient online educational experiences to support culturally relevant student learning. Online instructors need to be aware of these changing dynamics, and serve as change agents, providing appropriate leadership via cross-culture professional development, communities of practice, and educational reform efforts.

## REFERENCES

Becerra, D. (2010). Differences in perceptions of barriers to college enrollment and the completion of a degree among Latinos in the United States. *Journal of Hispanic Higher Education*, *9*(2), 187–201. doi:10.1177/1538192709359051

Bentley, J., Tinney, M., & Chica, B. (2005). Intercultural Internet-based learning: Know your audience and what it values. *Educational Technology Research and Development*, *53*(2), 117–127. doi:10.1007/BF02504870

Biggs, J. (1978). Individual and group differences in study processes. *The British Journal of Educational Psychology*, *48*, 266–279. doi:10.1111/j.2044-8279.1978.tb03013.x

Biggs, J., Kember, D., & Leung, D. (2001). The revised 2-factor study process questionnaire R-SP2-2F. *British Journal of Educational Research*, *71*, 133–149.

Bowker, A. (2003). *Sisters in the blood: The education of women in Native America*. Washington, DC: Office of Educational Research and Improvement.

Caine, R., & Caine, G. (1997). *Education on the edge of possibility*. Alexandria, VA: Association for Supervision and Curriculum Development.

Chen, S., & Macredie, R. (2002). Cognitive styles and hypermedia navigation: Development of a learning model. *Journal of the American Society for Information Science and Technology*, *53*(1), 3–15. doi:10.1002/asi.10023

Colon, Y., & Sanchez, B. (2010). Explaining the gender disparity in Latino youth's education: acculturation and economic value of education. *Urban Education*, *45*(3), 252–273. doi:10.1177/0042085908322688

Constantino, R. (Ed.). (1998). *Literacy, access, and libraries among the language minority population*. Lanham, MD: Scarecrow Press.

Edmundson, A. (Ed.). (2007). *Globalized e-learning cultural challenges*. Hershey, PA: Information Science Publishing.

Faiola, A., & Fatei, S. (2005). Cultural cognitive style and Web design. *Journal of Computer-Mediated Communication*, *11*(1). Retrieved from http://jcmc.indiana.edu/vol11/faiola.html. doi:10.1111/j.1083-6101.2006.tb00318.x

Fernandes, S. (2008). *Why do Native American males drop out?* Seattle, WA: University of Washington. Retrieved from http://www.nbowmanconsulting.com/Why_do_Native_American_Males_Drop_Out12.3.08%5B1%5D.pdf

Grant, R., & Wong, S. (2003). Barriers to literacy for language-minority learners. *Journal of Adolescent & Adult Literacy*, *46*(5), 386–393. doi:10.1598/JAAL.46.5.2

Gurubatham, M. (2005). Cognition, culture and effective e-praxis guiding principles. In Nicholson, P. (Eds.), *E-training practices for professional organizations* (pp. 121–128). Boston, MA: Kluwer Academic Publishers. doi:10.1007/0-387-23572-8_15

Hubbell, E. (2010). Using McREL's knowledge taxonomy for ed tech professional development. *Learning and Leading with Technology*, 20–23.

Irvine, J. (1990). *Black students and school failure*. Westport, CT: Greenwood.

Johnson-Bailey, J. (2002). A quarter century of African Americans in adult education. In R. Cervero, B. Courtenay, & C. Monaghan (Comps.), *The Cyril O. Houle scholars in adult and continuing education program global research perspectives* (vol. II) (pp. 90-110). Battle Creek, MI: Kellogg Foundation.

Joo, J. (1999). Cultural issues of the Internet in classrooms. *British Journal of Educational Technology*, *30*(3), 245–250. doi:10.1111/1467-8535.00113

Josey, E., & DeLoach, M. (Eds.). (2000). *Handbook of Black librarianship*. Lanham, MD: Scarecrow.

Kalyanpur, M., & Harry, B. (1999). *Culture in special education*. Baltimore, MD: Paul Brookes.

Livingston, G., Parker, K., & Fox, S. (2009). *Latinos online, 2006-2008*. Washington, DC: Pew Internet and American Life Project. Retrieved from http://pewinternet.org/Commentary/2009/December/Latinos-Online-20062008.aspx

Lockett, C., & Harrell, J. (2003). Racial identity, self-esteem, and academic achievement. *The Journal of Black Psychology*, *29*(3), 325–336. doi:10.1177/0095798403254216

Luevano-Molina, S. (Ed.). (2000). *Immigrant policies and the public library*. Westport, CT: Libraries Unlimited.

McMahon, C., & Bruce, C. (2002). Information literacy need of local staff in cross-cultural development projects. *Journal of International Development, 14*(1), 113–137. doi:10.1002/jid.864

Moller, S. (2001). *Library service to Spanish speaking patrons*. Westport, CT: Libraries Unlimited.

Morris, T., & Meinrath, S. (2009). *New media technology and Internet use in Indian country*. Washington, DC: New America Foundation. Retrieved from http://oti.newamerica.net/sites/newamerica.net/files/policydocs/New_Media_Technology_and_Internet_Use_in_Indian_Country.pdf

Muhammad, T. (1998). About this issue. *Black Enterprise,* 13.

Pew Internet and American Life Project. (2009). *Internet, broadband, and cell phone statistics.* Washington, DC: Pew Internet and American Life Project. Retrieved from http://pewinternet.org/Reports/2010/Internet-broadband-and-cell-phone-statistics.pdf

Pew Internet and American Life Project. (2010). *Understanding the participatory news consumer.* Washington, DC: Pew Internet and American Life Project. Retrieved from http://www.pewinternet.org/Reports/2010/Online-News.aspx

Rice, R. (2007). *The adolescent: Development relationships, and culture* (12th ed.). Boston, MA: Allyn & Bacon.

Seufert, S. (2002). Cultural perspectives. In Adelsberger, H., Collis, B., & Pawlowski, J. (Eds.), *Handbook on information technology for education and training* (pp. 411–424). Munich, Germany: Springer-Verlag.

Strand, J., & Peacock, T. (2002, December). *Nurturing resilience and school success for American Indian and Alaska native students.* ERIC Digest. Charleston, WV: ERIC Clearinghouse on Rural Education and Small Schools. (ERIC Document Reproduction Service No. EDO-RC-02-14).

Suefert, S. (2002). Cultural perspectives. In Adelsberg, H., Collis, B., & Pawlowski, J. (Eds.), *Handbook on information technology for education and training* (pp. 411–424). Munich, Germany: Springer-Verlag.

Tatum, A. (2003). All degreed up and nowhere to go: Black males and literacy education. *Journal of Adolescent & Adult Literacy, 46*(6), 476–481.

Teresi, J., Holmes, D., Ramirez, M., Gurland, B., & Lantiqua, R. (2001). Performance of cognitive tests among different racial/ethnic and education groups: Findings of differential item functioning and possible item bias. *Journal of Mental Health and Aging,* 7(1), 79–89.

Thompson, J. (1991, May). Resource-based learning can be the backbone of reform improvement. *Information Library. NASSP Bulletin,* 24–28. doi:10.1177/019263659107553506

United Nations Educational, Scientific, and Cultural Organization (UNESCO). (2002). *Universal Declaration on Cultural Diversity.* The Hague, The Netherlands: UNESCO. Retrieved from http://www.unesco.org/education/imld_2002/unversal_decla.shtml

Viadero, E. (2003). Study probes factors fueling achievement gaps. *Education Week, 23*(13), 1–12.

Zuvekas, A., et al. (1999). *Mini-environmental assessment of the health status and needs of the poor.* Washington, DC: George Washington University. Retrieved from http://www.gwumc.edu/sphhs/departments/healthpolicy/chpr/downloads/ascension99.pdf

# Chapter 16
# Summarizing Teaching Approaches in the Traditional Classroom and in the Virtual Environment

**Victor C.X. Wang**
*California State University Long Beach, USA*

## ABSTRACT

*Teachers in today's information society are required to rethink their teaching approaches to accommodate the learning needs of children and adults, either in the traditional classroom settings or the virtual environment. Logically speaking, children require instructors to teach them by using the pedagogical methods. Likewise, adults require teachers to help them learn by using andragogical approaches such as facilitation methods. When it comes to teaching children or helping adults learn in the online teaching and learning environment, it is the epistemological positions of the teachers that predetermine their instructional methods. In this chapter, the author compared and contrasted those pedagogical teaching methods with those andragogical approaches.*

## INTRODUCTION

Scholars and researchers have been examining historical trends of preferred teaching methodologies. As soon as graduate schools of education were established in the early twentieth century, scholars and researchers began to study why certain teaching methods might facilitate learning and why certain methods might stifle learning. Throughout the book, we have demonstrated to our readers that there exists "pedagogical teaching and learning" and that there exists "andragogical teaching and learning" because teachers are charged with responsibility of either teaching children or

DOI: 10.4018/978-1-60960-791-3.ch016

helping adults learn in the new century. Doctors have the responsibility to "prescribe" the right medicines to their patients. Likewise, teachers have the responsibility to "prescribe" the right teaching methodologies to their students, or clients in educational psychologists' terms. We do not want to prescribe the facilitation methods when we are teaching children who are so dependent on their teachers. Similarly, we would not want to prescribe the pedagogical model to adults who are self-directed in learning. These general directions or generational instructional modes should help teachers select the right teaching methodologies in either the traditional classroom or virtual environment.

In the virtual environment, it is all the more important for instructors to select accurate teaching methodologies because teaching online is compounded by the physical separation between course instructors and learners who may be at a remote learning site. School administrators, accreditation bodies, and course evaluators are always skeptical whether students actually learn in the online environment. Therefore, course instructors have the historic responsibility to demonstrate that their teaching methodologies online should facilitate learning, rather than stifle learning. To do so successfully, teachers need to know what kinds of epistemological positions they take because it is these positions that actually determine what to teach and above all how to teach. In writing this book, we posit that the popularity of online learning is driven by four epistemological positions: postpositivism, constructivism, advocacy/participatory, and pragmatism. Without interpreting the four positions, readers may wonder how learners engage in learning online via technology.

Postpositivists believe that knowledge is created by humans conjecturing and that, for learners to create an understanding, it is important that they work with and challenge the conjectures (Creswell, 2009). In the virtual environment, course instructors can arrange knowledge by specifying course syllabus, course assignments, discussion topics, course evaluation methods, and learning resources. Then, online learners come to the virtual environment to study, observe and even challenge these conjectures in order to determine effects or outcomes. Course instructors justify the course's existence by saying, "there are laws or theories that govern the world, and these need to be tested or verified and refined so that you, as learners, can understand the world." If we try to connect this position with instructional methods, we can likely say that this position is in agreement with andragogy instead of pedagogy simply because instructors link learners to learning resources. Learners do the "legwork" by embarking on Habermas's instrumental knowledge and practical knowledge in order to attain emancipatory knowledge—perspective transformation in Mezirow's terms.

Constructivists assume that individuals seek an understanding of the world in which they live and work. Individuals develop subjective meanings of their experiences—meanings directed toward certain objects or things (Creswell, 2009, p. 8). Creswell further indicates that these meanings are varied and multiple, leading the learner to look for the complexity of views rather than narrowing meanings into a few categories or ideas. Based on this position, online learners' tasks are clear: learners construct the meaning of a situation, typically forged in discussions or interactions with other persons. Then course instructors may arrange more open-ended questions, case studies, and analysis of personal experiences. These instructional methods all fit well with this position. In adult education, this epistemological position penetrated into the field many years ago. When scholars address "experiential learning," they want learners to make meaning out of their experience. Some universities in the United States grant college credits to adult learners based on experiential learning. If learners can turn their prior experience into knowledge, skills or attitudes, why require them to take redundant courses to waste their time or money? In the virtual learning environment, instructors may arrange learning activities around learners' prior experience. Again, we can tell that learners seek change in cognitive domain or affective domain based on the reflection of their experiential learning or prior learning. Technology is used as an external environment. To further elaborate on the constructivist position, we will focus on the following central themes:

1. Meanings are constructed by learners themselves as they engage with the virtual learning environment. Course instructors tend to use open-ended questions so that the learners can share their views and generate knowledge through their sharing.
2. Learners engage with the virtual learning environment and make sense of it based on their historical and social perspectives. Course instructors may remind learners to seek to understand the context or setting by visiting this context and gathering information personally via the use of technology.
3. The basic generation of meaning is always social, arising in and out of interaction with an online learning community. The goal of course instructors is to foster an online learning community.

Scholars and educators feel that postpositivist and constructivists do not go far enough in advocating for an action agenda to help marginalized peoples in society. Therefore, they developed advocacy/participatory worldview by drawing on the writings of Marx and Freire (Neuman, 2000). According to Creswell (2009), an advocacy/participatory worldview holds that learners need to become radical philosophers, that is, they need to have an action agenda for reform that may change the lives of themselves, the institutions in which they work or live, and perhaps the larger society. The course instructor's role is to have learners speak to important social issues of the day, issues such as empowerment, inequality, oppression, domination, suppression, and alienation. Learners should be considered equals of their course instructors. Therefore, learners may help design online learning questions, collect data, and analyze information together with their course instructors in the online learning environment. Since this epistemological position focuses on the needs of the learners and learners in society that may be marginalized or disenfranchised, we can tell the ultimate goal of this position is for learners to develop emancipatory knowledge. Specifically, learners can seek to do the following in order to develop a perspective change:

1. Learners advance an action agenda for change based on this worldview.
2. Learners seek to free themselves from constraints found in the media, in language, in work procedures, and in the relationships of power in educational settings.
3. Learners began with an important issue or stance about the problems in society.
4. Learners seek to create a political debate so that real change will occur.
5. Course instructors consider their learners as active collaborators in the learning process in the virtual environment.

The fourth epistemological position is pragmatism that maintains that a worldview arises out of actions, situations, and consequences rather than antecedent conditions as in postpositivism (Creswell, 2009). Learners are required to use all approaches available to understand problems. To understand problems, learners are free to choose the methods, techniques, and procedures that best meet their needs or purposes. Learners may use multiple methods to understand a particular problem. The emphasis in pragmatism is on hands-on application and practical solutions to problems rather than esoteric or theoretical approaches.

Clearly, the four epistemological positions predetermine what teaching methodologies teacher wish to employ in the traditional classroom setting or in the online teaching and learning setting. It is these positions that predetermine what kinds of teaching methods teachers have to select when they are teaching children or helping adults learn. Postpositivists are like behaviorists teachers we have addressed in other chapters. Likewise, constructivists and radical philosophers are akin to learning facilitators in adult education. When teachers take the fourth epistemological position, they have a propensity to vary their teaching approaches. The bottom line is that it is teachers' world views that determine their teaching methodologies, which have a huge impact on learners' learning.

## BACKGROUND

No one is to say that scholars such as Socrates, Plato or Confucius many years ago were aware of the four epistemological positions. However, we do know with a degree of certainty that their teaching methodologies can be interpreted by using the four epistemological positions. For example, the Socratic questioning is closely related to the facilitation method, via which both teachers and learners explore answers to a certain problem under discussion. Modern heuristic method is clearly derived from the Socratic questioning. The Platonic authoritarian approach to education is akin to the first epistemological position, that is, the postpositivist position. This approach is also similar to the behaviorist approach to education. As far as Confucius is concerned, his methods are more related to constructivist and radical approaches to teaching and learning. His "silent" reflection, on which Mezirow (1978, 1990, 1991, 1997, 2000) based his transformative learning theory, is much like experiential learning in adult education. When teachers are labeled as Confucian teachers, most likely, they may conform to the facilitation method in teaching and learning. But in many cases, Confucius is considered a pedagogue, who emphasizes the pedagogical model in education. Consider how Confucius emphasized experiential learning by saying this, "By nature men are nearly alike, but through experience they grow wide apart" (as cited in Chai & Chai, 1965, p. 44). Confucius or Kong Fuzi (551-479 BC).

The objective of this chapter is to compare and contrast the prevalent teaching methodologies available to contemporary teachers so that they can select the right ones when it comes to teaching traditional age and nontraditional age learning with information communication technologies. It is not our intent to bombard our readers with background information about Socrates, Plato or Confucius. However, some knowledge of these giant teachers and epistemological positions will equip our teachers with the right knowledge, skills and attitudes to succeed in their teaching careers. The following sections will lead our readers and teachers to the most used teaching methodologies, and perhaps the most abused teaching methodologies. By comparing and contrasting these methods, hopefully, our teachers and readers will select them accordingly and wisely in order to maximize learning in the virtual environment.

Pedagogical teaching methods are still useful in helping adults learn. Although the manner in which adults learn may be different from that in which children learn, the cognitive learning process may remain the same. We all use the five senses to acquire and absorb information and turn it into knowledge via critical reflection. We all have different learning styles. The more teaching approaches we can use, the better we can help adult learners learn. Pedagogical teaching methods, like andragogical teaching approaches, are geared towards maximizing adult learning. However, sheer application of pedagogical teaching approaches without modification may disappoint adult learners who yearn for andragogical teaching methods. Therefore, we suggest that instructors of adults rethink the traditional teaching approaches to ones more fitting the adult learning process. For example, if adult learners like to be considered co-learners in the learning process, instructors can try to turn their lecture into a lively discussion. Adult learners, like traditional age learners, may possess different learning styles. These range from independent, participant, competitive, collaborative, dependent and avoidant learning styles. It would be a mistake to claim that all adult learners are collaborative learners. In case they are dependent and competitive learners, instructors of adults may just need to switch to lecture or nominal group technique. Why? This is because dependent and competitive learners like rules and structure. Lecture and nominal group techniques offer clear rules and structure. This chapter attempts to provide an overview of pedagogical teaching approaches and to compare and contrast them. Then it is a teacher's responsibility to select appropriate teaching methods in order to facilitate adult learning or teach children.

## COMPARING AND CONTRASTING TEACHING METHODOLOGIES IN LIGHT OF INFORMATION COMMUNICATION TECHNOLOGIES

### Lecture

The lecture method was the most preferred and most used instructional method in adult education. Lecturing is informative speaking. Farrah (2004) suggested that instructors use the lecture method when the primary goal of the learning transaction is cognitive (information) transfer. However, it is not best to teach technical motor skills or modify attitudes. As noted by Farrah (2004, pp. 228-229), the lecture method can be used when the purpose is to:

1. Present information in an organized way in a relatively short time frame.
2. Provide a framework for learning activities and further study, which are to follow.
3. Identify, explain, and clarify difficult concepts, problems, or ideas.
4. Present an analysis of a controversial issue.
5. Demonstrate relationships between previously learned and new information, and among apparently dissimilar ideas.
6. Model a creative mind at work, an expert's thought process as the lecture "thinks out loud."
7. Challenge the beliefs, attitudes, and behaviors of the learners.
8. Stimulate or inspire the audience to further inquiry.

Lecturing is most suited to the transmittal of information for immediate recall; a short (less than 30 minutes), carefully constructed lecture with meaningful examples, frequent summaries, simple language, and appropriate speed of delivery is most effective. The specific learning task determines whether or not the lecture method is the method of choice. Augmenting the lecture with other instructional methods and devices facilitates learning.

The advantages of lecturing are that it is economical in time and energy. Lecturing well is an art. The material may be presented in a clear, precise, and orderly format. Lecturing is a well known and acceptable method. It is useful for participants who will not or cannot use printed materials. It may be used with large groups. It provides face to face contact with a talking, gesturing, feeling human being. Lectures are easier for participants to listen to than to read. It stimulates and motivates the learner to further study and inquiry.

The limitations of lecturing are that it may be misused and overused. The audience is exposed to only one person's views. Careless or irresponsible speakers may provide biased or inaccurate information. Lecturing may provide no verbal interaction between the audience and the speaker. It may discourage learner involvement in the teaching-learning transaction. It may be difficult to determine the effects of the lecture upon the audience in that feedback is often subtle. The speaker may not consider the audience's level of knowledge and education. Some speakers value "stage time" more than facilitating learning. Too often speakers are judged on whether or not they entertain the learners rather than on the quality of the content.

Adult educators need to have content expertise and ease in public speaking. This is true also online. Blackboard or WebCT programs have the power to include the "whiteboard" via which course instructors can talk to learners by using a microphone. During specified "synchronous" interaction between course instructors and learners, adult educators are required to have ease in public speaking. They need to be keenly aware of the importance of speaking loudly enough with clear diction, appropriate choice of words, and changing voice inflections for emphasis and variety. They also need to adapt the style of language (formal or informal, technical or commonplace) and level of content difficulty (basic or advanced) to the needs, interests, and background experiences of the learners. Most delivery problems occur when adult educators have insufficient preparation and insufficient self-confidence.

## Teacher Responsibilities

Before the learning encounter, educators need to engage in careful content planning and preparing to meet the specific learning objectives. During the learning encounter, they should be sensitive to the environment (temperature, illumination, excess noise). How does this translate to online learning? Educators can set the stage for collegial online learning environment by telling learners via texts or a microphone that they would use facilitation methods rather than possess a directing relationship between instructors and learners. Both educators and learners have the responsibility to reduce the noise level produced by microphones. Temperature can be translated into a "warm" "caring" atmosphere online. The learners' (nodding of head in agreement or from dozing, facial expression, body position) feedback should help guide the adult educators in meeting the particular needs of the group. This can also occur online via whiteboard by watching those computer "icons." After the learning encounter, educators need to make every effort to be available for follow up questions and interaction with the learners.

## Learner Responsibilities

Learners should attend the lecture with a readiness to learn, to more extensive preparation involving reading assignments, questions to be considered, or written work. Ideally, the learners move beyond listening and actively engage in critical thinking, identifying how the content relates to their own worldviews and what impact it might have on their lives. Learners also need take notes effectively. If questioning and discussions accompany lectures, Learners can participate by sharing their views and past experiences. Although these learner responsibilities apply to adult learners, teachers of children may try some of these techniques with teaching children.

## Guides for Preparation

A teacher needs to be flexible and adaptable. Always be sensitive to the needs of the learners; they should always take precedence over the teacher's original plan. Teachers should outline their lecture notes, but do not write out everything in full. Send the audience appropriate materials ahead of time so they can be prepared. Hand out a lecture outline with the key points, or place it on the board for students to copy. Intersperse intense, novel, or surprising information among the more mundane. Draw listeners into the discovery process as you make your journey through the material. The appropriate use of humor is a wonderful means of stimulating attention and imagination.

## Tips for Delivery

Set a learning climate: call the learners by name and maintain good eye contact. Limit the amount of information. Six or seven chunks of information are as much as can be handled in a fifty-minute class session.Speak clearly, loudly enough, and at a pace appropriate for the learner group. Use a conversational rather than pedantic, authoritative tone. Look at people. Keep moving, but don't overdo it. Complement the lecture with other instructional methods such as discussion and questioning. Provide an obvious end (Galbraith, 2004).

## The Anatomy of a Lecture

Say a lot about a little: requires narrowing of the topic and identification of the three or four essential concepts. Identify the most salient points. Use many examples, illustrations, and demonstrations. Keep moving about the room enhances both verbal and nonverbal communication. Capitalize on variety: change alone is a major factor in holding a group's attention (Farrah, 2004).

## NOMINAL GROUP TECHNIQUE

Group technique is defined as "...a pre designed pattern for human instruction that offers a better potential for progress toward goals than does unstructured random behavior" (Wang, 2006, p. 188). Effective leadership, instruction, democratic principle, adaptation, productivity and many other concepts are tied to the principles of effective group action. The choice of group method can be based upon a set of agreed principles (Wang, 2006).

- The appropriateness of the method in relationship to the knowledge, ability and skill of the participants.
- An understanding of the internal dynamics of groups in relation to the needs of the individual participants.
- The realization of the setting and organizational factors that are important to the process.
- The purpose to which the outcome is to be used.
- The understanding that group process should be used as an instructional or problem-solving method, not as recreational activity.

## The Development of Nominal Group Technique

This technique was developed as a problem solving technique. Strength is derived from the power of individuals each generating, exploring, and communicating ideas.

- Formulating the nominal group technique question.
- Generation of ideas.
- Round –robin listing.
- Discussion of ideas.
- Voting on individual ideas.
- Tabulating the voting.

### Adaptations of the Nominal Group Technique

- Individuals in the group work independently of others during the initial formation of responses although in the presence of others.
- All responses are written and the ideas generated are sequentially shared by the individual group members.
- Some form of ranking, ordering, or valuing is designed to fit the particular situation.

### Three Step Model

- Listing (of individual ideas)
- Recording
- Voting on ideas generated

### Four Step Model

- Participants are asked to respond to a question or statement by generating a written list of responses.

- The group facilitator asks each member to contribute an idea from their list in a round robin approach.
- Group members are given the opportunity to discuss and clarify any of the ideas that have been selected.
- Group members are asked to rank or rate each item.

**Five Step Model**

- Introduction to meeting.
- Select generation of ideas in writing.
- Round robin listing.
- Discussion for classification.
- Ranking of items.

## Advantages and Limitations of the Nominal Group Technique

The advantages include restriction of the influence of the group leader. It reduces, to a great degree, the influence of dominating group numbers. It provides a format for closure. By voting and ordering there is a calculated decision-making mechanism. Where other group processes demand a great deal of time, there is efficiency in this technique.

However, the technique also has limitations. It demands that the question posed to the group be well formed. It is not a consensus model. There exists the possibility that the decision reached will not provide the basis for entire group commitment. The group leader is limited to the role of facilitator. It limits the emergence of group leadership by restricting the decision making process.

It is best used when (a) there is a well-formed question; (b) a decision needs to be made; (c) time is a restricting factor.

## Group Leader and Participant Responsibilities

The responsibility to form the question and then facilitate the synthesis and tabulating. The learner's responsibility is to generate ideas, interact, and vote on the results of those processes.

## Nominal Group Technique for Evaluation

Nominal group technique restricts the influence of the group process leader by encouraging respondents to frame their own responses. It sustains individual autonomy during group pressure and provides the respondents with knowledge of the full range of possible responses.

Based on the characteristics of learners, educators can include a few basic elements for the adult-learner classroom in order to assume an effective role: Psychosocial Climate, Meaningful Tasks, Group Projects, Interactive Learning, and Choices, Support and Respect. To assume the same effective role online, educators can rely on cutting edge course rooms (Web 2.0 technologies) to create the same level of interaction as they would in traditional four walled classrooms.

## Psychosocial Climate

There are many different components or variables that contribute to the environmental climate of an educational encounter. Physical environment, a major component, includes the interaction of people with their physical and spatial environments. Some of the elements are the arrangement of classroom seating, lighting, ventilation, colorful decoration, appropriate temperature settings, and refreshment areas. Comparable arrangements in the online teaching and learning environment can be made if instructors are willing to take the time and effort. Although physical climate is important, in most cases it is not something an educator has a great deal of control over. The challenge is how we can translate this psychological climate into the online teaching and learning climate. Being good communicators means a great deal to online course instructors. They can send out collegial announcements, warm welcome letters and some ground rules without letting learners feel "threatened".

What seems to be most important is the development of a conducive psychosocial climate. This is something educators can control. The psychosocial climate, according to Knowles (1989), is concerned with the psychological aspects as well as the cultural dimensions of the educational encounter. This includes the relationship among the learners, rapport and systems that hold meaning for learners, expectations, and clarity of goals.

Knowles (1989) emphasized, educators first should establish a climate that suggests mutual respect, cooperation, mutual trust, supportiveness, openness to challenge and criticism, risk taking, pleasure, and friendliness. It is helpful to get participants involved immediately through introductory activities that provide personal and professional information, which can help everyone get acquainted and also create opportunities for informal conversations among the learners.

Then educators should maintain the conducive psychosocial climate by planning the process of assessing learning needs, establishing learning activities, and developing evaluation strategies. By using collaborative and challenging approaches that accept the learners' input, adult educators tell participants that they are important in the educational encounter and that their perceptions and contributions matter.

## Meaningful Tasks

From years of teaching, Konicek (1996) concluded that all students need meaningful and relevant information and useful skills. Tasks and assignments need to facilitate the development of the adult learner in accordance with the student's needs and goals. For online teaching and learning, these tasks and assignments can be text-based. Instructors can also incorporate audio/video clips to direct learners to see those meaningful and relevant information and useful stills. Therefore, it is necessary and vital that the instructor begins the term with a well-planned and organized schedule of class chapters and assignments. As a facilitator, the teacher can assume certain needs and goals based on previous experiences with similar audiences. However, the schedule of assignments and tasks should be prepared with the expectation that it will be changed to fit the students' needs and adjusted to fit their learning styles (Konicek, 1996).

## Group Process

Adult educators must recognize and respond to each individual's style of learning while recognizing group characteristics and applying basic principles of group process. Groups typically evolve through predictable stages (Wang, 2006). Implementing group process can be easily facilitated on the discussion board forum. Even under the Assignments Tab via web 2.0 technologies, group process can be implemented. During the first stage, members are polite and superficial as each seeks to establish safe patterns of interaction by choosing a role that is acceptable to himself or herself and to the group.

During the second stage, members seek to establish their power and influence within the group. Each member has some need to control and influence, but the need varies in degree from person to person.

In the third stage, the group becomes a cohesive unit and begins to establish the norms, roles, and processes it will use to accomplish tasks. Members begin to care for each other, and functional relationships develop.

Group experience is generally regarded as an effective educational method in adult education. If appropriate structure and supervision is made available, positive effects can be increasingly realized and negative effects can be studied and ultimately eliminated.

To increase the positive effects, the group facilitator believes in the worth and significance of each human being. He has faith in each person's potentiality to develop personally and interpersonally. He possesses genuine respect for the existence of both positive and negative characteristics within every group, but he believes that every person can achieve quality in his interpersonal encounters with others. As Cross (1976) stated:

The group facilitator protects the integrity and mental health of every person with whom he works and places the welfare of the individual member above the achievement of the group's goals. While demanding the freedom to work professionally, he accepts the responsibility for being a member of the helping professions. (p. 244)

The purpose of group facilitation is to help individuals in a group achieve fuller development as effective human beings and it is practiced in the service of others and in the presence of others. Educators can learn a great deal by observing learners in a group. By carefully observing communication patterns and task or maintenance behaviors, and by being cognizant of the underlying emotional issues of identify, power, and control, it is possible to determine what is going on in a group and what can be done to help.

## Interaction

Brookfield (1986) suggested that "in an effective teaching-learning transaction all participants learn, no one member is regarded as having a monopoly or insight, and dissension and criticism are regarded as inevitable and desirable elements of the process" (p. 24). Providing a personal atmosphere in the virtual classroom is helpful in establishing an interactive learning situation (Wang, 2005). The online learning environment is not a vacuum, but is filled with human interaction (p. 51). Students can serve as resources for each other and share their experiences and expertise. Ignoring an individual's experience or contribution may be considered as a rejection of the person rather than just the experience. Conversely, a safe environment is established by encouraging participation without judgment or criticism. Each person must be made to feel worthy and dignified.

According to Konicek (1996), collaborative and cooperative learning groups provide another opportunity for interaction and sharing. Problem solving projects give the adult student the experience and confidence needed to further their development of college level skills, analytical reading, and positive interaction with peers and instructors. He stated, "I have observed that many students are bolstered by their group experiences and more positive about their individual abilities and skills" (p. 13).

## Choices

Unlike traditional students, adult learners have their own ideas about what they most need to learn from their own experiences. They learn better when they are given choices that accommodate their own needs and goals. Transition and change are factors related to participation in adult education. Most adults want instructions that are problem-centered, and they desire to learn a particular skill for a specific reason (Konicek, 1996). Therefore, adult educators must discover the variables that will influence how course objectives will be delivered. The learners' learning styles, rate of learning, needs and goals are some of the elements that can assist an instructor in meeting course objectives and student needs. The sooner the variables are revealed the sooner the instructor can customize assignments. Based on the aforementioned characteristics of adult learners, online instructors can arrange "case studies" or meaningful problems (real world problems related to adult learners' careers) for adult learners to tackle via web 2.0 interactivity. In fact, the problem-based learning model is derived from principles of adult learning as adult learning is closely related to "orientation to learning." Translated into online learning, adult learners would enjoy instructors customizing assignments based on real life problems.

## Support

Individuals learn by receiving support from more experienced individuals and support requires a broader concept of instruction. Maslow's (1954) hierarchy of needs, Rogers' (1969) fully functioning person, and the stages and structures of other great psychologists provide the many assumptions for understanding the adult psyche. The adult student needs to feel safety, love, and belongingness in the classroom in order for learning to take place.

Learning situations that promote self-direction in learning, creativity, and non-stereotypical thinking are conducive to the successful acquisition of knowledge and skill. Konicek (1996) uses a variety of activities and techniques to foster a learning atmosphere in his classes, making them conducive to active participation, even by the least confident student. Questions are open-ended, every answer is "correct," any and all contributions are accepted. Group activities are relaxed and outside study groups encouraged. Once again, online instructors can do a lot by providing due support to learner in the virtual environment. Use your power of communication, power of expertise in the subject matter, power of empathy, power of enthusiasm, power of clarification and so on and so forth to create a sense of belongingness in the virtual environment.

## Respect

Rogers (1969) explained in his book, *Freedom to Learn*, that students can be trusted to learn and enjoy learning when the teacher creates and maintains a classroom environment that communicates respect through participation in selecting and reaching goals. People are able, valuable, and responsible and should be treated accordingly. No need to say that the online environment can be considered a special classroom where instructors and learners can form either a directing relationship or a helping relationship, depending on the actual course assignments (Wang, 2005). Naturally, respect is needed in order for learners to enjoy learning from course instructors, from text materials and from other fellow learners.

In a classroom or the virtual classroom, mutual respect is of vital importance. This respect is manifested by the teacher's caring and appropriate behaviors, as well as by places, policies, programs, and processes created and maintained by teachers. As Purkey and Stanley (1991) noted, "respect for people and respect for property are the foundations of invitational teaching" (p. 19).

Research shows that creating a classroom environment based on mutual respect is a highly effective way of encouraging student achievement. It is common sense that teachers who exhibit respect for students by starting and ending class on time tend to have students who view the class as important and therefore study more.

Teachers can show respect for students by developing an appreciation for each student's uniqueness and intelligence. The importance of using discipline not as punishment cannot be overstressed. It should be used as an opportunity to explore alternative behaviors that show respect for others.

Purkey and Stanley (1991) in their work with "disconnected" students found that effective teachers showed respect for students, maintained realistic expectations, offered helpful feedback, and encouraged students to ask questions.

## Exemplary Instructors

Exemplary instructors are most concerned about learners than things and events. Even though online learners are separated from course instructors by time and space, it is exemplary instructors' responsibility to show more concerns about learners rather than things or events. The distance between learners and instructors can be "shortened" if instructors can take the initiative to "call" their learners based on a certain course assignment or if the instructors just "feel like" talking to their learners about their personal needs and interests.

Online exemplary educators like their traditional classroom instructors know their subject matter. They relate theory to practice and their own field to other fields. They are confident instructors and are open to a wide variety of teaching approaches. They encourage learning outcomes that go beyond course objectives. Last but not least, they create a positive atmosphere for learning.

To help learn effectively, it is imperative that online educators adopt and adapt either andragogical style and method or pedagogical style and method accordingly. To try to restrict teaching/learning to the andragogical method is to fail to understand the teaching and learning process. Certain aims and objectives of a lesson and the content to be taught may leave adult learning professionals with no room for their andragogical preference. To restrict teaching exclusively to an andragogical method may allow for the possibility of irresponsibility and unacceptable eccentricities especially when andragogy is referred to more as an art rather than a science.

To try to say which of the two methods of teaching (pedagogical and andragogical) affects adults' transformation more is extremely difficult since each of us who teaches engages not only in a time-honored process but one that is quite unique to the immediate situation in which we are actually teaching. The more we understand the difference between pedagogical philosophies and andragogical philosophies, the more likely we are to understand those whom we are privileged to teach. Perhaps it is safe and beneficial to conform to Knowles' reminder that "an essential feature of andragogy is flexibility" (Knowles, 1984, p. 418). By being flexible, adult learning professionals accommodate both andragogical philosophies and pedagogical philosophies. A linear mode of teaching (either solely andragogical or solely pedagogical) can be detrimental in helping adults learn.

The issues of pedagogy and andragogy have ignited a tremendous amount of research into adult learning since Knowles advanced the principles of andragogy. These issues (i.e., pedagogy versus andragogy) will continue to spark further and subsequent research given the nature of the 21st century transformation and emancipation.

The final question remains how educators can apply these aforementioned teaching techniques to the virtual environment where educators and learners are separated by time and distance. All these teaching techniques apply to the online teaching and learning. Educators still can rely on texts, audio, video clips, discussion forums, email communications to implement these teaching techniques. The latest feature of Web 2.0 technologies has included "whiteboard" via which educators and learners can interact with each other synchronously. With the help of web cameras and other technology, educators and instructors can "view" each other's facial expressions, cues and so forth. Can educators teach pedagogically online? Yes, they can. As long as they rely more on lectures, written messages and a directing relationship, they teach pedagogically. How about teaching andragogically online? Yes, they can. As long as educators invite more interaction, more discussion, and prescribe independent learning projects or give out learning contracts, they become facilitators of learning online and they become andragogical instructors online.

## The Art of Questioning

It is well known that Plato's teacher was Socrates whose teaching method has influenced generations of people. What is the Socratic method of teaching and how effective is it? Cahn (1997) wrote that Socrates used his infamous method of questioning, and it proved to be applicable to other fields such as history and science. Indeed, the art of questioning is the most fundamental instructional methodology available, and it affords two-way communication. Educative questions are designed to advance pedagogical purpose and therefore require much thought to be effective. Everyday questions require no extra thought. Taba (1962) described questioning as the single most influential teaching act because of the ability of questions to influence the learning process. Questions may serve to gain the learner's participation in class, to determine what the learner knows about a subject; to focus the attention of the learner; to lead discussions, to review subject matter, to stimulate thinking, and to test the learner's knowledge of subjects covered in class.

Good questions should be clearly stated and easily understood by all learners, so common wording should be used. Good questions should focus on the major components of the chapter or other required texts. Good questions require much thought on both the part of the instructor and the learner. Finally, good questions should require the learner to take an active, reflective role in learning.

## A Questioning Procedure

A poor method of questioning is that when the instructor asks questions and allows the entire group to answer in chorus. It decreases individual thought and does not allow the instructor to monitor feedback from individual learners. Mental participation of the learners can be achieved through a simple five part questioning procedure. The procedure affords wait time, which stimulates thinking.

The correct questioning procedure should be: 1. Ask question; 2. Pause so that everyone will have time to think about the question; 3.Call on one learner by name or ask who will volunteer. Learners should be randomly selected to answer the question; 4. Listen to the answer; 5. Emphasize the correct answer (Galbraith, 2004; Wang, 2007/2008).

## Levels of Questions

Good questions are directed towards learning and evaluative thinking, rather than what has been learned in a narrow sense. Questions can be classified in several ways. A universally accepted classification of questions in the cognitive domain was developed by Bloom (1956). See Table 1.

Based on the levels of communication, Bloom's taxonomy and principles of instructional design, instructors should ask six levels of questions to generate meaningful discussions in distance education. See Table 2.

Questioning can be one of the most effective methods of teaching and is often used with other methodologies. Instructors should have a clear purpose in mind when asking questions. Pausing is essential for thinking about ideas and the formulation of answers, especially for higher order questions. When properly used, questioning can be a powerful tool for teachers. In online teaching, teachers can apply the same questioning techniques via "whiteboard" where instructors can ask the same questions related to Bloom's tax-

*Table 1. Classification of questions in the cognitive domain*

| | |
|---|---|
| Knowledge | Involves the recall of specifics and universals, the recall of the methods and processes, or the recall of a pattern, structure, or setting. It is the lowest level in the hierarchy. |
| Comprehension | Refers to a type of understanding or apprehension so that the individual knows what is being communicated and can make use of the material or idea being communicated without necessarily relating it to other material or seeing its fullest implications. |
| Application | Involves the use of abstractions in participation and concrete situations. The abstractions may be in the form of general ideas, rules of procedures, or generalized methods. |
| Analysis | Includes questions concerned with the breakdown of a communication into its constituent elements or parts. |
| Synthesis | Questions which focus on the putting together of parts to form a whole. |
| Evaluation | Develops judgments about the value of material and methods for a given purpose. |

*Table 2 Bloom's taxonomy and six levels of questions*

| | |
|---|---|
| To generate knowledge | Who, what, when, where how…? |
| To enhance comprehension | Retell… |
| To encourage application | How is…an example of…? How is… related to…? Why is… significant? |
| To achieve analysis | What are the parts or features of…? Classify…according to… Outline/diagram… How does… compare/contrast with…? What evidence can you list for…? |
| For synthesis | What would you predict/infer from…? What ideas can you add to…? How would you create/design a new…? What might happen if you combined…? What solutions would you suggest for…? |
| For evaluation | Do you agree…? What do you think about…? What is the most important…? Place the following in order of priority… How would you decide about…? What criteria would you use to assess…? |

onomy by using a microphone. Or the questions can be posted on the discussion board forum to generate meaningful discussions.

## FUTURE RESEARCH DIRECTIONS

### Social and Demographic Trends

There are more people over 65 than teenagers (Wang, 2007/2008) in American society. Minority populations are on the increase. Now we have about 29 percent of minority groups. Non-traditional families are on the increase. For example, we have more single parent families. More and more women enter the workforce. Now we have 61 percent of women that are employed (Merriam, Caffarella, & Baumgartner, 2007). Given this reality in our society, educators are faced with diverse learning needs that traditional classroom instructors may not be able to accommodate. Given the financial situations, these learners may require teaching and learning via technologies to save time and money. The conspicuous advantage of teaching and learning online is that technology offers flexibility and convenience. Although there are known advantages of teaching and learning online, there can be other hidden benefits that scholars and researchers may look into in the future. Learning is a complex phenomenon and learning online is more complex and controversial. The important task for scholars and researchers in the near future is to address more the issue related to advantages and disadvantages of teaching and learning via technologies.

### Economic and Technological Trends

Changes in the workplace have occurred. There are more and more high tech jobs in our society. An information society has already emerged. These trends have already changed the way people teach and learn. These trends have already changed the way people access knowledge. These trends have already changed the way people view themselves, others and the outside world. One trend could be that scholars and researchers will continue to address how this information society will continue to make an impact on people's daily lives and above all teaching and learning.

### Critical Issues for Education's Future

Educators need to provide accessible and equitable learning opportunities and adjust to the demands of an information society. Educators also need to make effective use of technology, and develop learning management skills. In fact, educators are already doing these either in their traditional classroom settings or in the virtual environment. Those educators who consider teaching and learning via technology a burden will be lagged behind.

Technology has the potential to provide equitable learning opportunities and it should be used by educators creatively based on those aforementioned teaching techniques. If used positively and creatively, technology should enhance teaching and learning greatly. If we say our knowledge increases exponentially, then technology is a huge contributor that cannot be under estimated in the information society.

## Trends for the Future

- Educators need to employ a wide variety of methods; they need to emphasize collaborative learning as well as individualized learning.
- Advances in artificial intelligence will provide greater individualization of instruction through information technologies.
- Methods that stress collaborative learning, problem solving, and critical and reflective thinking will increase in importance.
- The group will become an important vehicle for collaborative learning due to changes in the workplace.
- Computer assisted instruction will increase in importance.
- Educators will develop methods designed to help learners evaluate available information sources.
- Educators will also concentrate more on helping adults become better managers of their own learning. Specifically, educators can do the following to help adults become better managers of their own learning: A. Diagnosing learning style. B. Keeping logs and journals. C. Retrospective reports following episodes. D. Conducting critiques to analyze the process dimensions of such activities as group discussion. E. Providing relevant theoretical information through lecture and assigned readings.
- The development of learning management skills will be supported by computer software that will help adults learn while simultaneously making them aware of their own learning process.

## CONCLUSION

No single method is likely to dominate in the future. No one method is the best method. Our society is characterized by rapid and pervasive change. It is difficult to predict or forecast the future with any confidence. Educators may be disabling learners by preparing them for a future that has already passed. Richlin (2006) points out that teaching methods are associated with particular blends of teaching styles. To teach is either to create a match to student styles or to create a mismatch to student styles. Richlin (2006) identifies four major clusters of teaching styles based on learners' learning styles:

1. 38% of instructors consider themselves as experts and use formal authority because they believe their learners are dependent, participant and competitive;
2. 22% of instructors use personal models and formal authority because they believe their learners are participant, dependent and competitive;
3. 17% of instructors consider themselves facilitators because they believe their learners are collaborative, participant and independent;
4. 15% of instructors consider themselves delegators, facilitators because they believe their learners are independent, collaborative and participant.

The four clusters of teaching styles seem to contradict the fundamental andragogical assumptions in that adult learners are considered self-directed learners. If learners are self-directed, instructors need to be delegators and facilitators. As shown in previous chapters of the book, adult learners have a need for support and a need for direction. When this occurs, adult learners are not only independent learners, but also competitive and dependent learners. Therefore, instructors of adults need to be flexible in their instructional approaches. Traditional teaching approaches still have their place in the field of K-12 education. They are also useful and helpful in adult education. As learners live in the knowledge society and information age, they have multiple access to knowledge. It is natural that they will eventually become self-directed learners in learning of any kind. When this occurs, instructors do need to move from their pedagogical teaching styles to andragogical teaching approaches. In other words, instructors need to learn to be delegators and learning facilitators. Richlin (2006) argued instructors need to engage in the following if their learners are independent, collaborative and participant:

- Contract teaching
- Class symposium
- Debate formats
- Helping trios
- Independent study/research
- Jigsaw groups
- Laundry list discussions
- Learning pairs
- Modular instruction
- Panel discussion
- Position papers
- Practicum
- Round Robin interviews
- Self-discovery activities
- Small group work teams
- Student journals

The above teaching approaches possess the characteristics of andragogical teaching. It does not mean that we can not use them when we teach children. In fact, some of these approaches may prove more effective than those traditional teaching methodologies.

## REFERENCES

Bloom, B. S. (1956). *Taxonomy of educational objectives: Handbook I: Cognitive domain*. New York, NY: McKay.

Brookfield, S. D. (1986). *Understanding and facilitating adult learning*. San Francisco, CA: Jossey-Bass.

Cahn, S. M. (1997). *Classic and contemporary readings in the philosophy of education*. New York, NY: The McGraw-Hill Companies.

Chai, C., & Chai, W. (1965). *The sacred books of Confucius and other Confucian classics*. New York, NY: University Books.

Creswell, J. W. (2009). *Research design: Qualitative, quantitative, and mixed methods research* (3rd ed.). Los Angeles, CA: Sage.

Cross, K. P. (1976). *Accent on learning*. San Francisco, CA: Jossey-Bass.

Farrah, S. J. (2004). Lecture. In Galbraith, M. W. (Ed.), *Adult learning methods: A guide for effective instruction* (pp. 227–252). Malabar, FL: Krieger Publishing Company.

Galbraith, M. W. (Ed.). (2004). *Adult learning methods: A guide for effective instruction* (3rd ed.). Malabar, FL: Krieger Publishing Company.

Knowles, M. S. (1984). *Andragogy in action*. San Francisco, CA: Jossey-Bass.

Knowles, M. S. (1989). *The making of an adult educator: An autobiographical journey*. San Francisco, CA: Jossey-Bass.

Konicek, V. (1996). Adult-centered classroom. *Adult Learning*, 13.

Maslow, A. H. (1954). *Motivation and personality*. New York, NY: Harper.

Merriam, S. B., Caffarella, R. S., & Baumgartner, L. M. (2007). *Learning in adulthood: A comprehensive guide* (3rd ed.). San Francisco, CA: Jossey-Bass.

Mezirow, J. (1978). *Education for perspective transformation: Women's re-entry programs in community colleges*. New York: Teacher's College, Columbia University.

Mezirow, J. (1990). *Fostering critical reflection in adulthood: A guide to transformative and emancipatory learning*. San Francisco, CA: Jossey-Bass.

Mezirow, J. (1991). *Transformative dimensions of adult learning*. San Francisco, CA: Jossey-Bass.

Mezirow, J. (1997). Transformative learning: Theory to practice. In Cranton, P. (Ed.), *Transformative learning in action. New Directions in Adult and Continuing Education, no. 74* (pp. 5–12). San Francisco, CA: Jossey-Bass.

Mezirow, J. (2000). Learning to think like an adult. In Mezirow, J. (Eds.), *Learning as transformation: Critical perspectives on a theory in progress* (pp. 3–34). San Francisco, CA: Jossey-Bass.

Neuman, W. L. (2000). *Social research methods: Qualitative and quantitative approaches* (4th ed.). Boston, MA: Allyn & Bacon.

Purkey, W. W., & Stanley, P. H. (1991). *Invitational teaching, learning, and living*. Washington, DC: National Education Association.

Richlin, L. (2006). *Blueprint for learning: Constructing college courses to facilitate, assess, and document learning*. Sterling, VA: Stylus.

Rogers, C. R. (1969). *Freedom to learn*. Columbus, OH: Charles E. Merrill.

Taba, H. (1962). *Curriculum development theory and practice*. New York, NY: Harcourt, Brace and World.

Wang, V. (2005). Perceptions of teaching preferences of online instructors. *Journal on Excellence in College Teaching, 16*(3), 33–54.

Wang, V. C. X. (2006). *Essential elements for andragogical styles and methods: How to create andragogical modes in adult education*. Boston, MA: Pearson Education.

Wang, V. C. X. (2007/2008). *Facilitating adult learning: A comprehensive guide for successful instruction* (Rev. ed.). Boston, MA: Pearson Education.

# About the Contributors

**Victor C. X. Wang**, an associate professor, joined the faculty at California State University, Long Beach (CSULB) in 2002. Wang's research and writing activities have focused on workforce education, the foundations of adult education, adult teaching and learning, training, transformative learning, cultural issues in vocational and adult education, distance education, human performance technology, and curriculum development. He has published 125 journal articles, book chapters, and books during his eight years at CSULB and has been a reviewer for five national and international journals. Currently, he serves as the editor in chief of the *International Journal of Adult Vocational Education and Technology*. He has won many academic achievement awards from universities in China and in the United States, including the Distinguished Faculty Scholarly & Creative Achievement Award in 2009. Dr. Wang taught extensively as a professor in Chinese universities prior to coming to study and work in the United States in 1997. He has taught adult learners English as a second language, Chinese, computer technology, vocational and adult education courses, research methods, administrative leadership, human resource management and curriculum development for the past 21 years in university settings. Some of the books he has written and edited have been adopted as required textbooks by major universities in the United States and in China. In addition, numerous universities worldwide, including Ivy League universities in the United States, have cataloged his books and journal articles.

**Lesley Farmer**, Professor at California State University Long Beach, coordinates the Librarianship program. She earned her M.S. in Library Science at the University of North Carolina Chapel Hill, and received her doctorate in Adult Education from Temple University. Dr. Farmer has worked as a librarian in K-12 school settings as well as in public, special, and academic libraries. She chaired the Education Section of the Special Libraries Association, and is the International Association of School Librarianship Vice-President of Association Relations. Dr. Farmer is a Fulbright Scholar, and has received a university Distinguished Scholarly Activity Award, several professional association awards, and national/international grants. Dr. Farmer's research interests include information literacy, assessment, collaboration, and educational technology. A frequent presenter and writer for the profession, Dr. Farmer has published two dozen professional books, and over a hundred professional book chapters and articles. Her most recent books are *Your School Library: Check It Out!*, published by Libraries Unlimited in 2009, and *NealSchuman Technology Management Handbook for School Library Media Centers*, co-authored with Marc McPhee in 2010.

**Pamela M. Golubski** is the Director of Training and Development at iCarnegie (Powered by Carnegie Mellon University) and is an Assistant Professor of Business at Point Park University. She earned a PhD in Instructional Management, a MS in Educational Counseling, a BS in Management, and a certificate in Adult Learning. Prior to iCarnegie she was the Associate Director of Undergraduate Studies and Assessment in the College of Engineering at Carnegie Mellon University. Her 15 years of higher education experience extends into the areas of administration, curriculum development, academic and career advising, mentoring, specialized programming, first-year experience, accreditation, and assessment. She has been teaching since 1997, and her true passion is in teaching management (change, project, or strategic management, and organizational behavior) and soft skills courses (human relations, professional communications, research, and writing). Pamela's research has been and continues to be in the areas of traditional and e-mentoring, service-learning, virtual advising, probation counseling methods, and the use of Web 2.0 technologies in acclimating, communicating, engaging, onboarding, and retaining college students. Lastly, Dr. Golubski is on the Board of Directors for Dress for Success Pittsburgh, the Planning Board for Heinz History Center Uncorked, and Editor Board for the Journal of Student Affairs Research and Practice (JSARP). She also is the current Chapter Advisor for Alpha Kappa Psi Business Fraternity at Carnegie Mellon University.

**Judith Parker** has earned a doctorate degree, and an M.S. degree in Adult and Continuing Education from Teachers College/Columbia University in New York, an M.S. degree in physics from Purdue University in Indiana, and a B.S. degree in physics and mathematics from Notre Dame College in Ohio. Dr. Parker has over 20 years experience in leadership positions within business organizations emerging into the global market and has been instrumental in leading them toward becoming global learning organizations. She has worked extensively with technical managers and technical employees in Asia and Europe in leadership education and training and technical employee skill development. Dr. Parker's academic experience includes teaching adult learning and leadership theory and practice, staff development and training, and organizational development, in graduate programs at Teachers College/ Columbia University and St. Mary's University of Minnesota using totally on-line format, totally classroom format, and blended delivery. She also teaches college physics and astronomy at Muhlenberg College in Pennsylvania. She has presented numerous papers at conferences globally including the Academy of Management, American Association of Physics Teachers, American Society of Training and Development, College Industry Education Conference, Quality and Productivity Management Association, Business and Multimedia Conference in Ireland, Lisbon 2000 European Conference on ODL Networking for Quality Learning, and World Open Learning for Business Conferences in the UK. She has authored numerous articles in publications including the "Compendium on Uses of Distance Learning Technologies in Engineering Education" and the "Journal of the International Association for Continuing Engineering Education" and book chapters including "Cyber Action Learning and Virtual Project Teams for Leadership and Management Development" with L. Yiu in the book Workplace Training and Learning: A Cross-Cultural Perspective and the chapter "The Online Adult Learner: Profiles and Practices" in Handbook of Research on E-Learning Applications for Career and Technical Education by edited by Victor Wang. She has been elected a Fellow of the American Association for the Advancement of Science, and has received the American Association of Physics Teachers Innovative Teaching Award and the Park College Educational Partnership Award.

# Index

## Symbols



## A



## B



## C

## D



## E



## F

## G



## H



## I



## J



## K



## L



## M

CPSIA information can be obtained at www.ICGtesting.com
265051BV00008B/5-86/P